OXFORD LEGAL PHILOSOPHY
Series Editors: Timothy Endicott, John Gardner, and Leslie Green

The Nature of Legislative Intent

OXFORD LEGAL PHILOSOPHY

Series Editors: Timothy Endicott, John Gardner, and Leslie Green

Oxford Legal Philosophy publishes the best new work in philosophically-oriented legal theory. It commissions and solicits monographs in all branches of the subject, including works on philosophical issues in all areas of public and private law, and in the national, transnational, and international realms; studies of the nature of law, legal institutions, and legal reasoning; treatments of problems in political morality as they bear on law; and explorations in the nature and development of legal philosophy itself. The series represents diverse traditions of thought but always with an emphasis on rigour and originality. It sets the standard in contemporary jurisprudence.

ALSO AVAILABLE IN THE SERIES

Reason and Restitution
A Theory of Unjust Enrichment
Charlie Webb

Allowing for Exceptions
A Theory of Defences and Defeasibility in Law
Luís Duarte d'Almeida

The Ends of Harm
The Moral Foundations of Criminal Law
Victor Tadros

Corrective Justice
Ernest J. Weinrib

Conscience and Conviction
The Case for Civil Disobedience
Kimberley Brownlee

Why Law Matters
Alon Harel

The Nature of Legislative Intent

Richard Ekins

UNIVERSITY PRESS

Great Clarendon Street, Oxford, OX2 6DP,
United Kingdom

Oxford University Press is a department of the University of Oxford.
It furthers the University's objective of excellence in research, scholarship,
and education by publishing worldwide. Oxford is a registered trade mark of
Oxford University Press in the UK and in certain other countries

© R. Ekins 2012

The moral rights of the author have been asserted

First published 2012
First published in paperback 2016

All rights reserved. No part of this publication may be reproduced, stored in
a retrieval system, or transmitted, in any form or by any means, without the
prior permission in writing of Oxford University Press, or as expressly permitted
by law, by licence or under terms agreed with the appropriate reprographics
rights organization. Enquiries concerning reproduction outside the scope of the
above should be sent to the Rights Department, Oxford University Press, at the
address above

You must not circulate this work in any other form
and you must impose this same condition on any acquirer

Published in the United States of America by Oxford University Press
198 Madison Avenue, New York, NY 10016, United States of America

British Library Cataloguing in Publication Data
Data available

Library of Congress Cataloguing in Publication Data
Data available

ISBN 978–0–19–964699–9 (Hbk.)
ISBN 978–0–19–876620–9 (Pbk.)

Links to third party websites are provided by Oxford in good faith and
for information only. Oxford disclaims any responsibility for the materials
contained in any third party website referenced in this work.

Series Editors' Preface

Richard Ekins' book is a sustained argument for a well-integrated set of views: that a legislature is a rational agent, that it acts intentionally when it legislates, and that the task of the interpreter is to give effect to that intention. The intention in question is to adopt a reasoned proposal for law making. It is, in fact, the 'interlocking' intention of all the members of the legislature—to act on the reasoned proposal if the majority votes for it. It is a complex intention because it necessarily involves, in Ekins' view, the reasoning behind the proposal.

The result is an original work on the nature and effect of legislation. It has roots in political philosophy and in the philosophy of mind and of language. It presents elements of an account of the nature of law, drawn from the tradition of natural law theory and given new elaboration. The implications of the argument for the theory of interpretation are set out with Ekins' characteristic directness and clarity.

To some it has seemed that a legislature cannot act intentionally, because it is an assembly of individuals who have different intentions, and has no mind of its own. To others it has seemed that the legislature's law making power is simply to enact a text, and that the intention to do so offers no assistance to the interpreter who must determine the meaning of the text. Ekins responds to these theories of legislation with verve, arguing that they entail that legislating is collectively irrational.

The book puts central issues, long debated, in a new perspective. It is a step forward in legal philosophy, when you discover that a controversial position has more to it than you had thought. Readers who disagree with Ekins have that discovery in store.

This book will raise the standard of debate about the making and interpretation of legislation. It will also create new debates. We are delighted to publish Richard Ekins' book in *Oxford Legal Philosophy*.

Timothy Endicott
John Gardner
Les Green
August 2012

The Cover Picture

Althing in Session; oil on canvas by W G Collingwood (1897)

The Althing, the central institution of the Icelandic Commonwealth (930AD–1262AD), was a general assembly of the nation, in which the goðar (chieftains) met to settle disputes and to make new law. All free men were entitled to attend, and assemblies, held for two weeks in mid-summer, drew large numbers of farmers, traders, craftsmen, and storytellers, as well as quarrelling parties. The Althing met at Thingvellir, a magnificent rift valley some 45km east of what is now Reykjavík, and was formally opened and adjourned at Lögberg (law rock) by the assembly's presiding officer, the Lawspeaker.

At the Althing, laws were made and unmade by the Lögrétta (or law council), which consisted of the goðar and the Lawspeaker. The Lögrétta appointed the Lawspeaker, the only paid official of the Commonwealth, for a three-year term. At each assembly, he recited the procedural law of the Althing and one third of the substantive laws then in force. In Collingwood's painting, the Lawspeaker stands on the Lögberg, surrounded by goðar and others, perhaps reciting the law or opening or adjourning the Althing. In the foreground are two booths, stone structures tented over as dwelling or meeting places. From the Lögberg, the members of the Lögrétta would have moved down the slope seen on the left of the painting, to meet in a circular stone platform, the remains of which were discovered in 1742.

Collingwood spent three months in Iceland in the summer of 1897. He recorded his journey in *A Pilgrimage to the Saga-Steads of Iceland* (1899, with Jón Stefánsson), which included over 150 sketches intended, as the Preface says, 'to illustrate the sagas of Iceland . . . to supply the background of scenery which the ancient dramatic style takes for granted'.

Acknowledgements

This book is based on my Oxford doctoral thesis and I am greatly indebted to my supervisor, John Finnis, for his invaluable advice and support. No student could have had more careful, encouraging oversight, or a better model of scholarly rigour. For kindling my interest in the fundamentals of statutory interpretation, I thank Jim Evans, my first teacher of jurisprudence, on whose work I continue to draw deeply, as my final chapter attests.

Balliol College provided an ideal scholarly home throughout my studies in Oxford, for which I thank its members. I am grateful to the Tertiary Education Commission of New Zealand and the Marsden Fund of the Royal Society of New Zealand for financial support. While the thesis was largely conceived and written in Oxford, I completed it in Auckland. The main revisions were later undertaken again in Oxford, on leave from the Faculty of Law at The University of Auckland, for which support and to whose members, especially Paul Rishworth, I am very grateful. I also thank the Oxford Jurisprudence Discussion Group and the Statute Law Society for the opportunity to present my research and for helpful comments.

For reading and commenting on draft chapters and related work, I owe thanks to Larry Alexander, James Allan, David Baragwanath, Nick Barber, Paul Brady, Denis Chang, Timothy Endicott, Jim Evans, Miguel Garcia, Jeffrey Goldsworthy, Leslie Green, Grant Huscroft, John Ip, Maris Köpcke Tinturé, Matthew Kramer, Grant Lamond, Santiago Legarre, Martin Luteran, Bradley Miller, Matthew O'Brien, Philip Pettit, Joseph Raz, Edward Rock, Rodrigo Sánchez Brigido, Philip Sales, Matt Shapiro, Stefan Vogenauer, and Grégoire Webber.

I am especially grateful to Donald Hay, Jan van Zyl Smit, and Paul Yowell who have been tireless in their support. My doctoral examiners, John Gardner and Jeremy Waldron, provided careful and helpful criticism, as well as much encouragement. I thank also Alex Flach and Natasha Flemming of Oxford University Press, as well as an anonymous referee for the Press.

Finally, I thank my wife Rebecca for her constant love, friendship, and patience and our sons James, Alexander, and Henry, who have brought us untold joy.

Contents

List of Abbreviations	xiii
1. Introduction	1
2. Sceptical Arguments	15
I. Stipulating Legislative Intent	15
II. Hermes and 'the Catalogue of Mysteries'	20
III. The Unitary Model and Its Discontents	30
IV. An Alternative: the Voting Machine Model	34
V. Arrow's Theorem and the Legislative Process	40
3. Joint Intention and Group Agency	47
I. The Futility of Summing Intentions	47
II. Joint Intention and Group Action	52
III. Complex Group Action	57
IV. Discursive Dilemmas and Collective Irrationality	66
V. The Idea of Group Agency	71
4. Legislating Without Reasoning	77
I. The Forum of Policy	77
II. Technical Problems With Preference Aggregation	85
III. Reasons and Preferences	88
IV. The Authority of Unintentional Legislation	94
V. Rationality and the Voting Machine	99
VI. The Minimal Intention Argument	107
VII. Intelligible Legislating	112
5. What It Is to Legislate	118
I. Legislative Capacity	118
II. How One Reasons to Legislate	127
III. The Act of Legislating	135
IV. Legislative Integrity	139

6. The Legislative Assembly ... 143
   I. The Problem of the Sole Legislator ... 143
   II. Representation and Deliberation ... 146
   III. The Advantage of an Assembly ... 155
   IV. The Internal Hierarchy of the Legislature ... 161
   V. Washington and Westminster ... 169
   VI. Prospects for Reasoned Action ... 173

7. Language Use and Intention ... 180
   I. The Language Code ... 181
   II. Language Use Is Rational Action ... 193
   III. The Underdetermination Thesis ... 196
   IV. Pragmatics ... 205
   V. Legislative Language Use ... 211

8. The Nature of Legislative Intent ... 218
   I. The Standing Intention of the Legislature ... 219
   II. Parliamentary Procedure ... 224
   III. Legislative Intent in Particular Acts ... 230
   IV. Agency and Compromise ... 236

9. Intentions in Interpretation ... 244
   I. The Object of Interpretation ... 244
   II. Intentions, Purposes, and Applications ... 249
   III. Legislative Context ... 256
   IV. The Use and Misuse of Context: Some Examples ... 261
   V. The Relevance of Legislative History ... 268
   VI. Equitable Interpretation ... 275

Bibliography ... 285
Index ... 294

List of Abbreviations

Aquinas	J Finnis, *Aquinas: Moral, Political, and Legal Theory* (Oxford University Press, Oxford, 1998)
BAI	J Raz, *Between Authority and Interpretation: On the Theory of Law and Practical Reason* (Oxford University Press, Oxford, 2009)
BST	F A R Bennion, *Bennion on Statutory Interpretation*, 5th edn (LexisNexis, London, 2008)
ILT	A Marmor, *Interpretation and Legal Theory* (Oxford University Press, Oxford, 1992)
LD	J Waldron, *Law and Disagreement* (Clarendon Press, Oxford, 1999)
LE	R Dworkin, *Law's Empire* (Hart, Oxford, 1998)
NLNR	J Finnis, *Natural Law and Natural Rights* (Clarendon Press, Oxford, 1980)
ST	*Summa Theologica of St Thomas Aquinas* [A Summary of Theology]

1

Introduction

Legislatures enact statutes, the enactment of which (somehow) changes the law. Judges and lawyers, in interpreting a statute—adjudging its meaning and determining its lawmaking effect—very often try (and say that they are trying) to identify the legislature's intentions in enacting it. That is, they try (and say that they are trying) to reach a conclusion about what were or were not the meanings the legislature intended to convey and/or the ends (or purposes) it intended to pursue by means it intended to be followed. This *legislative intent* has traditionally been thought to be the central object of statutory interpretation. Much public discourse, too, takes for granted that the legislature is capable of forming and acting on intentions. This book elucidates the nature of legislative intent, explaining how and why the institution forms and acts on intentions. It shows intention's justified centrality in the very idea of having a legislature and recognizing acts of legislating, and in the historic and reasonable practice of statutory interpretation.

The central importance of legislative intent is defended by theorists as diverse as Aquinas and Hobbes. Transmitting one-and-a-half millennia of philosophical and juristic tradition, Aquinas taught that the adoption of laws requires the judge like anyone else to comply not with their letter (their wording) so much as with their maker's intentions.[1] Hobbes maintained that 'it is not the letter, but the intendment, or meaning; that is to say, the authentic interpretation of the law (which is the sense of the legislator), in which the nature of the

---

[1] Aquinas, *ST*, I–II q. 91 a. 1c, I–II q. 96 a. 6, and II–II q. 60 a. 5 ad 2; see further Finnis, *Aquinas*, 255–8, especially n 19.

law consisteth'.[2] And that was the position of great masters of English law, with Blackstone, to take just one instance, arguing that:

The fairest and most rational method to interpret the will of the legislator, is by exploring his intentions at the time when the law was made, by *signs* the most natural and probable. And these signs are either the words, the context, the subject matter, the effects and consequence, or the spirit and reason of the law.[3]

Today the leading English text on statutory interpretation states in no uncertain terms that:

An enactment has the legal meaning taken to be intended by the legislator. In other words the legal meaning corresponds to the legislative intention... [T]he function of the court is to find out and declare that intention [which] is the paramount, indeed only ultimate, criterion.[4]

Among countless judicial affirmations of this position, many emphasize *expressed* intention: 'The duty of the courts is to ascertain and give effect to the will of Parliament as expressed in its enactments'.[5] 'There are many so-called rules of construction that courts of law have resorted to in their interpretation of statutes, but the paramount rule remains that every statute is to be expounded according to its manifest or expressed intention.'[6] So some scholars contrast expressed with unexpressed or *subjective* intention,[7] a distinction I will consider and contest. What remains striking is the judicial willingness to declare legislative intent the central object of interpretive practice. At the end of a far-reaching set of comparative studies of statutory

---

[2] T Hobbes, *Leviathan*, ed A Martinich (Broadview Press, Peterborough, 2005) chapter XXVI ('On civil law').
[3] W Blackstone, *Commentaries on the Laws of England* (Oxford, 1765–9) cited to 9th edn (1783), the last revised by Blackstone, Book I, 59.
[4] Bennion, *BST*, 469.
[5] *Corocraft v Pan-Am* [1969] 1 QB 616 at 638, per Donaldson MR.
[6] *Attorney-General for Canada v Hallett & Carey Ltd* [1952] AC 427 at 449, per Lord Radcliffe.
[7] A Kavanagh, 'The Role of Parliamentary Intention in Adjudication under the Human Rights Act 1998' (2006) 26 Oxford Journal of Legal Studies 179, 181–3; J Manning, 'Textualism and Legislative Intent' (2005) 91 Virginia Law Review 419, 425–6.

interpretation, MacCormick and Summers observe that argument from intention is a central, trans-categorical type of interpretive argument in all systems[8]—trans-categorical because it informs and is informed by other types, which they term linguistic, systemic, or teleological/evaluative.[9] MacCormick and Summers note various tensions in the way legislative intent is understood in various legal systems and they are themselves somewhat sceptical about the idea's coherence or relevance.[10] Still, they emphasize that it is pervasive, even ubiquitous, in interpretive practice.

But all this is under challenge. Many judges, 'conservatives' and 'progressives' alike, and many scholars now doubt or flatly deny that the institution itself has intentions, reasoning that the modern legislature is typically an assembly of legislators rather than one legislator. Justice Scalia of the United States Supreme Court is a well-known sceptic.[11] Judges in New Zealand,[12] Australia, and the United Kingdom[13] have also all expressed doubts. For example, Michael Kirby, a Justice of the Australian High Court, writes:

So far as Acts of Parliament are concerned, it is unfortunately still common to see reference in judicial reasons and scholarly texts to the 'intention of Parliament'. I never use that expression now. It is potentially misleading. In Australia, other judges too regard the fiction as unhelpful. It is difficult to attribute an 'intention' of a document such as a statute. Typically, it is prepared by many hands and submitted to a decision-maker of many different opinions, so that to talk of a single 'intention' is self-deception.[14]

---

[8] D N MacCormick and R S Summers, 'Interpretation and Justification', chapter 13 in D N MacCormick and R S Summers (eds), *Interpreting Statutes: A Comparative Study* (Dartmouth Press, Aldershot, 1991), 511, 515 and 522–5.

[9] MacCormick and Summers (n 8) 512–21.

[10] D N MacCormick, 'Coherence in Legal Justification' in A Peczenik, L Lindhal, and G van Roermund (eds), *Theory of Legal Science* (Reidel Publishing Co, Boston, Dordrecht, 1984), 235, 240.

[11] A Scalia, *A Matter of Interpretation: Federal Courts and the Law*, A Gutmann (ed) (Princeton University Press, Princeton, 1998), 3, 16–23.

[12] K J Keith, *Interpreting Treaties, Statutes and Contracts* (Occasional Paper No 19, New Zealand Centre for Public Law, Wellington, 2009) 4–5; *R v Hansen* [2007] 3 NZLR 1 at [14], per Elias CJ; and New Zealand Law Commission, *A New Interpretation Act to Avoid 'Prolixity and Tautology'* (NZLC R17, 1990) at [73].

[13] J Steyn, '*Pepper v Hart*; A Re-examination' (2001) 21 Oxford Journal of Legal Studies 59.

[14] M Kirby, 'Towards a Grand Theory of Interpretation: The Case of Statutes and Contracts' (2003) 24 Statute Law Review 95, 98–9.

His speculation about other Australian judges now seems confirmed by the High Court's apparent consensus that legislative intent is a metaphor rather than a social fact.[15] These judicial qualms about and denials of the classic position rely in part on, and are echoed and extended in, scholarly scepticism. Cross for example argues that the expression 'the intention of Parliament' is 'not so much a description as a linguistic convenience',[16] for in truth '[o]nly human beings can really have intentions, purposes, or objects'.[17]

Much turns on whether legislative intent exists. The question plainly bears on the way in which judges and others interpret statutes. Should one aim to infer what the author(s) of the statute decided or intended? When, if ever, and on what grounds, may one depart from the literal or ordinary meaning of the statutory text? What place, if any, is there for 'purpose' in interpretation? How, if at all, may the statute's meaning or application change over time? The way in which we understand the nature of the legislature in general is also at stake. What should we expect of the institution? Is it an agent that responds to reasons with choice or is it a device—an arrangement or sort of machine—for producing outcomes? The nature of legislative intent informs how one should understand salient features of the legislative process (parties, offices), the character and point of the institution (representative, deliberative), and the duties of legislators. How one conceives of the institution frames political discourse, which in turn goes to questions about separation of powers, such as the grounds or scope of judicial review of legislation. My project is not to run all these implications to ground, but plainly the stakes are high.

The principal concerns about legislative intent which inform more recent judicial and scholarly scepticism are in fact not new. Gustav Radbruch argued in 1910 that it made no sense for statutory interpretation to centre on legislative intent, for:

...philological interpretation, striving to draw out of a mental creation the thought put into it by its creator, amounts to thinking about something

---

[15] *Momcilovic v The Queen* [2011] HCA 34 (8 September 2011).

[16] J Bell and G Engle (eds), *Cross on Statutory Interpretation*, 3rd edn (Butterworths, London, 1995), 28.

[17] Bell and Engle (n 16) 27. The quotes in the main text are found in the 1976 first edition, which was prepared by Cross himself. In the later editions, after his death, his editors add that 'an appeal to "the intention of Parliament"... is used as a statement of attitude or approach, not as an element of social fact to be researched' (at 31).

thought. The jurist can make no use of this in interpreting the statute, for the statute is not the creation of a single individual but is, rather, the product of many individuals acting in concert.[18]

The objection thus is that because the statute is not made by any one person, there may not be (and indeed, by implication, cannot be) one line of thought that animates the statute and could be discovered by an interpreter. Much the same concern informs Max Radin's very influential 1930 critique. Having noted the widespread view that the right way to interpret a statute is to discover the intent of the legislator, he scoffs:

On this transparent and absurd fiction it ought not to be necessary to dwell. It is clearly enough an illegitimate transference to law of concepts proper enough in literature and theology. The least reflection makes clear that the law maker, *der Gesetzgeber*, *le législateur*, does not exist, and only worse confusion follows when in his place there are substituted the members of the legislature as a body. A legislature certainly has no intention whatever in connection with words which some two or three men drafted, which a considerable number rejected, and in regard to which many of the approving majority might have had, and often demonstrably did have, different ideas and beliefs.[19]

His assertion that the lawmaker does not exist may seem absurd, for an assembly of legislators, which forms the institution of the legislature, acts to make law. However, Radin means that 'the members of the legislature as a body' do not constitute a single (natural) person and therefore do not have the relevant mental states.[20] He reasons that the institution has no intention if multiple persons draft the statute, if some reject it, and if the members of the enacting majority have different views.

Still, it is not immediately clear *why* these features of the legislative process entail that legislature has no intention. Interestingly, after this

---

[18] G Radbruch, *Einführung in die Rechtswissenschaft* (Quelle & Meyer, Leipzig, 1910), 118, cited in S Paulson, 'Statutory Positivism' (2007) 1 Legisprudence 1, 21–2.
[19] M Radin, 'Statutory Interpretation' (1930) 43 Harvard Law Review 863, 870.
[20] This reading is confirmed by his use of similar language elsewhere: 'Indeed, it was common to speak as though the law was the word of a single person, *le législateur*, *der Gesetzgeber*' (M Radin, 'A Short Way with Statutes' (1943) 56 Harvard Law Review 388, 393).

very direct and forceful critique, Radin shifts focus somewhat, and argues not that the 'legislature certainly has no intention' but '[t]hat the intention of the legislature is undiscoverable in any real sense'.[21] His two claims are incompatible. If the legislature has no intentions, then its intentions are not undiscoverable—they simply do not exist. To be difficult or even impossible to discover, something must exist. The reason he says the intention is undiscoverable is that '[t]he chances that of several hundred men each will have exactly the same determinate situations in mind as possible reductions of a given determinable, are infinitesimally small'.[22] This amounts to an argument that legislative intent does not exist, but it presupposes that under certain conditions it would exist. Radin later argues that one might discover the mind of the draftsman or of a very small committee that approves every word of the statutory text, but insists that this is simply not possible for the legislature. The reason is that:

Even if the contents of the minds of the legislature were uniform, we have no means of knowing that content except by the external utterances or behaviour of these hundreds of men, and in almost every case the only external act is the extremely ambiguous one of acquiescence, which may be motivated in literally hundreds of ways, and which by itself indicates little or nothing of the pictures which the statutory descriptions imply.[23]

Thus, Radin argues that too little information exists to conclude that all (or a majority of) the legislators had any particular pictures in mind. (There is, as was soon demonstrated, a wholly implausible understanding of intention at work here.[24]) The implication is that the legislature would, like a small committee, have an intention if a majority of its members held the same mental state. Radin's brief discussion here anticipates two ways in which some scholars have since sought to explain legislative intent—first, as an intention held by each member of the voting majority, or second, as the intentions held by some smaller group of legislators.[25] I shall argue that neither is sound, for neither explains how the legislators *act in concert*, to use Radbruch's

---

[21] Radin (n 19) 870. [22] Radin (n 19) 870. [23] Radin (n 19) 870–1.
[24] For incisive criticism, see L Fuller, 'American Legal Realism' (1934) 82 University of Pennsylvania Law Review 429, 445–7.
[25] These are sometimes termed the majority model and the agency model: G MacCallum, *Legislative Intent and Other Essays on Law, Politics, and Morality* (University of Wisconsin Press, Madison, 1993), 26–33.

phrase. The puzzle is to explain how the action of the legislators, plural, constitutes the action of the legislature singular.

Radin has another argument of interest, namely that legislative intent would in any case be irrelevant. The function of the legislature, he contends, is to enact statutes. The legislature need not form intentions to legislate and the judiciary need not find or defer to its intentions to interpret statutes. The irrelevance argument centres on the point or function of the legislature. Radin denies that the legislature has any right to rule over other citizens and officials. The modern legislature, he maintains, is not a sovereign but a democratic assembly and in law the function of the legislators 'is not to impose their will even within limits on their fellow-citizens, but to "pass statutes", which is a fairly precise operation. That is, they make statements in general terms of undesirable and desirable situations, from which flow certain results'.[26] The legislature's function is discharged, he concludes, when it has enacted some set of words, not when it forms intentions to supplement that text. That is, '[w]hen the legislature has uttered the words of a statute, it is *functus officio*, not because of the Montesquieuan separation of powers, but because that is what legislating means'.[27] In short, we are not subject to legislative will; but intention is a matter of will; so we are not subject to, and need not be concerned with, legislative intent.

This account of the legislative function is confirmed, Radin argues, by the way in which the legislature acts. The legislature, he says, is unable to legislate just by making clear an intention. Instead, the legislature must act by reference to the rules of procedure that constitute the legislative process, and so it must issue a text, rather than a diagram or illustration, and the text must be in English (for example). The formation of an intention, he maintains, does not suffice for legislation to be enacted, whereas following the procedural rules and

---

[26] Radin (n 19) 871; see also Radin (n 20) 388–95, in which he traces the historical importance of the idea of the sovereign legislature, but argues that the modern American legislature is not of this kind. He concludes, at 395, speaking of the American legislature: 'It was the business of the legislature to get the statute on the books. When that was completed the task of the coordinate branches began.' There follows a more explicit discussion, at 405–7, of the limited function of the legislature, which Radin argues has no authority higher than anyone else, is not the political superior of the judge or administrator, and has no right to have its will (if it had one) imposed on others.

[27] Radin (n 19) 871.

producing a text does suffice.[28] Radin thus again insists that forming (and acting on) intentions is not part of what it is to legislate.

The legislative function and process are of central importance in explaining legislating, but Radin's account of each is very weak. His claim that legislators may not impose their will on others is confused. Legislators may not have arbitrary power, but they do have authority to change the content of the law and presumably act to change the law in some way. To this extent, legislators have the right to impose their will—their choices about what direction should be followed in some aspect of their community's affairs—on others; it is difficult to explain how else their participation in legislating would be rational. Radin is also wrong to take the existence of procedural rules to prove that intentions are superfluous to legislative action. The rules are contingent. The Westminster Parliament, for example, is free to legislate as its members see fit, in accordance with procedures that they adopt and may change.[29] This control over procedure suggests that they legislate by making clear an intention to legislate and the procedures they adopt are a means to this end. Likewise, constitutionally fixed procedural rules are arguably best understood to be formal restrictions on how the legislature's intention is to be expressed rather than to entail that when acting within the rules, the legislature need have no intention. Their mere existence does not prove Radin's point.

Radin's pithy, pugnacious article anticipates many of the main lines of later scholarship. His initial, confident assertion that the institution of the legislature obviously does not act on intentions is undercut by his subsequent discussion, which rightly (if not clearly) attends to some important features of the legislative process and to the point of legislating. Radin's muddle is instructive. Untangling the nature of the legislative act, and determining what if anything might intelligibly be thought to constitute the legislative intent in that act, requires one to think through a range of related questions. The central puzzle, on which Radbruch and Radin and many others focus, is how an institution, which is a group of persons rather than one single person, may reasonably and accurately be said to have an intention, such that interpreters (and others) may profitably reflect on the line of thought

---

[28] Radin (n 19) 871.
[29] R Ekins, 'Acts of Parliament and the Parliament Acts' (2007) 123 Law Quarterly Review 91, 100–8.

that explains the statute, in the same way that the reasoning and choice of any author explains his text.

Related questions concern the nature of the legislative assembly (the scope of its authority, its procedures and capacities) and the nature of language use and legislating—of deliberate lawmaking (and so of law itself). Thus, to understand the legislature and its action, one must reflect on the philosophy of language and of social action, as well as political and legal philosophy.

My strategy throughout this book is to consider the reasons for instituting and maintaining the legislature, for participating in its action as a legislator, and for understanding its acts as in some way changing what one has duty to do. In this way, I aim to perceive and explain the shape of the well-formed legislature and its action, which is the exercise of its distinctive capacities. The legislature is the pre-eminent lawmaking body in any good polity, as well as the central political institution, the deliberation and action of which is the focus of democratic political life. The rationale for the institution is its capacity to act to change the law for good reasons. The book's central argument is that there are good reasons for the legislature to form and act on intentions, and that it is possible for it to do so and for these intentions to constitute the legislative intent. Legislative intent, I argue, is an intelligible idea, instantiated in countless legislative acts and central to how one should interpret the statutes the legislature enacts.

The main body of this work begins in chapter 2 with a close study of some leading sceptical arguments. The arguments powerfully elaborate the doubts that Radin (and Radbruch) sketched and many judges and other scholars now share. I focus on the most sophisticated philosophical sceptics, Ronald Dworkin and Jeremy Waldron, whose arguments are similar, to some extent mutually reinforcing, and yet subtly different. I also consider an argument from political science that concerns the implications of social choice theory for legislative action and intention. The sceptical arguments frame the discourse in a certain way, stipulating that legislative intent is (and could only intelligibly and plausibly be thought to be) an aggregation of the intentions of the many individual legislators. This stipulation begs the question, I argue. It also entails that the sceptical arguments have a narrower scope than is often recognized, not least by the sceptics in question. This aggregative conception of legislative intent Dworkin subjects to withering criticism for its arbitrariness and incoherence. Waldron argues that the central features of the legislative process, and their rationale, make unsound any conception of the legislature as a unitary agent, capable of forming and acting on complex intentions. Instead, he argues one should conceive of the legislative process as a voting machine, such that statutes are, per Radin's prescription, understood to be outcomes or products rather than the intelligent choices of some agent. Dworkin and Waldron's critique of legislative agency is reinforced, in broad brush if not in all details, by the argument from social choice theory that collective choices are incoherent, being determined more by an arbitrary institutional matrix than by stable majority will.

The sceptical arguments are forceful and say much that is true. They succeed, I contend, in discrediting aggregative conceptions of legislative intent, which I disavow and indeed criticize further. However, their scope is narrow—they do not address, and certainly do not refute, the possibility of the institution itself forming and acting on intentions, intentions which do not reduce to the aggregate of the intentions of each legislator, considered for his or her part only. Indeed, at various points the arguments suggest the importance and plausibility of such an understanding of what legislators do jointly, of how they act in concert. This puts in play the question of which theory of legislative action is sound, and I return in a later chapter to contest the understanding of legislating presupposed or made out in the work of the sceptics. Attending to the philosophical grounds of scepticism in this way helps frame my own argument in response to the strongest reasons for denying the legislature capable of forming and acting on intentions.

A sketch of that response. The sceptical arguments fail to see the possibility of and the need for the legislature to constitute an agent. They assume that institutions or groups at large are incapable of joint action, coordinated by joint intention. I explain the social reality of joint action and intention in chapter 3, rejecting as wholly unsound accounts (which have been extended to the legislature) of group intention as the sum of the intentions of each member of the group. Such accounts fail even to grasp the nature of the relevant type of group, which is an association whose members act for some common end. Joint intention is, I argue, the common plan of action adopted by all members of the group to that end. The plan of action arises out of the interlocking intentions of the members of the group, but does not reduce to the intention of any one or more individual members. More complex groups adopt plans to form and act on further plans, which means that they act on a series of nested intentions over time. Importantly, many groups have good reason to attend to the extent to which they respond to reasons like a rational agent. The use of majority vote, or indeed almost any other procedure, to decide on a series of interlinked propositions poses a standing risk of incoherence, of collective irrationality. For good reason, some groups are structured to avoid this risk, adopting procedures and dispositions to attend to the rationality of their actions (including over time). This is to form and maintain group agency. In this way I argue that there is no mystery in how institutions form and act on intentions or even constitute rational group agents.

The core of the book is set out in chapters 4–8, in which I aim to articulate the reasonable legislator's self-understanding. That is, I aim to see the point of legislating, which is to say the object of sound legislative action, and thence to understand the significance of legislative structure and the ways in which the legislator and legislators strive to use language and to cooperate to act together to change the law. I have said that the sceptical arguments fail to see the rational *need* for legislative agency. I substantiate this claim in chapter 4, in which I consider and evaluate theories of legislating in which the legislature is said to be incapable of responding to reasons with detailed, complex intention. The theories make out different claims about the legislative process and the rationale for legislating, but all fail to make intelligible the reasonable legislator's participation in the process, for they do not explain how legislating might change the law in some reasonable way. Indeed, the theories in question entail that legislating is collectively irrational and unreasonable.

Chapter 5 sets out my own understanding of what it is to legislate. The reason to form and maintain the institution of the legislature is, I say, to enable the exercise of the capacity to act deliberately to change the law when there is good reason for change. This capacity is valuable: the legislature's openness in principle to all that is relevant, and its freedom to act deliberately and comprehensively, make it well suited to be the polity's central or leading lawmaking body. For any one person to legislate well—say, a prince—he must undertake a complex chain of reasoning that finds its completion in the choice of some detailed plan of action, linking ends and means in a kind of chain and, to shift the metaphor, nesting ends within each other. The well-formed legislative act—bracketing questions about the assembly's capacity to act—is intentional, and indeed is defined by a complex intention that is at least closely relevant to the legal changes the act should be understood to introduce.

The modern legislature is of course an assembly rather than a prince and chapter 6 explores the nature of the legislative assembly. I reflect on the good reasons to authorize an assembly rather than a prince to legislate and argue that these reasons change who legislates, but not what it is to legislate. The assembly should be representative *and* deliberative, acting (like the prince) to change the law by way of coherent, reasoned choices. The assembly's size and diversity does constitute an obstacle to its acting well. For this reason, legislators introduce an internal hierarchy, conferring on some unequal access to the legislative agenda. The character of the particular legislature turns in part on the pattern of legislative offices and procedures that constitute the relevant internal hierarchy. There are important differences in this respect between the Westminster and Washington models, yet in both cases the structure of the legislature is intended to make possible reasoned action.

Theories of legislating without reasoning, some of which are considered in chapter 4, take for granted that one may understand language use without reference to intention, save perhaps the intention to adopt the conventional meaning of the text in question. I refute this assumption in chapter 7, in which I argue that language use is rational action and that the semantic content (the literal meaning) of the text underdetermines the meaning the author is likely to intend to convey in uttering it in this context. Thus, the central reality of understanding some instance of language use is inference about the language user's intended meaning. There are good reasons to think the same true for legislating, I suggest, because it would be irrational and impractical to aim to legislate by intending only the semantic content of the statutory text. The obvious way to use language to legislate is to act to convey one's intended meaning, which is inferred from one's utterance of the text in context.

These various lines of argument about the rationality of legislating, the nature of the assembly, and of language use, come together in chapter 8, in which I explain how the legislature forms and acts on intentions. My explanation differs sharply from the standard attempts to attribute to the legislature the shared intention of the majority or the intentions of leading legislators. Instead, applying my analysis of joint intention and group agency in chapter 3, I argue that the legislature develops and adopts a reasoned proposal for legislative action, which is open to legislators throughout the legislative process, and especially at the final vote on the third reading. The internal structure of the legislature, in which a subset of legislators enjoys agenda-setting power, is vital to enable coherent, reasoned proposals to be formed and put before the assembly. However, the legislature's act is an act on that open proposal. Reasonable legislators understand what is open not to be the literal meaning of the bill, but to be a complex, coherent proposal, which is a reasoned choice and has a certain meaning: this is the upshot of the conception of reasonable legislative action that I outline across chapters 4–7. *The interlocking intention of all legislators is to act on the proposal when a majority votes for it.* Therefore, the act of legislating is the joint act of all legislators, including those in the voting minority. Further, the plan on which the group acts, which is the intention that explains its joint act, is the proposal open to all, which does not reduce to the intentions of any one or more legislators. The assembly is thus capable of acting on an intention that is much more detailed and specific than that held by most individual legislators, many of whom may be ignorant about the statutory detail, for the legislative intent is the proposal held in common and open to all legislators, not the sum of their particular intentions. The legislature forms an agent, which is likely to act on coherent, reasoned plans of action, and this rational agency is, I argue, consistent with the possibility of legislative compromise.

This conception of legislative intent has important implications for interpretation and political practice. Chapter 9 begins to think through what follows for statutory interpretation. I argue that there is good reason to take the central object of interpretive practice to be the intended meaning of the legislature, the identification of which often turns in part on inference about the reasoned scheme the legislature acts to choose. However, this intended meaning does not collapse to the ends for which the legislature acted or to any beliefs or assumptions one or more legislator may make about its likely application. Legislative intent is not, I stress, one more source of evidence for the meaning of the statute, but is instead the basic object of interpretive reflection.

One infers legislative intent from the utterance of this text in context, a context that consists in what is known and of concern to legislature and community. Interpreters go wrong if they neglect the richness of the context in which the legislature acts and if they ignore or distort what it is plausible to think the legislature chose given this context and the detail of the statutory text. It is common to conflate legislative history—in the narrow sense of *travaux préparatoires*—with legislative intent. I argue that the centrality of the latter in no way entails the extensive, or even any, use of the former; indeed, my focus on legislative intent suggests reasons to eschew reference to legislative history. The chapter concludes by arguing that in some exceptional cases there are good reasons to recognize the qualification or extension of the intended meaning of the statutory text, by reference to the reasoned choice the legislature made in enacting the statute. I suggest then that equitable interpretation is licensed, and limited, by legislative intent.

The argument of the book is that there is reason to think that the well-formed legislature exercises rational agency in legislating, forming and acting on complex intentions to convey certain meanings and to change the law in the chosen way, for the common good. This theory of legislative intent makes plausible much of the orthodox or classic practice of statutory interpretation and warrants conceiving of that practice as a process of reflection on, and intelligent engagement with, the rational action of another—the agent that is the enacting legislature. It also makes clear what is sound in the concerns of those judges who have challenged the orthodox or classic formulae as a description of good judicial practice, but who can be seen to be conforming to that practice in substance. The truth of legislative agency should also inform wider reflection on the institution and the scope of its rightful authority. The nature of legislative intent is thus central to, and illuminates, the exercise of legislative authority and the interpretation of what results from that exercise: statutes. For to legislate well is to choose some plan to change the law for the common good, which the subjects of the law should adopt as if it were their own.

2
Sceptical Arguments

This chapter outlines the main grounds of scepticism about legislative intent, focusing on the work of the two leading modern philosophical sceptics, Dworkin and Waldron,[1] but attending also to relevant work in political science. The point of the chapter is to outline how these scholars understand the idea of legislative intent and the grounds on which they deny that it is possible for legislative intent to exist. The sceptical arguments all focus on the significance of the fact that the modern legislature is a group of legislators. I contend that the arguments refute a certain understanding of legislative intent, in which intent is thought to be the aggregate of the intentions of (some or all of) the individual legislators, but fail to disprove the possibility that the institution itself forms and acts on intentions.

I. Stipulating Legislative Intent[2]

Dworkin's argument against legislative intent is very well known.[3] He sets out his argument in its most sophisticated form in chapter 9

---

[1] John Gardner identifies Dworkin and Waldron as 'notable doubters' of the thought that an institution, such as Parliament, may have intentions: J Gardner, 'Some Types of Law' in D Edlin (ed), *Common Law Theory* (Cambridge University Press, Cambridge, 2007), 51, 56, n 14.

[2] The first two sections of this chapter draw heavily on sections II.1 and III of my 'Legislative Intent in *Law's Empire*' (2011) 24 Ratio Juris 435, 436–40, 442–50.

[3] It is routinely cited by sceptics about legislative intent, including judges and scholars of statutory interpretation: see, for instance, J Steyn, '*Pepper v Hart*; A Re-examination' (2001)

of *Law's Empire*,[4] in the course of elucidating his own theory of statutory interpretation.[5] The argument begins by stipulating that legislative intent is the aggregate of the intentions of the many legislators. This stipulation is important and frames Dworkin's main critique (see section 11 of this chapter).

For Dworkin, 'propositions of law are true if they figure in or follow from the principles of justice, fairness, and procedural due process that provide the best constructive interpretation of the community's legal practice'.[6] This theory he terms law as integrity. He explains the implications for common law adjudication in chapter 8 of *Law's Empire* and for statutory interpretation in chapter 9. At the start of chapter 9, he describes his method for reading statutes in the following way:

Hercules will use much the same techniques of interpretation to read statutes that he used to decide common-law cases... He will treat Congress as an author earlier than himself in the chain of law, though an author with special powers and responsibilities different from his own, and he will see his own role as fundamentally the creative one of a partner continuing to develop, in what he believes is the best way, the statutory scheme Congress began. He will ask himself which reading of the act... shows the political history including and surrounding that statute in the better light.[7]

This choice of language may initially seem surprising because Dworkin's subsequent argument is that it is a mistake to think that Congress is an author or to attempt to interpret statutes by responding to its intention. Although Hercules is to treat Congress as an author, Dworkin does not mean that Congress is in fact an author. The formulation 'treat Congress as an author earlier than himself in the chain of law' refers back to chapter 7, where Dworkin explains constructive interpretation in law by way of an analogy to a chain

---

21 Oxford Journal of Legal Studies, 59, 65 and J Bell and G Engle (eds), *Cross on Statutory Interpretation*, 3rd edn (Butterworths, London, 1995), 26.

[4] *LE*, 313–54. The argument in *Law's Empire* is the high point of Dworkin's scepticism about legislative intent. His earlier and especially his later work is much less sceptical and expounds what is to my mind a much more plausible account of how legislators act. For a helpful review of the shifts in Dworkin's position over time, see J Goldsworthy, 'Dworkin as an Originalist' (2000) 17 Constitutional Commentary 49.

[5] For a close restatement of the argument, see S Guest, 'Interpretation and Commitment in Legal Reasoning' in M Freeman (ed), *Legislation and the Courts* (Ashgate, Dartmouth, 1997), 133.

[6] *LE*, 225.   [7] *LE*, 313.

novel.[8] Law as integrity, Dworkin argued, requires the judge deciding a common law case 'to think of himself as an author in the chain of common law'.[9] That is, the judge should interpret the decisions of past judges, which are analogous to the contributions of earlier authors to a chain novel, deciding the present case in the way that best fits and justifies those decisions, thus showing the entire line of cases in the best light possible.

Dworkin notes that his argument for 'how judges should interpret statutes under law as integrity' faces 'an important objection'.[10] The objection is that 'Hercules' method ignores the important principle, firmly rooted in our legal practice, that statutes should be read, not according to what judges believe would make them best, but according to what the legislators who actually adopted them intended'.[11] Having stipulated the objection in this form, Dworkin says that it is true that American judges refer to the statements that legislators make about the purpose of an act and that they take this set of statements to be the 'legislative history', which they must respect.[12]

One may view this practice, he says, in one of two ways. The first is, like Hercules, to treat the statements as political acts, which, like the text of the statute, the best interpretation must fit and explain. The second way, which Dworkin says is presupposed by the objection, is to treat the 'statements not as events important in themselves, but as evidence of the mental states of the particular legislators who made them, presumed to be representative of the mental states of the majority of legislators whose votes created the statute'.[13] Dworkin terms this:

> ...the 'speaker's meaning' view because it assumes that legislation is an occasion or instance of communication and that judges look to legislative history when a statute is not clear on its face to discover what state of mind the legislators tried to communicate through their votes. It supposes, in short, that proper interpretation of a statute must be... conversational rather than constructive interpretation. The ruling model of this theory is the familiar model of ordinary speech.[14]

Dworkin does not cite any theorist or judge who has adopted this view. He stipulates the objection and the way he does so is telling. The stipulation in its initial form refers to what the *legislators* intended

---

[8] *LE*, 228–39. [9] *LE*, 238–9. [10] *LE*, 314.
[11] *LE*, 314. [12] *LE*, 314. [13] *LE*, 314. [14] *LE*, 315.

(at 314), which obscures the possibility that what matters is what the *legislature* intended. More significant still is Dworkin's shift from this initial statement to consider how and why American judges use legislative history. At first it seems that he has simply changed the subject. However, the effect of this shift in focus is to conflate the initial objection's concern with what the legislators (or legislature) intended with what the legislative history reveals about the mental states of particular legislators. This leads to Dworkin's conclusion that the speaker's meaning view is that when a statute is not clear one looks to the legislative history 'to discover the state of mind the legislators tried to communicate through their votes'.

There are two problems with this conflation. Many theorists and judges who might object to Dworkin's approach understand a statute to be clear or not to the extent to which one may identify the speaker's meaning. They need not adopt the view, which Dworkin attributes to them by implication, that the statute is clear or not on some basis other than the best judgment of what the speaker—the legislature— intended. Further, the conflation is parochial. The use of legislative history was long forbidden in England,[15] and yet judges and lawyers understood the meaning of the statute to be settled by what the legislature intended to communicate in this or that act.[16] This alternate possibility establishes that the speaker's meaning objection to constructive interpretation does not reduce to studying legislative history to reveal the mental state of individual legislators. Dworkin is aware of the English practice. He later relies on its contrast with the American practice to argue that the latter is only justified if the statements of legislators have some role intermediate between open debate and enacted text.[17] What he has not acknowledged is that the intelligibility of the English practice means that refuting the stipulated objection is not the same as refuting the use of legislative intent in general.

The stipulation continues. Dworkin attributes the following line of thought to the person who accepts the speaker's meaning view:

He will present his conclusions as statements about the intention of the statute itself. Is it the purpose or intention of the Endangered Species Act to give the secretary a certain power? But he regards the intention of

---

[15] The rule was relaxed somewhat in *Pepper v Hart* [1993] AC 593.
[16] See further nn 4–6 in chapter 1.   [17] *LE*, 344.

the statute as a theoretical construction, a compendious statement of the discrete intentions of particular actual people, because only these can have conversational intentions of the sort he has in mind.[18]

This attribution is worth unravelling. What is attributed is the proposition that the intention of the statute is a compendium of the intentions of particular individuals. The interpreter has to understand speaker's meaning in this way, Dworkin argues, because only individual persons have mental states. The implication is that the legislature itself, not being an actual person, cannot have conversational intentions. This assertion entails that the intention of the statute has to be constructed out of the 'discrete intentions of particular actual people'. That is, the interpreter cannot find speaker's meaning but must construct it.

Later, he makes this conclusion explicit:

It seemed a metaphysical mistake to take the 'intention' of the legislature itself as primary so long as Hermes was in the grip of some mental-state version of the speaker's meaning theory of legislative intent. So long as we think legislative intention is a matter of what someone has in mind and means to communicate by a vote, we must take as primary the mental states of particular people because institutions do not have minds, and then we must worry about how to consolidate individual intentions into a collective, fictitious intention.[19]

That is, Dworkin asserts that it is a tacit premise of the speaker's meaning theory that the legislature cannot have an intention because it is an institution. This way of framing the problem is critical because it rules out any serious inquiry into how or if the legislature as an institution might have intentions and it commits the speaker's meaning theorist to the conclusion that what is termed 'legislative intent' is a construction, a fiction. Dworkin never advances an argument for this critical premise. He takes its truth to be obvious. Elsewhere in *Law's Empire*, he does address the metaphysics, as he terms it, of groups.[20] Specifically, he discusses the personification of groups, which is relevant to the central place that the community personified has in law as integrity. That discussion is intriguing, but it does not establish that institutions cannot have intentions; instead, it too assumes

---

[18] *LE*, 315.   [19] *LE*, 335–6.   [20] *LE*, 167–71.

that premise and then struggles to explain intelligibly what it is to personify a group.[21]

The way that Dworkin stipulates the speaker's meaning theory is important. Over the next twenty-one pages, Dworkin argues that interpreters should abandon the attempt to aggregate the intentions of actual people into some fictional collective intention.[22] The argument repays close attention. However, it also begs the question. If the premise is true, then the conclusion is true also. What needs to be determined is precisely whether it is true that the legislature cannot have an intention so that any talk of legislative intent is 'a compendious statement of the discrete intentions of particular actual people'.[23]

II. Hermes and 'the Catalogue of Mysteries'

I now turn to Dworkin's main critique of legislative intent, which is effective against the stipulated theory. However, close reflection on the detail of the argument makes clear that it does not refute the possibility of the institution of the legislature forming and acting on intentions but rather gives one reason to think that a plausible possibility. Dworkin's method is to trace the reasoning of Hermes, a judge 'who is almost as clever as Hercules and just as patient, who also accepts law as integrity but accepts the speaker's meaning theory of legislation as well'.[24] Hermes, Dworkin argues, must answer a series of difficult questions, the plausible answers to which push him to depart from the speaker's meaning theory and finally to collapse into Hercules' method.

The first decision that Hermes must make is whose intentions to aggregate. This may seem an unlikely problem. Thus far, I have followed Dworkin in assuming that the relevant persons are the legislators who enacted the statute.[25] However, Dworkin now suggests that

---

[21] The discussion equivocates between discovery and make-believe, opting in the end for make-believe. Dworkin considers corporate liability, which is a much better example than the community personified, but here he just assumes that the corporation has the capacity to act (he asserts that it controls its operations), argues persuasively that one cannot reduce the corporation's action to that of any individuals, and then asserts that this cannot be discovery because the group has no distinct metaphysical existence (that is, no mind): *LE*, 170–1.

[22] *LE*, 317–37.

[23] *LE*, 315.

[24] *LE*, 317.

[25] In stipulating the objection he refers to the intentions of the legislators that enacted the statute and to those who voted at the time of enactment: *LE*, 314–15. He does note that the

this is too hasty.[26] Not all of the members of the enacting legislature voted for the statute, so Hermes must decide whether to count the intentions of the minority who voted against it and whether to give more weight to those legislators who spoke, or spoke more often, in debates. He must also decide whether to count, and if so how to weigh, the intentions of the officials or staffers who helped draft the bill, as well, if applicable, as the president who signed it into law. More widely still, Hermes must decide whether to count private citizens who sought to influence how their legislators voted or lobby groups who participated in the legislative process. After asking whether lobby groups count, Dworkin says:

Any realistic view of the legislative process includes the influence of these groups; if they contributed to making the statute law, does Hermes have any good reason for not counting their intentions in determining what law they made?[27]

I say yes, Hermes has good reason. When Dworkin talks of the 'law they made', he must mean 'they' to refer to the lobby groups. But the 'they' that make law are the legislators, perhaps in association with the president or queen. Dworkin implicitly concedes this when, a few sentences earlier, he suggests that the president's intentions are relevant because it is his act of signing a bill (to which Congress assents) that makes it law. Not all those who participate in the legislative process make law. The legislature enacts legislation and only its members, the legislators, have authority to legislate. Therefore the persons who made the statute law are the legislators and it is only those persons whose intentional action may constitute the act of lawmaking; this is why they are lobbied. A persuasive lobbyist may prompt a legislator to form certain intentions, but the lobbyist's intention is only relevant to the law that was made if he is persuasive, in which case his intention drops out.

---

speaker's meaning theory must answer the question 'Which historical people count as the legislators?': *LE*, 315. However, he does not make it clear at this point why this is a live question and directly after posing the question, in his account of Hercules' method, he refers to the legislators at the time of enactment (*LE*, 316) and in his discussion of the evidential problems he refers to statesmen, senators and congressmen (*LE*, 317).

[26] *LE*, 318.
[27] *LE*, 318.

Dworkin advances another possibility as to whose intentions might count. He says '[a] statute owes its existence not only to the decision people made to enact it but also to the decision of other people later not to amend or repeal it'.[28] He agrees that it is too strong to term this a decision, but argues that common understandings may grow up about a statute that differ from the understanding of those who enacted it and thus he says Hermes must decide whether to consider the intentions of the legislators who might have repealed the statute but did not. I say that the intentions of subsequent legislators are irrelevant. Any subsequent legislature could of course have amended or repealed the statute and if it had done so, then the statute would have changed or ceased. However, Dworkin's assumption is that the subsequent legislature did not act. In the absence of any lawmaking act the intentions of the legislators are just the intentions of those who did not legislate. They have the same relevance as the intentions of other persons who did not legislate: none at all. The enacting legislature acted to make the law. If subsequent legislatures do not act to repeal or amend the law that has been enacted, the intentions of the legislators who belong to those legislatures are not relevant to the content of that earlier statute.[29] For the intentions of legislators to be relevant (somehow) to the law, the legislators must act jointly to change the law: legislative intent arises only when the institution of the legislature acts.

Dworkin says that Hermes must decide whose intentions to count and that he has no alternative but to think 'about the influence that the attitudes, beliefs, and ambitions of particular groups of officials and citizens ought to have in the process of legislation' and make whatever choices 'would, if generally accepted by judges, bring that process closer to his ideal'.[30] I maintain that a rule of legislative competence authorizes the institution of the legislature, which has a defined membership, to make law.[31] The legislature acts when its members act in certain ways so if anyone's intentions are relevant, which has yet to be proved, it is the intentions of those members, because they may be relevant to what the enacting legislature did. If the legislature has authority to make law, as Dworkin's argument thus far takes for granted,

---

[28] LE, 318–19.
[29] See F Easterbrook, 'Statutes' Domains' (1983) 50 University of Chicago Law Review 533, 538–9.
[30] LE, 319.
[31] H L A Hart, The Concept of Law, 2nd edn (Oxford University Press, Oxford, 1994), 95–6.

Hermes should attend to the intentions of the persons who form the legislature—the legislators—who when they act together act as the legislature and make law.

To my mind, the truly difficult choices that face Hermes in attempting to apply the stipulated theory are whether to count the intentions of the legislators in the voting minority and what weight to give the intentions of various legislators. The choices are difficult because although there is good reason to focus on the members of the enacting legislature it is not clear what reason there is to differentiate further. That is, all the legislators have some connection to the lawmaking act, but it is difficult to identify a basis on which to count only some of those legislators.

Dworkin goes on to assume that Hermes will limit his attention to the voting majority in the enacting legislature, each counted equally.[32] This assumption is unsurprising; most theorists maintain that if the majority shared an intention it would be the legislative intent.[33] The formal equality of legislators and the majority voting rule seem to make the voting majority in the enacting legislature the salient subset whose intentions should count. It is true that if one aggregates intentions, it would seem difficult to account for legislators in the minority whose intentions were likely to be to defeat what was enacted. The different members of the majority may have different intentions and Hermes must thus also decide how to combine their intentions into a corporate intent.[34] Hermes, Dworkin argues, does not respond to any fact about what the legislature intended, but makes a political choice about how best to combine the intentions of the legislators.

There is, I say, good reason to focus on the intentions of legislators who were members of the enacting legislature, for only when that institution acts may legislators change the law. However, this reason to focus on the enacting legislature implies that what is significant is the action of the legislature itself, and how it should be understood, rather than the intentions of each member of the legislature considered for his or her part only.

---

[32] *LE*, 320.
[33] G MacCallum, *Legislative Intent and Other Essays on Law, Politics, and Morality* (University of Wisconsin Press, Madison, 1993), 17–18.
[34] *LE*, 320.

The next choice facing Hermes is how to decide for any legislator, say Senator Smith, 'which of her beliefs, attitudes, or other mental states constitutes her "intention"'?[35] The speaker's meaning theory, Dworkin says, 'ties intention to the picture of legislators intending to communicate something in particular' and thus understands the legislator's intention to be what he 'actually had in mind as he spoke through his vote'.[36] Dworkin also refers to the 'state of mind the legislators tried to communicate through their votes'.[37] It is unclear whether Dworkin thinks that legislators in fact attempt to communicate their state of mind when they vote; his conclusion concerns how judges should interpret statutes not what legislators do in enacting statutes. Nevertheless, he chooses a curious formulation because it suggests that the legislator's vote is a communicative act, a form of speech.

I take it that one casts a vote intending that it be counted, which is to say publicly aggregated, and it is important that certain classes of vote are not anonymous.[38] But it is odd to think that what one does when one votes is to communicate some proposition apart perhaps from the simple proposition that one votes for or against some proposal. The point of voting, the reason for which one acts to vote, is to make it the case that the option for which one votes has one more vote than it would otherwise have, which in ordinary cases means that it is more likely that this will be the course of action that the voting group adopts. The legislator may in legislating communicate something to someone, but presumably the text of the statute is central to the means of the communication and the vote pertains to whether that communication should be made. Thinking of legislative intent as the aggregate of the intentions of the legislators may encourage one to think that each legislator intends to speak through his vote, but this would seem to be a clear wrong turn because it ignores the logic of the legislator's vote, which directs one towards that for which he votes.

Dworkin is aware of the problem and denies that the legislator is like an ordinary speaker. He notes that ordinary speakers 'choose words they expect to have the effect they want. They expect to be understood the way they hope to be understood'.[39] (This description

---

[35] LE, 321.   [36] LE, 321–2.   [37] LE, 315.
[38] G Brennan and P Pettit, 'Unveiling the Vote' (1990) 20 British Journal of Political Science 311.
[39] LE, 322.

of the ordinary speaker is not quite right, for the ordinary speaker expects to be understood in the way that he intends to be understood.[40]) Not all speakers, Dworkin says, are 'in charge of their own words': for example, 'someone who signs a group letter he cannot rewrite for the group' or 'the author of that letter who drafts it to attract the most signatures possible'.[41] The example approaches a group letter from two perspectives, signatory and drafter, and as with the enactment of a statute, the feature that marks it out from the ordinary case is that a group rather than an individual sends the letter.

The ordinary legislator, the backbencher, is in the same position. That is, he:

...might well expect that the act would be interpreted to realize his worst fears, but he would hope that it would not be. He is therefore not like someone choosing to communicate some thought or idea or wish. He occupies a position intermediate between speaker and hearer. He must decide what thought the words on the paper before him are likely to be taken to express and then decide whether he wishes that message to be sent to the public and its officials, including judges, given the only realistic alternative of sending no message at all. That change of role is important, for he treats the document, not himself, or any other person, as the author of the message he agrees to send.[42]

This is an insightful analysis. It is an important truth that no single legislator is free to adopt whatever words he chooses and it follows that no rational legislator may form whatever communicative intention he wishes apart from the content of the statutory text that the legislature acts to enact. In other words, the legislator is like a signatory to a group letter. The group letter example and the extract just quoted rightly shift the focus of attention away from the mental states of each person considered independently and towards the message that they adopt together. It is a mistake to assume that each legislator is an independent speaker and that legislative intent is the aggregate of what the many legislators each sought, for his or her part only, to communicate. What matters is what the legislators do together, how they understand their joint act.

---

[40] See further chapter 7, sections II–IV.   [41] *LE*, 322.   [42] *LE*, 322.

Dworkin says that the legislator 'is not like someone choosing to communicate... [but] occupies a position intermediate between speaker and hearer'. It would be more accurate to say that the legislator, like the signatory to a group letter, is not like someone who communicates on his own. The legislator is a member of a group and is therefore both hearer (of the bill or draft letter) and speaker (of the statute or final letter). Not all legislators lack control over the content of the statutory text. Dworkin implies as much when he limits his focus to backbenchers. Ministers or committee leaders enjoy more control, but that control is not absolute—it is exercised subject to rules and at the sufferance of the majority—and if the group letter analogy is extended they stand, roughly, in the position of drafters. The 'author' of a group letter is not in charge of her words, to adopt Dworkin's term, not because she writes to attract signatories, as he suggests, but precisely because she is not the author of the letter: the group is. She is the drafter but not the author and even if she signs the letter she is but part of the author. Dworkin is wrong to think either that the legislator treats the document as the author of the message he agrees to send or even that he agrees to send the message. The legislature sends the message. The legislator votes for the legislature to send the message but does not himself send it save to the extent that he is part of the legislature that acts. Dworkin is driven to conclude that the document is the author, which is absurd (an author is a person who writes a document to convey something), because of his prior assumption that the institution does not act.

The (stipulated) speaker's meaning theory requires Hermes to combine the mental states of each legislator into a corporate intent. Therefore, Dworkin argues, Hermes must choose whether to count a legislator's hopes or expectations when they come apart. Hopes or expectations may of course have no connection to action at all. I may hope that tomorrow is a sunny day and I may expect it to rain, but neither thought is in any sense my intention. I may plan to take action based on that thought, in which case I would form a conditional intention, say to go the beach if it is sunny or to carry an umbrella if it is rainy. Even when one acts, what one hopes or expects to follow from, or to be caused by, one's act is not one's intention. I may deliver an argument in court, intending to put before the judge my client's argument, hoping that my skilful advocacy will impress my peers but expecting the opposite. Neither the hope nor the expectation takes the place of my intention in explaining my action. My hopes and expectations are states of mind that I may hold about my action; they are not the state that explains how and for what I act, which is my intention. Dworkin reduces the legislator's intention to her hope or expectation because he has no explanation as to how and for what the legislator acts. That is, in place of an account of why legislators act, Dworkin substitutes their opinions about what may yet happen. Dworkin's awareness of the importance of legislators attending to the meaning of the document open to them all, which they will on a majority vote jointly author, has dropped away. This is unfortunate because what is open to all may be central to how legislators understand legislating.

Dworkin argues that Hermes will turn away from hopes because they 'may reflect selfish ambitions that have no place in any acceptable theory of legislative interpretation',[43] for example to curry favour with lobbyists or business associates. Likewise, the legislator's 'expectations may be based on predictions that have no place in any such theory either',[44] for example the legislator's belief that the first case to be decided under the new statute will be heard by a judge who has a certain bias. There is no good choice to be made between hopes and expectations, Hermes will conclude. The situation is no better when the legislator's hopes and expectations coincide because the arguments that applied against each in isolation continue to hold when the two come together. That is, Senator Smith may hope for a particular interpretation because it benefits her cronies and also expect this because of the political dispositions of the relevant judge.[45] Thus, even when the legislator hopes to be understood as he expects to be, which is how Dworkin describes the ordinary speaker, Hermes should not attend to his opinions.

Very often of course the legislator will have no relevant hope or expectation. The issue before the court will not have occurred to him. Hermes might consider asking what the legislator would have intended if the issue had occurred to him. The problem with this response, Dworkin argues, is that neither hopes nor expectations are attractive, whether real or counterfactual.[46] Hermes might instead ask whether the legislator would have voted for a hypothetical amendment, resolving the issue in one way or another. Dworkin argues that there is no non-arbitrary answer to this question because the legislator could have

[43] *LE*, 323.   [44] *LE*, 323.   [45] *LE*, 324.   [46] *LE*, 325.

voted for or against the amendment for any number of reasons.[47] For example, he might have voted for it because he wanted to delay the congressional recess, because he did not want to offend the bill's sponsor, or because he was being blackmailed. It would be wrong, Dworkin says, to let these reasons settle how the statute should be interpreted. Further, whether he would vote for or against the amendment would turn on when in the legislative process it was introduced and whether it was bundled with other amendments that he supported.

The hypothetical amendment discussion is interesting. It means that Hermes has again turned his attention towards the action of the legislature, which might have enacted that amendment. The shift in focus fails to rescue the stipulated theory for two reasons. First, it concerns what the legislature might have enacted, rather than what it did enact. Second, legislators cannot make law by each forming an intention for his part only; they must join together in a legislative act. Hermes never reflects on what the legislature did enact and Dworkin never pursues the question—to which his analysis of the difference between legislators and other speakers gives rise—of how legislators understand the bill that they enact.

Dworkin argues that Hermes will turn away from the legislator's hopes, expectations and counterfactual votes and look instead to 'the political convictions out of which she voted, or would have if she had been voting on principle'.[48] Attending to convictions, Dworkin says, avoids the arbitrariness of the counterfactual approach and is well suited to a community of principle, for:

Members of such a community expect their legislators to act on principle and with integrity, and that goal is promoted if legislation is enforced in the light, not of personal ambitions prominent among legislators, but of convictions dominant in the legislature as a whole.[49]

Note that Dworkin shifts from (the ambitions of) the legislators to (convictions dominant in) the legislature.[50] This foreshadows Hermes' imminent collapse into Hercules. (It is quite unclear how political

---

[47] *LE*, 326. [48] *LE*, 327. [49] *LE*, 328–9.
[50] See also *LE*, 330 where a very similar phrase is used: '...they should be read to express a coherent scheme of *conviction dominant within the legislature* that enacted them' (emphasis added).

convictions may be dominant in an institution that lacks the capacity to form conversational intentions.)

If Hermes adopts the convictions approach he has jettisoned the speaker's meaning theory. He now understands 'Smith's votes [to] be evidence of her convictions... not statements of them in the way a speaker's sentences are statements of the thoughts he uses them to express'.[51] (This analysis does not explain why legislators vote.) Smith, like any other person, has a jumble of convictions which Hermes has to corral into 'a structured system of ideas, made coherent so far as this is possible' before they are fit to use.[52] That is, he constructively interprets her political convictions. The evidence that Hermes has for her convictions is the record of her votes and statements in office and he must therefore ask 'what system of convictions provides overall the best justification for what she has done in office'.[53] At this point, 'the combinatorial problem' resurfaces, for Hermes has to interpret each legislator's record one by one and then aggregate the set into the convictions of the legislature.[54] An alternative exists: '[h]e can train his interpretive imagination... on the record of the legislature itself, asking what coherent system of political convictions would best justify what *it* has done'.[55] Thus, Hermes will grasp that 'he interprets the record of the institution not their records one by one'.[56] This is Hercules' method, which Hermes at last adopts. The *reductio* is complete.

It is striking that Dworkin's conclusion is that Hermes, following Hercules, should focus not on the hopes, expectations or convictions of individual legislators but on the legislature itself, aiming to 'justify what *it* has done'.[57] I argue elsewhere that Dworkin does not have a plausible account in *Law's Empire* of what the legislature has done when it enacts a statute.[58] But what is significant about this shift in focus is that it rightly perceives that it is the legislature's action that is of central importance, rather than the action of the individual legislators considered each for his or her part only.

No strategy of aggregating the mental states of each legislator, considered apart from the action of the legislature itself, can succeed in picking out legislative intent. This conclusion is unsurprising given the initial stipulation that institutions cannot form and act on intentions, and that there is thus in truth no legislative intent, just a fictional

[51] *LE*, 329.   [52] *LE*, 330.   [53] *LE*, 335.   [54] *LE*, 335.
[55] *LE*, 335.   [56] *LE*, 337.   [57] *LE*, 335.   [58] Ekins (n 2) 450–5.

construct. However, the futility of attempting to aggregate the intentions of legislators, each considered for his or her part only, does not prove the stipulation. Indeed, much of Dworkin's argument, including the difference between ordinary speakers and legislators which he notes but does not explore, suggests reasons to think plausible the proposition that the institution forms and acts on intentions, which intentions are not the mere aggregate of the mental states of (all or some of) its members. Thus, 'the catalogue of mysteries'[59] that afflict the hapless (stipulated) speaker's meaning theorist, who sets out to discover an intention that by hypothesis does not exist, does not discredit the theory that the institution, which is the legislators acting jointly, acts on intentions.

III. The Unitary Model and Its Discontents

Waldron shares Dworkin's scepticism about legislative intent. However, his own argument against legislative intent consists in a sophisticated explanation of how the legislature acts. The argument is set out in most detail in chapter 6 of *Law and Disagreement*,[60] and forms part of a wider body of work, the point of which is to redress the neglect of legislation and legislatures in the legal academy.[61] There is, Waldron says, relatively little work by legal philosophers on the legislature,[62] and what little there is, addressing statutory interpretation, has for the most part 'proceeded without reference to the structural features of legislatures'.[63] The notable exception, he says, is Dworkin's discussion in *Law's Empire*.[64]

The structural features in which Waldron is interested are 'size, diversity and disagreement, together with the institutional arrangements that frame decision-making in that context—party organization, deliberative structure, formal debate, rules of order and voting'.[65] That is, the legislature is an assembly, a large gathering of persons who disagree with one another and who represent a divided community.

---

[59] *LE*, 348.
[60] *LD*, 119–46; the chapter is entitled 'Legislators' Intentions and Unintentional Legislation'.
[61] See also J Waldron, *The Dignity of Legislation* (Cambridge University Press, Cambridge, 1999), especially chapter 2, 'The Indignity of Legislation', 7–35.
[62] *LD*, 21. [63] *LD*, 27.
[64] *LD*, 27–8, citing *LE*, 313–54. [65] *LD*, 24–5.

They meet to discuss what laws, if any, to enact and they employ formal rules and voting procedures to that end.

Legal philosophers, Waldron argues, ignore the importance of the internal structure of the assembly and instead adopt a unitary model, 'treating "the legislature" as a single entity, or actor, or author of statutes'.[66] He discusses two examples of jurisprudential neglect of the nature of the legislature. The first is Raz's argument that the legislature is not essential to a legal system,[67] and the second is Hart's willingness to interchange the Queen-in-Parliament and Rex in explaining the rule of recognition.[68] (I return to the first example in chapter 5, section I.) Waldron then concludes that legal philosophers are indifferent to how the legislature is structured, instead assuming that the legislature is like a single individual, and so has a will and acts on intentions.[69] This line of thought has, he says, been refuted by Dworkin,[70] but, mysteriously, jurists continue to maintain it.

The point of Waldron's initial analysis was to explain the need for a theory of legislating and legislation that attends to the structure of the assembly. In the chapters that follow he explains why the legislature is a large body and why it has to adopt formal rules of procedure to discuss and then vote on a specified text. The discussion is rich and complex, but may be summarized as follows. The legislative assembly has the form it has because this makes it capable of authoritative action in the face of disagreement about how best the community is to settle its common problems. The assembly has to have a large and diverse membership if it is to represent the views of those who disagree and thus to act fairly in response to those views.[71] The assembly needs to follow detailed procedural rules and focus on a specified text because without this ordered focus, action will be impossible.[72] And the assembly needs to employ majority voting procedures because this is the only way to respond fairly to the views of the millions of citizens who constitute the divided community.[73] Legislation has authority, he concludes, because it is the product of a respectful way of addressing problems that call for common settlement.

---

[66] *LD*, 28.
[67] *LD*, 34–5, citing J Raz, *Practical Reason and Norms*, 2nd edn (Oxford University Press, Oxford, 1990), 129–31.
[68] *LD*, 42, citing Hart (n 31).   [69] *LD*, 42–3.   [70] *LD*, 43, citing *LE*, 313–54.
[71] *LD*, 49–68.   [72] *LD*, 69–87.   [73] *LD*, 88–118.

Finally, in chapter 6, Waldron turns to the implications that the close study of the structure of the assembly has for how statutes are to be interpreted. He introduces the chapter by noting the 'initially appealing' proposal 'that we should interpret the statute in the way the legislators intended, resolving any vagueness or ambiguity by finding out as much as we can about what the legislators had in mind'.[74] Reference to intent, he argues, is common in America, but prior to *Pepper v Hart*[75] at least, less common in England.[76] Yet, whatever judges and lawyers may say:

Philosophically, however, the idea of appealing beyond the statutory text to independent evidence of what particular legislators are thought to have intended has been subject to such powerful criticisms, most notably by Ronald Dworkin, that one is surprised to find it appearing again in anything other than a trivial form in respectable jurisprudence.[77]

The conflation of legislative history with legislative intent is unsound.[78] In England, judges have continually understood their duty to be to identify the legislative intent conveyed by the statutory text.[79] The judges ask what meaning the legislature intended to convey, given, inter alia, the detail of the statutory text, other statutory or common law rules, relevant legal principles, and the nature of the mischief that it seems the statute was enacted to address. Waldron, I suggest, objects to interpreters making any inference about what the legislature intended, even if not grounded in legislative history. The interpreter, in his scheme, should take the assembly to have enacted just the statutory text, understood in its conventional meaning.

Waldron structures chapter 6 to respond to the argument that a statute's authority turns on the authority of its maker, so that when the statute is unclear the interpreter should refer to the intentions of the legislator.[80] This line of argument, he contends, assumes the unitary model. It may be that if the legislature is a single person his intentions are relevant to the scope and meaning of his

---

[74] *LD*, 119.   [75] [1993] AC 593.   [76] *LD*, 119, n 1.
[77] *LD*, 119, the extract ends with a reference to *LE*, 312–37.
[78] See also *LD*, 140–1.
[79] Bennion, *BST*, 469–86.
[80] He responds specifically to Andrei Marmor's argument to this effect: Marmor, *ILT*, chapter 8. Waldron addresses Marmor in particular at *LD*, 119–21, 130–1, 138–9, 143, and 146.

enactments.[81] Indeed, Waldron does not dispute Hobbes' observation that one ought to conform to the will of the lawmaker, rather than the letter of his instruction.[82] However, Waldron contends that this conclusion is relevant only to a very simple polity, in which the legislature is a single person. In the modern world, the legislature is an assembly, the structure of which distinguishes it sharply from a sole legislator.[83] That is:

> ...modern statutes are not the products of single expert authors. They are produced by the deliberations of large multi-member assemblies whose claim to authority in Raz's sense (if indeed they can make any such claim at all) consists in their ability to integrate a diversity of purposes, interest, and aims among their members into the text of a single legislative product. The modern situation, in other words, is not that of a *person* having authority, but (at most) of a *group* having authority, and of its having that authority only by virtue of the way in which it combines the interests and knowledge of its members in the act of legislating.[84]

The authority of legislation, for Waldron, is not that it is what any reasoning person chooses, but that it is the output of a fair group process that there is reason to think will produce reasonable outcomes. (I consider in chapter 4, section IV the reasons to which Waldron refers.)

Waldron thus asks what 'the most helpful general model of the legislative process [is], so far as theories of authority are concerned'.[85] His answer is that 'we will do better by eschewing any model that regards legislation as most commonly the intentional product of a single law-making author'.[86] For, 'it is often implausible to describe legislative acts as intentional acts, even though they take place in an intentionally organized context'.[87] Yet, such 'legislative acts, despite the fact that they are not conceived as intentional acts' might still have Razian authority.[88]

---

[81] *LD*, 120; although see J Waldron, 'Legislation by Assembly' (2000) 46 Loyola Law Review 507, 531, n 72: 'But even in the case of the single lawmaker, we would still face the problem of deciding which mental states exactly—hopes, expectations, wishes, counterfactual wishes, etc.—of the legislators we were trying to plumb. See [Dworkin, *LE*], at 321–33.'

[82] *LD*, 120.   [83] *LD*, 41–5, 49–51, 67–8.   [84] *LD*, 121.   [85] *LD*, 121.
[86] *LD*, 121.   [87] *LD*, 121–2.   [88] *LD*, 122.

IV. An Alternative: the Voting Machine Model

I term Waldron's own understanding of the legislative process 'the voting machine model'. He outlines it in section 3 of chapter 6, which is entitled 'Unintentional Legislation'. Waldron imagines a possible statutory text:

Vehicles in the Park Act 1993. (1) With the exception of bicycles and ambulances, no vehicle shall be permitted to enter any state or municipal park. (2) Any person who brings a vehicle into a state or municipal park shall be liable to a fine of not more than $100.[89]

It is, he says, deeply confused to think that interpreting this text must be 'a matter of determining what the intentional being who produced it meant'.[90] The reason that it is a mistake to think that modern legislation can be read to identify what its maker meant is that:

Legislation ... is the product of a multi-member assembly, comprising a large number of persons of quite radically differing aims, interest, and backgrounds. Under these conditions, the specific provisions of a particular statute are often the result of compromise and line-item voting. It is perfectly possible, for example, that our imagined Vehicles in the Park Act, considered as a whole, does not reflect the purposes or intentions of any of the legislators who together enacted it.[91]

Imagine that the assembly that enacted the Vehicles in the Park Act formed three factions and that only the first section was controversial. Let the exception for bicycles be B, the exception for ambulances A, and the inclusion of state parks S. Faction one might have voted for A and B and against S; faction two, for B and S and against A; faction three, for A and S and against B. Thus, '[s]uccesive majority voting on these various questions would produce our familiar statute—B & A & S—even though that combination corresponded to nobody's preference'.[92]

There is an obvious rejoinder, which Waldron anticipates. The rejoinder is that after various possible amendments have been voted on, that is after the machine has determined the content of the bill,

---

[89] *LD*, 124.   [90] *LD*, 125.   [91] *LD*, 125.   [92] *LD*, 126.

legislators will vote on the overall package—so 'even if they initially disagree, the enacted statute will at least reflect the intentions of a majority at that last stage, taking into account their awareness of what was politically possible'.[93] Waldron's response is to claim that this final reading 'is purely an artefact of our particular parliamentary procedures'.[94] The legislative process, he asserts, could just as easily take the following form:

There might be a preliminary discussion during which all the issues likely to provoke a division were identified. General debate would ensue, at the conclusion of which members would feed their votes on the various issues into a machine which would produce the statute in its final form on the basis of the voting and promulgate it automatically to judges, officials, and the population at large.[95]

This voting machine, he says, is like Wollheim's democracy machine.[96] However, Waldron does not explain in much detail how the machine is to work.

The point of the model is to make it possible to conceive of a statutory text as the output of a process, like a machine, rather than the choice of an agent.[97] The legislators may each have reasons for their votes and intentions beyond the text of the statute, but the statute is just the text that survives the vote. The machine aggregates votes on texts, not intentions or reasons.[98] That is, the legislators may each have complex, coherent plans about what should be done, but the legislature 'acts' by aggregating those individual plans into a corporate act, the content of which is exhausted by the strict meaning of the statutory text. The contributions to the machine are intentional, because the legislators are persons, and the machine is intentionally designed. The legislators and the programmers of the machine share an 'expectation about how the machine's output—whatever it is—will be understood by those to whom it is sent: they will read it as a set of English sentences'.[99] It follows, Waldron argues, that statutory provisions may have a fixed meaning without reference to the intentions of any particular language user.[100] Therefore, the thought that legislation is

---

[93] *LD*, 126.   [94] *LD*, 126.   [95] *LD*, 126.
[96] R Wollheim, 'A Paradox in the Theory of Democracy' in P Laslett and W Runciman (eds), *Philosophy, Politics and Society*, 2nd series (Blackwell, Oxford, 1962), 71.
[97] *LD*, 126–7.   [98] *LD*, 128, 142–3.   [99] *LD*, 127.   [100] *LD*, 128–9.

in some sense a speech-act should not, Waldron maintains, tempt us to think that the assembly has to form intentions to legislate. The machine takes advantage of the stability of language in that the particular texts it produces have linguistic meaning despite the fact that there is no language user.[101]

It is not clear whether Waldron means that 'preliminary discussion' begins with an otherwise complete legislative proposal already before the legislators for consideration.[102] This is significant because it is not clear whether the machine is intended to form entire proposals or to be a means to amend otherwise complete proposals. The former reading is a better fit with Waldron's concern, which is to show how legislation may be an indirect function of the choices of individual legislators, without being in any important sense the object of choice of a reasoning person (as an already formed proposal would be, to some extent at least). However, this would make the model more artificial, for Waldron is well aware that proposals are ordinarily drafted in detail in advance of legislative deliberation.[103]

The legislators are to identify issues, debate and then vote. It is not clear what it means to identify 'issues likely to provoke a division'.[104] An issue may mean part of an existing proposal that is controversial or it may mean a possible amendment to that proposal. Alternatively, an issue could be a specific point that is relevant to a general question (say, public taxation) that is to be considered. The legislators are to debate and then vote on these issues and this implies that the issue is a textual formulation that if adopted on majority vote will form part of a statute. That is, what are at issue are the possible provisions (what will be sections if enacted) that the legislators wish to consider. Waldron does not discuss whether all legislators are free to contribute possible provisions or if agenda-setters control who may contribute.

Much later in his argument, Waldron says that he has 'assumed implicitly that any bills [the legislature] considered and any statutes it enacted would be complex in their contents'.[105] This assumption does not clearly inform his presentation of the voting machine. The only example that Waldron uses is the Vehicles in the Park Act 1993, which is a two-section statute.[106] The issue for the legislators, he stipulates, was just the content of the first section. (I argue in chapter 4 that the machine cannot explain how legislators reason and act even in this

---

[101] *LD*, 128–9.   [102] *LD*, 126.   [103] *LD*, 81.
[104] *LD*, 126.   [105] *LD*, 142.   [106] *LD*, 124.

AN ALTERNATIVE: THE VOTING MACHINE MODEL 37

simple example.) Most modern statutes are vastly more complex than this simple example. The Finance Act 2008 (UK) for example has 166 sections and 46 Schedules. There are of course a great many subsections and the number of issues, in Waldron's sense, that arise in the various sections and subsections must be very high indeed. If the proposal is formed in the assembly then there may well be thousands of issues (every section, subsection, or variation to a section or subsection that may be contentious). The number of issues that may arise make it impractical either to form proposals on the floor or to debate all the issues at once and then to vote. It also makes it impractical to debate all the issues at once and then to vote. Legislative time is a scarce resource, which the legislative process is structured to use efficiently.[107]

The most important ambiguity in the model is whether the vote is (a) simultaneous, so that the legislator enters his votes on the five or fifty issues into the machine all at once, or (b) sequential, so that the legislator votes on each issue one after another, knowing how the earlier issues were decided. The extract set out above implies that the vote is to be simultaneous.[108] However, in his earlier discussion of the Vehicles in the Park Act, Waldron says that '[s]uccessive majority voting on these various questions would produce our familiar statute'.[109] He also says that the evidence for the model's explanatory force is 'the large part that is played by compromise, logrolling, and last-minute amendments in contemporary legislation'.[110] Both remarks suggest sequential voting.

It may be that if forced to settle the ambiguity he would opt for sequential voting. Yet there is also reason to think Waldron might opt for simultaneous voting: this would limit tactical voting and focus the legislator on whether he should support each particular provision. Waldron's arguments that the output of the machine is authoritative, which I discuss in chapter 4, section IV, assume that each legislator responds in this focused way.

If the voting machine model is sound, the legislature acts without forming intentions and legislation cannot rightly be understood to be the coherent choices of an intentional agent. Instead, statutes are sets of isolated provisions, having no purpose beyond what follows from

---

[107] G Cox, 'The Organization of Democratic Legislatures', chapter 8 in B Weingast and D Wittman (eds), *The Oxford Handbook of Political Economy* (Oxford University Press, Oxford, 2006), 141, 142–4.
[108] *LD*, 126.   [109] *LD*, 126.   [110] *LD*, 127.

the conventional meaning of the text, and not having been intended for a certain end. Waldron accepts that the model is to some extent artificial, but maintains that it captures the nature of the legislative process:

> Of course, this is just a model: in the real world, statutes are never produced exactly like that. But also, in the real world, statutes are never produced exactly as the product of one person's coherent intention. The interesting question is which picture is more helpful for our thinking about the intentionality of statutes under modern legislative conditions. Given the large part that is played by compromise, logrolling, and last-minute amendments in contemporary legislation, my money is on the machine.[111]

Waldron does not doubt that the legislature acts. He follows Radin in saying that it 'is the job of a legislature to pass statutes not form intentions',[112] and takes the legislature's action, as the term Act of Parliament entails, to be the enactment of a statute. What Waldron insists, however, is that it is a mistake to take 'the language of agency' to entail that there must be a legislative equivalent to the mental states of individual agents.[113] He argues that just as it is odd to think that the legislature has motives, so it is unnecessary to think that the legislature has intentions. That is, he asserts that the legislative act is an artificial act constituted by the intentional acts of legislators but not itself the product of any person's intention.[114] This move is not convincing. Motives are abstract or distant intended ends and so the question of whether the legislature has motives is a subset of the question of what intentions it has.[115] Waldron is quite likely right that there is no absolute equivalence between artificial and natural agents (artificial agents, I suggest, do not have emotions), but it remains an open question precisely what an artificial agent needs to intend, if anything, if it is to act at all or, more importantly, if it is to act well. The merit of his conception of the legislative process as a voting machine turns on the extent to which it suffices to explain (reasonable) legislative action.

---

[111] *LD*, 127.
[112] *LD*, 128; paraphrasing M Radin, 'Statutory Interpretation' (1930) 43 Harvard Law Review 863, 871.
[113] *LD*, 128.   [114] *LD*, 128.   [115] Finnis, *Aquinas*, 64–5, n 20 and 277.

Later in the chapter Waldron helpfully restates his understanding of legislative action. He says again that the defining structure of the legislative assembly—its large and diverse membership, its reliance on formal procedures, and the complexity of the statutes it enacts—serves 'to undermine any talk about "the intentions of the author" of a statute'. He then goes on, however, to say that '[t]o the extent there is one author, it is the legislature...as distinct from the individual members'.[116] The legislature's intentions as author are exhausted by 'the meanings embodied conventionally in the text of the statute' and '[t]here simply is no fact of the matter concerning a legislature's intentions apart from the formal specification of the act it has performed'.[117] It seems then that the legislature does act with an intention, or at least its 'action [is] under a certain intentional description', namely 'that such-and-such words were used with their conventional English meaning. That, however, is *all there is to say* about the institution's intentions'.[118] Thus, the legislature's act is defined by a certain intention, but the intention is very thin.

Waldron's position is that while the assembly needs a rule for aggregating votes if it is to act (majority vote), 'it does not need, in addition, any rule for combining their thoughts, hopes and understandings into something that would count as the thoughts or purposes of the institution'.[119] He says that '[i]t is one *decision* we need, not necessarily one personality, and so it is not merely as a matter of logic that we should refrain from attributing mental states to the legislature'.[120] And '[w]hat the decision is—what *we* have done—is the text of the statute as determined by the institution's procedures'.[121] The legislators do not intentionally make decisions, if Waldron is right. Instead the text that emerges from the series of votes is what they have done. Hence 'a legislator interested to know what he and his colleagues "decided"' will, like the citizen or judge, just read the text that the machine produces.[122] Waldron concludes that the function and structure of the legislature entail that the legislature has no intention apart from the conventional meaning of the enacted text. It follows that interpreters should not read statutes as if they were the objects of any person's coherent, intentional choice.[123] If a court

---

[116] *LD*, 142. [117] *LD*, 142. [118] *LD*, 143. [119] *LD*, 143.
[120] *LD*, 144. [121] *LD*, 145. [122] *LD*, 128. [123] *LD*, 145.

imposes coherence on the statutory text, 'it is slighting the political process by virtue of which alone the statute has its legitimacy'.[124]

This account of legislative action is plausible and important. It denies that the legislature is an intentional agent, instead conceiving of the acts of the legislature as the unintentional output of the intentional system that is the legislative process. Waldron adopts, to my mind, the right approach to studying the legislature. He reflects on the objects for which a well-formed legislature acts and the capacities it exercises to that end. And he reflects first and foremost on what it is that the legislators do together, rather than, as Dworkin does, starting with the question of how interpreters should consider statutes. Further, he attends to some of the problems that legislators face in acting together and hence grounds his theory of legislative action in plausible solutions to those problems.

The live question is whether it is true that the assembly has no capacity to form and act on intentions that go beyond the bare intention to enact the words of the statutory text with their conventional meaning. The argument for this limited conception of legislative action turns on an assumption about how groups act, namely that what the group does is exhausted by formal rules, and an assumption about the nature of language use. It also turns on the truth of Waldron's conclusions that the voting machine model is a sound account of the nature of the legislative process and that the machine is likely to produce reasonable legislation, such that the legislature may be said to exercise lawmaking authority. In the chapters that follow, I question each of these points, outlining my own theory that the legislators act jointly like a single legislator. This theory—a form of the unitary model—I aim to ground in the structure by which a group legislates, to which Waldron rightly draws attention.

V. Arrow's Theorem and the Legislative Process

Waldron's critique of legislative intent finds support from an unlikely source. Political scientists and others working out the implications of social choice theory for the legislative process argue that the legislature has no intention because the legislative process does not produce

---

[124] J Waldron, 'Legislating with Integrity' (2003) 72 Fordham Law Review 373, 386.

coherent collective choices, which could be termed the will of the majority. Instead, agenda-setting and procedural rules determine the output of the process.

Kenneth Shepsle, a senior political scientist, is the author of the leading article on social choice theory and legislative intent.[125] He argues that Arrow's impossibility theorem entails that '[l]egislative intent is an internally inconsistent, self-contradictory expression [that] has no meaning'.[126] (Many legal scholars have deployed similar arguments.[127]) Arrow's theorem is in part a generalization of Condorcet's voting paradox.[128] The paradox is that if a group of three or more persons adopts a majority voting procedure to decide amongst three or more options, the majority vote may fail to yield a result. That is, the majority vote may cycle amongst the alternatives. For example, a majority may vote for A over B, a different majority may vote for B over C, and another majority may vote for C over A. There is thus no unique majority vote winner. The group either does not choose or its choice is settled by something other than what the majority wants, such as the order in which the alternatives are considered. Arrow generalizes this finding to show that no collective decision-making procedure that meets certain minimal fairness conditions can avoid the possibility of cycling.

I do not propose to survey the vast literature on Arrow's theorem and social choice theory. Instead, I outline Shepsle's account of, and argument from, Arrow.

He explains the theorem's findings in this way:

In the context of majority rule voting, this theorem implies that it is not possible to guarantee that a majority rule process will yield coherent choices. Put differently, if the preferences of the members of a voting body display a modicum of diversity, then majority voting need not generate a transitive ordering of the alternatives available for choice; the alternatives cycle, even

---

[125] K Shepsle, 'Congress is a "They," Not an "It": Legislative Intent as Oxymoron' (1992) 12 International Review of Law and Economics 239.

[126] Shepsle (n 125) 239.

[127] See, for instance, J Mashaw, 'The Economics of Politics and the Understanding of Public Law' (1989) 65 Chicago-Kent Law Review 123, Easterbrook (n 29) at 547–8, F Easterbrook, 'The Role of Original Intent in Statutory Construction' (1988) 11 Harvard Journal of Law & Public Policy 59, 64, and J Manning, 'Textualism and Legislative Intent' (2005) 91 Virginia Law Review 419, 423 and 430–2 (citing Shepsle at nn 35 and 43).

[128] K Arrow, Social Choice and Individual Values (Wiley, New York, 1963).

though individual preferences are quite coherent. Indeed, incoherence will often take the form of the nonexistence of a collectively 'best' alternative; the final outcome may be arbitrary (for example, a function of group fatigue) or determined by specific institutional features of decisionmaking (for example, rules governing the order of voting on motions). In either case we may be able to provide *positive explanations* of these results, but rarely will we also be able to provide *normative justifications*.[129]

He equates coherence with transitivity, so that a collective choice is coherent if it is the uniquely best option, the only option the majority prefers. The italicized term, 'normative justifications', it later becomes clear, refers to majoritarian preference satisfaction. The shift from 'need not' in the second sentence to 'will often' in the third is important. Various scholars, including Farber and Frickey,[130] observe that legislatures are not as unstable or indecisive as one would expect if alternatives often cycled. (Waldron cites Farber and Frickey's later work for this proposition.[131]) However, Shepsle argues that this observation is confused. Arrow's theorem entails not constant indeterminacy or instability but rather that cycling is resolved arbitrarily, that is, without a normative, for which read majoritarian, rationale.[132]

Shepsle asserts that 'the Arrowian dilemma' has two implications.[133] The first is that there is no unbeatable policy, which is to say that there is always another possible proposal that could win majority support. The second is that the outcome turns on the voting order, so that a clever agenda-setter can produce any of the possible majority results. It is unclear whether Shepsle is asserting that legislative preferences always cycle or whether he just aims to explain the situation when they do cycle. The latter would avoid begging the question of frequency. However, the former reading seems more likely, as he asserts, in a footnote, that it is very rare for the preferences of legislators to be

---

[129] Shepsle (n 125) 241–2.
[130] D Farber and P Frickey, 'The Jurisprudence of Public Choice' (1987) 65 Texas Law Review 873, 904 and W Panning, 'Formal Models of Legislative Processes' (1983) 8 Legislative Studies Quarterly 427, 438–40.
[131] D Farber and P Frickey, *Law and Public Choice: A Critical Introduction* (University of Chicago Press, Chicago, 1991), 47–62, cited in *LD*, 31, n 24 and 89, n 4 and accompanying text.
[132] Shepsle (n 125) 242, n 6.
[133] Shepsle (n 125) 243–4.

'single-peaked', in which case there would be a unique majority winner.[134] And the rest of the article assumes cycling is ubiquitous.

The legislature enacts a bill on majority vote. Shepsle says that '[it] is evident that Congress is composed of *many* majorities'.[135] What this entails is that when a bill is enacted, a particular majority supported a particular change to the status quo. It is unclear, Shepsle says, why this majority prevailed rather than any of the other majorities that could have been assembled. He suggests that the reason may be either interest-group action or that this majority had some procedural advantage. His point is that:

Many policies, in principle, can topple an existing status quo. That some are more likely than others to actually do so is dependent on idiosyncratic, structural, procedural, and strategic factors, which are at best tenuously related to normative principles embraced by democratic theorists and philosophers.[136]

The policy that a majority votes to enact is largely the result of what Mashaw terms 'the institutional matrix',[137] that is, the internal structure that determines how the legislature votes on various policy proposals. Shepsle takes it to be obvious that if the outcome that the legislature produces turns on procedural or strategic factors rather than any unique majority preference, the outcome lacks legitimacy. He asserts this point repeatedly throughout the article.[138]

Shepsle argues that there are no reasons that explain any particular majority's policy choice. Each legislator has reasons, but the majority does not: many legislators make up the winning majority and 'their respective reasons for voting against the status quo may well be as varied as their number'.[139] Later, he argues that legislators reveal little when they vote for a motion.[140] The nominal logic of the vote, he says, is that the legislator prefers the world in which the motion passes to one in which it fails. But this is consistent, he maintains, with the legislator acting to express: a personal taste, a value judgment, a reflection of the desires of particular constituents or the wishes of a majority of her constituents, or consideration for the interests of her benefactors, or some mix of these. (It is unclear why he focuses on what one expresses by way of one's vote rather than what one acts for.[141])

---

[134] Shepsle (n 125) 244, n 10. [135] Shepsle (n 125) 244.
[136] Shepsle (n 125) 244. [137] Mashaw (n 127) 134.
[138] Shepsle (n 125) 246–8. [139] Shepsle (n 125) 244.
[140] Shepsle (n 125) 248. [141] See my discussion in section II of this chapter.

Strategic action also complicates matters, because legislators have good reasons to vote not to express a sincere preference but to act strategically, changing the order of decision for some further end. Thus:

With $(n + 1)/2$ or more individuals in the winning coalition, there is not a single legislative intent, but rather many *legislators'* intents. Congress is a 'they', not an 'it'. Legislator A may have voted for an amendment that ultimately became part of the winning policy because he favored the 'plain meaning' of the text. Legislator B, on the other hand, may have voted for it because he thought (incorrectly as it turned out) that the amendment would undermine support for the final bill or draw a presidential veto, thereby allowing the status quo to survive. Finally, Legislators C, D, and E may have supported the amendment, disinterestedly, as a reasonable compromise among competing interests. To ask, in this circumstance, what Congress 'intended' is to invite a non sequitur.[142]

Shepsle concludes that the winning majority consists of legislators acting for different reasons, to express different preferences or acting strategically. There is a majority for this bill, but the majority does not make a coherent collective choice for reasons in the way that a single person does.

He now turns to explain the internal structure of Congress that shapes outcomes. The proposals on which Congress votes are largely formed and selected by subsets of legislators, members of the committees that exercise disproportionate agenda power. A bill that a committee forms enjoys various advantages.[143] It has the lead position in the voting order, because it is the principal motion before the house. The committee bill also frames deliberation, with debate largely centring on how the bill compares to the status quo and how or if that bill should be amended. The bill may also enjoy special procedural protections, such as restrictions or even prohibitions on amendment. The agenda-setters thus exercise proposal and veto power, in that they help determine on which bills the house will vote.[144] Committee membership is a function of seniority rather than election. The majority retains capacity to change the rules allocating committee places, but the exercise of this capacity is costly, and so in practice agenda-setters have wide discretion.[145] What this means is that:

---

[142] Shepsle (n 125) 244–5.
[143] Shepsle (n 125) 245–6.
[144] Shepsle (n 125) 246.
[145] Shepsle (n 125) 246, n 15.

... there is no strong or obvious relationship between the exercisers of agenda power and the preferences of majorities. To the extent such exercises of agenda power affect the content of legislation, as I claim they do, they cannot be traced to majoritarian preferences. Thus, as noted, a relationship between the content of legislation and the preferences of majorities is attenuated; the capacity of a bill to enjoy the normative gloss of majoritarianism is likewise diminished.[146]

The committee structure is central to how Congress proceeds. Other procedures are also highly significant, including the rules that structure legislative debate (who may speak and for how long) and the resolution of differences between House and Senate. Committee members occupy privileged positions in relation to each procedure. Shepsle observes that these procedures 'have a number of salutary effects on the process of legislating, but they also diffuse any bright line that might otherwise connect the preferences of majorities to final outcomes'.[147] That is, the 'impact of procedures, like the impact of agenda setters and multiple majorities, loosens the coupling between legislative outcomes and majority preferences'.[148] Shepsle does not detail these 'salutary effects' and indeed he never explains what reasons legislators might have to adopt and maintain these procedures. At best, he implies that legislators need agenda-setters to resolve cycles, but he always says explicitly that this resolution lacks legitimacy because it departs from majority preference.[149]

Shepsle concludes that the most that one may infer from a majority vote for a bill is that a majority preferred the bill to the status quo. It is not clear why and indeed each legislator may have different reasons for his preference. The outcome does not ground any inference about what the majority wants in relation to bills that were not put before them. The available evidence, including 'legislative history, does not permit us to differentiate the "will of the majority" from the machinations, both ex ante and post, of agenda setters'.[150] It is a mistake then to think that the legislature intends anything, specifically it is to 'commit a fallacy (the false personification of a collectivity)'.[151] The problem, Shepsle insists, is that even if the legislators are reasonable, 'it is still fruitless to attribute intent to the product of their *collective*

---

[146] Shepsle (n 125) 246.
[147] Shepsle (n 125) 247.
[148] Shepsle (n 125) 248.
[149] Shepsle (n 125) 241–2, 244, 246–8.
[150] Shepsle (n 125) 248.
[151] Shepsle (n 125) 239; see also 249.

efforts. Individual intents, even if they are unambiguous, do not add up like vectors. That is the content of Arrow; that is the malady of majority rule'.[152]

The argument from social choice theory establishes that the act of the legislature is not a direct expression of majority preferences, which (often) cycle, but is instead transformed by the institutional structure of the legislature, in which agenda-setting, limits on time, and strategic action (including logrolling) are of central importance. These conclusions are very important for understanding legislative action, and I explore them further in chapters 4, 6 and 8. However, Shepsle's argument only refutes an account that provides that legislative intent is the true will of the majority, understood to be a unique majority preference. Shepsle assumes that this is the only way in which one could 'attribute intent to the product of their *collective* efforts'. Indeed, this way of framing the point further begs the question, for it assumes that the intent is *attributed* to the action—to the product of their efforts (a formulation that studiously avoids explaining what exactly the legislators do together)—rather than *recognized* in the action, in the way that the legislators jointly act.

It is not sound to understand the intention of the legislature to be the aggregate of the intentions of the legislators. Attempts to aggregate individual intentions are arbitrary and ungrounded precisely because the aggregation is detached from the way in which legislators act together, which is to say from the action of the institution. I explain further in chapter 3, section I why joint intention is no mere aggregation. However, the forceful criticisms levelled at the aggregative conception of legislative intent do not refute the alternative possibility that the legislature itself is capable of forming intentions. Indeed, the strength of the sceptical arguments is very often that they draw one's attention away from what each legislator intends for his part only towards what is done together. In the chapters that follow I develop this possibility further, outlining in chapter 3 how groups form and act on intentions, arguing in chapters 4–7 that legislating requires intentional action, and drawing these lines of argument together in chapter 8 to explain legislative intent.

---

[152] Shepsle (n 125) 249.

3
Joint Intention and Group Agency

The aggregate of the intentions of each legislator does not constitute the intention of the legislature. However, this truth does not entail that legislative intent is an incoherent idea, for it is possible for groups to form and act on joint intentions, which do not reduce to the sum of the intentions of each member of the group. The joint intention on which the group acts is the plan of action that coordinates and structures the joint action of the members of the group. This chapter explains how groups reason and act. I begin by making clear precisely why the aggregate of the intentions of each member does not constitute the intention of the group. I then proceed to explain how groups form and act on joint intentions, how complex groups adopt complex plans to act over time, and how and why some groups are disciplined to respond to reasons. My focus throughout is on the well-formed group, on the central case of joint action, in which there is good reason to participate.

I. The Futility of Summing Intentions

Andrei Marmor argues that sceptics about legislative intent are wrong to assume that a group may not have intentions in the absence of attributive conventions for, he contends, they have ignored the possibility of shared intention:

Even the sceptic would probably agree that many people can have the same (or very similar) intentions. Arguably, this is often what we mean when we attribute intentions to a group in a non-representative manner. In saying, 'the Nation aspires to independence', for instance, we mean that the relevant intention is shared by all or most individual members of the group in question. Similarly, we often attribute intentions to political parties, minority groups, artistic genres, sports clubs, and the like.[1]

An intention held by all or most members of the group, he says, may be attributed to the group so that the shared intention is the group intention. His proposal then is that a group's intention—what we attribute to the group—is an intention held by each member of the group, which is shared in the sense that each person holds it. On this approach, group intention is the sum of the intentions of most or all members of the group.[2] The group may thus be a convenient way of referring to many individuals, who share some characteristic or other, and who perhaps somehow act together, but may itself have no distinct existence or capacity for action.[3] Margaret Gilbert has termed accounts of this kind 'summative'.[4] One may imagine (at least) two variants: the first provides that a group has a certain intention if all or most of its members hold that intention; the second provides that all or most members must hold that intention and this must be common knowledge. On either variant, this approach provides that group intentions are mere shorthand to enable us to refer to the intentions of many individuals at once. For example, to say that the working class intends to vote Labour is just to say that most or all members of the working class intend to vote Labour.

The first variant of the summative accounts is plainly false as a general explanation for group intention. The following example shows why.[5] Several people seated in a park may all run for the same shelter in the event of rain, each intending for his part to shelter there from the rain. Here, there is no group intention and no group act. But if the persons form part of an outdoor dance company and run for the

---

[1] Marmor, *ILT*, 162.
[2] A Quinton, 'Social Objects' (1975) 75 Proceedings of the Aristotelian Society 67.
[3] Dworkin, *LE*, 168: 'We personify groups in ordinary conversation. We speak casually of the interests or goals of the working class, for example. But these expressions are often only convenient figures of speech, shorthand ways of talking about the average or representative members of a community.'
[4] M Gilbert, *On Social Facts* (Routledge, London, 1989), 19.
[5] J Searle, 'Collective Intentions and Actions' in P Cohen, J Morgan, and M Pollack (eds), *Intentions in Communication* (MIT Press, Cambridge MA, 1990), 401, 402–3.

shelter intending to perform a particular choreographed movement, then there is a group act. The difference lies not in the bodily movements, but in the content of the intentions of the relevant persons. In the former case there is a mere coincidence of intention; in the latter there is coordination. The example shows that a group's intention is not just the sum of the isolated intentions of individual members of the group. The intentions of the various members cannot yield or support a group intention unless they are, in some way yet to be explained, connected to the intentions of other members of the group. Thus, the simple fact that all members intend to perform an act cannot establish that there is a group intention to that effect.

The second variant is somewhat more plausible, but remains in the end unconvincing. The fundamental problem is that the addition of common knowledge still does not enable us to distinguish the intention of a group from a series of unconnected, even if publicly known, individual intentions. The insufficiency of common knowledge is made clear by Gilbert, who points out that one set of individuals may adopt different group intentions in their capacity as members of different groups.[6] If common knowledge were decisive, this would not be possible. Michael Bratman provides an interesting counter-example to this variant. He imagines two painters who set out to paint the same house, who are aware of the other's presence and intention, but who use different coloured paint and paint over one another's work. The painters, Bratman contends, do not constitute a group that intends to paint the house. They each intend to paint the house, but there is no joint intention: they do not intend to paint the house together.[7] The painters do not form a group that acts intending to paint the house. Intentional group action requires cooperation not mere common knowledge.

The central objection to summative accounts is that they fail to distinguish coincident intention from jointly held intention. That is, summative accounts are false because group action cannot be explained by pointing to the fact that several individuals acted in a certain way, unless those individual actions are in some way coordinated, cooperative, and understood by the individuals involved to constitute a group action. No strategy of noting isolated individual

---

[6] Gilbert (n 4) chapters IV and V.
[7] M Bratman, *Faces of Intention* (Cambridge University Press, Cambridge, 1999), 109–29.

intentions can explain how those individuals act together. And the strategy cannot be salvaged by stipulating common knowledge because the sum of many individual intentions is just many individual intentions, not a group intention.[8]

The summative accounts may derive what plausibility they have from an ambiguity in the term 'group'. We use group to refer either to sets of individuals who share a common feature (the group of taxpayers earning over £100,000 per annum, the group of all men on death row in the United States, etc.) or to associations united by their coordinated pursuit of a common purpose.[9] Summative accounts explain our attribution of intention or action to groups of the first type only. And they succeed in this way only because groups of the first type do not form intentions or act together. There is no harm in speaking of them as having intentions when that is understood as a shorthand reference to what is common amongst members of the group. In no sense, however, does the group act together (if it did it would be a group of the second type). Its members do not seek to coordinate their actions towards some end and therefore they do not form group actions or intentions. It is groups that are able to act—purposive groups—that are of central interest to social action theory and it is for this reason that the summative accounts fail.

In the passage quoted above, Marmor does not draw this distinction: political parties and sports clubs are purposive groups, but minority groups are not, even if members of those groups may form purposive groups (I am not sure in what sense artistic genres are groups). However, the account of group intention he goes on to develop is more plausible than the pure summative account and does implicitly focus on a subset of groups.[10] He insists that there must be a connection between the identity of a group and the shared intentions of its members before those intentions may be thought to be the group's intentions. He puts the requirement this way: 'An additional element must obtain, establishing a non-accidental connection between the identification of the group and the pertinent intention'.[11] The members of the group, he says, share an expectation that they will all

---

[8] Searle (n 5) 402–6.
[9] Finnis, *NLNR*, 150–3; D Ruben, *The Metaphysics of the Social World* (Routledge, London, 1985), 21.
[10] For a very similar line of argument, see L Alexander and E Sherwin, *Demystifying Legal Reasoning* (Cambridge University Press, Cambridge, 2008), 171.
[11] Marmor, *ILT*, 162.

hold a particular intention and it is this expectation (which partly determines the identity of the group) that makes the intention significant for all members. By contrast, some other intention common to all members of the group, say an intention to eat strawberries, may be unconnected to the group's identity and so does not count as a shared intention to eat strawberries.[12]

This focus on the nature of the group and its connection to what is shared is undeveloped. Marmor does not explain how members of a group are to form the necessary expectation or identity and it remains the case that the sheer fact that each individual intends to act in a certain way is insufficient to establish that the group does likewise. The account's application to the legislature is unconvincing. Marmor argues that legislators may share intentions in respect of the law they have enacted because those intentions are connected to their identity as a lawmaking group. While for most groups the intention that is to be shared must be held by most or all members, the shared intention of the legislature, Marmor contends, needs to be held only by a majority of legislators, because this 'is in accord with the rules which determine whose actions, and in what combination, count as an act of legislation'.[13] Just as the actions of the majority suffice to enact statutes, so too, he asserts, the legislative intent need only be held by a majority of legislators.[14] MacCallum outlines, but does not wholly endorse, a similar argument, saying that because a coincidence of votes suffices for the legislature to act, a coincidence of intentions by those voters, in relation to the bill and their votes, should suffice for the legislature to intend something by that act.[15]

The argument begs the question. Majority vote settles how the group that is the legislative assembly acts, but that does not entail that the majority acts for the group. One might imagine a group that made provision for the majority to act as the group: for example, a majority of partners might jointly act as if they were the partnership, disposing of assets, and only notifying the minority after the fact. The legislature is not like that. It is the assembly that acts to make law, not the majority. The vote of a majority of legislators settles whether the assembly adopts

---

[12] Marmor, *ILT*, 162. [13] Marmor, *ILT*, 163.
[14] Marmor, *ILT*, 163–5; a similar idea, in which the majority is said to have intention votes, is mooted in P Brest, 'The Misconceived Quest for the Original Understanding' (1980) 60 Boston University Law Review 204, 212–13.
[15] G MacCallum, *Legislative Intent and Other Essays on Law, Politics, and Morality* (University of Wisconsin Press, Madison, 1993), 26.

or rejects a bill, but the vote concerns the action of the assembly. The majority has no authority to legislate alone. It is a mistake to take the importance of majority voting within the legislative process to establish that the majority has legislative authority such that intentions that are shared amongst its members count as the legislative intent. The legislators who form a majority do not have authority to make law. Only the legislature has that authority.[16] The legislators who form a majority may, under the procedures adopted by all legislators, act so that the legislature enacts some proposal.

The majority intention model goes wrong in conceiving of legislative action as a sequence of individual communications, which amount to group action when they happen to overlap. On this view, legislators only decide or communicate together if they each happen to decide or communicate the same point in the same way. This confusion is also evident in Marmor's concern that different groups of legislators may attempt to implicate different, incompatible content by way of the same statutory text.[17] In truth, no subgroup of legislators may implicate anything, because it is only the legislature that acts to legislate. Explaining legislative action requires analysis of how and in what sense the members of the group act together. Majority voting procedures are important means to joint action, but they are not fundamental. I turn now to the foundation of group action, which is joint intention.

II. Joint Intention and Group Action

A group is an association of two or more persons who unite in the coordinated pursuit of a common purpose.[18] I aim to explain the structure of group action, to clarify how groups act. Group action, I argue, is action by the members of the group on a group intention. That group intention, or joint intention as I also term it, is a plan of joint action adopted by all members as the means to the shared end that defines the group. In complex cases, groups adopt authority procedures that determine who may set the plan and so direct joint

---

[16] In this I agree with Waldron, *LD*, 143–4.
[17] A Marmor, 'The Pragmatics of Legal Language' (2008) 21 Ratio Juris 423, 437.
[18] Aquinas understood the acting group to be a unity of order in which acts of individual persons are unified by (i) their coordination and (ii) the point or purpose of that coordination: Finnis, *Aquinas*, 24–5.

action. The group acts when its members execute the plan of action. Thus, group action is the coordinated pursuit of a common purpose by means of a jointly accepted plan of action.

My aim is to understand the nature of group intentions, which is to understand how they coordinate individual acts into a group action and how they relate to the reasoning of individual members. I shall consider two promising non-summative accounts of group intention. The first, advanced by Michael Bratman, provides that group intentions arise out of a structure of interlocking individual intentions. The second approach argues instead that group intentions are irreducible, such that they cannot be explained in terms of a supporting or constitutive structure of individual intentions. John Searle and Margaret Gilbert advance variants of this second approach, although I shall focus only on Searle's account.[19]

Searle rejects the summative accounts, arguing that no set of individual intentions ('I-intentions') may combine to yield the group intentions ('we-intentions') that characterize group action. His explanation for group action provides instead that the capacity for collective behaviour is primitive, as can be seen in collective behaviour amongst animals, and that humans are simply able to form we-intentions, which are distinct from and not reducible to I-intentions.[20] Group action occurs when persons form and act on we-intentions. The group intention, he says, is formed in the mind of an individual (there are no group minds) and he takes it to follow that a single individual who fundamentally mistakes his situation (say, a brain in a vat) and falsely imagines that there are others with whom he may act may form we-intentions even though he is alone.[21] It is more than a little odd to think there may be group intentions without a group and I maintain that only an association of persons who coordinate their action to some end forms and acts on group intentions.

Searle is somewhat vague about the conditions under which the formation of we-intentions may result in group action. Specifically, he does not comment on whether the we-intentions must be identical (or coherent) or even whether their existence and substance must be common knowledge or open to the other members of the group. By failing to provide an alternative explanation, his account suggests that we-intentions merely need to coincide.[22] That would be

---

[19] J Searle, *The Construction of Social Reality* (Penguin Press, London, 1995).
[20] Searle (n 5) 402–6.   [21] Searle (n 5) 406–8.   [22] Searle (n 19) 23–6.

problematic for it would entail the unlikely conclusion that group action is possible even when one person does not know that the other, to whom his we-intention is to apply and who forms the same intention, plans to do likewise. Yet it is irrational for an agent to form a we-intention without having grounds to believe others intend to do likewise and this suggests that the intentions must interlock in some way.

I find Bratman's account more persuasive. He argues that group intention[23] is not a mental state existing in any one mind, but is instead a state of affairs that arises when two or more persons hold a particular set of interlocking intentions. He summarizes his approach thus:

To understand shared intention, then, we should not appeal to an attitude in the mind of some superagent; nor should we assume that shared intentions are always grounded in prior promises. My conjecture is that we should, instead, understand shared intention, in the basic case, as a state of affairs consisting primarily of appropriate attitudes of each individual participant and their interrelations.[24]

That state of affairs is as follows:

We intend to J [a joint action defined in cooperatively neutral terms] if and only if:

1. (a) I intend that we J and (b) you intend that we J.
2. I intend that we J in accordance with and because of 1a, 1b, and meshing subplans of 1a and 1b; you intend that we J in accordance with and because of 1a, 1b, and meshing subplans of 1a and 1b.
3. 1 and 2 are common knowledge between us.[25]

The structure is built on Bratman's understanding of intentions as commitments to future action which have a certain stability that allows us to act as planning agents. When two or more persons (his model is explicitly limited to simple social settings lacking authority structures[26]) seek to act together they form intentions with respect to their putative joint action, which intentions, while individual (as there is no group

---

[23] Bratman refers to shared intention, but to avoid confusion I shall speak only of group, or joint, intention.
[24] Bratman (n 7) 111.   [25] Bratman (n 7) 121.   [26] Bratman (n 7) 94.

mind) are common to both parties and by virtue of their content and contingency enable the agents to plan joint action. That is, my intention that we J interlocks with your intention to similar effect and this means we may rationally plan on the basis that we will J, although that commitment may be revised or abandoned prior to action. This approach avoids the failure of the summative accounts because the intentions interlock (our intentions are caused by and are contingent on one another) rather than coincide and because the group intention arises out of and is not reducible to any one individual intention.

That the intentions must interlock rather than coincide is also seen in the requirement that members of the group intend to act together by means of meshing subplans. This requirement arises because intentions are plans that may be more or less specific. Joint action is possible because members of the group do not just form relatively abstract intentions to act together but instead intend also to structure their further (more specific) plans to enable joint action. Our interlocking intentions that we J establish a plan that we share, but we each have subplans that we hope to fulfil in executing our shared plan.[27] If those subplans were inconsistent, and neither of us was prepared to revise them in the event of conflict, then our joint intention would not be capable of fulfilment. Thus, for group intention to ground group action, Bratman contends both agents must intend to mesh their respective subplans, which is to refrain from frustrating the other's subplans and instead to include the relevant subplans within a unified coherent plan of action.

On this approach, every member of the group must hold the relevant interlocking individual intentions before group intention may arise. Unanimity in the supporting structure of intentions is thus a precondition of group intention. This is not to say that an individual's intention to participate in group action may not be coerced. Jointly intentional action requires certain states of mind amongst all participants, and while these states of mind may arise from manipulation or force, if they do not exist, or at least appear to exist, there is no group action.

A basic objection to Bratman's account, which he anticipates, is that it seems prima facie irrational for anyone to 'intend that we'. Rational agents intend to act only to the extent that they have some prospect of

---

[27] Bratman (n 7) 98–103, 119–20.

performing the act, which means they have some control over what is to be done. Hence, I may intend to run a marathon, even if there is a good chance I will fail, but I may not intend to fly like Superman. The objection then is that no rational agent may intend that the group act because the individual agent cannot control the actions of others. If sound, this would mean that no rational agent would ever intend that the group act in a certain way and so interlocking intentions to that effect could not ground group action.

Bratman's response is compelling. He argues that a rational agent may intend that another person act in a certain way if the agent is in a position to influence, support, or enable that action. Then the agent's intention that another person acts is not akin to a bare wish or fancy but is instead a plan on which the agent may act. The agent's plan is not fulfilled unless the other person does so act, but that does not mean the formation of the intention is irrational: everything does not have to be under my control for it to be rational for me to intend to act. My intention that we J is conditional on your intention to similar effect.[28] Thus we both retain sufficient control over our joint act for it to be rational for us to form the interlocking intentions that support group intention.

This approach to group intention provides a plausible account of how individuals may form group intentions to act together, thereby explaining at least simple cases of group action. The explanation is attractive in part because it does not rely on the mysterious (or at least quite incomplete) idea of we-intentions. The Bratmanian approach is reductive, in that it reduces group intention to a certain pattern of I-intentions. In two other ways, however, it is non-reductive. First, the group intention is not reduced to an intention held by an individual; instead, it is a plan that arises from the intentions of individuals and is open to them as the shared plan. Second, while his account differs from that of Searle or Gilbert in that it explains group action in terms of a supporting structure of intentions, it is non-reductive in that it does just assume there is a capacity for joint action. That is, the group act J is stipulated to be a joint action, even if described in cooperatively neutral terms, and Bratman never explains how that act might be further reduced to a series of individual actions. I shall assume that the capacity

---

[28] J Finnis, 'On Conditional Intentions and Preparatory Intentions' in L Gormally (ed), *Moral Truth and Moral Tradition* (Four Courts Press, Dublin, 1994), 163, 164, 169–70.

for joint action is basic and arises from our recognition that other agents are also rational.

I take group intention, as outlined by Bratman, to be the foundation of the structure of group action. Thus, group action is action on a common plan that is constituted, and supported, by a set of interlocking individual intentions. This common plan is the joint intention of the members of the group, the group intention. However, I am under no illusions that I have proved that Bratman's theory is true. I have at best provided sufficient reason to proceed for now with Bratman's approach, reserving the possibility that further analysis might establish that group action rests on irreducible we-intentions. Still, if that did prove to be the case, I do not think my account of the structure of group action would require radical revision. The disagreement between Searle and Bratman concerns the foundation of group intention and how, if at all, it is constituted by the intentions of individual agents. Both theorists understand the group intention to be the means by which the group secures its shared end, to be a joint plan of action. Therefore, while my analysis adopts Bratman's starting point, the account I provide of group action has wider support than just his theory alone.

III. Complex Group Action

Bratman limits his account to simple cases where the group is small and informal. In cases of this kind the group intention arises directly from the unanimous intentions of the members of the group and concerns the group's plan of action for the particular case only. However, my concern is with more complex groups that use procedures and exist over time. Therefore, I shall extend Bratman's account to explain those cases in which the group intention is formed in part by procedures, especially authority procedures.

In his book *The Construction of Social Reality*, Searle argues that the crucial device in explaining complex social facts is the formula 'X counts as Y in C'.[29] This formula enables the imposition of status functions on objects, events, or persons that previously had no such function. The process iterates, so that a Y from a previous instance of

---

[29] Searle (n 19) 28–9.

the formula may be the X in another use: thus, social facts are nested within one another.[30] The formula works, argues Searle, because of collective intention, so that we all intend X to count as Y in C and by virtue of our joint intention to that effect the new status is indeed conferred.[31]

Complex groups impose status functions on the outcome of particular procedures, which may be used on a single occasion or, more interestingly, may form part of a plan to act over time. A procedure, such as majority voting, is adopted by a group when all the members of the group form interlocking intentions that the outcome of that procedure shall count as the act of the group. Authority procedures are used to direct the group to act in the absence of unanimity by providing how the group's plan is to be selected. This is valuable for any group that cannot wait on unanimity before acting.[32]

A group uses an authority procedure to select the plan of action on which it is to act when the group intends the application of the procedure to count as its act. We may thus distinguish two types of group intention. The first is the primary or particular intention of the group, which is the intention (the plan, the means-end package) that explains and defines the particular action of the group on this occasion. The second is the secondary intention of the group, which is the group's general intention to use certain procedures to determine its particular intentions: that is, the group's general plan to select particular plans, which are to be the means to its defining purpose. I term this secondary because it is a plan about plans, but it might also be termed the group's standing intention and indeed this better captures the framing and enduring nature of the plan, to which members of the group conform over time and within which particular plans are formed. We understand the particular intentions of a complex group in light of its standing intentions.

The following example may clarify how authority procedures feature in complex group action. A company is a group (employees, management, and shareholders) that exists to profit in commercial enterprise. The group acts by reference to a corporate structure that includes a rule authorizing the CEO to set future company strategy. The rule provides that the intentional action of the CEO counts as the act of the group in deciding on strategy. The group's standing intention

---

[30] Searle (n 19) 80.   [31] Searle (n 19) 43–51.   [32] Finnis, *NLNR*, 232–3.

is to pursue its purpose, to profit in commercial enterprise, by means of a general plan that includes this rule, which will in turn be used to generate further, particular plans on which the group will act. It follows that irrespective of the consequences that the law may attach to the action of the CEO, his intentional action is truly part of a group act: the group intends the individual act to be its act, the CEO acts intending to direct the group, and the other members of the group coordinate their further action as his act directs.

Authority procedures are not the only procedures that groups may adopt. For instance, groups may also adopt procedures that enable competitive behaviour, so that a prize fight or game of chess is an instance of competition nested within a structure of group action.[33] With games, the group adopts a structure of rules that stipulates the significance of various individual actions and within that structure the members of the group compete as individuals (or teams, which are subgroups). Thus, all the participants in the game must form interlocking intentions to adopt the rules of the game before the group may play.

To direct group action a procedure must be adopted by all members of the group: departures from the starting norm of unanimity must be unanimous. No procedural rule, including majority vote, has any automatic application, as a simple example illustrates. Imagine a group of five friends deciding how to spend the afternoon together. Three of the friends grow impatient and purport to vote for a certain plan. The vote does not settle how the group acts and if the three friends (who purport to be 'the majority') went ahead and acted as though it did then the two friends could rightly insist that they were not participants in the resulting group act: there would be an act of three friends but not of all five. Of course, putting the matter to a vote might result in the two friends either acquiescing in the result, or, alternatively, accepting the use of majority vote as the group's procedure. But until all the members of the group adopt the relevant procedure, its use cannot settle how the entire group is to act.

It follows that authority procedures are not fundamental to group action. Instead, procedures are relevant only to the extent that they have been adopted by the group as part of the group's general plan to attain its defining end. The complex case shares the same structure as

---

[33] Bratman (n 7) 107, 122; Searle (n 5) 413–14.

the simple case in that the general plan or standing intention of the complex group must arise from the unanimous interlocking intentions of its members. The complex group differs from the simple in that the particular plans on which it acts need not be directly unanimous; instead those plans, the particular intentions of the group, may have been generated by the application of authority procedures.

I make no claim that the members of a complex group always believe that their intention to adopt an authority procedure creates either the procedure (say, hereditary succession to the kingship) or an obligation to accept the outcome of the procedure. My claim is just that when the members form interlocking intentions to adopt a certain procedure, then its application counts as a group act, but in the absence of that structure of supporting intention, no such group act is possible. Similarly, individuals often have good reason to participate in certain group actions or to adopt certain procedures. Their failure to do so may not remove that reason, but it does shape the way things are. That I ought to join the army does not mean that even without forming the relevant intention I have done so, even if for some purposes I may rightly be dealt with as though I had (perhaps being deemed to have joined and now to be a deserter). My concern is with the reality of social acts, and that reality turns on the actual intentions of individuals.

To explain group action, one must clarify the relationship between intentional individual acts and the group act, which is to explain when and why an individual action 'counts as' the act of the group. It is not the case that all individual acts that count as group acts are exhaustively defined as such by the group's procedures. Very few groups, if any, employ the full set of procedures that such exhaustive stipulation would require. For example, a company may have explicit rules that effectively stipulate that the decision of the board counts as an intentional action of the company, but the act of a company clerk or the guard at the gate will still, without reference to procedures, also count as acts of the group. And the same individual act may also count as the act of multiple groups, again without the need for procedures. To adapt John Finnis' example, the guard at the gate is a member of the complex group that is the factory and all its workers and yet he may also, simultaneously, form a simple group with truck drivers to the extent that they cooperate towards the shared end of ensuring that several trucks are able to enter and exit without accident.[34] The guard's act in raising the security barrier is thus at once the act of the factory authorizing entry, and also the act of the drivers and guard coordinating entry and exit.

That procedures are not fundamental to the structure of group action further confirms that specific procedures are not needed for an individual act to count as a group act. Still, it is not immediately clear what else may determine whether an individual act counts as a group act. Indeed, if an act counts as a group act only if the group intends it to so count, then it would seem impossible to identify an act as a group act without the use of procedures: if the group intends the particular act to count as its act it would seem to have adopted a procedure to that effect. The problem dissolves if we recall that group action is the coordinated pursuit of a common purpose by means of a jointly accepted plan of action. The group acts when its members execute the plan of action that the group has adopted (whether directly as with a simple group or via procedures as with a complex group) and it follows that each individual action taken to execute the plan counts as a group act. The member of the group intends his particular act to be a means to the end of executing the common plan. His individual action thus stands as means to the end of joint action and is only explicable as part of the larger group act.

An example of Searle's also makes this point. The individual intention of a member of a football team (I intend to tackle X), he says, stands in relation to the group intention (we intend to execute the particular play) as means to end, just as pulling the trigger of a gun stands to the firing of a bullet.[35] We execute a particular play (in part) by means of my tackling X. For the members of the group to adopt a certain plan of action is for each member to adopt it as his plan of action, intending and being understood to intend to play his part, acting as needed to execute the plan. Therefore, any individual act that is taken to execute the plan counts as a group act.

The following example may help illustrate the structure of complex group action.[36] An army is a group defined by the shared end of military victory. The standing intention of the group is to seek military victory by acting on plans that are generated by the complex set of authority procedures known as the chain of command. The members

---

[34] Finnis, *NLNR*, 151–2.   [35] Searle (n 5) 408–13.
[36] Finnis, *Aquinas*, 33–5.

of the group (soldiers of all rank) form interlocking intentions to act by means of those procedures. The procedures authorize the general to direct the joint action of other soldiers by choosing a plan of action, a strategy, as a means to victory. Soldiers lower in the chain of command further specify the plan and their directives coordinate the action of lower-ranking soldiers. The full group act is the execution of the overall plan of action, which is increasingly specified at lower levels but stands to all soldiers as a means to the shared end. The individual soldier acts to play his part in the plan and his action is rightly understood by other soldiers to count as the act of the group. The general's formulation of strategy is a group act that constitutes the group's particular plan (at a high level of abstraction). Likewise, a platoon's execution, at the direction of its platoon leader, of a highly specified plan to defeat a particular enemy outpost is a group act of the army, as well as of the platoon, which forms one of the many subgroups within the group.

The group intends to execute a certain plan to fulfil its purpose. The plan is the proposal that was adopted by the members of the group, either unanimously or on the basis of authority, to direct their joint action. For the plan to direct joint action, it, like the shared purpose, must be an end in the reasoning of each member. But neither the plan nor the purpose need be accepted by all members for the same reasons. Fulfilment of the group purpose will often be a means to different ends for the various members, and this is not fatal to group action. To cooperate, the members must act on one proposal and they therefore need to know only that the proposal stands in the practical reasoning of each member as a means to the shared end that defines the group. The further reasons that the members have for acting are irrelevant to group action.

The group act is constituted by the reasoning and action of the members of the group, but the act, and the group intention that defines it, are also detached from that reasoning.[37] The reason for this is that in participating in the group act the members need not intend to realize all the ends that define and direct the particular group act. For the group to act each member must play his part in the plan, which is a means-ends package; however, a member may do so while intending to realize only one of the ends that the group act seeks, accepting the other(s) as an unintended side-effect of his action. This reasoning does

[37] J Finnis, 'Persons and their Associations' (1989) 63 Aristotelian Society Supplementary Volumes 267, 271–3.

not negate group action because the group act is defined by the plan that is open to all members. The group act is not an amalgam of the full chain of reasoning of each individual member. Instead, the act is a set of actions that are coordinated by reference to a commonly accepted plan of action. To say that the group intends to act on the plan is not to say that each member intends the entire plan: the member may intend only to coordinate with others in accordance with the plan, but that is sufficient for group action.

This detachment of the group act from the full chain of reasoning of each member is confirmed by the existence of a group perspective.[38] It is perfectly comprehensible for an agent to participate in the group act and yet to insist that his individual action is not defined by the group intention in which it takes its place. This may be a self-serving rationalization, but it need not. An example may clarify my point. Two soldiers may be ordered to operate a howitzer to destroy a certain building in order both to destroy a military target and to terrorize the civilian population: for example, a command post within a school. The group act of the army is defined by its intention, which is to win the war by means of (1) destroying a military target and (2) terrorizing civilians, where (1) and (2) are to be accomplished by means of destroying this building. The soldiers carry out that group act. Both soldiers accept the group purpose (victory in war). Yet the reasoning of each soldier may differ in that one may intend to destroy the military target and to terrorize while the other intends to destroy the military target but only accepts the terror as an unintended side-effect. The difference in reasoning determines how the individuals have acted but the group act is defined by the group intention, which is a plan adopted to realize both ends.

In Bratman's account, the group plan must be common knowledge. My account loosens that stricture. It is plain that complex group action is not always action on a plan known by all members. The general's strategy is secret and yet his intention directs the army and defines its action. The standing intention of the group is constituted by unanimous interlocking intention and so it must be common knowledge. However, the particular plans on which the group acts need only be open to members at the level of specification at which they are called upon to act. That does not mean they must know or understand

---

[38] Cf. P Pettit, 'Collective Persons and Powers' (2002) 8 Legal Theory 443, 462–3.

its content, but it must be open and accessible at the level at which they are called to act. Ignorant members of the group may participate in the group act if they act in accordance with the plan, either by following the lead of other members or by being directed by others to act as appropriate. The group act then is defined by the proposal for action that was open to members and on which the group intends to act.

The account I have set out is I think consistent with the classical understanding of social action found in Aquinas[39] and restated by Finnis, Grisez, and Boyle.[40] I accept Aquinas' insight that groups are associations that coordinate the action of individuals to some defining end. And I have argued for the central importance of the open plan in the same way that Finnis argues that group acts are defined by the 'public' proposal that is put to the members of the group for them to participate in or not.[41] Where I have sought to extend the classical account is in setting out in some detail the relationship between the intentional act of the group and the reasoning of the individuals who constitute the group. My aim has not been to reduce group action to a series of individual acts, but rather to ground group action on a supporting structure of individual intentions and so explain how the action of the group may truly be said to be defined by its intention in acting.

My analysis suggests that the individual action of a member of the group does not count as an act of the group when the action is inconsistent with the common plan. For example, a soldier's act of torturing prisoners (for entertainment rather than for military advantage) does not count as an act of the army, even if the army is responsible for some reason (such as a failure to supervise). Further, if a member of the group openly manifests an intention not to act as part of the group, then his actions do not count as acts of the group. Indeed, for the purposes of group action he is not part of the group. That conclusion follows from the unanimous jointly intentional structure of group action and is consonant with experience: for the purposes of determining whether the army or platoon has acted, a reluctant soldier counts as a soldier, and may thus count as the army or platoon, but a person who flatly refuses to bear arms (or a deserter) does not.

---

[39] Finnis, *Aquinas*, 23–37.
[40] J Finnis, J Boyle, and G Grisez, *Nuclear Deterrence, Morality and Realism* (Oxford University Press, Oxford, 1987), 120–3, 288–91, 344–7.
[41] Finnis (n 37) 273.

It is possible that a member of a group, who purports to participate in its joint action, does not truly form the interlocking intentions on which the group act is premised. This 'secret defector' rejects the group purpose. He does not intend to coordinate his actions in accordance with the common plan to the shared end, but still wishes to maintain the illusion of being an ordinary member. For example, a spy in the general staff participates in the formation of strategy to open up the possibility of wrecking the plans of the army. There are good reasons in such cases to say that the acts of the defector do not count as the group act: he does not intend to coordinate and the purported coordination of others rests on a false premise. However, secret defection is distinguishable from open defection. The secret defector participates in the group act, even though his action is parasitic on that of a good member. To avoid detection and to carry out his own purpose, he must take the plan into account and on occasion he may even have to act to further the common purpose.[42]

It follows that secret defection need not frustrate execution of the common plan or nullify the group act, although it does mean the act is a non-central case. In the central, well-formed case all members of the group truly do form the necessary interlocking intentions and adopt the plan of action as their own. But apparent compliance is sufficient to enable a type of group action. The same is true where a member of the group intends the group to act on the basis of a plan other than that which was open to all members and has been adopted by all other members of the group. The member's mistake is not necessarily fatal to the group act so long as his action is in fact coordinated by reference to the common plan.

Another variation on the central, well-formed case is where one or more members intend only to contribute to the group action rather than to fulfil the shared end that defines the group. Christopher Kutz argues that collective action in large groups is possible because members of such groups need only intend to contribute rather than to intend to fulfil the group purpose.[43] Scott Shapiro adapts Kutz's notion and gives as an example Microsoft employees hired to work on part of a complex technological project who do not intend the project's final or overall success, but who do intend to contribute to the

---

[42] Finnis, Boyle, and Grisez (n 40) 120–3.
[43] C Kutz, *Complicity: Ethics and Law for a Collective Age* (Cambridge University Press, Cambridge, 2000), 94.

project, as that is a precondition of their being paid.[44] Another example might be the reluctant soldier who will march where directed and fight as required (he is not a deserter and he will coordinate with other soldiers to execute the army's strategy) but is indifferent to the goal of victory, intending instead only that he survive without being court-martialled.

This psychology is certainly possible. And I agree with Kutz and Shapiro that a group may act even when certain of its members do not share the group's defining purpose. However, this is certainly a non-central case (being a reluctant solider, for example, is just to be a non-central variant of the committed soldier). It can be understood as a form of group action because it shares common features with the central case, most notably that the members of the group still adopt the common plan as their own, which plan takes its point and meaning by reference to the group purpose. Therefore, while in the central case all members act intending to fulfil the group's purpose by means of the open plan, neither secret defection nor the bare intention to contribute preclude group action.

IV. Discursive Dilemmas and Collective Irrationality

Joint intentions are plans held in common by members of a group to structure their joint action to their shared end. The group's intention is the rational order that explains and structures its action, just as an individual person's intention defines and explains his action. The intentions of a rational person follow from and are explained by the individual agent's response to reasons, which there is good reason to expect to be coherent and at least somewhat stable over time. I consider now whether there is good reason to expect the intentions of groups to be coherent and consistent and to follow from the group's response to reasons. The plans of any group arise in some way from the intentional action of its members. When the group acts on related propositions, there is a standing risk that integrating the rational intentions of individual members of the group into the joint intentions of the group will result in collectively irrational action. That is, the group

---

[44] S Shapiro, 'Law, Plans, and Practical Reason' (2002) 8 Legal Theory 387, 412.

may form an incoherent, inconsistent or unreasoned plan that is an unfit means to the ends for which the group acts. I maintain that a group may avoid this outcome if its members attend to the relations amongst propositions and aim to act jointly like a rational agent.

The problem of collective irrationality is explored with care in List and Pettit's important work on group agency. They begin by discussing groups that use majority voting procedures, but their argument is, as they make clear, of more general application.[45] Their discussion proceeds by way of a reflection on the so-called doctrinal paradox in appellate court decision-making.[46] The paradox may arise when a court of three or more judges has to decide an issue that turns on two or more premises, say, the issue of the defendant's liability which turns on (i) whether he caused the loss and (ii) whether a duty of care existed. The court decides by each judge taking a view on the premises (causation and duty of care) and then voting on the conclusion (liability). There is a doctrinal paradox if the pattern of votes is as follows:

	Causation	Duty of care	Liability
Judge 1	Yes	No	No
Judge 2	No	Yes	No
Judge 3	Yes	Yes	Yes
Majority	Yes	Yes	No

A majority of judges conclude that the defendant was not liable. That conclusion is not supported by the view of a majority of judges on the relevant premises. Instead, a majority of judges believed that there was causation and another majority believed that there was a duty of care. Despite a majority of judges believing that there was causation and a duty of care, the aggregation of the rational votes of each judge yields the conclusion that there is no liability. Yet if the court had decided by voting on the relevant premises and taking the premises to dictate the conclusion, it would have reached the opposite decision. Hence, the choice of decision-making procedure can be very important, for a premise-based procedure leads to one outcome, and a conclusion-based procedure to another.

---

[45] C List and P Pettit, *Group Agency* (Oxford University Press, Oxford, 2011), 43–50.
[46] List and Pettit (n 45) 44–5.

This example is important and illuminating, but also somewhat obscure. In reflecting on the doctrinal paradox, List and Pettit argue that:

Relative to the given legal doctrine—that obligation and action are jointly necessary and sufficient for liability—the set of propositions accepted by a majority, namely that the defendant had an obligation, did the action, and yet is not liable, is inconsistent. If adherence to legal doctrine is considered a requirement of rationality in a court, then majority voting will prevent the court from meeting this requirement in the present case.[47]

The point of the court is to decide the dispute, which is to reach a conclusion on the appellant's liability. The court uses majority vote to reach this conclusion. List and Pettit take the court to form judgments on each premise and on the conclusion. However, the court need not use majority vote to reach a position on each premise: the judges may each form *views* on the premises and then *vote* on the conclusion. Hence, the pattern of votes—or rather of views on premises and then the vote on the conclusion—does not entail that the court's decision is inconsistent. The decision would be inconsistent if, as List and Pettit present the example, the court were to decide on the premises by way of majority vote and then on the conclusion in the same way, for then the court would decide 'yes, causation and duty of care, but yet no liability', which is flatly inconsistent. Inviting the court to vote on premises *and* conclusion would be to invite just such inconsistency, because if the court is to take a position qua court on the premises, this will entail a consistent conclusion. The subsequent vote on the conclusion would then offer only an opportunity to affirm the entailed conclusion or to decide inconsistently with the premises that support a particular conclusion. Importantly, however, the court need not decide on premises and on conclusion. Each judge must decide on all three propositions, but the court may settle the dispute by asserting just that the defendant is not liable. The court's decision is then not collectively irrational because inconsistent. However, it is irrational to the extent that it is incomplete. That is, the court's decision does not follow from reasons that the court itself adopts and takes to justify its decision.

---

[47] List and Pettit (n 45) 45.

The court is able to attain its end, the fair adjudication of disputes, without itself adopting reasons. Instead, the dispute may be settled by the intersection of the rational decisions of each judge, each of whom takes a consistent view on premises and conclusion. The court's decision is complete and follows from reasons that the court itself adopts when the majority's conclusions follow from the same chain of reasoning. It is not unfair for a dispute to be settled by the conclusions of judges, each of whom reasons carefully, notwithstanding that the court itself does not act for reasons. Still, there are good reasons to think this adjudicative act less than satisfactory—if the court itself acts on reasons, it is clearer that the dispute was settled rationally and the merits of the settlement are open to scrutiny. Further, the secondary point of adjudicative decisions in the common law world, to restate legal doctrine and perhaps to change it in relevant part, cannot be secured if in articulating and applying the law the court itself fails to act on a complete set of reasons. I do not mean that an incomplete decision unsettles the content of the law, although it may, but rather that it fails to constitute what the common law method of legal change requires, which is reasoned judgment.

The doctrinal paradox, List and Pettit argue, is just one instance of a more general discursive dilemma, which is the standing possibility that 'majority voting on interconnected propositions may lead to inconsistent group judgments even when individual judgments are fully consistent'.[48] In earlier work, Pettit argued that this possibility poses a dilemma because groups could be structured to reach decisions either by a conclusion-centred approach (voting on the conclusion) or a premise-centred approach (letting the vote on the relevant premises be decisive), and each approach has its advantages and disadvantages.[49] In his recent and most sophisticated work with List, he argues that groups should resolve the dilemma by forming rational agents, although this need not call for a strict premise-based approach.

To form plans of action by way of majority vote on a series of related propositions is to risk adopting plans that are inconsistent. This means that the group may form a plan that is an unsound means to the ends for which the group acts. To illustrate the point, consider another example of Pettit's, a political party formulating policy.[50]

---

[48] List and Pettit (n 45) 46.   [49] Pettit (n 38) 450–1.
[50] Pettit (n 38) 453–4.

	Increase taxes?	Increase defence spending?	Increase other spending?
Politician A	No	Yes	No
Politician B	No	No	Yes
Politician C	Yes	Yes	Yes
Majority	No	Yes	Yes

Pettit stipulates that if defence spending were increased, other spending could not be increased without raising taxes (there is no deficit borrowing and/or the point of the policy is to balance the budget). Therefore it would be irrational (as impossible) for anyone to set out to increase defence spending and other spending without also raising taxes. Yet the pattern of votes above would lead the party to adopt this policy. The joint plan is inconsistent, such that it is not fit to be chosen by any rational person. The plan is not an intelligible response to the relevant reasons for action. It is collectively irrational because it is an inept, incoherent means to the group's end—developing credible policy proposals, which may serve as the platform on which to contest and win elections and then to govern well.

Interestingly, Pettit imagines each of these questions being considered at different points in time. Assume that per the table above the members of the party have at T1 voted not to raise taxes and then at T2 voted to increase defence spending. He argues that a discursive dilemma arises at T3, when the question is whether to increase other spending. The decisions at T1 and T2 provide a reason for the group not to increase other spending. However, if the party reaches its decision at T3 on the basis of ordinary majority vote, without adopting procedures to take T1 and T2 into account (which may include repudiating either decision reached at T1 or T2, or letting the issue at T3 follow from the prior two decisions), then, as the pattern above indicates, the party will adopt an irrational policy platform. The individual members of the party, Pettit asserts, have voted rationally, but their votes yield a collectively irrational decision.[51] (I argue below that the votes at T3 are not reasonable.)

This discussion makes clear that there are two dimensions to collective irrationality—incompleteness and inconsistency—and that the

---

[51] Pettit (n 38) 453.

importance of joint action being consistent and reasoned turns on the point of the group. The group that maintains collective rationality is thus a group structured to adopt plans that constitute intelligible responses to reason, and which are consistent, coherent, and complete.

The use of majority vote to form complex plans risks collective irrationality. This risk generalizes from majority vote to other procedures, such as supermajority or unanimity rules. Indeed, List and Pettit establish that it is impossible for any group acting in response to some set of propositions to maintain collective rationality if the procedure it adopts meets three other conditions.[52] The first is universal domain, which is to admit all possible consistent and complete individual attitudes. The second is anonymity, which is to treat all individuals equally in forming group attitudes. The third is systematicity, which is to provide that:

The group attitude on each proposition depends only on the individuals' attitudes towards it, not on their attitudes towards other propositions, and the pattern of dependence between individual and collective attitudes is the same for all propositions.[53]

The upshot of this impossibility theorem is that one cannot square collective rationality with universal domain, anonymity, and systematicity.

V. The Idea of Group Agency

List and Pettit consider various ways in which groups might adopt procedures that depart from the conditions so as to make possible collective rationality. One possibility is to institute dictatorship, such that the plans of one person are the plans of the group. This is to relax anonymity.[54] However, this is in general no solution to the problem of how to enable reasoned joint action, for it achieves coherence at the cost of integration. Alternatively, one can restrict the range of rational individual attitudes that are admissible, which is to relax universal

---

[52] List and Pettit (n 45) 47–50. Strictly they say that four conditions are incompatible, one of which is collective rationality.
[53] List and Pettit (n 45) 49.   [54] List and Pettit (n 45) 53.

domain.[55] However, while deliberation about attitudes may narrow the range of attitudes, it is unlikely to remove the prospect of discursive dilemmas if the set of propositions is sufficiently diverse. It follows that limiting the set of inputs, so to speak, to avoid collective irrationality will curtail the group's capacity to act on its members' attitudes.

The most attractive way to maintain collective rationality, suggest List and Pettit, is to liberalize systematicity, which means to take into account how different propositions relate to one another.[56] This could be achieved by way of a sequential priority procedure, in which propositions on the agenda are arranged in some order, with earlier propositions taking precedence over later to the extent they are inconsistent.[57] Premises might be understood to be earlier than conclusions for example; that is, the premise-based approach is an instance of a sequential priority procedure. The problem with this approach is its rigidity, with much being settled by the initial ordering and hence on how propositions are categorized. This mode of settling which propositions the group adopts is thus somewhat arbitrary and liable to distort joint action. Further, the premise-based approach is difficult to extend to domains in which propositions are not neatly distinguishable into premise and conclusion.[58] Where the agenda is large and complex, and the relationship amongst propositions complex and contested, strict procedures of this kind, while in principle a means to maintain collective rationality, fail to be an intelligent measure to make possible reasoned joint action.[59] The type of group agent these procedures form lacks the openness in response to reason that characterizes well-formed individual agency, in which the relationship between propositions is open to be revisited, by way of reflective equilibrium.

More promising are procedures that are less rigid and depend instead on making provision for feedback, wherein members of the group are alert to and respond to inconsistency and incompleteness, drawing out such inconsistency and resolving it. This feedback may be realized by some members of the group privately changing their votes, but more interestingly the group will make provision for inconsistencies to be made public within the group, to be discussed, and then to be resolved to maintain collective rationality (and hence avoid frustrating the objects of the group action).[60] For example, the group may use a

---

[55] List and Pettit (n 45) 51–2.
[56] List and Pettit (n 45) 54–8.
[57] List and Pettit (n 45) 56.
[58] List and Pettit (n 45) 57–8.
[59] List and Pettit (n 45) 60–1.
[60] List and Pettit (n 45) 62–4.

straw poll procedure, in which propositions are considered in turn and approved on majority vote if consistent with other propositions.[61] If inconsistent, then the group considers (and if need be votes on) the various ways in which one might revise either the later or earlier proposition to ensure consistency. When the members of the group attend to the relations amongst propositions in this kind of way, and strive to settle on a joint position that is complete and consistent, the group is in one sense reasoning about what should be done. One need not say, as List and Pettit do, that the group takes a view on the relation amongst propositions when it considers possible inconsistencies.[62] The group may instead be structured to allow its members to each form a view, such that when they settle on a common plan, that plan is likely to be coherent and reasoned rather than contradictory and arbitrary.

The group that is structured to adopt reasoned plans, which are complete and consistent, forms an agent, which there is reason to think is likely to act rationally. If it acts irrationally, this constitutes a poor exercise of its capacities rather than all that is to be expected from a group incapable of disciplining itself in response to reasons. The foundation of this group agency is the joint intention to form and maintain a group that responds coherently to reasons. That is, the members of the group act for a shared end and the means to that end, which thus forms an intermediary end in its own right, is to form rational plans that are supported by a stable response to the relevant reasons. The means to that intermediary end consist in a set of dispositions on the part of members of the group and procedures that make it possible for the group to attend to the consistency and completeness of the propositions it adopts. While List and Pettit argue that group agency is possible, even if unlikely, without joint intention, I disagree.[63] Their example—terrorist cells which are coordinated by unknown handlers—seems to me unsound, for the joint intention of the terrorists is to coordinate their actions by way of plans developed by the unknown handlers, who are trusted to pick out means to the shared end that unites the members (say, defeating some enemy).

That group agency is grounded in joint intention is significant. Members of the group aim to act jointly by way of coherent, reasoned plans. Hence they have good reason to adopt and maintain procedures that make inconsistencies salient and provide for their resolution. They

---

[61] List and Pettit (n 45) 62.   [62] List and Pettit (n 45) 64.
[63] List and Pettit (n 45) 33.

also have good reason to change what they would otherwise do, including the option for which they would otherwise vote, in order to maintain group agency. This is implicit in the rationale for the procedures and in their successful application, for when inconsistencies are brought to light, members of the group strive for consistency. Indeed, even in the absence of procedures allowing the relations amongst propositions to be revisited, it would be unreasonable for members of the group to insist on their ex ante plans, ignoring what the group has otherwise decided up to this time. Recall the political party example. Politicians B and C do not act reasonably if they vote to increase other spending, ignoring the party's earlier decisions (the plan thus far . . .) not to increase taxes and to increase defence spending. The politicians foresee that their votes will make it the case that the party has an inconsistent platform, which fails to achieve its end, which is to balance the budget and/or to constitute a credible policy on which to contest elections and to govern. Their vote is thus only rational if one discounts the importance of the joint action in which they are engaged. And indeed this is the point: acting together for some end changes how one should act.

The joint intention to form a reasoned agent, which acts on coherent and consistent plans, changes how members of the group should reason. Consider another example, in this case the members of a company's board deciding whether to purchase an attractively priced company X, in the specialty chemicals sector.[64] The decision involves three propositions.

	Specialty chemicals?	Expand by acquisition?	Acquire X?
Board A	Yes	Yes	Yes
Board B	Yes	No	No
Board C	No	Yes	No
Majority	Yes	Yes	No

The company has to decide whether to expand into this sector, whether to do so by acquisition (or by internal growth), and whether to acquire an attractively priced company in that sector. If one decides

---

[64] E B Rock, 'The Corporate Form as a Solution to a Discursive Dilemma' (2006) 162 Journal of Institutional and Theoretical Economics 57, 58.

to expand into this sector and to expand by way of acquisition, then one should acquire X. If the company votes on each proposition, the company decides to expand into this sector, by acquisition rather than internal growth, yet decides not to acquire X. To this extent the company is unable to formulate a reasoned strategy: it adopts reasons that warrant acquiring X, yet fails to acquire X. This is plainly a problem, because it means the company is incapable of executing a coherent strategy, which frustrates profitable action and undermines the company's credibility as an agent in the marketplace (it cannot be relied on to respond to reasons or to act consistently over time). Members of the board should grasp this and bring the company's reasons and action into line. The problem is especially acute if the decisions are made over time, for then the vote by B and C not to acquire X would be to abandon the plan thus far. This is not to say that the plan cannot be revisited, but until it is, it stands as the group's plan. Hence, when members of the group perceive the importance of reasoned action they have good reason to discipline themselves and to attend to the coherence of their joint action.

The prospect of collective irrationality is a standing problem for any group that acts on interlinked propositions, especially over time. Many groups cannot attain their defining end without maintaining collective rationality and responding to reasons with complete and consistent joint action. The way to maintain rationality at the group level is first to recognize the problem, to take it to change how one should reason and vote (that is, with an eye to the coherence and intelligibility of the resulting joint action), and to adopt procedures to bring out inconsistencies and to resolve them. When one acts on these procedures, with these dispositions, the group is reasoning and it is well placed for reasoned action. The action of such a group is thus not the mere intersection of private reasoning, for the members of the group are concerned to make it the case that the group acts on a workable plan for sound reasons, and this changes what they have reason to do together.

The intention of the group is not the aggregate of the intentions of its members, for joint action is not the overlap of individual action. Instead, members of some association act for some common end, adopting plans of action that coordinate their joint action. More complex groups adopt complex plans, such that the group has standing intentions and particular intentions. And some groups have good reason to attend to the consistency and completeness of the plans they adopt, such that the group should and may be structured to respond to reasons with coherent, reasoned joint action. Thus, many groups form and act on intentions and some constitute rational agents, which may be expected to act coherently.

4

Legislating Without Reasoning

The well-formed legislature, I argue, is an institution capable of reasoned choice. Many scholars maintain, however, that the legislature makes law without making reasoned choices, without intending to change the law for some reasons. I argue that theories of this kind fail to explain how the legislature acts well. Any 'legislature' that aggregates preferences, constitutes a voting machine, or acts on a minimal intention to change the law would fail to exercise legislative authority and would be unlikely to enact reasonable legislation. Theories of this kind depart from how reasonable legislators understand the joint act of legislating, which understanding (taken up further in chapters 5–8) illuminates the nature of the institution.

I. The Forum of Policy

Dworkin's work, especially his earlier work, discloses a theory of the legislature. His arguments about the nature of rights and the capacity of judges to enforce rights feature various claims about the nature of the legislature. Those claims may not be fully consistent with the rest of his jurisprudence. Following Dworkin's lead,[1] however, I do not attempt

---

[1] 'I have made no effort to discover how far this book alters or replaces positions I have defended in earlier work.' Dworkin, *LE*, viii. 'I make no effort here to discover how far my argument qualifies or expands my discussion of liberty in my book *Taking Rights Seriously*.' R Dworkin, *Sovereign Virtue: The Theory and Practice of Equality* (Harvard University Press, Cambridge MA, 2000), 481, n 9.

to trace the coherence of his overall line of thought, but instead consider particular arguments that he has deployed.

The distinction between principle and policy is central to Dworkin's account of adjudication. Principles describe rights and are requirements of justice or fairness, whereas policies describe goals and are concerned with the general welfare and public interest.[2] The distinction entails an institutional division of labour.[3] Dworkin signals this in the preface to *Taking Rights Seriously* where he says that:

... the promotion of the highest average welfare ... might be advanced more securely by assigning different types of questions to different institutions according to some theory of institutional competence, rather than by supposing that all institutions are equally able to calculate the impact on overall welfare of any particular political decision.[4]

Later he argues that the judiciary is the forum of principle.[5] The implication is that the legislature is the forum of policy.[6] That is, the judiciary settles questions of principle and right and the legislature settles questions of policy and general interest. For Dworkin, rights qualify the general interest, hence the need for judicial review.

Kyritsis argues that despite initial appearances Dworkin does not limit legislatures to policy alone. He has two arguments why any such limit would be a misreading of Dworkin and an unsound account of legislation.[7] The first is that 'it must be false to say that principle-based justifications don't figure in legislative proposals'. Dworkin acknowledges this when he says that '[t]he justification of a legislative program of any complexity will ordinarily require both sorts of argument'.[8] One might add that Dworkin says that legislators have a duty to advance the integrity of the law.[9] The second is that 'it would cast legislatures in an

---

[2] R Dworkin, *Taking Rights Seriously* (Duckworth, London, 1977), 22.
[3] B Miller, 'Justification and Rights Limitation' in G Huscroft (ed), *Interpreting the Constitution* (Cambridge University Press, Cambridge, 2008), 93, 101.
[4] Dworkin (n 2) ix.
[5] R Dworkin, *A Matter of Principle* (Harvard University Press, Cambridge MA, 1985), 69–72.
[6] P Yowell, 'A Critical Examination of Dworkin's Theory of Rights' (2007) 52 American Journal of Jurisprudence 93, 108.
[7] D Kyritsis, 'Principles, Policies and the Powers of Courts' (2007) 20 Canadian Journal of Law and Jurisprudence 379, 386–7.
[8] Dworkin (n 2) 83.
[9] See R Dworkin, *Freedom's Law: The Moral Reading of the American Constitution* (Harvard University Press, Cambridge MA, 1996), 31, 345 and *LE*, chapter 6.

irredeemably bad light to suggest that all they are institutionally bound to do is to aggregate interests'. Legislators, he contends, would fail to do their duty if they ignored principle or rights; it is at least as much part of their institutional function to consider such questions as it is to debate issues of policy. He suggests that it would be deeply counter-intuitive to think that legislators had discharged their duty if they made considered policy judgments even if they were insensitive to rights and principle.

I agree with Kyritsis' two arguments, but I do not think this settles the question of whether Dworkin understands the legislature to be merely the forum of policy. For while it is true that Dworkin does say that legislators do and should engage with principle, the weight of argument in his theory is for a conception of the legislature in which principle, and indeed reason, has no place. His argument for how the legislature is structured to decide policy would seem to preclude, or at least to curtail severely, the possibility of legislators reasoning about principle. Specifically, the point of the legislature, on Dworkin's understanding, is to aggregate the preferences of members of the community and this leads to rights and principles being approached as questions of preference to be decided by numbers rather than reason.

This conception of the roles of judge and legislator is found in Dworkin's early formulation of rights. In *Taking Rights Seriously*, and work of a similar time, he defined rights in response to otherwise legitimate utilitarian goals, which constituted the general welfare. In one passage he says:

The concept of an individual political right...is a response to the philosophical defects of a utilitarianism that counts external preferences and the practical impossibility of a utilitarianism that does not. It allows us to enjoy the institutions of political democracy, which enforce overall or unrefined utilitarianism, and yet protect the fundamental right of citizens to equal concern and respect by prohibiting decisions that seem, antecedently, likely to have been reached by virtue of the external components of the preferences democracy reveals.[10]

In a contemporaneous, but less well-known paper, Dworkin is yet more explicit:

---

[10] Dworkin (n 2) 277.

[A]ny political judgment about what makes the community better as a whole must count the impact on each particular person as having the same importance. As Bentham said, 'Each man [and woman] to count for one and none for more than one'.

The political process in a democracy is meant to translate that requirement into legislation through the institutions of representative democracy. The welfare economists have worked out a theory to how that is achieved. Each individual, through his votes and other political activity, registers or reveals a preference. The political process is a machine which is calculated, though imperfectly, to reach decisions such that, though some individuals suffer and others gain, the *overall* preferences of all the people, considered neutrally with the same consideration for the preferences of each, is improved.

In a community which has a settled prejudice of one sort or another... the machine will inevitably break down because there is no way of excluding these preferences based on prejudice from affecting the process. If prejudicial preferences are counted, then the personal preferences of those against whom the prejudice acts are not counted equally in the balance; they are discounted by the effect of the prejudice. Therefore constitutional rights are needed.[11]

Thus, Dworkin argued that the courts refine the legislature's coarse utilitarian calculation by enforcing rights that filter out external preferences, paradigmatically prejudicial preferences (although altruistic preferences fall on a similar logic).

He later steps away from utilitarianism and adopts instead resource-egalitarianism. However, common to both is the concern to count each person equally, and policy continues to be defined in terms of what members of the community want:

Most conceptions of equality, including utilitarianism and resource-egalitarianism, make the public interest, and therefore proper policy, sensitive to people's tastes, preferences, and choices. A community committed to such a conception will think that certain decisions of policy are sound simply because preferences and choices are distributed in a certain way...[12]

This is consistent with the further distinction he later introduces between choice-sensitive and choice-insensitive issues, a distinction

---

[11] R Dworkin, 'Social Sciences and Constitutional Rights—the Consequences of Uncertainty' (1977) 6 Journal of Law and Education 3, 10.
[12] Dworkin, *LE*, 384.

he explicitly says corresponds to policy and principle.[13] The point of the distinction, which I discuss further in section III of this chapter, is to ground his argument that the practice of judicial review is better suited to the resolution of choice-insensitive issues, where moral truth rather than preference distribution constitutes accuracy.

For Dworkin then, the point of the elected legislature is to aggregate preferences, thus identifying the general welfare against which rights may later have to be upheld. Easterbrook also sees legislatures 'as the mechanisms for aggregating preferences'.[14] And David Miller asserts that: '[i]n the liberal view, the aim of democracy is to aggregate individual preferences into a collective choice in as fair and efficient a way as possible'.[15] Dworkin does not explain in detail how the legislature aggregates preferences, but the following extract is suggestive:

Policy decisions must therefore be made through the operation of some political processes designed to produce an accurate expression of the different interests that should be taken into account. The political system of representative democracy may work only indifferently in this respect, but it works better than a system that allows non-elected judges who have no mailbag or lobbyists or pressure groups to compromise competing interests in their chambers.[16]

The implication is that legislators are responsive to the majority of constituents because to be re-elected they must act to satisfy the preferences of their constituents. The competition and bargaining amongst various legislators is a means—imperfect but the best available—to aggregate overall preferences. The political process is designed then to place pressure on legislators to maximize the preferences of (at least a majority of) their constituents. This responsiveness is critical to the legislator's capacity to play his part in the utilitarian machine, but it is also what leads to the inevitable malfunction of that machine, because the legislature necessarily counts prejudicial preferences, hence the need for judicial review.

---

[13] Dworkin, *Sovereign Virtue* (n 1) 204–5.
[14] F Easterbrook, 'Method, Result, and Authority: A Reply' (1985) 98 Harvard Law Review 622, 627.
[15] D Miller, 'Deliberative Democracy and Social Choice', chapter 9 in J Fishkin and P Laslett (eds), *Debating Deliberative Democracy* (Blackwell, Oxford, 2003), 182, 182–3.
[16] Dworkin (n 2) 85.

The above extract implies, as does Dworkin's earlier reference to the inevitability of the machine's malfunction, that legislators are unable to do other than advance majority preferences. It follows, he says, that they do not reason about principle:

[A]n argument of principle fixes on some interest presented by the proponent of the right it describes, an interest alleged to be of such a character as to make irrelevant the fine discriminations of any argument of policy that might oppose it. A judge who is insulated from the demands of the political majority whose interests the right would trump is therefore in a better position to evaluate the argument.[17]

His point is that the very features of legislative structure that are critical to the legislature acting fairly to find the general interest—responsiveness to majority will, ongoing pressure from constituents and lobbyists—tend to preclude the legislature from responding reasonably to moral argument.

Dworkin's statements that the legislature also has a role to play in protecting principle should be read in light of the above account. The logic of his argument is that the legislature should aggregate preferences and leave principle to the courts. The alternative is that they attempt to do more than just aggregate, but are structured to fail. Dworkin is quite explicit that whereas courts decide on principle, 'ordinary politics [turns on] the weight of numbers or the balance of political influence.'[18] This is consistent with his conclusion that '[j]udicial review insures that the most fundamental issues of political morality will finally be set out and debated as issues of principle and not political power alone, a transformation that cannot succeed, in any case not fully, within the legislature itself'.[19] In the final chapter of *Freedom's Law*, he reflects further on how legislatures make decisions:

[W]hen political controversies are decided by legislatures...the decision is likely to be governed by what most people want. That is desirable when an issue turns on what is in the best interests of the community as a whole, and the gains to some groups are balanced by losses to others. In such matters,

---

[17] Dworkin (n 2) 85; see also Dworkin (n 9) 344.
[18] Dworkin (n 9) 30.
[19] R Dworkin, *A Matter of Principle* (Harvard University Press, Cambridge, MA, 1985), 70.

numbers should count. But they need not count, at least not for that reason, in matters of fundamental principle...[20]

Ordinary politics generally aims... at a political compromise that gives all powerful groups enough of what they want to prevent their disaffection, and reasoned argument elaborating underlying moral principles is rarely part of or even congenial to such compromises.[21]

That is, the judiciary is structured to reason about principle and the legislature to respond to numbers. The legislature's general incapacity to reason about principle follows from the fact that the point of the legislature is to aggregate preferences, which is a complex exercise in counting what others think, and it is therefore structured to treat points of principle as if they were questions of preference. The legislators thus do not reason about what should be done, but instead invoke the fact that a majority of persons want a certain decision as if it were a reason.[22]

Dworkin's account of the legislature as a machine is strikingly similar to the public choice theory of legislation. Public choice scholars analyse legislation as a commodity and the legislative process as a market. Their critical assumption, which Dworkin shares, is that legislators are driven by the aim of re-election.[23] Their central claim is that interest groups procure legislation from legislators, whom they support with campaign contributions, bribes, endorsements, information, and the like. The legislative process, then, is a 'transmission belt for the translation of interest group preferences into public law'.[24] This conception of the legislative process is absurd. Shepsle, who, whatever the merits of his own theory of legislative action, is an astute observer of legislative politics, characterizes its principal failure as 'its asymmetric, *demand-side reductionism*' by which he means its focus on lobbyists and assumption that legislators are passive agents who respond to stimuli (usually venal).[25]

More sophisticated economic analysts of the legislative process step away from the focus on demand and attend also to what they term 'the

---

[20] Dworkin (n 9) 344. [21] Dworkin (n 9) 344–5. [22] Dworkin (n 19) 368.
[23] D Mueller, *Public Choice II* (Cambridge University Press, Cambridge, 1989), 1.
[24] D Rodriguez, 'Legislative Intent' in P Newman (ed), *The New Palgrave Dictionary of Economics and the Law* (Macmillan, London, 1998), vol 2, 563, 565 (Rodriguez does not endorse the public choice conception); see R Tollinson, 'Public Choice and Legislation' (1988) 74 Virginia Law Review 339–71.
[25] K Shepsle, 'Congress Is a "They," Not an "It": Legislative Intent as Oxymoron' (1992) 12 International Review of Law and Economics 239, 240.

supply side', which is to say how legislators think and act.[26] It is plain, argue these political economists, that legislators may have a wide variety of preferences beyond re-election or personal enrichment: professional accomplishment, partisan objectives, and moral or ideological policy goals. This alternative, more plausible economic approach models the legislative process as a site of strategic action, but understands the interaction of legislators to be significant and grants that legislators are capable of self-directed action.

Dworkin does not adopt the public choice conclusion that legislation is a commodity and the legislative process just another market. What he adopts is the public choice conception of the legislator, a passive agent who responds to stimuli, and, in modified form, the thought that the legislative process is a machine that produces legislation. The modification, and thus his difference from the public choice theorists, is that he takes the legislative process, while imperfect, to be fair because it counts each citizen equally. Public choice theory, by contrast, maintains that the legislative process is captured and corrupted by private interests. Dworkin is more confident that the legislative process is not, or at least need not be, wholly corrupt. It is hard to know what grounds his confidence, however, given that he relies on the mechanisms central to public choice—the spur of re-election and the activity of interest groups—to explain why legislators aggregate preferences.

The public choice conception of the legislator, which Dworkin largely adopts, is reductive and unsatisfying. It is false as an empirical claim—legislators are not passive agents, but persons acting for ends that explain their action, sometimes justifiable (the common good of their community) and other times not (personal enrichment or career advancement). And even if it were empirically plausible, this would not settle how the theorist should explain the legislative process. An account of how legislators enact legislation should explain how legislators understand what they do together. That is, the theorist should adopt the internal point of view. For this reason, Dworkin should argue that the legislator has good reason to aggregate the preferences of his constituents, because this is a requirement of democratic fairness. Dworkin should then focus on this reason for action to explain what it is to legislate, setting aside as of less central importance the other

---

[26] Shepsle (n 25) 240–1.

courses of action that are in fact open to legislators—say, taking interest group bribes while manipulating the electoral process (targeting benefits to pivotal voters, imposing barriers to entry for political competitors, gerrymandering electoral boundaries) to be re-elected.

II. Technical Problems With Preference Aggregation

My argument is that the legislator has no general reason to aggregate the preferences of his constituents and should not understand the legislative process that he helps maintain to be a machine that aggregates the preferences of the community. I noted above that in adopting the depiction of the legislative process as a machine, Dworkin purports to rely on a theory put forward by 'the welfare economists'.[27] He does not cite any particular economist. The assertion is curious because Arrow's principal findings were well known in the late 1970s, although it may be that their significance was not well known by political theorists prior to Riker's work on the political process.[28]

The importance of Arrow's theorem is that no voting rule applied to a profile of individual preference orderings can guarantee a unique majority preference. An outcome that a majority votes for may be problematic in two ways. First, it may be 'unstable' because the particular outcome may be one of many that are consistent with the application of the voting rule to the profile of preference orderings.[29] That is, it is possible that the outcome is one instance of a cycle, in which case it is not true to say that fairness to the majority requires this outcome. Fairness alone does not stipulate a decision, because the application of fair procedures is consistent with, and so leaves open, a range of possible decisions. Second, the outcome may be 'ambiguous' in that another fair voting rule would have produced an alternative outcome, equally consistent with the underlying preferences.[30] Again, fairness alone is consistent with both voting rules and so with each outcome. The point then is that social choice theory gravely

---

[27] Dworkin (n 11) 10.
[28] W Riker, *Liberalism Against Populism* (W H Freeman, San Francisco, 1982) and *The Art of Political Manipulation* (Yale University Press, New Haven, 1986).
[29] J Coleman and J Ferejohn, 'Democracy and Social Choice' (1986) 97 Ethics 6, 11.
[30] Coleman and Ferejohn (n 29).

86 LEGISLATING WITHOUT REASONING

undermines the coherence of preference aggregation as an end for collective action. Whenever preferences cycle, which may be very often for a large, diverse group that faces many choices, there is no unique majority preference and therefore no ground in fairness alone to choose any particular outcome.

There are further difficulties with preference aggregation. Voters may, and often have good reason to, act strategically, increasing their own preference satisfaction at the cost of majority preference satisfaction or to break a cycle in their favour. The possibility of strategic voting undermines the connection between fair voting rules, the underlying preference profile and the collective outcome. Whereas cycling defeats the assumption that the outcome of fair voting procedures is necessarily the unique majority preference, strategic voting defeats the assumption that the outcome is the majority preference. The outcome has to be what the majority prefers in one limited sense, because it is adopted by a fair vote, but it is not what follows from the preference orderings of a majority of members of the group. The minority that vote strategically engineers an outcome that is not otherwise the majority preference.

Legislators may have good reason to act strategically. Anscombe showed that when a series of issues are decided by majority vote, it is possible for a majority of voters to be in the minority for a majority of the issues.[31] Anscombe demonstrated this point by way of a ten-member committee voting on eleven successive motions. Dummett has simplified her demonstration to five members (A–E) voting on three motions:[32]

	A	B	C	D	E	Result
Motion 1	Pro	Con	Con	Pro	Pro	Carried
Motion 2	Con	Pro	Con	Pro	Pro	Carried
Motion 3	Con	Con	Pro	Pro	Pro	Carried

A, B, and C form a majority (A–C) and yet each is outvoted on two of the three motions. The minority of D and E are in the majority in all three motions. In this situation, which there is no reason to think

---

[31] E Anscombe, 'On Frustration of the Majority by Fulfillment of the Majority's Will' (1976) 36 Analysis 161.
[32] M Dummett, *Voting Procedures* (Oxford University Press, Oxford, 1984), 14–15.

uncommon, A, B, and C have good reason to vote tactically, that is, not to vote their sincere preferences, but instead to change votes to ensure that they are in the majority more often than not. For the table above, for example, A could change his vote for Motion 1, B for Motion 2 and C for Motion 3. In this case, each motion would be defeated, placing A–C in the majority in a majority of cases.[33] However, while the defeat of the three motions is better for A–C than the previous scenario, what was otherwise the majority preference is defeated. A majority supported each motion, and yet A–C's strategic action means that each motion is defeated. The outcome of the vote when A–C act strategically is not what follows from the sincere preferences of a majority.

If the point of the process is to maximize preference satisfaction, then strategic voting is suboptimal. Assign a preference value of one to each sincere preference that is satisfied. Without tactical voting, A, B, and C each have +1, while D and E each have +3; the preference aggregate is +9. After tactical voting, A, B, and C each have +2, while D and E each have 0; the aggregate is +6. The preference values I assigned are stipulative, but the problem is clear. One might insist that A–C act immorally, because the point of the process is to aggregate sincere preferences. This is superficially true if the premise is true. However, if legislators are more attached to their preference than to the preference aggregating exercise, they will vote tactically. Knowing that others may vote tactically, other legislators have good reason to counteract this by voting tactically themselves. That is, the legislator's justified insistence that his sincere preferences be counted equally gives him a reason to vote tactically. Preference aggregation is thus highly unstable.

Further, if legislators act for reasons and not to express and maximize joint preferences, as I argue below, then the action of legislators A–C is not immoral but rational. The legislators have in effect formed a faction, jointly adopting a compromise policy platform, and acted to make it the case that the motions, which they jointly have reason to oppose, are defeated. Legislators form parties for this reason, among others. Of course, legislators D and E may act strategically as well, and different majorities and factions are possible. The possibility of strategic action defeats the assumption that fair voting uncovers the majority preference, even when preferences do not cycle. Legislators have good

[33] Dummett (n 32) 15–17.

reason to counter the problem that a majority may be in the minority a majority of times by forming factions that are better means to the ends they value. The rational appeal of organizing in this way, confirmed by the ubiquity of political parties, suggests that legislators do not understand the legislature to be a machine designed to identify majority preference.

It would be irrational for the legislator to aim to aggregate the preference of his constituents (or the community at large), because very often there is no unique majority preference to find. There is no guarantee that the electorate or any constituency has a unique majority preference on any issue. It would be foolish then for the legislator to understand his function to be to identify and act on that preference.

III. Reasons and Preferences

The electorate's preferences are not fit to govern. This is in part because they cycle, but also because, as I explain below, they are not sufficiently responsive to the reasons for and against changing the law. The legislators' preferences will be similarly unfit if legislators aim to aggregate their constituents' preferences. However, even if each legislator forms his own views of what should be done, the preferences of legislators will also often cycle. The legislature is a much smaller group than the electorate, but the legislators are also likely to have more complex preferences on many more public issues than the average citizen. If, as is often likely to be the case, the preferences of the legislator cycle, then the legislature will be unable to reach a decision, or it will reach a decision, which it will then promptly reverse. That is, the particular decisions it makes will be unstable and arbitrary. It will be difficult, if not impossible, to determine whether a particular legislative outcome is a unique majority preference, one point in a cycle, or the result of strategic action.[34] The prospect of cycling and the inevitability of strategic action defeat the assumption that fair voting will identify the will of the majority. It follows that '[l]egal theory must make its way in a world in which we know that fair

---

[34] Riker (1982) (n 28) 115–36 and J Finnis, 'The Authority of Law in the Predicament of Contemporary Social Theory' (1984) 1 Notre Dame Journal of Law, Ethics & Public Policy 115, 125.

procedures cannot guarantee outcomes which are fair in the sense of accurately representing, say, majority preferences'.[35]

It is true that legislative assemblies do not seem to be plagued by Arrovian cycling and that they make stable decisions. The social choice theorists argue, plausibly, that this stability is a structure-induced equilibrium, to which agenda-setting is central and in which outcomes cannot be traced directly back to majority preference.[36] Thus, one way for the legislature to address the problem of Arrovian cycling is to adopt an internal hierarchy that authorizes some legislators to set the agenda. Agenda-control is not unfair, I argue, if agenda-setters are subject to scrutiny and sanction. However, while a majority may have good reason to adopt an internal hierarchy, the decisions that are made in this framework, subject to the unequal influence of leading legislators, do not follow straightforwardly from majority preference. It is not open to those who conceive of legislating to be fair preference aggregation to rely on agenda-control, for this is a response that is different in kind.

Another way to respond to cycling is for the legislators to deliberate together about what should be done. The significance of deliberation is that it filters preferences—not all may be defended publicly—and it may lead legislators to change their minds. Deliberation may reduce the instances of cycling by focusing disagreements amongst legislators on relevant issues. Legislators do not deliberate about what the majority prefers, but about what the good of the community requires. If legislators address the problem of cycling by deliberation, which changes how they vote, the legislature does not act on the ex ante preference profile. Instead, 'preferences' are formed in response to the reasons put forward by legislators.

I discuss agenda-control and deliberation in more detail in chapter 6. I mention them now because it is important that the two ways in which the legislature acts despite preference cycles—the source of legislative stability—both abandon the conception of the legislature as the machine that aggregates the existing preferences of legislators or citizens. Instead, agenda-control and deliberation entail that what takes place inside the legislature matters. The legislature is a space for reasoning about what should be done and making decisions; it is not

---

[35] Finnis (n 34) 125.
[36] K Shepsle, 'Institutional Arrangements and Equilibrium in Multi-dimensional Voting Models' (1979) 23 American Journal of Political Science 27.

a mere description of whose preferences count and a formal decision rule for aggregating their preferences.

Dworkin's conception of the general welfare as the preference aggregate is not attractive. His strategy is to avoid as far as possible making any controversial judgments of value, instead explaining law-making by reference to the fairness of counting each person's preferences equally. The approach is impractical because preferences may cycle. The approach is also unappealing because the reasonable legislator is interested in reasons for and against proposals for legislative action; his constituents' preferences are not in general decisive reasons for him. The reasonable legislator aims to act for the good of his constituents, which is in some sense to act in their interest(s). His responsibility is to decide what the good of the community, which includes his constituency, requires, and how or if the law should be changed deliberately to that end. He would be failing in his duty if he simply ascertained and enacted the preferences of his constituents.

A legislator who reflects thoughtfully on what his community needs may well depart from the preferences of citizens. His intelligent decision may track their preferences, but only to the extent that they are well formed. The preferences are well formed if they are grounded in sound judgment about what is good for all and therefore what should be done. That is, citizens should prefer the common good of their community. The legislator could not reasonably assume that what citizens prefer is what ought to be done. However, it would be open to the legislator to reason about what should be done and to outlaw a practice, say because it is harmful. In this case he would be acting for a reason not because of the fact of another's preference. It might well be that the reason on which he acts is the reason why many of the members of the majority disapprove of the practice. That is, he would track the majority preference because both he and they found the same reason persuasive.

Dworkin's own discussion suggests reasons to doubt that the legislative function is to identify and enact preferences. He says that the correct solution to choice-sensitive issues 'depends essentially on the character and distribution of preferences within the political community'.[37] He explains how this is so by discussing how the question of whether to build a new road system or a sports centre should be decided. (The example trades to some extent on the possibility that there are good reasons for

---

[37] Dworkin, *Sovereign Virtue* (n 1) 204.

either choice, so that the options are in some sense incommensurable. However, the reasons should be irrelevant for Dworkin, so I set this reading aside.) It is not clear how and why, and with what detail, it is these two alternatives that confront the decision maker.

Dworkin notes that 'a variety of issues may merge in that decision, from issues of distributive justice to those of sound environmental policy'.[38] The former is a matter of principle, of course, but the latter, as the term suggests, is policy, so it is curious how this could have standing apart from the preferences of members of the community. Indeed, in *Law's Empire*, Dworkin remarks that the question of whether to conserve another species, a subset of environmental policy, is paradigmatically a question that should turn on what people want, that is, on their preferences.[39] That example makes stark the truth that counting preferences treats each person equally at the cost of failing to respect anyone's reasons. For example, the person who opposes the action that threatens extinction is likely to insist that there is good reason not to take this action, say that it is immoral to wipe out another species for no good reason.[40] Dworkin argues that the relevant decision-maker, in this case the legislature, should count the fact that this person has a preference, but ignore his reasons. His irrational or vicious preferences would count just as much. This is hardly an approach that respects persons as reasoning agents.

Having introduced a mysterious category of policy that does not turn on preferences, Dworkin goes on to say that 'information about how many citizens want or will use or will benefit directly or indirectly from each of the rival facilities is plainly relevant, and may well be decisive' to whether to build the road system or the sports centre.[41] He then restates this as the question of 'whether a new sports stadium or a new road system will better match the needs and desires of the population as a whole'.[42] Therefore, he concludes, questions of this kind are most accurately decided by 'a process in which the wishes of most people are recorded directly, as through a referendum, or

---

[38] Dworkin, *Sovereign Virtue* (n 1) 204.
[39] *LE*, 340.
[40] Other possibilities are open. He could think it was dangerous to undermine biodiversity when little is known about long-term effects or that it is wasteful to destroy a species that may be an economic resource for some later generation (assuming changes in technology that we cannot foresee) or that it is sacrilegious to wipe out another species. But these are all reasons.
[41] Dworkin, *Sovereign Virtue* (n 1) 204.
[42] Dworkin, *Sovereign Virtue* (n 1) 205.

indirectly through the decisions of representatives elected and re-elected by popular majorities'.[43]

This discussion is revealing in two ways. First, Dworkin's account of preference is highly unstable. It equivocates between what citizens want, what they will use, what will benefit them, what their needs are, and what their desires are. Only the first of these—wants—are preferences in the strict sense. One need not prefer what one desires, or vice versa, and what one needs or will benefit from is not settled by what one prefers. If the question should be decided by reference to what citizens need, as is plausible and as Dworkin perhaps implies, then what citizens prefer does not settle what should be done. The aggregate preference of citizens, even if it existed, would not constitute the standard for sound legislative action.

Second, Dworkin, in this context at least, is indifferent between direct and indirect representation. This apparent indifference is consistent with his public choice premises and his reductive account of legislative action. There is no material difference between referenda and legislation if choice-sensitive issues should be settled by citizen preferences. If preferences constitute the standard for sound decision, then the legislators are pure delegates, acting either as ciphers for public opinion or as negotiators for parties who have already settled their position on all questions that fall to be decided.

The preferences of each citizen are private. They are not formed in response to ongoing public reasoning about what should be done because the citizens are not for the most part engaged in such reasoning. Hardin explains why:

Citizens rightly do not waste their time and resources learning even more information about all of the issues that might have effects on their lives... They rightly choose to leave those decisions vaguely to political officeholders. For this massive range of issues, it would be practically incoherent to suppose that officeholders had any charge other than to serve their electors' interests well.[44]

Highly salient public issues may, and should, receive detailed public scrutiny by citizens, who may then have fairly well-developed

---

[43] Dworkin, *Sovereign Virtue* (n 1) 205.
[44] R Hardin, 'Democratic Epistemology and Accountability' (2000) 17 Social Philosophy and Policy 110, 117.

judgments on point. This is the exception rather than the norm and for good reason. Most questions that fall to be decided require reasoning in response to the detail of those questions, rather than abstract ex ante preference formation that is then taken by the persons who are authorized to decide (the legislators) to settle what should be done. That is, Dworkin is wrong to be indifferent between direct and indirect democracy: he should choose the indirect. His indifference is consistent with his argument that the legislature is a machine rather than a body, the members of which reason, deliberate, and decide. A sound theory of the legislature, I say, must acknowledge and explain the legislature's character as a deliberative and representative body.

Legislators should reason, deliberate, and act to change the law for good reasons. The centrality of voting and compromise to the legislative process does not support Dworkin's assertion that the legislature responds to power and numbers whereas the judiciary responds to reasons.[45] The use of a rule of majority vote tells one little about how members of the group decide. Judges should decide cases for the right reasons, namely that the law requires, or at least is consistent with, a particular resolution. Yet as Waldron argues the balance of reasons does not settle the outcome in a multi-member appellate court: instead, the outcome is settled by the vote amongst judges, each of whom should have voted for reasons they found persuasive.[46] Likewise, in the legislature the outcome of the process, the question of whether a particular proposal is enacted, is settled by a majority vote, but the reasonable legislator, like the reasonable judge, acts for reasons.

It is true that compromise has an important place in legislative reasoning in the way that it does not in judicial reasoning. But this is not a difference that tracks one institution's openness to reason and another's capture by preference and power. The courts act in response to cases brought before them and the options open to them are for the most part narrowly curtailed by doctrine. The legislature by contrast acts on its own initiative and has a very wide range of possible courses of action open to it. Therefore, the possibility of legislators discussing what should be done and adopting a compromise that attracts wide support is not evidence that the legislature is a place in which, at best, preferences are aggregated and reasons subdued.

---

[45] Dworkin (n 5) 70.   [46] LD, 90–1.

I have assumed thus far that preference aggregation is in some way democratic. However, a lawmaking process that counts each person's preferences is not necessarily democratic. Estlund points out that a clever dictator may accurately track the preferences of the electorate and yet is not democratically legitimate.[47] Richardson argues that the same is true of a want-collation machine that registers and aggregates each person's preferences.[48] I address this issue further in chapter 6, sections I–III, but in very general terms, political equality, the driving ideal of democratic theory, is a reason for law to be made in a way that is open to popular participation, with persons being free to act for reasons in ways that help settle what law is enacted. Having one's preferences taken into account is not sufficient; the law should be made by way of a process that is open to the reasoned participation of members of the community. Individuals participate in the political process intending to effect certain changes. It follows, Estlund says, that '[h]eeding votes is different... from tracking the voters' views or preferences. It is doing as they say, not merely as they want'.[49] The point of the legislative process then is not to identify 'the will of the people' that exists apart from, and prior to, the legislature's public deliberation and action.

IV. The Authority of Unintentional Legislation

Recall Waldron's voting machine model.[50] Waldron takes it to be obvious that the output of the machine has authority in the sense that it is a fair and respectful response to the need for action in the circumstances of disagreement.[51] His argument in chapter 6 of *Law and Disagreement* is that the output of the machine, which he earlier refers to as 'majoritarian outcomes',[52] might also have authority in Raz's sense. Elsewhere, the arguments that he makes to this end he says go to the question of whether an assembly enacts better laws than one or a

---

[47] D Estlund, *Democratic Authority: A Philosophical Framework* (Princeton University Press, Princeton, 2008), 76–9.
[48] H Richardson, *Democratic Autonomy: Public Reasoning about the Ends of Policy* (Oxford University Press, Oxford, 2002), 63–4.
[49] Estlund (n 47) 78.
[50] See chapter 3, section IV.
[51] LD, 130, n 35 and accompanying text; n 35 also refers back to 99–101.
[52] LD, 99, n 36.

few enlightened legislators.[53] That is, they are arguments about 'the relative wisdom of the lawmakers' and 'wise and well-informed decision-making'.[54] He argues in chapter 6 that there are good reasons to take the output of the machine to settle what one has reason to do.

Waldron aims to establish that authority does not turn on authorship. He sets out the following thesis:

[J]: A statute (or any text) S has authority over a person Y only if person Y is likely better to comply with the reasons which apply to him by following the provisions of S, than if he tries to follow those reasons directly.[55]

He says that '[J] may be true on account of something about the views or the intentions of the person X who authored or voted for S', but that need not be so.[56] Before turning to the voting machine, he gives as an example a bank helpline which one telephones, entering one's account details, and hearing in response an automated voice saying 'your account balance is four hundred dollars' or some such. The customer knows that no person is speaking to him and yet he does better if he relies on the voice for his available balance than if he calculated this himself.[57]

At best, the bank example concerns theoretical authority. The machine's output no more directs my action than does the astronomer who tells me that a comet will be visible in the night sky this evening. She may be a theoretical authority for me, because her knowledge exceeds my own and I have reason to defer to her reasoning. Yet she does not make it the case that I have a reason to watch the night sky, but only changes my reasons for believing that a comet will be in the sky. The line between practical and theoretical authority is often hard to draw, but the machine has neither. Birds flying south are not an authority that winter is coming, they are just evidence that winter is coming. Likewise, the output of the machine is good evidence that my bank balance is $400, but if my reason for taking the output to be true is that it is good evidence then I am not responding to it as one responds to an authority, that is to say, adopting the reasoning of another as my own. If I took the astronomer's interest in some portion of the sky to be evidence of where to see a comet, on the grounds that she is a lucky

---

[53] J Waldron, 'Legislation by Assembly' (2000) 46 Loyola Law Review 507, 525–7.
[54] Waldron (n 53) 527.   [55] *LD*, 131.   [56] *LD*, 131.   [57] *LD*, 132.

stargazer, then I would not be responding to her as an authority. I should defer to her as a theoretical authority only if I have good reason to adopt her reasoning and only if she acts to change my reasons for knowledge.

Waldron's point is that authority need not be personal or reasoned or deliberate. However, the bank example trades on the extent to which the machine takes the place of a person, such as a bank teller, who otherwise reasons and speaks. His argument extends much more widely. If he is right, my wristwatch is an authority for the time and my car's petrol gauge is an authority for how much petrol remains in the tank. These claims are false, but they differ from the birds flying south example in that the wristwatch and petrol gauge are devices, machines that have been designed to generate certain outputs based on certain inputs. If the designer is successful, the machine he creates will generate an output based on certain inputs that I have reason to take to be accurate. The machine is evidence of a true state of affairs because it is a good device; if it were not, if I had reason to think it was malfunctioning, then it would not be good evidence. A device's mode of operation is starkly different to that which characterizes theoretical or practical authority. The device tracks reasons in some limited field, to the extent that it functions well, and so I may have good reason to use its conclusions. But because the device is not a reasoning person, I have no reason to adopt its 'reasoning' as if it were my own.

Thesis [J] thus cannot distinguish evidence from authority, because it does not perceive how authority is a response to reasons. More than this, [J] double counts. Waldron says that S may have authority because of the views or intentions of X, the author of S. This formulation misstates the relationship between X and S: they do not both have authority. The authority is X. I should follow S because this is how X has chosen to express (perhaps imperfectly) what I am to do. S is an act of X and I should interpret that act—I should not interpret S as if it were a freestanding object. If the reason why I should follow S is that X is well placed to decide what should be done, that is, if X has authority, then it is a mistake (if often harmless) to think that S is an authority. And it is doubly a mistake to take the distinction between S and X to entail that one may have a text that is an authority without an author that has authority. The exercise of authority is a reasoned action to change the reasons of another. It follows that one cannot be an authority or exercise authority unless one is capable of reasoning and that there are no authoritative texts or utterances without an agent that exercises authority in making or otherwise adopting that text or utterance.

The bank machine is the only example other than the voting machine model that Waldron introduces to justify [J]. He sets out three arguments for the authority of the voting machine's output. The arguments appeal to the good consequences that follow, indirectly, from the participation by a group of persons in a process that aggregates their votes on a series of particular provisions. The arguments do not rely on the wisdom of the group understood to be a person that acts directly.

The first is 'the Utilitarian Argument'. If the right thing to do (sometimes, always) is to aggregate preferences, then, Waldron says, an output that is the sum of the preferences of each legislator, counted by means of the voting machine, settles what should be done, if each legislator to some extent aggregates the preferences of his constituents.[58] There will be nothing behind the voting machine's aggregation of preferences—no intelligent, coherent choice by a reasoning agent—yet there remains good reason to defer to the machine's output. If an interpreter were to refer to the intention of any one legislator, prioritizing his particular preference, this would unravel the aggregation and defeat the utilitarian rationale.[59] I argued against this conception of the legislature above. The legislature is a poor utilitarian counting machine and the object of legislative action is not the aggregate of citizen preferences, but the common good, in its full scope and complexity. Waldron, rightly, does not think utilitarianism relevant to that wider inquiry.[60]

The second argument is 'Condorcet's Jury Theorem', which holds that where the odds of any one person reaching a true or correct decision are greater than 0.5, adding further members to a decision-making body increases the prospect of deciding rightly. One would have good reason to defer to the output of the group because its size increases the chances that the decision that emerges is correct.[61] This approach is unintentional, however, because the group conclusion emerges from the process and to take the view of any one person to be the intention of the group would undermine that conclusion. That is, there is no way to know if the individual member whose intention is

---

[58] *LD*, 133–4.   [59] *LD*, 139.   [60] *LD*, 134.   [61] *LD*, 134–6.

given priority was in the right or not. The probabilistic rationale for authority points just to the result of the process.[62]

The third argument, and the one in which Waldron is most interested,[63] is the 'Aristotelian Synthesis', which holds that a group of persons, sharing their knowledge and testing one another's views, may know more than any individual member of the group.[64] This argument is promising because it addresses how the size and diversity of the group may improve decision-making. Waldron argues that the synthesis of the skills and experience of the members of the group is a reason to respect the output of the group's interaction. He argues further that while the synthesis may be realized in the reasoning of the individual members, so that each is better placed to think and decide what should be done, 'if the issue is a complex and subtle one, an authoritative synthesis may emerge at the level of group action without necessarily emerging at the level of individual understanding at all'.[65] Waldron suggests that this group synthesis is analogous to Mill's marketplace of ideas. Later he pulls back, making clear that his emphasis on the legislature acting explicitly by formal procedures is at odds with any invisible hand. However, he argues that the group synthesis idea is useful because it indicates that the individual synthesis is unlikely to arise until voting takes place, at which point it will be captured in the text of the statute itself.[66]

Neither the Condorcet nor Aristotelian arguments succeed. The arguments require each member of the group to attend carefully to one question that has an objective answer. The voting machine does not conform to this stricture and neither does legislative reason in general. The central instance of legislative action is not settling a contentious moral issue where the alternatives are already salient. Instead, it is identifying one amongst many opportunities to introduce a valuable state of affairs and adopting a plan to that end. Waldron's discussion often seems to take the legislative function to be just to settle controversial moral disputes.[67] I agree that legislatures must settle what should be done in the face of disagreement, but more importantly, they

---

[62] LD, 140.
[63] He refers to the argument before chapter 6: LD, 72, 85 and 98. See also J Waldron, *The Dignity of Legislation* (Cambridge University Press, Cambridge, 1999), 92–123.
[64] LD, 136–8.
[65] LD, 137.   [66] LD, 141–2.
[67] Waldron (n 63) 36–9, 65–70; cf. A Marmor, *Positive Law and Objective Values* (Oxford University Press, Oxford, 2001), 95–6.

must act for the common good when the possibilities for action are open and what is called for is intelligent, creative decision-making.

The voting machine requires action on a series of questions. The set of provisions that the machine produces was not selected by a majority vote that satisfies Condorcet's theorem or follows from an Aristotelian synthesis. The question of whether to adopt all the provisions that survive majority vote was never put before the group—that is the defining feature of the voting machine. Therefore, while there may be a Condorcet reason to respect the vote on A, B or C, there is no Condorcet reason to respect the output of A–B–C. Enacting a set of provisions is starkly different to approving each in turn. Likewise, the voting machine gives rise to a set of provisions that the legislators do not deliberate about as a set. Therefore, there is no Aristotelian synthesis about the merits of the set and if such a synthesis were to be formed (as it might be if there was deliberation and voting on a final complete proposal), then that synthesis would be open to legislators at the time of voting, rather than a function of their interaction that they themselves cannot identify before voting.

V. Rationality and the Voting Machine

The fundamental problem with the voting machine is that rational voting by each legislator on various related issues is likely to give rise to a collectively irrational outcome. That is, the legislature may enact sets of provisions that there is no good reason to choose, apart from the fact that they were generated by a process that is responsive to the views of each legislator. If no legislator should choose the set of provisions that constitutes the statute, even if each had majority support on its own, then it is unreasonable to make law by way of a voting machine.

The statute that the machine produces is the set of provisions that survived majority vote. Two (or more) provisions may sometimes be contradictory in that the citizen cannot adopt both to frame his reason. If no person intends to enact both provisions, then there is no non-arbitrary way to read one subject to the other or to read both to avoid the contradiction. The provisions survived majority vote and therefore each was enacted; they were not enacted together as parts of one act intended, all the way through to the end, to be non-contradictory. That is, one cannot appeal to the intention of the authority to settle the contradiction. Simultaneous voting might often give rise to contradiction. Imagine that one legislator proposes a provision, while another legislator proposes a rival formulation that is similar but a little different: say, one proposes a three-week time limit on applying for leave to appeal, the other a four-week time limit. A rational legislator might vote for both on the grounds that either is worth adopting and he does not know which is more likely to attract majority support. He does not want both proposals to fail because he only voted for one. Yet if both are enacted, the legislative output would be unreasonable, because contradictory.

Any statute that emerges from the voting machine may also be incoherent. That is, the parts of the statute may work against each other, while falling short of outright contradiction. With shifting majorities having settled different issues, it is quite likely that the set of provisions that emerges does not form a consistent response to the reasons that bear on how this particular community need should be addressed. The set may also be incomplete, by which I mean that an otherwise appealing scheme is frustrated, or even wrecked, because one or more provisions that are necessary if the scheme is to retain its rational appeal did not survive the majority vote. The point is that if the content of the statute is settled by aggregating a series of discrete votes, rational voting on the part of each legislator may give rise to a statute that is unworkable. The resulting statute is collectively irrational, to use Pettit's term,[68] which means that it is not a response by the legislature to the relevant reasons. No person would think the statute fit to be chosen because it is contradictory or incoherent or incomplete, which means that it is a poor means to valuable ends. Therefore, the legislature should not produce the statute. The group of legislators—the legislature—is collectively irrational if its group act, the enactment of the statute, is not a good means to the ends for which the group exists to act.

To some extent, Waldron anticipates my line of argument. But he does not address it. He says:

Now, theorists of public choice are familiar with various tangles of cyclicity that such a machine might get into. Let us assume, however—as Wollheim did—that these are not a problem for the cases we are considering. The point of this thought-experiment... is that it enables us to envisage a piece

---

[68] P Pettit, 'Collective Persons and Powers' (2002) 8 Legal Theory 443. See further chapter 3, section IV.

of legislation that cannot be conceived as, in Fish's words, something produced 'by an intentional being' ... situated in some enterprise in relation to which he had a purpose or a point of view.[69]

The assumption is unsound. The voting machine is a model of general application and so it is not clear what Waldron takes to be the limited set of cases he is considering. Majority cycling is quite possible in a series of votes on a large number of issues and this is a further reason to expect the voting machine to issue contradictory directives. If alternatives cycle, then ordinarily the legislature would be unable to reach any stable decision. The voting machine might well enact all of the cycling alternatives. Resolving this problem requires agenda-control, as well as deliberation and decision-making that focuses on one complete proposal.

For Waldron's thought-experiment to succeed, it is not enough for it to be possible to envisage a statute that cannot be conceived of as produced by an intentional being. The statute in question must be a reasonable exercise of legislative authority, such that it is a well-formed instance of legislative action, rather than a distorted or corrupted instance. Possibility is not what is at issue.

In a footnote within the last extract (at the end of the second sentence), Waldron also notes and purports to avoid the coherence objection:

I also want to evade a complaint that Dworkin might make, that the Wollheim machine is capable of yielding something like 'a checkerboard statute', that is, a statute that lacks internal coherence ... Even if Dworkin is right in thinking that there is something objectionable about a statute so compromised that it does not reflect any coherent set of principles or policies, he can hardly deny that it is a text and that a judge might make a good faith effort to interpret it. Remember too that 'integrity', the value which Dworkin says is at stake here, is just one legal value among several, and must often be considered alongside justice and fairness ... In any case, the Wollheim machine *need* not produce statutes that lack integrity. At most, a requirement of integrity would imply only that the machine's output *could* be interpreted as the product of someone's intention, not that it *must* be so interpreted.[70]

---

[69] LD, 126–7.
[70] LD, 126, n 24.

My concern has not been with integrity in Dworkin's sense. The common good requires the choice of rules that will serve as adequate and rational responses to some particular community need. There may well also be value in the community speaking with one principled voice, to use Dworkin's term, but this is not my interest and it is not the only sense in which coherence matters. A plan of action, to succeed in attaining some valued end, has to be sufficiently coherent and complete to serve as a means to an end. This is a truth of practical reason that the machine fails to respect.

Waldron's account does not attend closely to the importance of complex plans of action, which work together as a means to valuable ends. The contrast he draws between compromise, justice, and fairness on the one hand, and integrity or coherence on the other, is telling. Justice is often secured by complex, coherent action in response to reasons. Not all questions of justice are isolated and capable of abstract resolution. Instead, framed by general moral truths, the legislator responds to the detail of the particular situation. Further, it is not always unreasonable to compromise and a reasonable compromise is consistent with, and forms part of, a scheme that helps serve the common good. Reasonable legislators may choose to compromise. Even a checkerboard statute might be a suitable object of legislative action. A statute that uses birth dates to settle who is to be called up for military service, for example, would not be contradictory, but would be a reasoned response to the problem at hand (a choice to adopt a somewhat arbitrary resolution). The voting machine does not sacrifice coherence to compromise; it precludes the legislature from acting deliberately in response to reasons for compromise.

The three arguments for the authority of unintentional legislation did not establish that the machine is likely to produce reasonable legislation. If a statute is a set of inconsistent, contradictory provisions that lacks what is needed to form a coherent plan of action, then I say that the statute is unreasonable. There is no reason to think it any more reasonable because it is the product of a series of majority votes.

Statutes are complex decisions. Yet the voting machine stipulates that neither legislators nor interpreters can understand different provisions to explain and inform one another, to form part of a plan that is larger than a series of discrete independent 'choices'. Each provision has its conventional sentence meaning, and barring explicit reference to another provision (which is possible but not well suited to the voting machine), it is to be given effect strictly in accordance with that meaning. This is what Waldron means when he says that the statute is not the product of any person's coherent intention. The reason for the stipulation is that each provision is part of the statute solely because it survived majority vote. Each could have been adopted independently and the interpreter frustrates the voting machine if he understands the fact that both survived the vote to mean that one informs the meaning of the other.

This stricture demonstrates that the voting machine is an unreasonable model of the legislative process. Various provisions are very often chosen precisely because of how they inform the scope and meaning of the other, so that the legislators understand them as being related to one another. That is, legislators act for more than just each provision read in isolation. And it is valuable that legislators are able to form proposals in this way, with the content of the proposal being settled not just by the meaning of each provision read in isolation, but read as part of a larger, reasoned plan, which is at least capable of being chosen by a reasoning person.

Waldron's own example, the imaginary Vehicles in the Park Act 1993, proves the point.

Vehicles in the Park Act 1993. (1) With the exception of bicycles and ambulances, no vehicle shall be permitted to enter any state or municipal park. (2) Any person who brings a vehicle into a state or municipal park shall be liable to a fine of not more than $100.[71]

There are two problems with this Act. The first is that if (1) is read literally, then it does not prohibit persons taking vehicles into the park. The section denies permission to any vehicle, apart from bicycles and ambulances, to enter the park. This is an unfortunate formulation for two reasons. First, vehicles are incapable of action; persons are the proper objects of legislative direction. Second, if one assumes that the section is (intended to be) directed towards persons, the phrase 'no vehicle shall be permitted' purports to remove someone's power to grant permission to another person to take his vehicle into the park. No such power is likely to exist and yet removing permission or power to grant permission is not the same as prohibiting; whatever is not prohibited is permitted. It follows that in these two ways, the

[71] *LD*, 124.

conventional meaning of the statutory language does not explicitly prohibit a person from taking a vehicle into the park: instead it denies vehicles permission to enter. The legislators that enact this section are likely to intend to prohibit a person from taking a vehicle into a park and those legislators might think that even if the statutory language does not state this explicitly, it conveys it by implication. However, this conclusion is not dictated by the conventional meaning of (1), but is instead a reasoned inference about what the legislators are likely to mean in uttering (1).

The second problem concerns the relationship between the two sections. Assume that a person who takes a vehicle into a park breaches (1). The Vehicles in the Park Act does not impose any consequence on him for that breach. The person also happens to breach (2), which is somewhat better formulated: the section imposes liability for a fine on the person who brings a vehicle into the park. Thus, (1) is not necessary to ground liability for a fine. Now imagine that a person takes a bicycle or an ambulance into a park. The person has not breached (1), but he has breached (2), which applies to 'a vehicle'. The cyclist or ambulance driver may argue that (1) limits the scope of (2), but neither section says this, and the conventional meaning of 'a vehicle' is just a vehicle, which includes bicycles and ambulances. It is true that the legislators probably enacted (1) to limit the scope of (2). It is unclear why else they would enact (1). The section was not well formulated to that end. It would have been better to say: 'For the purposes of section two of this Act, "a vehicle" does not include an ambulance or a bicycle'.[72] However, the interpreter asks why the legislature would enact these two sections together and infers that it intended (1) to qualify (2). That is, the interpreter reads the Act as if it were the object of the legislature's coherent, reasoned choice.

The Vehicles in the Park Act is Waldron's only example of a statute that the voting machine might produce. He concludes that 'when the statute is read for the first time ... [one] is not entitled to say that the aim of the reading must be to determine what somebody meant.'[73] This conclusion is undercut by his assumption, quite likely shared by the (imaginary) legislators, that (1) qualifies the scope of (2). Waldron, I think, took the two sections to constitute a coherent, reasoned

---

[72] It would be wise to be yet more specific, making it clear that an ambulance is not a vehicle for the purposes of this Act only when it is being used for emergency relief.
[73] LD, 128.

scheme, in which (1) limited the scope of (2) despite neither section saying this directly. This coherent reading is entirely reasonable. Of course, one might argue that the legislators chose to word (2) to make clear their decision that (2) should have a wider scope than (1), with the difference in word choice grounding the inference that 'any vehicle' in (2) meant any vehicle. The weight of argument favours the reading that Waldron assumes because it is reasonable to infer that the legislators understood and intended the point of (1) to be to qualify (2). Interpretive argument thus centres on what it was that the legislators did together when they enacted the two sections.

If the legislature were a voting machine, it would be impossible for rational legislators to understand a statutory scheme in the way that Waldron reasonably understood the Vehicles in the Park Act. It follows that it would also be impossible for those legislators to act to secure the common good by intending to enact a scheme of various provisions that inform and support one another.

The effect of the voting machine is to make it difficult (or almost impossible, if voting is simultaneous) to take a broad view of what should be done and to adopt coherent, complex plans to that end. The voting machine model and the three arguments for indirect authority privilege episodic, isolated responses to particular questions. The voting machine thus frustrates the central task of the reasonable legislator: thinking about what complex, reasoned approach the legislature (and the community) should take to address this or that question. Instead, it forces the legislator to respond to a series of provisions, considered in turn with little capacity to keep at the forefront of one's reason how the resulting set will work in the community. The machine forces the legislator to respond to each successive proposition, rather than to the more detailed, comprehensive, and unified proposals that he can see are needed.

The legislator in such an environment has good reason to try to game the machine, predicting how his fellows will act, and voting tactically in an attempt to secure a workable final set of propositions. Thus, his reasonable action undermines Waldron's arguments for unintentional legislation.[74] It will be very hard to act rationally if

---

[74] Tactical voting undermines Waldron's three arguments for indirect authority. If a legislator votes tactically he would not act for his or his constituents' preferences on this issue, which would undermine the preference aggregate and defeat the utilitarian rationale. Insincere voting would also defeat the Condorcet rationale, because the legislator's vote

voting is simultaneous, because one's vote on this or that proposition rightly turns on whether others are adopted, and yet whether they are adopted is not known until after the vote. The voting machine stops the legislators—any of them—seeing the complete proposal on which the legislature is to act, because the only point at which the final proposal emerges is after voting, at which point it is too late to consider its merits. The legislator has to vote and take his chances or vote very conservatively, rejecting provisions for which he would otherwise vote unless he is confident, somehow, of how his fellows will vote. Sequential voting is a little better, because the legislator is in a better position to vote tactically, aiming always to develop a proposal that is fit for choice by one (reasonable) person. However, the structure of the machine still makes it very hard for legislators to form reasonable proposals. The sequence of votes may often determine the success of particular provisions, so that the legislator's reasoning would change markedly depending on the result of the previous vote. Thus, if Waldron were to opt for sequential voting in specifying the model, agenda-control would become all the more important.

A majority may support one provision, a different majority a second, and another majority a third and yet it may be that no majority supports all three provisions taken together. The lack of majority support for all three provisions may be precisely because that support would not be collectively rational. That is, the majority sees that it would be unwise to adopt all three together. Insisting that the group decide what is to be done by aggregating a series of votes on various issues is to set aside concern for the rationality that the final decision would have if the legislature were conceived to be a person responding to reasons. Yet the propositions that a statute sets out must at least be capable of being the choice of a reasoning person, such that the citizen has good reason to adopt that choice as if it were his own.

The legislators rightly consider whether a final complete proposal is one that they should support. The voting machine keeps this proposal from view, by preventing the legislators from formulating a complete proposal in advance of the final vote: their votes create the proposal

---

would not improve the accuracy of the collective outcome, and the Aristotelian rationale, because his vote would not contribute to the wisdom of the multitude. In each case, the legislator who votes tactically does not participate in the legislative process in the way that the model's three rationales require. Therefore, Waldron has reason to opt for simultaneous voting in specifying the model because this would tend to frustrate tactical voting.

that is then adopted. The legislators therefore lack the advantage of debating a complete proposal for action, deciding that in some sense it is lacking, and revising it accordingly. The voting machine makes the legislature highly responsive to individual legislators, but prevents them from talking, reasoning, and acting as a purposive group. Reasonable legislators are interested in how the legislature should act and thus they would reject a process that forces them to reach decisions by voting on a series of particulars (all at once or in some arbitrary sequence) rather than on final proposals. The voting machine is not an intelligent way to make use of the reasoning and judgment of the many legislators.

The model may perhaps be modified to enable it to produce reasonable legislation. If one took the results of the voting machine to be provisional and permitted the legislators to revisit various issues, then they would be much better placed to enact statutes that are reasonable, sufficient responses to community need. The revisiting would end when a majority of legislators agreed that the proposal in its latest amended form was fit to be enacted. However, that would be to return more or less to the status quo in which the final vote occupies central place. The final vote on a stable, complete proposal is not 'purely an artefact of our particular parliamentary procedures',[75] but an essential feature of the well-formed legislature.

VI. The Minimal Intention Argument

I argued in chapter 2, section IV that Waldron effectively concludes that legislating is intentional in a very limited sense. Specifically, the 'intention' on which the legislature acts is just to enact the conventional meaning of the statutory text, which minimal intention is thus not practically relevant to interpretation. Joseph Raz has set out a more detailed argument to similar effect, as has John Gardner. I argue that legislative action should not be conceived to be action on this minimal intention.

Raz explains what it is to legislate:

To give a person or an institution law-making powers is to entrust them with the power to make law by acts intended to make law ... It makes no

---
[75] *LD*, 126.

sense to give any person or body law-making power unless it is assumed that the law they make is the law they intended to make.[76]

If the law that the legislator made was not what he intended to make, Raz argues, it would have to be the case that he could not predict what law he was making when the legislature enacted a bill. But if this were so, Raz insists that it would be irrelevant who the legislators were and it would not matter that their intentions were reasonable or unreasonable.[77] This conclusion, he implies, is absurd. It matters who the legislators are and what their intentions are because this is relevant to the law they make. There is, he asserts, no invisible hand mechanism that produces law as a function of their beliefs or intentions (he refers to Waldron's early work and asserts that it is implausible).[78] Therefore, 'the very idea of law-making institutions is that of institutions which can make the law they intend to make'.[79]

Gardner argues that legislating is intentional because those who have legislative authority must respond to reasons:

An agent acts intentionally inasmuch as it does what it does for (what it takes to be) reasons. Those who legislate, whether they are human beings or institutions, must do so for (what they take to be) reasons for and against changing the law. If they did not, there would be no sense in having wider public debates about legislative policy, nor the general elections in which these debates are brought to a head. Such debates make sense only on the footing that whoever it is that legislates will, in legislating, respond to at least some supposed reasons for and against changing the law.[80]

I agree with this analysis, but it is framed too strongly. Legislators cannot legislate well unless they act for reasons that bear on whether the law should be changed. They may legislate in a secondary, non-focal sense without reasoned choice, perhaps by taking bribes or legislating for private interest or partisan advantage.

---

[76] Raz, BAI, 274.   [77] Raz, BAI, 274–5.
[78] Raz, BAI, 275, n 10; the reference is to J Waldron, 'Legislators' Intentions and Unintentional Legislation', chapter 9 in A Marmor (ed), *Law and Interpretation* (Clarendon Press, Oxford, 1997), 327.
[79] Raz, BAI, 275.
[80] J Gardner, 'Some Types of Law' in D Edlin (ed), *Common Law Theory* (Cambridge University Press, Cambridge, 2007), 51, 57.

Attaching legal consequences to some act is not, Raz says, enough to make it an act of legislating, for that would be like attaching legal significance to some natural event (say an earthquake of a certain severity which creates a public duty to compensate those who suffer loss).[81] What this means is that a legislative act must be an act on the intention to legislate, which is to change the law:

The reason is that the notion of legislation imports the idea of entrusting power over the law into the hands of a person or an institution, and this imports entrusting voluntary control over the development of the law, or an aspect of it, into the hands of the legislator. This is inconsistent with the idea of unintentional legislation.[82]

It follows, Raz argues, that legislating requires knowing what it is that one legislates. For, '[o]ne is hardly in control over the development of an aspect of the law, if, while one can change the law by acts intending to do so, one cannot know what change in the law one's action imports'.[83]

Raz recognizes an obvious objection: 'surely legislators do not have to know the precise details of the legislation they vote for'.[84] He says—and I agree—that many legislators will know only the general outline of the legislation and others will have little idea what they are voting for. Gardner puts the point more strongly: legislators 'invariably had diverse and conflicting intentions concerning its meaning, application, use and effect' and '[i]ndeed, some...possibly had no intentions at all concerning any of these matters (they were just lobby fodder who voted when they were told to by their political masters)'.[85] Therefore, Gardner concludes, that 'Parliament usually had no intentions concerning the meaning, application, use, or effect of the statute in question'.[86] However, all that is necessary for legislating to be the intentional action of the legislature, Raz and Gardner argue, is for legislators to act on the minimal intention to change the law by enacting this text.

Raz describes the minimal intention in this way:

---

[81] Raz, *BAI*, 281–2.
[82] Raz, *BAI*, 282. [83] Raz, *BAI*, 282.
[84] Raz, *BAI*, 283. [85] Gardner (n 80) 56.
[86] Gardner (n 80) 56.

A person is legislating (voting for a Bill, etc.) by expressing an intention that the text of the Bill on which he is voting will—when understood as such texts, when promulgated in the circumstances in which this one is promulgated, are understood in the legal culture of this country—be law.

On this understanding the required intention is very minimal, and does not include any understanding of the content of the legislation. We can expect that this intention is almost universally present in acts of legislation.[87]

The minimal intention on which the legislator acts, and which he expresses in legislating, is that the text of the bill on which he votes is to be law. This formulation might appear to explain how it is that all the legislators may share the intention: the legislator in the minority also intends that the text of the bill on which he votes, against which he votes, is to be law, if a majority votes for it. However, Raz does not understand the intention in this way. He says '[l]egislators who have the minimal intention know that they are, if they carry the majority, making law, and they know how to find out what law they are making'.[88] This implies that only legislators in the voting majority hold the minimal intention and that the legislature only has this intention because the intention shared by the majority is attributed to the institution. That is, the legislature's intention is likewise minimal. To be clear, the minimal intention is not a choice to enact specific changes to the law for reasons that justify those changes, for if this were the intention it would not be minimal.

Gardner's account is similar but not identical. He argues that Parliament could adopt rules that settled whose intentions constituted its intentions on 'the meaning, application, use and effect of a statute'. (He cites *Pepper v Hart*[89] as a hesitant move in this direction.[90]) But, he says, 'for the most part there are no such rules, and hence Parliament has no such intentions' and '[s]o Parliament often has no intention to make the particular changes in the law that it ends up making when it legislates'.[91] However, the absence of any specific, particular intentions does not entail 'that, when it legislates, Parliament has no intention to change the law. Worries about the diverse and conflicting intentions of individual parliamentarians do not apply to this more humble intention'.[92] The humble intention is just the intention to change the law,

---

[87] Raz, *BAI*, 284.
[88] Raz, *BAI*, 284.   [89] [1993] AC 593.   [90] Gardner (n 80) 56, n 15.
[91] Gardner (n 80) 56.   [92] Gardner (n 80) 56.

which is either identical to the minimal intention or more minimal still, for Raz's formulation at least refers, explicitly, to the way in which the text will be understood in the legal culture.[93] Drunken accidents aside, all legislators intend to participate in Parliament's act of changing the law, Gardner says. This is true even for legislators in the minority, who intend the law to be changed if Parliament intends this, 'where what counts as Parliament's intention depends in turn on the actions and intentions of at least some members of Parliament'.[94] He takes it then that Parliament's constitution attributes the humble intention held by each member of the majority to Parliament itself, so that Parliament acts intending to change the law.

This approach to explaining how legislators in the minority stand in relation to the legislature's act is an advance on Raz. The minority members participate in the lawmaking act because they intend the legislature to enact the statute if a majority votes for it. However, it is not the case, I shall argue in chapter 8, section III, that the intention held by each member of the majority is attributed to the legislature. The legislature acts on majority vote, but its intention is different to that of any one legislator.

Raz anticipates the objection that the minimal intention is insufficient to explain how the legislator acts to make the law that he intends to make. He argues in response that '[t]he minimal intention is sufficient to preserve the essential idea that legislators have control over the law', because the legislators are able to 'establish the meaning of the text in front of them, when understood as it will be according to their legal culture assuming that it [is] promulgated on that occasion'.[95] It follows that legislative intent is not practically relevant to interpretation. The legislators in the majority intend, and so the legislature intends, to enact the bill 'when understood as it will be according to their legal culture'. The content of the statutory text, in other words, is settled by the conventions of interpretation that prevail at the time of enactment. This argument, which he contends is consistent with the nature of language use in general,[96] 'requires one to understand the legislation as meaning what the legislators said'.[97]

---

[93] I think it likely that Gardner intends the humble intention to be read to be identical to the minimal intention. His discussion of the canons of interpretation and how they relate to the meaning of the statutory text supports this reading: Gardner (n 80) 53.
[94] Gardner (n 80) 56.   [95] Raz, *BAI*, 284–5.
[96] Raz, *BAI*, 286–7.   [97] Raz, *BAI*, 288.

After arguing that the minimal intention suffices to explain how legislators retain voluntary control over the content of the law, Raz makes this observation:

> Of course, it is hard to imagine a theory of authority which will not demand much more—that is, which will not demand that authorities form an informed judgment about proposed legislation before endorsing it. But it is intelligible that the law would leave the judgment as to what exactly one needs to know and to intend in order to satisfy this moral requirement to the legislators themselves. Therefore, a legal system which does not require any more specific intention is intelligible.[98]

Raz thus distinguishes the conditions that the law imposes on how legislators legislate from what legislators must do to exercise legitimate authority ('form an informed judgment . . .'). He implies that legislators acting on the minimal intention succeed in legislating, but perhaps do not exercise legitimate authority.

VII. Intelligible Legislating

I argue that a theory of legislating must explain how, or if, legislating is an exercise of authority. The legislature may legislate unreasonably as well as reasonably. My theory of legislative action aims first to explain reasonable legislating and then to understand unreasonable legislating as a distortion of that which is reasonable. Raz aims to explain the concept of legislating itself. I argue that his theory of legislative action entails that legislating cannot intelligibly be thought to be an exercise of legitimate authority, and so also lacks de facto authority. Raz would agree, I trust, that a theory of legislative action that cannot explain how legislators might intelligibly be thought to exercise legitimate authority must be unsound.

A person who exercises legitimate authority responds to reasons by reasoning about what should be done and directing how lawmaking subjects are to act. My argument is that if the legislature acts only on the minimal intention, it does not respond to reason and so does not exercise legitimate authority. The legislature's intention is just to

---

[98] Raz, BAI, 285.

change the law by enacting this text, which is to be understood by reference to prevailing convention. The minimal intention argument is precisely that the legislature need not intend to change the law in any specific way for any particular reasons. Thus, the legislature has not acted to make it the case that the law will be changed in the way that its act is taken to change it, and it also has not acted for reasons that would justify those changes. If this is what the legislature does, then I say that it is not an authority: it does not respond to reasons with reasoned action. The legislature acts, and it acts for an end—making the conventional meaning of the text the law—but the end lacks the precision for which an authority acts and it is not supported by reason.

It is not rational to intend just to change the law in general, in the same way that it is not rational for an author to intend to convey some meaning in general. Rational lawmaking is action to change the law in specific ways for (what the legislature takes to be) good reasons. Gardner makes this argument himself when he explains what it is to act intentionally and when he argues that the institution of the legislature must respond to reasons for changing the law. On the logic of his account, which I endorse to this extent, the legislature does not even act intentionally if it acts only on the humble/minimal intention to change the law.

The legal norms that a legislative text expresses are norms because the legislature acted to make them law. That is, the point of the act was to introduce these norms. If the legislature acts only on the humble intention, then the norms that interpreters 'find' in the legislative text are not legislated law: they are not legal norms that one agent, the legislature, has intentionally and expressly made. Instead, the legislature's act would be the limited, irrational act of adopting texts, which have legal effects.

Raz might respond that his argument is that action on the minimal intention suffices to legislate, but that to legislate reasonably requires more detailed intentions. However, Raz's assumption that the intention of the legislature just is the intention held by each legislator in the majority makes it impossible, as a general matter, for the legislature to change the law in specific ways for specific reasons.

Not all individual legislators know or understand the full detail of the statutory text they vote to enact; they also do not grasp fully the reasons for the changes in the law the text introduces. It is a mistake to think that this ignorance is necessarily unreasonable. It may be unreasonable and certainly legislators who never read bills or think about what should be done are poor legislators. However, the modern legislative agenda is complex and legislators rightly focus on particular problems and statutory responses. What this means is that the legislators have to rely on their peers, among others, to help monitor the contents of bills. The committee structure helps legislators act reasonably despite the limitations on their time and legislators also form factions and parties in part to enable close scrutiny and intelligent responses to many bills. Thus, it is not at all surprising that particular legislators, such as those who drafted, sponsored, or debated bills, may be better informed than others about the detailed content of and reasons for bills. It will almost never be the case that all the legislators in the majority will share the same detailed knowledge as those particular legislators (some of whom may be in the minority).

For Raz then, as for Gardner, it has to follow that the legislature almost never acts on more detailed intentions, which identify specifically the changes to the law that the statute is to make and the reasons for those changes. That is, the legislature cannot do more than act on the minimal intention. It is thus impossible for the legislature to exercise legitimate authority and so it is unintelligible for it to be thought to have authority. This conclusion cannot be right. Raz and Gardner are driven to it, unnecessarily, by the unsound assumption that the legislature's intention must be an intention held by each legislator (or each legislator in the majority). I say that the legislature is a group and so its action must be grounded in the intentions of its members, but this does not mean that its intention reduces to intentions held by each legislator that are attributed to it. The legislature acts on intentions that are formed in part by, but also do not reduce to, the intelligent activity of particular legislators. And ordinary, relatively ignorant legislators participate in the legislature's act, which is an act on a joint intention that is more detailed than their own intention.

Imagine that only one person exercises legislative authority. This legislator could not exercise his authority, I argue, by acting just on the minimal intention. The legislator would not be responding to reasons; he would not be acting to make the law that he intended to make. Instead, he would be acting to make as law whatever legal effects, if any, follow from the conventional meaning of the text, which by hypothesis he does not know and has not chosen to bring about. If he did know what the text meant (bracketing for now the ground of that meaning) and acted to introduce the changes that it expresses, for reasons that seemed to him good, his intention would not be minimal.

The legislator who acts only on the minimal intention would not intend to make whatever specific legal changes his act is taken to make. His act is a failure to legislate in the focal sense. One legislates in the focal sense by making a specific, complex choice in response to reasons, which choice is expressed in the text. If one person cannot exercise legislative authority by acting only on the minimal intention, it follows that a group of persons is similarly incapable. The legislature must act on intentions that are more detailed than the minimal intention if it is to legislate.

One might respond to my argument by contending that while the legislature acts only on the minimal intention, the legislators respond to reason and this is sufficient. That is, the legislature is an authority because (some) legislators reason individually; its authority follows indirectly from their reasoning about what it should do. I maintain, however, that the institution itself has to act in response to reasons. The legislature's authority to direct others turns on whether there is good reason to expect its directives to be reasonable. There is no reason to think that the legislature will enact good law if legislators do not respond to reasons as a group, as an institution. Particular legislators would reason and act to vote, but there is no reason to think that the indirect aggregation of the reasoning of various legislators will be reasonable. This is true even if each legislator is reasonable because the aggregation may still yield a choice that no reasonable sole legislator should adopt. The point is that one cannot devolve the legislature's response to reasons to each legislator considered as an individual. The legislators do have to reason and choose individually to some extent, but they reason about and choose what they should do together as the legislature.

Reasonable legislative action is a unitary response to reasons because if it is not it cannot posit coherent, reasonable sets of propositions. Unless the legislature responds to reason directly, the community cannot reasonably understand the legal norms that it introduces to be the exercise of authority, which is the reasoned choice of reasons for action. Raz rightly argues that there is no way to legislate indirectly, as a function of how legislators think and act.[99] Therefore, a group of persons legislates by structuring their interaction so that they together act like a single reasoning, choosing person. In other words, they

---

[99] Raz, *BAI*, 275–5.

reason and decide jointly in a way that unifies them in the decision to enact these changes for those reasons.

The legislature must respond to reasons as a group if it is to settle how others should act. There are two further reasons why the legislature must respond to reason as an institution if it is to exercise legitimate authority. The first is that interpreters identify the legal changes that the legislature has acted to introduce by understanding the intended meaning of the statutory text. Interpreters understand what was intended by inference, which in turn requires reflection on why the speaker acted. If the legislature were not structured to form reasoned decisions, it would be absurd for interpreters to infer what meaning was intended and legislators would be unable to communicate joint decisions by way of a statutory text. I take up this point in further detail in chapter 7, section V, and again, indirectly, in chapter 9.

The second reason is that the legitimate scope of the legislature's directive may turn on the reasons for which the legislature acted. That is, exceptional cases may arise in which the reasons for a legislative decision are unexpectedly absent or outweighed by some decisive new factor. In either case, it may be reasonable for the courts to recognize an equitable exception, qualifying the rule that the legislature adopted by reference to the legislature's choice. It may also be reasonable, even in the absence of a judicial practice to this effect, for citizens to understand their duty to follow the law in this way. Again, this mode of response to the legislative act, which explains the relevant case law,[100] requires the legislature itself to act for reasons. (I consider this mode of 'interpretation' further in chapter 9, section VI.)

There are many ways to fail to legislate well. The hapless lawmaking body might aim to aggregate preferences rather than respond to reasons, which is to act for an impossible and unattractive end. It might aim to aggregate majority responses to a series of propositions, which is to stumble headlong into collective irrationality. Or the institution might make only the minimal decision to enact the text of the bill whatever its content, which is to fail to exercise authority at all. What unifies the failures is their eschewal of a full, direct response to

---

[100] J Evans, 'A Brief History of Equitable Interpretation' in T Campbell and J Goldsworthy (eds), *Legal Interpretation in Democratic States* (Ashgate, Aldershot, 2002), 67.

reason, of the kind I outline in chapter 5. What is striking is that each misconception of legislating is driven in part by a theory of group action, in which the relevant course of action is all one can expect of an assembly. My own theory of legislative action, outlined across the chapters that follow, provides that legislating is centrally the making and promulgation of reasoned choice and that the well-formed legislative assembly is capable of such choice.

5

What It Is to Legislate

I aim to explain the nature of the legislature. The key to understanding the nature of a dynamic reality is to understand its capacities, which one understands by understanding its acts, which in turn one understands by understanding its objects—that for which it acts.[1] The classical method of social theory is to adopt the perspective of the practically reasonable person to identify the ends, or objects, of fully reasonable human action and thence to understand more or less confused or in other ways rationally defective purposes, actions, and institutions.[2] The central case of the legislature, which I seek to identify, is the form that the legislature has, if any, when it is chosen and maintained by practically reasonable persons. Thus, I ask what reasons, if any, there are to establish the legislature, serve as a legislator, and follow legislation as a citizen. This course of reflection leads in this chapter to an account of what it is to legislate, in which one chooses to change the law for reasons, and in the following chapter to an account of the way in which the legislative assembly is structured to legislate.

I. Legislative Capacity

Law is a distinct and valuable form of social order in part because legal rules are structured in a system that authorizes some person or body to modify the system by changing one or more of its component rules, or

---

[1] Finnis, *Aquinas*, 29.
[2] Finnis, *Aquinas*, 40–51; Finnis, *NLNR*, chapter I.

at least changing the application, or likely application, of one or more of those rules. The content of the law should be open to change in this way, most obviously when and because a particular rule may be unreasonable so that the common good of the community is best served by its removal. The rule in question may always have been unreasonable so that it should never have been adopted. Alternatively, a rule may have become unreasonable so that it should now no longer be maintained. For example, a rule permitting common land use may become unreasonable when the population grows and economic conditions change. Legal change also extends to introducing new rules. There is reason to introduce a new rule when this would serve the common good. When an unreasonable rule is removed, there may often be good reason to create a new rule. The repeal of a rule permitting common land use may warrant introducing a rule to enable that land to be divided and alienated. Further, there may be reason to adopt new rules to instantiate some aspect of the common good not addressed by the existing law. For example, discovering a certain type of pollution may be a reason to introduce new rules to regulate the relevant activity.

Hart argued that the static character of rules in the pre-legal society is a defect that warrants the introduction of a particular type of secondary rule, the rule or rules of change.[3] This type of rule, he said, authorizes some person or persons to repeal old rules and to introduce new rules. Hart did not explain in detail the need for rules of change, taking it to be obvious that a society would be in bad shape if it had no means to modify the content of the rules that directed social life. And he thought it plain that the person or body that is authorized to change the law would be a legislature.[4] This understanding is consistent with the ordinary meaning of legislate, which is to make law.

The rule (or rules) of change has not been the focus of close academic study. Hart's later argument centred on the rule(s) of recognition, which sets out criteria for legal validity and unifies the legal system.[5] The third type of secondary rule, the rule(s) of adjudication, sets up a procedure to settle disputes, with officials impartially applying valid rules.[6] Hart rightly thought that the rule(s) of change and recognition had to be closely linked: for the legislature to change the law, the changes that it enacted had to be identified as valid law. A rule of

---

[3] H L A Hart, *The Concept of Law*, 2nd edn (Oxford University Press, Oxford, 1994), 95–6.
[4] Hart (n 3) 96.   [5] Hart (n 3) 94–5, 100–10.   [6] Hart (n 3) 96–8.

change identifies a person or body with authority to change the law; the rule may also specify the authority's jurisdiction to legislate and the procedure it has to follow to legislate.

A rule of recognition may overlap with a rule of change. In the Westminster constitution the doctrine of parliamentary sovereignty, conveniently stated by Hart in the formula 'whatever Parliament enacts is law', constitutes part of the rule of recognition as well as the rule of change.[7] Elsewhere, the rule of change is not part of the rule of recognition. In the United States, the legislative authority of Congress is conferred by Article I of the Constitution. The rule of recognition is that the Constitution is law. The Constitution provides for its content to be changed by way of amendment. The rule authorizing Congress to legislate is contingent and may itself be varied by exercising the rule of change that is the Constitution's amendment procedure. The wide (but not unlimited) jurisdiction that Congress has makes it the federal legislature and Article I the leading rule of legislative competence and rule of change. The American example confirms that there may be more than one rule of change in a system. The state legislatures in the United States and the regional assemblies in the United Kingdom exercise legislative authority under a rule of change. In the latter case, the authority of the legislative body is itself grounded in the act of the national legislature, Parliament.

The appropriate response to the community's need for deliberate legal change, evident in every modern legal system, is to institute a body to make law deliberately. Such a body is a legislature. The need for change may be answered by a legislature that has limited jurisdiction, especially if the limits exist to preserve the legislative authority of a subsidiary body that acts for a local community. However, the common good will not be well served if the lawmaking body lacks sufficient freedom to change the law as reason demands. Therefore, while constitutional limits are not objectionable per se, they should be closely specified and adopted with caution. The alternative is that the lawmaking body—indeed, the whole set of such bodies in a community—may lack the capacity to act to serve the common good. The separation of legislative powers amongst lawmaking bodies and the extent of legitimate constitutional limits are highly contingent. The point of general application is that the common good requires an institution that has the capacity to change the law when need be.

---

[7] Hart (n 3) 106–8.

I argue that the legislature, with its capacity to change the law deliberately, is an institution that is fundamental to the central case of law. Raz argues that a legal system can exist without norm-creating institutions, but not without norm-applying institutions.[8] His concern is with the minimum conditions that must obtain for a set of norms to be a system. This focus is not sound. One may imagine a community that shares a set of norms and yet lacks an official means to apply the norms, with self-help being the order of the day. The community has a form of law and yet lacks much that is valuable about the central case of law, including impartial official application of its rules. Raz's minimal system is likewise a semblance of law, merely analogous to the central case. Any community structured in this way could not respond to the need for legal change and would lack one of the valuable, distinctive features of a worthwhile legal order, viz. the capacity for a community to act to modify the rules that structure its social life. The latter point suggests a further feature of the central case of the legislature: it is the body that is set up to legislate for this community. It may be that it need not be representative—I consider this later—but the object of its action is to change the set of legal rules that the community adopts to further the common good of that community.

My claim that the legislature is the institution that is set up to change the law does not entail that legal change by other means is unreasonable. Customary rules may change over time, and one need not be Hayekian to think that sometimes those rules will be reasonable. However, the slow and ad hoc development of custom alone is insufficient to serve the common good; this is the reason why a rule of change is needed.[9] In many jurisdictions, the decisions of courts are a source of law, so that legal change may follow judicial action. The primary point of an adjudicative decision is to settle a dispute about what the law is, or how it applies or is to be applied to particular facts involving the parties to the dispute. The point is not to change the law.[10] Thus, case law arises as a consequence of another activity, the adjudication of disputes,

---

[8] J Raz, *Practical Reason and Norms*, 2nd edn (Princeton University Press, Princeton, 1990), 129–48; cf. Waldron, *LD*, 34–5.

[9] Cf. Waldron's argument that legislation by assembly is more closely analogous to customary change than to legislation by a single person: *LD*, 45–8, 55–68.

[10] This may be the reason for the dispute or at least the litigation, as when campaigners prompt the court to change the law, but this does not change the structural position of the court: it decides the particular dispute and its decision may have the consequence of changing what had been the content of the law.

whereas the point of legislating is to change the law. Legislatures may serve other purposes but their distinct function, that which explains why they are instituted and maintained, is to change the law by enacting legislation.[11]

It would be unreasonable to rely solely on case law development to change the law. The case law method is for the judge to decide the particular case, often by analogy to previous cases, with that decision bearing on the weight of argument in later cases. This is an incremental and indirect approach to legal change. It may permit judges over time to develop a set of reasonable legal rules. However, the approach runs into difficulty in certain circumstances. The common good may call for comprehensive, decisive legal change, rather than piecemeal, incremental reform. And often, reasonable change will require processing complex information and choosing amongst open alternatives. Judges largely lack the capacity to respond in this way.[12] A line of cases may be grounded in error or have been overtaken by rapid social change. It is difficult, for good reason, for judges to correct long-established errors or to respond decisively, and if need be radically, to new circumstances. The central judicial task is to decide disputes by reference to existing law. It would be unfair to the parties to the dispute, as well as to other members of the community, for the dispute to be the occasion of deliberate lawmaking, fully open to reason. In any event, the judge is not well placed to respond to the reasons that settle what the law should be. His concern is rightly with this particular dispute rather than the general state of the law and its connection to the common good. And he lacks the time, expertise, and information needed to deliberate and choose the content of the law.

The reason for a legislature does not entail that it must legislate frequently. I make no claim about how much legislation a community needs, as that is highly contingent. It may be that the legislature may not have to act often or that it has to act repeatedly and radically to reform the law. It is consistent with the legislative function for the legislature to permit secondary forms of legal change—case law and custom—to proceed. The legislature has the capacity to act to correct or to supplement case law or customary legal rules and the reason for

---

[11] J Waldron, 'Legislating with Integrity' (2003) 72 Fordham Law Review 373, 379.

[12] J Waldron, 'Judges as Moral Reasoners' (2009) 7 International Journal of Constitutional Law 2, 19–24; and A Vermeule, *Law and the Limits of Reason* (Oxford University Press, Oxford, 2008).

this capacity is precisely so that some body is able to intervene to ensure that the content of the law serves the common good. It follows that the reasonable exercise of legislative authority requires oversight of the content of the law and judgment of the extent to which that law realizes the common good.

Gardner argues that legislation is the paradigmatic case of law because it is the clearest case of posited law, which is to say law that is deliberately made.[13] This is true, but obscures the more important point that the capacity to posit new rules is valuable. The key advantage of making law deliberately is that the lawmaker is able to respond directly to the reasons that bear on changing the law. If there is good reason to repeal a law, that is if it is obsolete, unworkable, or pernicious, then one may repeal it; if there is good reason to introduce a new rule, in that it helps restrain wrongful action or opens up valuable new opportunities, then one may act on those reasons to adopt law to that effect. This direct and open responsiveness to all relevant reasons distinguishes legislating from lawmaking by other means.[14] A judge deciding a case responds to that dispute and the existing legal materials limit his decision. It is not open to him simply to change the law to be as he thinks it should be if it were open to him to posit the law anew. The judge understands that he is not a legislator and that it is not his task to oversee the content of the law and to act freely to change it as is required to instantiate the common good.[15]

The legislature responds to the reasons to change the law. That is, it decides when there is good reason to act and how, if it acts, the law is to change. The capacity to legislate entails the freedom to settle the content of the law by acting for that end. Freedom does not mean that legislating is arbitrary. Rather, it means that the way in which the legislature acts, including whether it acts and the content of the law it makes, is settled not by rules but by how the person exercising legislative authority chooses to respond to the reasons that he or it perceives. The legislature is self-starting and self-directing. It need not wait for a

---

[13] J Gardner, 'Some Types of Law' in D Edlin (ed), *Common Law Theory* (Cambridge University Press, Cambridge, 2007), 51, 76.

[14] M Atienza, 'Reasoning and Legislation', chapter 14 in L Wintgens (ed), *The Theory and Practice of Legislation: Essays in Legisprudence* (Ashgate, Aldershot, 2005), 297, 311; A Oliver-Lalana, 'Legitimacy through Rationality: Parliamentary Argumentation as Rational Justification of Laws', chapter 11 in L Wintgens (ed), *The Theory and Practice of Legislation: Essays in Legisprudence* (Ashgate, Aldershot, 2005), 239, 247–8.

[15] Hart (n 3) 273; Waldron (n 11) 379.

case to adjudicate or a petition to arrive before it acts, and within jurisdiction it may legislate as it sees fit. The exercise of legislative authority is thus under the voluntary control of the institution itself.[16] For the legislature to act in this way it must have the capacity to formulate proposals for legislative action, and to evaluate and revise them in response to reasons that bear on the common good. To legislate, one must consider the common good, propose a legislative response, reason about its merits, and perhaps modify it accordingly, before deciding whether to adopt the response. In short, for an institution to be a legislature it must deliberate about what should be done and it must have the capacity to shape legislative proposals. An institution confined to endorsing or rejecting the content of proposals put forward by another body, as the head of state or perhaps one house of a bicameral parliament might do, would have a limited legislative function but would not itself be a legislature.

The community is not able to legislate itself, because the community at large lacks the capacity to consider the reasons that bear on legal change and to formulate proposals for legal change that are responsive to the relevant situation. The community might participate in legislating if it adopts procedures to act on direct legislative proposals—referenda. This would only be participation in legislating because the shape of the proposal for legal change would not be within the control of the community itself. A legislature that was structured to overlap the community, as to some extent the Athenian assembly was, would have great difficulty exercising authority in a rational fashion. The reasonable person has good reason to help authorize an individual person or a group smaller than the entire undivided community to legislate. And indeed, at different times and places, legislatures have been established that have one member or many; I discuss this further in chapter 6, sections I–II.

Reasonable persons accept the authority of the legislature because they recognize the need for law and for an institution to oversee and change the law when necessary. The exercise of practical authority is deliberate action in response to reasons—reasons that have directive force for reasonable acting persons by identifying and directing towards intelligible goods which stand as worthwhile goals for effective and available means prescribed by these reasons. Where the reasons address

[16] Raz, *BAI*, 258–9.

a community, goods to which they direct will be common goods or elements in a or the common good. The common good of the community is complex and there are many ways to attempt to serve or realize it. The legislature is needed to settle the content that the law of this community shall have, amongst otherwise open alternatives. The community needs the legislature to act in response to the reasons that bear on these alternatives, selecting that which it judges should direct the community: that is, which will serve or realize the common good.

There is good reason to think that only an institution that is free to deliberate and to act as and when it chooses is well placed to make good law. The legislature responds directly to the complexity of the common good in that its deliberation is open to whatever is relevant to the good of the community, including moral argument, empirical findings, and the interests of various members of the community; I discuss legislative reason in detail in the next section. The reasons for change may justify a complex, comprehensive decision as to what shall be done. The legislature is able to act to introduce a detailed set of legal rules—a code—that addresses an aspect of the common good in this comprehensive way. The legislative act is also able to settle decisively what shall be done, in a way that is not open to challenge or argument. Legislation is posited at a certain point in time in a canonical formulation and is prospective in effect. It is thus a form of law that is suited to the rule of law. Public promulgation and canonical formulation make the legal change easier to locate and grasp than that found in unwritten custom or in the best understanding of a line of cases. This advantage is contingent as particular rules of case law or custom may be extremely clear and well settled, whereas legislation may be vague or impenetrable. However, the structure of the legislative act is directed towards positing law in the best form possible, by way of a public, canonical text, which is the focus of legal reasoning.

To change the law is to change the set of propositions that constitute the law. The law is this set of propositions in the sense that its primary reality is that it provides reasons for action for the members of the community whose law it is. That is, a law is a prescription of practical reason promulgated by a legal authority, a prescription which the person subject to the authority is to adopt as if it were self-prescribed.[17]

---

[17] Aquinas, *ST*, I–II q. 91 a. 1c, q. 92 a. 1c; Finnis, *Aquinas*, 255–6.

I talk of propositions because what matters is the reason for action, the directive conceived of as a rule that is fit to be adopted in my own deliberation and action. The particular textual formulation in which that proposition is expressed does not have this same importance in action and is of secondary interest, even when the form of words is canonical, so that interpreters must engage with that form of words. The same legal proposition may be set out in various alternative formulations and much of legal reasoning seeks to distinguish that proposition from its contingent formulation and to identify the proposition that is made legally true by the interaction of the formulation with other formulations and with propositions of law already accepted as true. It follows that in acting to change the law the legislature should aim to change the existing set of propositions, otherwise the law will not change.[18]

In modern legal systems, the legislature acts by enacting a particular statutory text, known thereafter as an Act of Parliament, an Act of Congress, or the like. The connection between the text and the legislative act is complex. The statutory texts that the legislature enacts are both sources of law and the law itself. This is not a contradiction. The enactment of the statute is the legislative act. The statute is a set of provisions, united in a single written text under a particular title, which stipulates what is to be done. That is, the statutory provisions are promulgated as, and will be understood to be, the legislatively chosen standards. However, simply restating the text of the provisions does not capture the legal effect of the statute.[19] Rather, the legal effect of the statute is the set of legally true propositions that the statute stands for and by its enactment introduces and establishes. There are two reasons for this. First, the legislative function is to formulate and communicate prescriptions of practical reason that citizens may internalize as directive of their own conduct: that which is formulated, legislation, must therefore take propositional form. Second, the statute is a contribution to an existing legal order, in which there are prevailing assumptions, antecedent rules, and general qualifying principles. The statutory text is not freestanding and it is formulated and understood to be a particular legislative act, which together with other such acts constitutes a scheme of social coordination towards the common good. Thus, the text of the

---

[18] Gardner (n 13) 54.
[19] J Finnis, 'Helping Enact Unjust Laws Without Complicity in Injustice' (2004) 49 American Journal of Jurisprudence 11, 16.

statute is the form in which the legislative act—the exercise of authority to select certain standards—is made known. But the content of the law that has been enacted is the set of normative propositions that the statute brings into being.

II. How One Reasons to Legislate

The legislature is an institution that is established to act deliberately in response to reasons to change the law. For legislation to be reasonable, the legislative act must in some sense follow from sound reasoning about what should be done. The legislature has capacity to respond to reasoning of this kind in that it deliberates about how to act and it forms and revises proposals for legislative action in light of that deliberation. I now ask how one should reason to legislate. My aim is to outline the reasoning that grounds the central case of legislative action and to clarify how the legislative act is a response to that reasoning. That is, I explain how a well-formed legislature responds to reason. I will assume that one person, the prince, is authorized to legislate and ask how that person should reason. This assumption brackets the problem of group action. I discuss in chapter 6 the extent to which authorizing a group—an assembly—to legislate changes what it is to legislate. The prince is a natural person and he may reason and choose; relying on my argument in the previous section and the argument yet to come in chapter 6, I take it that he thus has the capacity to legislate. Analysis of how he should reason may help clarify the way in which any legislature must reason if it is to legislate well.

The reasoning of the prince is the deliberation of the legislature. The practically reasonable sole legislator understands that he is authorized to legislate because the capacity for deliberate legal change is valuable. Therefore, the prince acts to change the law for the common good. Like any person, he may be corrupted and act for his private good, which is to be a tyrant, but in the central case he serves the community. The prince exercises voluntary control over the content of the law so that his action determines what the law shall be. He exercises this control reasonably if he identifies and responds to the reasons that bear on whether, and if so how, the law should be changed. That is, the prince should determine the extent to which existing legal propositions support the valuable states of affairs that constitute the common good and, if need be, should act to amend the set of propositions so that it better instantiates the common good. The sole legislator's act is to choose, and to promulgate his choice, that the law shall be a certain way. The act is a choice because the prince is free to act otherwise, or not to act at all, and he acts by exercising his will to adopt the conclusion of his practical reasoning as to what should be done. The act is a reasoned decision as to what should be done. The form of the act is the enactment of a statutory text that promulgates the legislator's choice, his decision, that certain propositions are to be repealed or introduced. Thus, when the legislature is one person, the legislative act is a choice that follows from a chain of reasoning and is intentional under a certain description.

The sole legislator has a duty to oversee the content of the law and to act to change the law when this serves the common good. The prince acts when he judges that he may address a community need by means of a reasonable course of legislative action. That is, he sets out to identify the common good and to determine how or if legislative action on his part may help realize it. The object of legislative deliberation, and thus the reasoning of the prince, is a proposal for legislative action, a proposal to change the law in a certain way. The prince forms a proposal to meet a particular community need. He may revise it to avoid certain unintended consequences or to realize a further, subsidiary end. If the prince concludes that the proposal is fit to be chosen, which is to say that it helps secure the common good, then he will adopt the proposal, making a reasoned choice that the new set of legal propositions that it sets out shall direct the community. The point of legislative deliberation is to form, reflect on and refine proposals for legislative action, so that the legislator is able to choose well what should be done.

It is helpful to sketch in outline how one should reason to legislate. In the set of points that follow, I state each stage in the prince's reasoning as a proposition that he adopts. At various points, in parentheses, I refer to two examples.

1. This particular state of affairs is valuable and is an aspect of the common good. The state of affairs is not yet—adequately or at all—realized in the life of the community. I have good reason to consider further whether I should act to instantiate this state of affairs, which, as an aspect of the common good, is the proper object of my legislative action. (For example, one valuable state of affairs is an absence of driving accidents; a second is a flourishing public forum for art, journalism, and entertainment.)

2. The relevant state of affairs may be realized if the community is coordinated in a certain way (driving carefully in coordination with other drivers; establishing a public non-commercial broadcaster). I propose to introduce that state of affairs by adopting a scheme of particular propositions of practical reason that direct the action of relevant persons in the following way (detailed, public rules of the road; an operating charter, and licence fee). The scheme will direct reasonable persons as to how they should act and will shift the incentive structure of unreasonable persons (obligations to drive safely, sanctions for breach; public service duties backed up by a regulatory structure, plus an obligation on various persons to pay a licence fee, with sanction for breach).
3. This proposal is a means to the end that I seek, which is the state of affairs I perceive to be valuable and the reasons why it is valuable. It does not damage other ends that I value (efficient travel, just punishment, control of official discretion; commercial freedom, open media, prosperity of citizens, especially the poor) and indeed it is not just a means to one end but to a complex of valued ends (efficient transport, safer travel, simple law enforcement, salient rules; public control over broadcasters, space for private commercial operations, political neutrality, commitment to value, control of bureaucracy).
4. The content of the scheme is to be developed—elaborated, specified, revised—in response to the ongoing question whether this particular course of action—the lawmaking proposal—is a reasonable way to secure the cluster of valuable ends for which I act, as well as the various side-constraints that I recognize. My adoption of the proposal, duly elaborated and revised, will change legal propositions in the way that will direct action to these ends by means of this scheme.
5. The proposal is fit to be chosen and I choose to adopt it.

This outline is somewhat artificial. I do not imagine that the reasonable legislator proceeds in precisely this fashion, just that the various points capture much that is at play in his reasoning. I set out an extended example below that explains further how this general scheme serves to clarify reason and action in particular instances. The outline is useful to the extent that it helps pick out what it is that a sole legislator should consider in reasoning about how he is to act and what form his reasoned action should take.

Aquinas identified four orders of knowledge: knowledge of the nature of things (centrally, of empirical facts), logic, moral evaluation, and technical craft.[20] This identification is useful at least as an aide-memoire or checklist, an obstacle to reductivist oversights. The reasoning of the prince is complex and partakes in all four. (I do not consider the second order in any detail.) Like any legislator, he has to decide what should be done. His legislative act is a moral choice made in response to reasons, which directs the reason and action of others. The prince cannot legislate well without sound moral judgment. However, he should not aim to identify and give effect to an ideal legal code, fit for any community: no such code exists.[21] The reasonable legislator will perceive that there are goods valuable for all persons, which are the object of practical reason and which constitute the common good. He will also recognize one entailment of those goods when they are soundly understood, namely some exceptionless moral norms against, inter alia, intentional killing, rape, and lying. Further, he will grasp that some general conclusions may be drawn about how communities should be ordered, conclusions that are the subject of political and legal theory. These truths frame good legislative reasoning but do not exhaust it. Indeed, as I argued above, there is good reason for the legislator to address the contingent needs of his particular community, acting to remedy the insufficiency of moral norms alone—even when negative norms are supplemented by the many norms identifying positive responsibilities—to facilitate human flourishing.

Legislative action is necessary in part because very many of the goods that moral reasoning picks out as worthy of choice cannot be realized in the life of the community without law. The reason and action of the prince is framed by general moral truths, but his duty as the legislator is very often to 'specify' these truths, choosing in what specific forms they shall be given effect in the law of this community. This kind of specification Aquinas terms *determinatio*.[22] He explains it by analogy to architecture, where the architect has to make specific general forms, such as 'house' or 'door', if the project is to be completed. The architect's choice(s) settles the precise form that is adopted and in

---

[20] Finnis, *Aquinas*, 21–2.
[21] Finnis, *NLNR*, 27–8; cf. W Cyrul, 'How Rational is Rational Lawmaking?', chapter 5 in L Wintgens (ed), *The Theory and Practice of Legislation: Essays in Legisprudence* (Ashgate, Aldershot, 2005), 93, 94–5.
[22] Aquinas, *ST*, I–II q. 95 a. 2c, q. 99 a. 3 ad 2; Finnis, *Aquinas*, 267–71 and *NLNR*, 284–9, 295–6.

virtually every case his choice(s) could reasonably have been more or less otherwise. The legislative act is a very complex series of *determinationes*. The specifying choice may occasionally be so open that one could call it 'indifferent' or even 'arbitrary'.

The prince cannot choose well, specifying general moral truths for the good of this community, unless he knows the relevant facts, the relevant nature of things. He must confront the state of the world as it is if he is to serve the community. The legislator should inquire into whatever facts bear on the question of how the community should be structured. This may include straightforwardly empirical judgments about physical facts and relationships. The legislator could not act to settle how water rights are to be allocated without understanding the relative scarcity of water, the way in which liquid moves, and detailed facts about rainfall patterns, aridity, topography, soil formations, and the like. Not all of these facts require careful investigation and the legislator need not always understand them in their full complexity. However, the facts are relevant to the scheme the community adopts to coordinate access to water and therefore the legislator should identify and understand them to the extent of their relevance. The detail of various human practices is also very often relevant. Here the knowledge is not of facts that exist apart from our reason, but facts that concern a certain kind of human action. The technical details concerning how steel plants operate, or how fishermen trawl for mackerel, may be highly relevant to how the legislator should act. Knowledge of this kind is in the fourth order. The object of law is the good of persons, which is understood by practical reason and judgment, in the third order. The nature of persons, including their limitations and dispositions, may be studied in the third order but also in the first order, as human physiology and psychology may be understood as physical phenomena. Inquiry into the facts is necessary to sound practical reasoning. The legislator has to reflect on the existing state of the world and the causal relations that govern it because he acts to bring into effect certain valuable states of affairs.

Legislating is a complex practical choice in response to moral reasons and empirical facts. It is also an exercise in technical reason. In enacting statutory texts to make law, the legislator participates in the complex cultural practice that is the law and must engage in the technical reasoning that characterizes it. His act is a technical choice, similar in form to stipulating the rules of any systematic social activity (games, cryptography), as to the propositional content of the standards that make up the community's body of law. Note that as the choice is promulgated, and so is in some sense a communicative act, he must also reason about language, choosing formulations that convey the meaning he intends to convey. (I discuss this in detail in chapter 7.) The legislator cannot formulate and enact his practical conclusions about what is to be done without attending to the craft of legislating. That craft requires detailed knowledge of the existing law together with an understanding of the relationship between overarching (or background) legal values and default rules, the specific statutory text, and the ultimate legal propositions the legislator wishes to introduce. The law is in part a technical system, which the legislator should understand, so that the content of the law remains under his voluntary control.

The craft of legislating is the practice of forming proposals that capture the practical choice as to what should be done in a form that both changes the law to this effect and is fit to be adopted by officials and citizens. That is, legislating well requires technical skill, for the prince's legislative act must be precisely tailored to change the law and to introduce the state of affairs the legislator seeks. The process of crafting a set of legal rules to capture the moral conclusion that a problem ought to be addressed in a certain way may itself generate new alternative courses of action or require revision of the prior moral choice. That is, specifying the scheme by introducing it into the technical practice of law may transform its content and form. Feedback of this kind is central to legislative deliberation, with the legislator working through a proposal, identifying its strengths and weaknesses, and refining its content to meet any problems that detailed specification reveals.

Adherence to the ideal of the rule of law is central to legislating well and the rule of law serves as a powerful rational constraint on legislative reason. What the prince might otherwise choose may sometimes be rightly limited by the need for easy enforceability and clear guidance: the legislator may choose strict rules, which deliberately over or under reach the reasons for the rule. In this case, the sound practical choice is to adopt a strict rule. At other times, there may be good reason to adopt a vague standard that frames but does not exhaust subsequent decision-making. The anticipated use of a standard in adjudication may also bear on the content of the choice.[23] Part of the craft of legislating is also attending closely to how to direct the action of the persons one seeks to

[23] J Gardner, 'Rationality and the Rule of Law in Offences Against the Person' (1994) 53 Cambridge Law Journal 502.

coordinate. This is a complex judgment that requires reflection on how and why certain kinds of persons—whom one aims to direct—are likely to act under certain conditions. (Atienza notes this aspect of legislative reason, which he terms pragmatic rationality, but he does not explain it in detail.[24]) Reasonable citizens take the legislator's act, and the content of the law, to change their reasons for action. Unreasonable citizens may conform without good reason, perhaps responding to incentives for action: inconvenience, shame, sanction, or rewards. The reasonable citizen and the unreasonable citizen are not distinct classes of person, for any person may choose to respond to reason or not. The law that the legislator enacts constantly appeals to the reason of citizens, while very often (but not always) including measures that compel or induce the unreasonable to comply.

The prince should structure his proposal to direct the reasonable and to compel the unreasonable. However, he may often act expecting, but not intending, many persons to fail to comply and yet rightly refrain from adopting measures that would tend to increase compliance, if they are otherwise not fit for choice: for example, if they are too harsh or require a complex or costly public enforcement scheme. The prince should do more than foresee likely compliance and frame sanctions accordingly; he should also judge whether some scheme he introduces will be taken up by reasonable persons. That is, is this scheme for, say, corporate liability one that would be of value to reasonable persons such that they would make use of it? Thus, to legislate well, one must consider carefully how the set of interlinked propositions one proposes to introduce is likely to change how persons—reasonable and unreasonable—act, and one should reflect further on whether, in light of one's judgment on this point, this proposal is fit to be chosen.

I propose to explore the complexity of legislative reason by imagining a prince who addresses a particular problem, namely how the law should respond to a person's failure or incapacity to meet his debts, and specifically, whether the status quo, debtor's prison is a reasonable response. There is reason to think the response unreasonable: it is harsh, it wastes the industry of the debtor, it harms his dependants, it often fails to make good the creditor's loss, its impact is arbitrary in that the extent to which one suffers is contingent on family resources, and it hurts the economy by discouraging what might otherwise be beneficial

---

[24] M Atienza, 'Practical Reason and Legislation' (1992) 5 Ratio Juris 269, 280.

risk-taking. However, imprisonment is not an irrational response to non-payment of debts. It punishes the debtor for his presumable defaults in prudence and care, creates an incentive for repayment and for families to make good the creditor's loss, and it may protect the public from trading with those unwilling to meet their debts. For these reasons, it would be unreasonable to prohibit imprisonment if no alternative response to default on debts were available. In any event, the legislator has good reason to consider whether to change the law.

The legislator may be aware of this problem himself or it may be brought to his attention by a petition or by officials. He cannot respond reasonably without understanding debt, how debtor's prison operates, and its impact on the community. Therefore, he will aim to find out: the availability of credit and the extent of debt in the community, how many persons are unable to pay debts, how many are imprisoned, the impact of imprisonment (and the threat thereof) on the lives of debtors, their dependants and creditors, the cost to the public of maintaining the debtor's prison system, the popular and elite interest in alternatives, and the economic consequences of defaulting on debt and imprisonment (economic theory as well as empirical study). The legislator will also assess the social science of economic decision-making and consider the reasons, good and bad, why persons in general, and the typical debtors in his community in particular, incur, and then fail to discharge, debt.

The prince deliberates by forming and evaluating proposals for action. The proposal is formed in response to many valuable ends, including the creditor's right to recover, the importance of economic growth, the value of the debtor's personal relationships, the interests of the debtor himself, and the need to avoid corrupting commercial relations. The legislator must consider closely how the rights of debtors, the interests of creditors and other commercial parties, and the public at large may best be served. He might propose: (1) to introduce new forms of trading, which limit personal liability for debts, (2) that a debtor's affairs be administered, so that he continues to trade and repays debt on a structured basis, or (3) that in certain cases the debtor's liability be extinguished so that he may make fresh start, perhaps subject to various temporary disabilities. These proposals are not necessarily exclusive, but may take their place in a complex response to the problem of the inability to meet one's debt. Reflection on why persons take on debt, and its social impact, may lead the legislator to perceive a new end for which he should act, and he may modify his proposal to that extent, adopting say a special procedure in cases of usury or limiting how or if persons may take on debt. (Or he may propose reform and expansion of the debtor's prison, in combination with changes to the criminal law, to address organized criminal abuse of the arbitrariness and laxity of the present system.)

The legislator continues to specify the proposal, making the subsidiary choices necessary for it to structure adequately how the community is to act. He may adopt various complex limits on the scheme to avoid distortion of other valued ends. For example, the prince may deem certain otherwise valid transactions to be voidable if the debtor continued to trade when he knew that he was insolvent. He might also modify other legal and social arrangements (family property say) to avoid persons using those arrangements to frustrate the scheme that he proposes to adopt. He will consider how the legislative scheme will act in the reasoning of reasonable and unreasonable persons and thus will ask what the social order will be like with this scheme in place. That is, he will think about how the adoption of his scheme will shape commercial life, and the lives of debtors and creditors. It remains open to him to adjust the proposal in light of this reflection.

If the legislator concludes that the proposal will further the common good, he will choose the proposal for the reasons that explain how it would serve the common good. The scheme is usually introduced prospectively and the prince and his successors will monitor its impact on the life of the community. He may respond to pathologies (abuse of the scheme, or distortions of valuable ends) or unintended consequences with legislation that amends or even repeals the scheme. In this way the legislator addresses a social problem that may not be settled by abstract moral reasoning alone, but which instead requires deliberation in response to existing legal and social arrangements and the reasons that exist to create new alternatives. He forms and develops a proposal for action in response to the reasons he perceives and he evaluates the proposal by reference to its impact on existing arrangements, aiming to bring valuable order to social life.

III. The Act of Legislating

The legislator acts to legislate when he communicates or promulgates his choice that certain propositions shall be law. The form of the choice is the statutory text and the act of enactment is thus both the adoption of the text as law and, more importantly, the exercise of authority to introduce into the law the propositions of which the text is a formulation. The choice is an action that is intentional under a means-end description. The choice is that certain propositions shall be introduced into the law and those propositions stand as a complex means to the end of the realization of patterns of coordination that the legislator perceives to be valuable. Thus, the intention on which the legislator acts in legislating is:

I intend that this set of particular legal propositions shall direct citizens to act in certain ways, such that a certain pattern of social coordination is achieved, which shall be a means to the end, or the instantiation, of a state of affairs in the community that I perceive to be valuable.

The propositions that the legislator chooses are part of the plan on which he acts, hence he acts intending that they be law, but they are also the plan on which the members of the community are to act. Thus, the intentional act of the legislator in legislating is to direct others to act on the plan of action that he has chosen for them.

The legislative act should not be understood to be first and foremost a communicative act. It is necessarily communicative, because the act of a legislature is always to choose standards that direct the community and for those standards to be known they must be made known, which is to say, communicated.[25] My point, however, is that the act of legislating is not a communicative act that has consequences for the content of propositions that direct the community. The act of legislating is the act of settling on those propositions. That is, just as law in general is seen most clearly in the bearing it has on—the meaning and force it has in—the deliberation and action of those it addresses, so too the primary reality of legislating is in the practical reasoning and choice of the legislator. The object of choice is not a course of action on which the legislator is himself to act, save as a proposal to advance, but rather on which the community is to act.[26] The legislator aims at the action of

---

[25] Cf. N Stoljar, 'Survey Article: Interpretation, Indeterminacy and Authority: Some Recent Controversies in the Philosophy of Law' (2003) 11 Journal of Political Philosophy 470, 476–7 and 'Is Positivism Committed to Intentionalism?' in T Campbell and J Goldsworthy (eds), *Judicial Power, Democracy and Legal Positivism* (Ashgate, Aldershot, 2000), 169–83; H Hurd, 'Sovereignty in Silence' (1991) 99 Yale Law Journal 945.

[26] This includes the legislator of course, but not qua legislator. Whereas in most cases of practical reasoning our focus is directly on how I should act, with legislating (and analogous

others and his method is to formulate and adopt propositions that are fit to be adopted and to direct the practical reasoning of those others. The central aspect of the act of legislating then is the exercise of reason and the response of will, which culminates in the act of choice, adopting a proposition (a series of inter-related propositions) as if for myself.

The legislative acts of the prince should be understood by perceiving his intentions in acting. That is, one only fully understands how the legislator exercises his authority, and how one is directed to act, when one understand the means-end package on which he acts. It may be that in many cases there is no practical need to grasp the reasons for the legislator's choice or the ends he intended to seek: the propositions he has chosen may seem clear. However, there is often good reason to be unsure what exactly the legislator has chosen or how it fits with other choices. Purposive interpretation, the correction of legislative mistakes, implied repeal, identifying side-constraints on statutory powers, and the practice of recognizing equitable exceptions to statutes all require the interpreter to reflect on the reasoning of the legislator to identify the law. Arguably one person cannot perceive another's intended meaning without understanding, to some extent, the reasons for which that person acted; I take up this point in detail in chapter 7. I have made no argument yet for how legislative intent should inform statutory interpretation. My claim is just that when a sole legislator acts, one has reason to reflect on his reasoning to understand how he has exercised his authority to direct one to act. As with any individual action, interpretation or assessment of the act's significance may focus on or discount the remotest intentions, and/or the more proximate intentions (means) and/or the consequences including foreseen, foreseeable, and 'direct' or 'indirect' consequences.

The prince acts intending to choose a plan of action for the community, or for an official and/or non-official part of the community. However, his legislative act, and therefore the content of the standards that have been chosen to be law, does not reduce to his full chain of reasoning. This is an important point and is central to my later account of how the many legislators act like a sole legislator. The prince may choose a certain plan for the community for a variety of further

---

actions: commands, advice) the focus is on how another should act. The question of how I should act remains fundamental, for I must decide how, if at all, I should direct others, but the main object of deliberation and choice is a course of action for you, and only secondarily for me (as the proposal that I should choose to direct you to adopt).

(private) reasons, none of which need be relevant to the content of the plan of action. For example, the legislator might enact a certain public standard intending either to do his religious duty, to deter citizens from violent rebellion, to attract favourable comment from historians, or to indulge his capricious whims. The legislator may act for these or other ends and yet the public standard may remain the plan of action that is found in the structure of intentions outlined above.

This detachment from the legislator's full chain of reasoning is possible because the act of legislating, which is intentional as explained, is itself a means to the legislator's own ends. An individual's acts are fully explicable only as part of an extended chain of reasoning and yet any particular act may also be understood by reference to the more limited means-end package that it executes. The legislative function requires the legislator to reason and choose, and the plan that he chooses must be capable of coordinating the community to the ends that define the plan. It follows then that the legislative function requires and authorizes the enactment of a plan that is intentional under a means-end description, but that plan forms only part of, and therefore does not collapse into, the legislator's full reasoning. Thus, the act of legislating is a public act, in which the legislator's intentions are determinative—but only those intentions that constitute a publicly sufficient ground and justification for the specific provisions in the enactment. The legislator's private intentions, and also his hopes and expectations, are relevant to historians seeking to understand him, not to members of the community seeking to ascertain how he has directed them to act.

It would be a mistake then to think that in the central case the legislator's full chain of reasoning must be understood before the authoritative standard is known. It would be equally mistaken to think that citizens and officials will have to search for extraneous evidence of the legislator's intent before they know how to act. The legislator has very good reason to ensure that his intentions—up to the level at which they constitute a publicly justified and justifiable set of provisions—are transparent to members of the community. The statute is to coordinate and direct and so its content must be clear and accessible. The legislator knows that the community should (for rule of law reasons and to reduce costs) understand his statutes as sufficient public standards within a technical system, rather than as partial steps in a private game of 'guess what was in my mind'. Therefore, the rational legislator who is concerned to ensure conformity between the standard he chose and the statute he enacted will strive to ensure that the text manifests his choice as to what propositions shall be law. And he will accept as consistent with the authority of his office formalization of the interpretive process that deems the legislator's reasonably apprehended intention to be his actual intention.

The mistaken but common assumption that the legislator's further, private intentions define the legislative act may perhaps be explained thus. Some princes will certainly have abused their authority by insisting that their legislative acts create as law not those propositions that they chose in legislating but rather those propositions they would rather they had chosen, which better suit their present needs and private plans. The fact of such abuse may suggest the false conclusion that all the prince's mental states are decisive so that his hopes and expectations for the statute are always to be fulfilled. The analysis above of the partial detachment of the plan from the legislature's full reasoning shows this conclusion to be unsound. The conclusion is also unsound because it is often impossible to adopt both the legislator's past choice and his present inclination. Further, an agent's hope or expectation is not his intention in acting.[27] The legislative function requires only an authoritative public choice. A practically reasonable sole legislator will note and insist on the distinction and thus so too will the sound authority structure that exists in the central case of legislative action.

IV. Legislative Integrity

The coherence of the legal order is relevant to legislative reason. The prince aims to change the law in response to reasons, which means that the object of his act is, at one level, the set of legal propositions in force. Therefore, he has very good reason to avoid contradiction and gaps in the law, for these would defeat his rational lawmaking act. I follow Marmor and take a set of propositions to be coherent if they 'are somehow mutually supportive [and] somehow fit together in the overall scheme of things'.[28] He distinguishes pragmatic in-coherence, 'when the law promotes aims, policies or patterns of

---

[27] See further the discussion in chapter 2, section II.
[28] A Marmor, *Law in the Age of Pluralism* (Oxford University Press, Oxford, 2007), 40.

conduct which practically conflict',[29] from moral incoherence, when the law's 'various prescriptions and their underlying justifications cannot be subsumed under one coherent moral theory'.[30]

The moral coherence of 'the law' is not a proper object of legislative action. That is, the prince should not act for legislative integrity for its own sake.[31] The legislator should change the law when there is reason to change the law. If he responds to reasons consistently, and has sufficient time to reason and act to change whatever law he judges warrants change, the legal order might be quite coherent. However, he would have good reason not to change laws enacted by other legislators, which he himself might not have enacted, if those laws are well settled and ground good states of affairs.[32] The rule of law may cut against legislative integrity.

The prince has good reason to make pragmatically and morally coherent choices. He chooses a plan of action in order to realize valuable states of affairs in the community and therefore the various propositions that he chooses are likely to form part of a coherent—mutually supporting—plan of action that manifests a consistent response to the relevant reasons and is not contradictory. The prince is likely to have chosen a coherent plan because he intends the plan to be a means to certain ends, and it will be an inept or unworkable means, in extreme cases even self-defeating, if it is incoherent or otherwise irrational. However, the coherence of the prince's choices should not be overstated. There are good reasons to expect his choices to be coherent on certain issues, that is, to be locally coherent,[33] but it is much less likely that all of his choices will be entirely consistent or explicable by reference to a full and unified scheme of principle.

The legislator's complex choices, which constitute a single statute, may fail to cohere fully for at least three reasons. First, the legislator may have made a reasoning error, failing to perceive the lack of full coherence between his choices: that the legislator is a single rational agent does not entail that he is incapable of error. Second, the legislator may have rationally decided to adopt a different rationale for a particular provision or set of provisions, so as to undertake a partial experiment

---

[29] Marmor (n 28) 27.
[30] Marmor (n 28) 28.
[31] Cf. Dworkin, *LE*, 176.
[32] Marmor (n 28) 55–6; see also Finnis, *NLNR*, 287.
[33] J Raz, *Ethics in the Public Domain: Essays in the Morality of Law and Politics*, revd paperback edn (Oxford University Press, Oxford, 1995), 291–2.

(or to hedge his bets). Third, political or economic pressures may drive the legislator to make choices that cannot all be justified on one scheme of principle. It is mistaken to assume that a prince is an absolute sovereign, with complete practical freedom to choose what the law shall be. To function as an authority in a real community, the legislator must take account of political considerations and this may rightly (or wrongly) lead to choices that do not fully cohere.

The prince may also have reason to choose a compromise. This may sound odd—his unity of decision would seem to dispense with the need to compromise. However, the legislator acts for his community and he should legislate in ways that do not unnecessarily disturb the peace or provoke widespread non-compliance. For this reason, the prince may refrain from choosing the option he would otherwise adopt and instead choose a compromise. (This may be a compromise between him and some group or between two or more groups.) One does not compromise reasonably by failing to make a decision, alienating one's decision to another or splitting the difference in some arbitrary way. A well-formed compromise is a course of action that respects the commitments of the compromising parties and which constitutes a second-best alternative that each is willing to choose to adopt.[34] A compromise is not irrational, but it is also not fully coherent.

There are also good reasons not to expect full coherence across the prince's legislative acts over time. It is true that the legislator is likely to adopt roughly consistent approaches to various social problems over time. For all the reasons noted above, however, this may not be the case. Further, the legislator may repent of earlier choices and deliberately depart from them. Also in most monarchical systems, as I noted above, more than one legislator will have made the law. Each successive legislator will act within a system partly constituted by the acts of his or her predecessors, and the choices he or she makes may be more or less coherent with that past body of law.[35] Thus, the rational legislator's choices will not necessarily cohere with past legislative choices.

The legislative function is to exercise voluntary control over the content of the law so as to provide the coordination (of conduct

---

[34] H Richardson, *Democratic Autonomy: Public Reasoning About the Ends of Policy* (Oxford University Press, Oxford, 2002), 143–61 and R Bellamy, *Political Constitutionalism* (Cambridge University Press, Cambridge, 2007), 192–4 and 241–2.

[35] Raz (n 33) 292; J Ferejohn, 'Law, Legislation, and Positive Political Theory', chapter 7 in J Banks and E Hanushek (eds), *Modern Political Economy: Old Topics, New Directions* (Cambridge University Press, Cambridge, 1995), 191, 211, n 5.

in the community) that the common good requires (including, as always, the 'negative coordination' of avoiding strife, collisions, neglect, etc.). The prince acts to fulfil this function by reasoning about what should be done, crafting standards that serve as means to the end of states of affairs perceived to be valuable, and by making a public choice that those standards shall be law. The legislative acts of the sole legislator are thus reasoned choices amongst options that are defined by means–end packages. His intention in acting is likely to be transparent to citizens and his acts are likely to be, but are not necessarily, coherent. In this way, the sole legislator, the prince, exercises legislative capacity.

6

The Legislative Assembly

The legislature acts for the common good by legislating when need be, which is to act to modify the set of legal rules that direct the community. The legislature exercises its capacity to legislate by choosing in response to reasons. Legislative reason requires accurate knowledge of facts, sound moral judgment, technical skill, and coherent practical choice. The legislature may be a single person, a prince, or a group of persons, an assembly. A well-formed assembly, I argue, represents the community and deliberates about what is to be done. There is very often good reason to authorize an assembly to legislate, for the assembly is: less likely than a prince to be a tyrant, open to popular participation, and more likely to legislate well than a prince. Yet these advantages do not change what it is to legislate. The assembly exercises legislative capacity well if, like the prince, it considers relevant reasons and chooses reasonably how to change the law. The assembly's internal hierarchy assists rather than frustrates this exercise.

I. The Problem of the Sole Legislator

A prince is able to legislate and this capacity is valuable. There is reason to authorize one person to legislate and in many classical and medieval polities the will of the prince was the law. Yet in almost all modern states, an assembly, which may have two chambers (each of which is itself a subordinate assembly) and perhaps acts in concert with the head of state or chief executive officer, exercises legislative authority. The Westminster Parliament is the House of Lords and the House of

Commons, but it is the Queen-in-Parliament that legislates. The United States Congress is the House of Representatives and the Senate, and Congress enacts legislation subject to presidential veto. The bicameral structure of these and many other legislatures is an important object of study in its own right, but is not of central concern for present purposes—in this chapter I set it aside and focus on a unified assembly. I now consider why an assembly should be authorized to legislate. I argue that the reasons for an assembly change who it is that legislates, but not what it is to legislate. If the assembly is to legislate for the common good, I maintain, it must reason and choose like the prince.

The prince is able to legislate for the common good because he is able to reason and choose in response to the reasons that bear on what should be done. In communities that would otherwise lack the rule of law, it is thus reasonable to authorize one person to legislate, to be a prince. However, there are three reasons to be wary of vesting legislative authority in the prince. The first and most obvious is that the prince may yield to corruption and become a tyrant, and tyranny is the worst form of government. Even if the prince is a reasonable person, his successor in office may not be, especially if, as is often the case, the polity adopts the clear, salient rule of hereditary succession. The second is that members of the community do not participate in legislating, save as subjects petitioning for relief. This detachment from the legislative process limits the valuable opportunity for persons to participate in politics as equals, to share in government as citizens. It may also alienate many persons from the law, and lead them to disobey it, which is inimical to the common good. The third reason is that it may be difficult for a prince to legislate well. Acting alone, he may lack the time or expertise to understand the relevant facts or the breadth of experience and judgment needed to reason practically about what is to be done.

Electing the sole legislator would not adequately address the three problems of tyranny, exclusion, and incompetence. The electors may remove a tyrant at the next election, which is an important protection. The prospect of having to contest the next election may also restrain the legislator somewhat. However, this remedy may only be exercised after the fact and the capacity for the legislator to abuse his authority in the interim remains very wide.[1] Indeed, the electoral constraint may be

---

[1] J Linz, 'Presidential or Parliamentary Democracy: Does it Make a Difference?' in J Linz and A Valenzuela (eds), *The Failure of Presidential Democracy* (Johns Hopkins University Press, Baltimore, 1994), 3, 12–14, 16–18.

altogether ineffective, for as Brennan and Hamlin argue the common knowledge that the electoral constraint is ineffective in the final term of office works its way backwards, undermining the effectiveness of the constraint in any term.[2] With but a single legislative office, elections will focus on the quality of the individual candidate, which means there is no space for parties to contest elections. This is unfortunate for the political party is an important device for restraining self-serving legislators.[3] There may be almost as much to fear, in short, from an elected president as from a prince.

The community may choose the sole legislator, but the exercise of legislative authority by just one person continues to limit the extent to which citizens may participate in or contribute to lawmaking. The office of legislator may be open to competition, but opportunities for meaningful participation are limited because there is only one office and the incumbent of that office may exercise legislative authority as he alone thinks best. One may petition the legislator and attempt to influence his decision-making but, as with the prince, the members of the community approach the sole legislator as supplicants. The winner takes all on this approach,[4] with the loser(s) in the electoral contest, even if supported by a majority of the electorate,[5] having no stake at all in the exercise of legislative authority, or any institutional position from which to monitor and comment on that exercise.[6] This allocation of authority is not a good means to enable citizen participation.

Finally, the elected legislator has the same limited capacity as the prince. The extent to which the law serves the common good is in both cases dependent on the judgment of one person. Election may help select for competence, but the main problem remains the limits of any one person's practical intelligence. Also, in one sense, the elected legislator may be at a disadvantage to the prince: the former may perhaps serve only a short term (if term limits obtain or if he is ousted

---

[2] G Brennan and A Hamlin, *Democratic Devices and Desires* (Cambridge University Press, Cambridge, 2000), 208.

[3] The relative unimportance of political parties makes it more likely that political outsiders will be elected and this in turn is a significant factor in the tendency of presidential regimes to regress to authoritarianism: Linz (n 1) 10–14.

[4] Linz (n 1) 14–16.

[5] Assume that three candidates run for office and that there is no run-off election. A and B have 30 per cent support each. C wins with 40 per cent support and is the sole legislator, despite lacking majority support.

[6] Brennan and Hamlin (n 2) 194–5.

at election), which may frustrate the development of the experience and judgment needed to legislate well. That is, there are gains to be had from having a long-serving legislator.

The reason to authorize an assembly to legislate is that an assembly is a legislator that is capable of answering each of these three problems.

II. Representation and Deliberation

An assembly is a certain kind of purposive group—a gathering of persons to some end[7]—and a legislative assembly is a group that meets to legislate together.[8] For a group to be a legislative assembly, it must have the capacity to deliberate and decide. In a small community, all adult citizens may meet—assemble—to decide what the content of the law shall be. They would legislate in their official capacity as members of this assembly, with the decision of the assembly settling how they would act as ordinary members of the community.[9] The assembly of all citizens *is* the community acting for the common good. This community directly exercises self-rule, because its members, in association with one another, settle what is to be done.

For most communities, it is impractical for all citizens to assemble to legislate. This is an obvious conclusion, but it warrants careful explanation. There are far too many citizens to meet together in one location. More to the point, even if they were to assemble in some physical or virtual location, the resulting group would be far too large to deliberate intelligibly and to act together rationally. The members of this assembly of all citizens would be unable to talk to one another or to coordinate their action and so would be unable to form, evaluate and revise proposals for legislative action. Also, most citizens would not be sufficiently well informed to participate as equals in the assembly's decision-making process. The members of a small community are more likely to have direct acquaintance with and thus to engage rationally with the limited number of issues that fall to be decided. They are also likely to hold one another to account for how they

---

[7] This is not a tautology, for not all groups 'gather': think of a team of salesmen or an international research group.

[8] Again, the group may consist in two (or more) subgroups, which are chambers in an assembly, and an executive officer.

[9] Finnis, *NLNR*, 252–4.

vote,[10] with the relative size of the community making each vote salient. In a large, modern society, by contrast, each vote is less decisive and legislative issues are complex, which entails that voters are rationally ignorant of the facts that are relevant to how one should legislate.[11] I do not mean that most voters are fools, unreasonable, or selfish, just that each voter is less well placed to participate in legislating than his counterpart in the small community; the former voter would also not be subject, as the latter is likely to be, to the discipline that follows from being publicly answerable for one's vote.[12]

Voters in large, modern polities do settle various questions. Most importantly, they settle who is elected to office. The term electorate refers either to the body of voters eligible to vote or to those who do vote. The electorate, I contend, does not have the capacity to legislate. The electorate does not act at all, not even to settle who is to be elected to office. Voters, who together constitute the electorate, vote for a particular candidate or candidates (depending on the voting rule), sometimes in one national contest for a single office, but more often in a number of contests across particular locales for a number of offices. The election is decided by aggregating votes. The electorate does not make one decision; it is just the body of persons whose individual acts are counted. The voters do not jointly elect a particular candidate. They participate together in a collective scheme for holding an election, in which votes are counted, with the aggregate of votes settling who is elected. It is quite misleading, for example, to say that the electorate chose to elect a hung parliament.

Voters may also settle the outcome of referenda. The approval of a proposal in a referendum may directly change the law. It would seem then that the electorate decides the referendum and in this way legislates. However, the electorate does not deliberate to decide and the electorate is not a body that is capable of giving reasons for its decision: its membership is too large and inconstant for the members to jointly form an act in response to reasons. It lacks the procedures necessary for members to discuss what they should decide as a body.

---

[10] Brennan and Hamlin (n 2) 198–9.

[11] Brennan and Hamlin (n 2) 172–3; R Hardin, 'Democratic Epistemology and Accountability' (2000) 17 Social Philosophy and Policy 110, 115–17.

[12] There is good reason for elections to be held by secret ballot—to avoid voter intimidation—but the reverse is true for the assembly. The legislators should decide by open vote, because this means they are held publicly responsible for the positions they adopt: G Brennan and P Pettit, 'Unveiling the Vote' (1990) 20 British Journal of Political Science 311.

The rational limits on citizen time, interest, and energy also serve to make it the case that the electorate cannot deliberate and therefore, in the focal sense, cannot decide. Moreover, the electorate is not capable of ordering its decisions over time in the way that reason may demand.[13] Each voter may reason, but the electorate is not a group that reasons and acts as one. Pettit concludes that the electorate is not conversable: it does not respond to reasons like a person and cannot be held to account for irrationality.[14] The electorate cannot respond to reasons as reasons and so it cannot legislate. It may 'decide' in a series of referenda, but like the output of Waldron's voting machine, the set of 'decisions' is quite likely to be collectively irrational.[15] I conclude that the electorate is not capable of legislating and is not a suitable candidate to replace the prince.

Direct democracy, where all citizens share in legislative authority, is in general unreasonable, I contend, unless the community is of a size where the electorate may form an assembly. This is not the case in most polities and it follows that direct democracy is not an ideal that one should approximate as best one may. For the common good to be realized, some person or body within the community must legislate. That person or body has no natural right to rule but has authority because he or it acts for the common good. The obligation each citizen has to obey that which is enacted is owed not to the legislature but to one's fellow citizens. This set of moral truths, Aquinas argues, is what it means to say that the legislature represents the community; it acts for the community to choose the law.[16] It does not follow that the consent of the community is a condition of legitimate authority. The case for a representative legislative assembly is not that this institution approximates direct democracy,[17] but that this institution is likely to exercise legislative capacity reasonably. The assembly is thus not a second-best alternative to direct rule by the electorate, but an improvement on rule by the prince.

Instituting an assembly shifts lawmaking authority from a person to a group. This group jointly exercises the capacity that the prince

---

[13] P Pettit, 'Deliberative Democracy, the Discursive Dilemma, and Republican Theory', chapter 7 in J Fishkin and P Laslett (eds), *Debating Deliberative Democracy* (Blackwell, Oxford, 2003), 138, 148–9.
[14] Pettit (n 13) 154–5.
[15] See also T Kousser and M McCubbins, 'Social Choice, Crypto-Initiatives, and Policy-making by Direct Democracy' (2005) 78 Southern Californian Law Review 949, 961–6.
[16] Finnis, *Aquinas*, 264.
[17] Brennan and Hamlin (n 2) 180–1, 183.

exercises alone. However, the assembly is not just a group, as is any committee or council. It is a large group that is structured to represent the community, not only in the important sense noted above—acting for the common good and having no natural right to rule—but also in the sense that it is drawn from the community. Its members are selected in such a way that the assembly acts not just for but also in some sense on behalf of all citizens. The reason for the large size of the assembly is that with several hundred members it is practical for individual legislators to represent particular groups or districts.[18] The assembly may 'represent more accurately [than a president] the range of diversity in the polity and ... foster closer connections between representatives and voters'.[19] While the assembly has many members, the point of the group, which is to legislate well, limits its size; the assembly would frustrate that point if it had thousands of members.[20] The representative assembly, by virtue of its size and membership criteria, is structured to reproduce the community in a form that can reason and act well.

Each member of the assembly is a representative. Membership criteria vary but include democratic election, selection by lot, or holding a salient office or status (lord of the manor, burgher, or sheriff). The early practice of the English Parliament is instructive.[21] The King summoned notable persons, religious and secular, to form one assembly. He directed the various political districts to send persons competent to consent on their behalf, to form a second assembly. Across the land, those subsidiary communities employed different selection procedures, including partly democratic election, with those selected forming a second assembly. The point of the exercise was to form a body that was capable of giving the consent of the realm to the proposal of the King so that once that proposal was adopted everyone would comply. It was judged critical that the assemblies speak for the different parts of the realm.

---

[18] This line of thought is implicit in Waldron's work, but he does not discuss representation in any detail: LD, 54, 109–10, n 60.

[19] J Carey, 'Legislative Organization', chapter 22 in R Rhodes, S Binder, and B Rockman (eds), *Oxford Handbook of Political Institutions* (Oxford University Press, Oxford, 2006), 431, 432.

[20] A possible counter-example, the Chinese national assembly, which has almost 3,000 members, I take instead to prove my point. The assembly's size has not been limited by reference to what would permit meaningful deliberation and decision. See also J Waldron, 'Legislation by Assembly' (2000) 46 Loyola Law Review 507, 509.

[21] F W Maitland, *Constitutional History of England* (Cambridge University Press, Cambridge, 1908), 60, 69, 74–5, 78.

Membership of the modern assembly is largely settled by election;[22] appointment is possible for a second, politically inferior chamber. The individual legislator represents some part of the community. He participates in the legislative process on behalf of that group, which is to say that he has a special responsibility to act to place their legitimate interests before the assembly. In the modern polity, legislators very often form parties and contest elections in these parties. The legislator thus represents a constituency that elected him, forms part of an institution (the legislature) that represents the entire community, and belongs to a party that coordinates the actions of its members by reference to a shared manifesto and leadership.

The assembly does not fail to represent the community just because the set of judgments and preferences of its members does not reflect in direct proportion the set of judgments or preferences of the voters. Electors choose representatives for reasons. The voters should not choose representatives to be mere spokesmen for public opinion, who translate voter preferences or judgments into votes in the assembly. They should choose a person, in their electoral district, whom they think competent to legislate well, where competence includes moral probity and sound judgment on public issues.[23] Voters will of course assess candidates differently, choosing, other things being equal, the candidate who approaches public issues in ways that the relevant voter thinks sound. The voter has reasons for acting to elect this person and ideally the election will select a person who will legislate well. The point of election is to select the best candidate. The selection method is democratic, because all adult citizens share in it, but the criterion for selection is aristocratic.[24] Thus, 'elections [are] primarily...selection devices, which function to create what might be thought of as a democratically elite assembly—democratic in its mode of selection but elite in its civic virtue and in its competence'.[25]

If the electoral system is sound,[26] and voters choose well, the assembly will over-represent virtue, selecting persons who aim to, and are competent to, serve the common good. The prevalence of

---

[22] B Manin, *The Principles of Representative Government* (Cambridge University Press, Cambridge, 1997), 79–93.

[23] It is no good selecting a perceptive and careful legislator if he will sell his vote to the highest bidder.

[24] Manin (n 22) 132–60; 'aristocratic' in this context means 'best' and does not refer to wealth or title.

[25] Brennan and Hamlin (n 2) 180.

[26] The detail of electoral systems is very complex and I set it aside.

disagreement in the polity also means that the assembly will be likely to include persons who share and reflect the range of different, credible political groups and views salient in the community. Each legislator forms part of the decision-making body and to some extent identifies with and has interests in common with the part of the community he represents. It follows that the assembly is a body that brings the interests and views of the community together, in the person of intelligent participants, in a forum that may deliberate and decide.

The assembly is a deliberative body. Its members meet to deliberate in public about what should be done and legislative proposals are introduced, debated, revised, and then finally adopted or rejected on majority vote. Authorizing an assembly to legislate means that the legislature reasons in public. The content and rationale of a particular legislative proposal has to be presented and defended to the assembly. The legislators form and respond to proposals by finding relevant facts, which they discuss together, thinking about how best to resolve particular questions, and arguing about whether this or that proposal is fit to be adopted. Thus, the legislators reason like the prince, asking how they may exercise their authority to serve the common good. The prince reasons and chooses; the members of the assembly reason, argue, and then vote to settle whether they make this or that choice. The assembly hears different views, forces proposals to be defended, and makes law after reasoned argument.[27]

The initial selection of legislators frames, but does not exhaust, the assembly's subsequent argument and action. How the legislators reason and argue in response to particular questions settles how the assembly acts. The key difference between the assembly and the prince (elected or otherwise) is that whereas the prince reasons and chooses alone, lawmaking by assembly enables a microcosm of the community, those selected by other citizens to be competent legislators, to continue to argue about what should be done. Election may result in a party winning a majority of seats in the assembly, so that until the next election the members of this party, if they act together, may settle what the assembly does. Yet even when the party is relatively unified, the assembly is starkly different to the (elected) prince. The electoral losers continue to participate in the legislative process, arguing with the majority about what should be done, presenting new facts and questioning proposals. All the legislators, who together represent the community as a whole, participate in an ongoing argument about how best

---

[27] J Waldron, 'Legislating with Integrity' (2003) 72 Fordham Law Review 373, 383.

to serve the common good. The majority, the electoral winners, enjoy an advantage in settling that argument, but they cannot dispense with it.

Each legislator knows that he is a representative, but may be unsure whether this means that he is a trustee, charged with exercising independent judgment, or a delegate, authorized only to execute the wishes of his electors. Both alternatives are species of representation.[28] The reasonable legislator, I argue, should see that he is a member of a legislature, which acts for the common good by deliberating about and acting on proposals. His duty is to contribute to the legislative process so that the assembly legislates well. The openness of legislative deliberation militates against the delegate conception, as does the extent to which legislative reason involves specification and detailed response to contingent facts. The legislator cannot participate meaningfully without exercising his own reason and judgment in the assembly in response to particular proposals. However, the delegate conception is not without all force. An election may involve debate about particular proposals and—save in very exceptional circumstances—the legislator should not abandon an explicit commitment to the electors.[29] Likewise, if he contests an election as a member of a party, the manifesto is a commitment that he and the party should not lightly set aside.

Burke's argument is instructive:

If government were a matter of will upon any side, yours, without question, ought to be superior. But government and legislation are matters of reason and judgment, and not of inclination; and what sort of reason is that in which the determination precedes the discussion, in which one set of men deliberate and another decide, and where those who form the conclusion are perhaps three hundred miles distant from those who hear the arguments?... Parliament is not a *congress* of ambassadors from different and hostile interests, which interests each must maintain, as an agent and advocate, against other agents and advocates; but Parliament is a *deliberative* assembly of *one* nation, with *one* interest, that of the whole—where not local purposes, not local prejudices ought to guide, but the general good, resulting from the general reason of the whole.[30]

---

[28] H Pitkin, *The Concept of Representation* (University of California Press, Berkeley, 1967), 112–43; see also D Kyritsis, 'Representation and Waldron's Objection to Judicial Review' (2006) 26 Oxford Journal of Legal Studies 733, 741–4.

[29] Knowing that circumstances change, he should be reluctant to give a wholly unconditional commitment.

[30] E Burke, 'Speech to the Electors of Bristol' [1774] in R Hoffmann and P Levack (eds), *Burke's Politics, Selected Writings and Speeches* (AA Knopf, New York, 1949), 115.

The assembly of elected representatives should deliberate to legislate. This requires the participants to be willing and able to act in response to reason, for the alternative is not deliberation, but a negotiation amongst hostile parties. Interestingly, surveys confirm that most American legislators understand themselves to be trustees rather than delegates;[31] legal philosopher Neil MacCormick, reflecting on his own service as a member of a legislative assembly, understood his role in the same way.[32]

Thomas Christiano argues that citizens should set the ends of legislative action, which he terms 'aims', while legislators determine the best means to those ends.[33] Citizens must select ends, he says, because 'those who choose the aims of the society are the ones who hold decision-making authority'.[34] The selection of means, he says, is not necessary for self-rule and requires technical, complex choice that citizens cannot make in advance. Christiano recognizes that ends may conflict and argues that citizens should also transmit judgments about priorities amongst ends. The ends of legislative action are thus fixed at election. Parties are useful because they set out 'packages of aims and trade-offs', which citizens may choose.[35] The function of the assembly, Christiano argues, is to find compromises when the aims of citizens differ and to determine the means to those aims.[36] These are technical tasks, he says, requiring skill and expertise, but do not require legislators to second-guess the aims citizens have chosen.[37]

My argument in section II of chapter 5 suggests that Christiano's proposed division of legislative labour assumes an atrophied account of legislative reason. One cannot legislate abstractly in isolation from relevant facts or argument about specific proposals. It would be unreasonable for citizens to stipulate ends to be sought unless those ends were so abstract, and subject to such wide qualifications, that they did

---

[31] E Uslaner and T Zittel, 'Comparative Legislative Behavior', chapter 23 in R Rhodes, S Binder, and B Rockman (eds), *Oxford Handbook of Political Institutions* (Oxford University Press, Oxford, 2006), 455, 461.

[32] D N MacCormick, 'Legislative Deliberation: Notes from the European Parliament' in L Wintgens (ed), *The Theory and Practice of Legislation: Essays in Legisprudence* (Ashgate, Aldershot, 2005) 285, 290–1.

[33] T Christiano, *The Rule of the Many: Fundamental Issues in Democratic Theory* (Westview Press, Boulder, 1996), 169–71.

[34] Christiano (n 33) 216, see also 175–7.

[35] Christiano (n 33) 199–201.

[36] Christiano (n 33) 208–9.

[37] Christiano (n 33) 215–17, 218–19.

little to constrain legislative deliberation. The stipulation of ends in isolation from means-end packages would compel the legislators to adopt unreasonable means if no reasonable means exist. Further, the specification of an abstract end very often involves reflection on other ends that may be realized or damaged in this process. Christiano's limited conception of the assembly's deliberation also unravels when one considers how legislators are to compromise competing ends. Reasonable legislators cannot aim to maximize realization of citizen ends, but will instead make the best they can out of the set of ends. That is, they will reason about what should be done, but will reason within the ends that citizens stipulate. At best then, Christiano's argument reduces to an insistence on public reason, with legislators framing their choices by reference to arguments that have some traction in the community. This may often be prudent, but it is not a condition of justice: legislators in a complacent slave-owning polity have good reason to prohibit slavery even if no major constituency (assume that the disenfranchised slaves are a minority) adopts this as an end.[38]

The legislators need not be delegates for the electors to have real political power. The electors choose their particular representative knowing that that he sees the world in a certain way and belongs to a party that has a programme of legislative action. He does not betray their trust when he proceeds to reason and act in the common good; however, if he radically changes his previous political views or party allegiance in fairness he should—save in very exceptional circumstances—resign. The proper object of the legislator's action is the common good of the community, of which his constituency is part. He may not legitimately sacrifice the former for the interest of the latter, although it is his duty as representative to forcefully place the interests of his constituents, which are relevant to the common good, before the assembly at large. The reasonable legislator speaks for those he represents but may at times rightly act in ways that are not in their proximate interest.

---

[38] The lack or fragility of popular support may be relevant to how aggressively legislators should move: consider the incremental progress of abolition in the British Parliament, first outlawing the slave trade (the Slave Trade Act 1807), then the institution of slavery (the Slavery Abolition Act 1833), with important transitional provisions and compensation for slave owners.

III. The Advantage of an Assembly

The Burkean model of the legislator, Russell Hardin says, 'owes its central conception to the prior form of government by monarch'.[39] This is true; the legislator, like the prince, should reason and act for the common good, not for what citizens stipulate are their interests. Hardin argues that this conception is inconsistent with '[t]he point of representative democracy [which] is to put these interests in contest to decide policy'.[40] If each legislator is an enlightened monarch, Hardin argues, then they would all choose alike, which would make representation unnecessary. Thus, one might as well elect a monarch as an assembly; the only advantage of the latter, he continues, is that, by analogy to Condorcet's Jury Theorem, it may be less likely than the former to make a mistake.[41] Legislating well is no small advantage, to my mind, but Hardin does not explain adequately why an assembly is better placed to legislate than a prince. Also, he neglects the other good reasons for authorizing many Burkean legislators rather than just one to legislate. I now explain why one should authorize a representative, deliberative assembly to legislate.

The assembly is less likely than the prince (or president) to be a tyrant. The assembly reasons and chooses in public and therefore legislators must justify their acts with arguments that at least seem to be in the interests of the community at large, which rules out various proposals they might otherwise advance.[42] This 'civilizing force of hypocrisy', as Elster terms it, is valuable.[43] It deters obvious abuses of power, grounds possible criticism of unjust legislation, and may even lead legislators to adopt sincerely the arguments they initially mouth.[44] Reasoning in public discourages, even if it does not deter altogether, abuse of authority.

Public scrutiny is an important check on the abuse of power. However, the risk of tyranny is not answered by forcing the prince to explain his legislative acts to a public gathering. More important is

---

[39] Hardin (n 11) 120.
[40] Hardin (n 11) 120.
[41] Hardin (n 11) 120.
[42] See Manin's analysis of 'Trial by discussion': Manin (n 22) 183–92.
[43] J Elster, *Explaining Social Behavior* (Cambridge University Press, Cambridge, 2007), 424, 435; see also D Miller, 'Deliberative Democracy and Social Choice', chapter 9 in J Fishkin and P Laslett (eds), *Debating Deliberative Democracy* (Blackwell, Oxford, 2003), 182, 189–90.
[44] R Goodin, *Motivating Political Morality* (Blackwell, Oxford, 1992), chapter 7.

the distribution of legislative authority to many (often several hundred) persons, amongst whom it is held in common.[45] Each legislator has a duty to act for the common good, as well as to speak for a particular constituency, to whom he is answerable at the next election.[46] Each legislator thus has good reason to scrutinize proposals closely, objecting to injustice and proposing alternatives. Even if many legislators are corrupt, the difficulty of securing majority consent and the importance of election may restrain the naked pursuit of private good that characterizes the rule of the tyrant. If the people are corrupt and elect fools and rogues, then legislation by assembly may be tyrannical. This risk, while real, is less sharp than that posed by reliance on the character of one person, and his successors, whose moral character may be wholly unknown.[47]

Legislators have good reason to form parties to seek legislative objectives and to contest elections. The political party is a response to and a form of strategic action. The action of parties is vital in any modern legislature, as I explain further in section IV below. The large number of legislators in the assembly means that there is space in which parties may operate, whereas they are effectively irrelevant to the office of prince or president. The party is a purposive group that always intends to contest the next election and therefore the party has good reason to guard its reputation.[48] The members of the party should, and are likely to, discipline one another, adhering to a common platform in a way that enables them to maintain electoral support. Thus, legislators who form parties are more trustworthy than any one of them alone.[49] Parties help restrain self-serving legislative behaviour and the assembly is less likely than the prince to abuse its authority because it is open to parties.

The assembly's structure also helps restrain tyranny by enabling the losing parties to share in the exercise of legislative authority. The minority cannot formally check the united majority, but it may

---

[45] J Locke, *Two Treatises on Government*, ed P Laslett (Cambridge University Press, Cambridge, 1988), II, para 143, 364.

[46] This is contingent on the electoral system; some legislators may be elected by a national party vote, as in Germany or New Zealand, rather than by the electors of a particular constituency.

[47] Locke (n 45) II, para 94, 329–30.

[48] Brennan and Hamlin (n 2) 207.

[49] Brennan and Hamlin (n 2) 209; for a wider defence of the virtues of parties, see N Rosenblum, *On the Side of the Angels: An Appreciation of Parties and Partisanship* (Princeton University Press, Princeton, 2008), chapters 7 and 8.

constantly monitor and critique the majority from a position inside the institution that exercises authority.[50] And the minority's location in the assembly, engaging directly with the majority at each stage of the legislative process, means that it is able to present itself as an alternative 'majority in waiting', thus maintaining the electoral constraint on the majority throughout the legislative term.[51] The active presence of the minority and the size of the assembly also make it unlikely that legislators will attempt to exempt themselves from the laws they enact. This is a live possibility for a president, who may take his office to distinguish him from citizens, but is less likely for the many legislators who identify more closely with the community.[52] The subjection of legislators to the rules they enact sharpens deliberation and makes self-serving legislation less likely.

I conclude that sharing legislative authority amongst many legislators rather than conferring it on one person is an important check on tyranny. Locke overstates the case only a little when he says that the people 'could never be safe nor at rest, nor think themselves in civil society, till the legislature was placed in collective bodies of men, call them senate, parliament, or what you please'.[53]

The assembly is a lawmaker that is structured to bring forward and to consider the interests of citizens and to permit as many citizens as possible to share in legislating. The large number of legislators makes it possible for a range of perspectives and arguments to inform the legislature's deliberation. Instead of periodically choosing who is to be prince, citizens choose representatives whom they think likely to legislate well, perhaps in part because of the candidate's personal record of judgment or achievement, as well as because of the party to which the candidate belongs. When legislators argue for positions that citizens share, as is likely if the electoral process selects a range of persons whom the electors think show sound judgment, then the citizens' case is made in the legislative process. The case will often not be decisive, yet it is still valuable that the arguments that citizens find persuasive have been made. Crucially, the arguments are made in the forum that decides:

---

[50] Brennan and Hamlin (n 2) 195.
[51] Brennan and Hamlin (n 2) 196.
[52] Locke (n 45) II, para 138, 360–1.
[53] Locke (n 45) II, para 94, 329–30. It is an overstatement because a sole legislator need not be a tyrant and because the assembly may be a tyrant, which means, alas, as Locke was well aware, the people are never safe: Locke (n 45) II, paras 135–9 and 149, 357–62 and 366–7.

they inform deliberation and are live, not just symbolic, contributions to the process.[54]

The large number of legislators is relevant to how citizens relate to them. Whereas the prince or president is the decision-maker—the political superior—each legislator is just one person amongst the many who share in decision-making, none of whom have authority to legislate until they persuade the legislature to act as one.[55] It follows that citizens may approach the legislative assembly not as supplicants but as participants once removed, setting out reasons for legislators to argue in this or that way. Kutz argues that the large number of legislators, together with their democratic credentials, makes it possible for citizens to understand themselves as participants in the assembly's deliberation in a way that is not possible where a much smaller group acts.[56] I would add that part of the point of the representative assembly is to make it possible for citizens to identify with the reasoning and action of a group to which they do not formally belong. The group understands its reasoning and action to be for the community and to some extent to be by the community, in the person of those representatives whom the electors have selected to serve. The assembly is thus a forum that is open to the community and authorizing an assembly to legislate is consistent with the political equality of all citizens.

The sheer number of legislators itself also increases popular participation. Waldron doubts this, arguing that as far as participation is concerned the difference between one and several hundred legislative offices is insignificant in a large community.[57] I disagree. It is fundamental to democracy that anyone may contest election for public office. The opportunity for the ruled to serve as ruler is valuable. A polity that elects one person to legislate has much less competitive politics and is less open to community participation than a polity that elects members of an assembly. The implicit criterion for electing a sole legislator is that he is best, the most fitted to be prince. Electing one of several hundred persons, none of whom is to be prince, is different. The electors reasonably choose someone who will act for their interests

---

[54] See Waldron, *LD*, 289–91 on the irrelevance of public debate that is unconnected to decision.

[55] In practice, this means persuading a majority of legislators to support a bill on its final reading.

[56] C Kutz, 'Parliamentary Self-Government: Comment on Waldron' in E Villanueva (ed), *Legal and Political Philosophy* (Rodopi, New York, 2002), 39, 44–8.

[57] *LD*, 54–5.

and contribute ably to the legislative process. Membership of the assembly is a much more open prospect to all members of the community than is election as president. The barriers to entry are lower and the skills required are different, because the whole burden of legislating does not fall on one individual.[58]

Electing legislators in a contest that is open to all to compete, and in which all persons have the franchise, respects the equality of all persons. The electors and the elected are not separate classes of person and the latter's entitlement to exercise authority turns on the decision of the former. The community needs authority, so each person should support whoever has the basic capacity to direct others and acts for the common good.[59] However, there is good reason to introduce a structure of authority in which those who exercise authority are chosen periodically by those they direct and where any person may compete to exercise that authority. This alternation of legislators is a means to hold them to account, forcing attention to be paid to the common good.[60] The process may of course fail, with a corrupted populace acting to punish and remove legislators who act for the common good rather than for private (if widely held) interests.

The assembly has the capacity to secure consent.[61] The assembly's openness to argument and capacity to represent difference mean that authorizing it to settle what is to be done is a fair way to legislate in a divided community.[62] The reasonable person should authorize an assembly to legislate, if political circumstances make this feasible and if the assembly is likely, or at least as likely as alternative possibilities, to legislate well. Members of the community are likely to accept as authoritative decisions made by a body that respects their views and extends them an opportunity to participate in deciding what is to be done. The capacity to secure consent is valuable not because consent grounds political legitimacy but because an institution that people accept and support has the say-so necessary to posit law. Further, securing consent maintains the stability of the legal and political system, which serves the common good.

---

[58] Kutz (n 56) 48.
[59] Finnis, *NLNR*, 245–9.
[60] Locke (n 45) II, para 138, 360–1.
[61] S Beer, 'The British Legislature and the Problem of Mobilizing Consent', chapter 4 in P Norton (ed), *Legislatures* (Oxford University Press, Oxford, 1990), 62, 74–8.
[62] Waldron, *LD*, 105–16, 307–9.

An assembly may be better placed than the prince (or president) to legislate well, choosing well in response to reasons for changing the law. The large number of legislators means that the legislature is well placed to find facts. The many legislators know, and may discover, certain facts directly. Different legislators may also be able to respond intelligently to various types of information. For example, a legislator who has been a doctor, while not an expert on all things medical, is well placed to question medical experts or reports, just as a legislator who has been an economist may better address economic consequences or arguments. The assembly features multiple intelligences, many of whom are able to scrutinize closely a particular proposal, while their fellows work on other proposals. The size and diversity of the assembly enables an informal and partly formal (committees) division of labour to take place, which permits the assembly to reflect in more detail and on many more proposals than would be possible for a sole legislator.[63] Further, the number of legislative offices reduces the pressure for term limits and makes it possible for legislators to pursue a career in politics and to specialize in certain issues.[64] It is likely then that a large assembly has greater capacity than a single individual to find facts and to respond to them intelligently.

Argument in the legislature about particular proposals may inform and clarify decision, forcing legislators to confront unforeseen problems. Legislators may challenge or qualify proposals, adding new perspectives to the reasoning process. The division in the assembly forces a defence of a proposal in the face of opposition. Not all reasoning is done within the assembly, and certainly not on the floor of the house. Persons outside the assembly may reason like a sole legislator, articulating proposals fit for enactment: private citizens, interest groups, and government bodies all act in this way. They may put their reasoned proposal to a legislator who should, if he judges it sound, seek to put it before the assembly. Again, the size and diversity of the assembly opens multiple channels for reasoned contributions to the process, and for ongoing community participation in what is to be done.

The legislative assembly thinks in public for the community. Its open deliberation is central to that process, not so much because that is where the thinking has to be done as because it is an opportunity to

---

[63] Carey (n 19) 432–3, 440–1.
[64] Carey (n 19) 440–3.

present arguments, raise issues, and request clarification, all as a prelude to a decision by the legislators as to what is to be done.

The assembly divides legislative power amongst several hundred persons, although its exercise is corporate and the act of the legislature is the act of a single institution, a unified agent. What this means is that the possibility of compromise, of adopting and responding to the views of multiple persons, is built into the decision-making process. The prince has reason to take into account the views of his subjects, and sometimes to adopt a position that is a compromise. However, the legislative process by which an assembly acts is structured to permit multiple inputs, thus moving the interests of the community from outside the deliberating body (to whom they are relevant but not constitutive) into the deliberating body. Thus, the person doing the reasoning is now an artificial person, the community personified in the assembly. This capacity to reason and to act in response to reasons explains why I insist that the assembly must have authority to propose, amend, and shape proposals. If the assembly simply affirms or declines to affirm the proposals of another, then it is a check on someone else's legislative capacity, rather than the body that chooses what is to be done. An assembly that was structured in that way would not be a legislature (in anything like a focal sense).

IV. The Internal Hierarchy of the Legislature

The legislative assembly is the central case of the legislature. The reasonable person should choose an assembly rather than a prince to legislate for the reasons set out above. The assembly should legislate like a prince to the extent that it responds to reasons for changing the law with a unified, reasoned decision. Nonetheless, I do not doubt that it is difficult for an assembly to legislate well. The reason for the difficulty is that for the assembly to act well, a large group of persons—several hundred—must coordinate their joint action in such a way that they together respond to reasons with a unified, intelligent decision. In this section I explain how the assembly is structured to respond to this difficulty.

Doubts about the capacity of assemblies to legislate are not new. Waldron says that there is 'a very clear consensus, in the canon of western political theory, that the size of a legislative assembly is an obstacle rather than an advantage for lawmaking'.[65] He usefully surveys the consensus.[66] Hobbes provided that the sovereign might be an assembly but argued that a monarch, with his unity of decision, was preferable to the assembly, the internal disunity of which could lead to civil war.[67] Rousseau argued that it was very difficult for the people to organize effectively their use of plenary time, hence the need for a 'Lawgiver' to act as agenda-setter, bringing sense to the otherwise uncoordinated actions of the people.[68] Condorcet took his theorem to entail that a large assembly would legislate poorly, because he thought that as an empirical matter, when numbers rose the average competence of the legislators would be likely to be less than 0.5.[69] Mill argued that an assembly was well placed to discuss issues of great concern and to decide whether to adopt a legislative proposal, but that it lacked the coordination necessary to form reasonable proposals itself.[70] Madison concluded that 'after securing a certain number for the purposes of safety, of local information, and of diffusive sympathy with the whole society', the number of representatives should be held constant to avoid mob rule.[71] Locke and Aristotle, Waldron argues, are the few exceptions to this consensus.[72]

This consensus is important but it is hardly univocal. Hobbes and Condorcet oppose legislation by assembly; the others think that the legislature should be an assembly, but express doubts about its capacity to legislate. Hobbes is wrong. Incorporating rival factions into an assembly, where they may argue about what should be done, is very often a better strategy for maintaining peace than authorizing an individual to rule. The much greater relative stability of democratic over authoritarian regimes in the modern world proves the point. Madison's argument is consistent with adopting a large assembly, as

---

[65] J Waldron, 'Legislation by Assembly' (2000) 46 Loyola Law Review 507, 512.

[66] Waldron (n 65) 512–15; Waldron, LD, 51–3.

[67] T Hobbes, *Leviathan*, ed A Martinich (Broadview Press, Peterborough, 2005), chapter 19, 141–2.

[68] J Rousseau, *The Social Contract*, ed G Cole (Everyman, London, 1973), II, chapters 6–7, 23–8.

[69] M Condorcet, *Selected Writings*, ed K Baker (Bobbs Merrill, Indianapolis, 1976), 49; Waldron, LD, 51–2, 135.

[70] J Mill, *Considerations on Representative Government* (Longman, London, 1865), chapter V, 34–43.

[71] J Madison, A Hamilton, and J Jay, *Federalist Papers*, ed I Kramnick (Penguin, Harmondsworth, 1987), Number LVIII, 351.

[72] Waldron (n 65) 514–15.

large as is necessary to achieve the ends he notes. His point that an assembly may be too large to legislate well is plainly true: if there are too many legislators to deliberate intelligibly then the assembly is too large. (It is groups that lack the capacity or motivation to reason that are likely to descend into mobs.) The live questions are how many are too many and why are that many legislators unable to legislate well. Mill and Rousseau advance a common line of argument, taking the mass of legislators to be unable to form reasonable decisions. Mill proposes a Commission of Legislation and Rousseau a Lawgiver to bring order and unity to the decisions of the assembly. The assembly would deliberate and either adopt or reject the proposals put forward by the legislative intelligence. I am not sure that Locke is an exception to the consensus. He thinks there is good reason for the legislature to be an assembly, but then so do Madison, Mill, and Rousseau. The question is how the assembly is to succeed in legislating well. Mill and Rousseau's proposals respond to that question.

The consensus in political theory, Waldron maintains, is mirrored in political science. Referring back to an earlier discussion,[73] he says 'empirical political scientists are likely to' explain away the size of the assembly 'by highlighting the efforts that are made in most legislatures to limit the number of members who participate actively in the drafting and consideration of a given measure'.[74] The executive drafts proposals in the United Kingdom and specialist committees oversee proposals in the United States. The political scientists will conclude, Waldron says, that '[i]t may *look* like we prefer legislation by assembly ... but our *real* legislators are party bosses and committee managers'.[75] This conclusion may be good political science, Waldron argues but it is inadequate political theory:

Certainly the members of legislative assemblies participate in law-making to greater or lesser degrees ... And certainly there are power structures within parties and within legislative assemblies that belie the formal equality of their members. But though these practices are important, they do little to undermine the continuing association of the authority of a statute as law with its emergence from an institution comprising hundreds of representatives. Despite all the structures and hierarchies, despite the committees, cabals, and corridors, the constitutional requirement that a bill be deliberated

---

[73] *LD*, 29.   [74] *LD*, 50.   [75] *LD*, 50.

upon and passed by (say) Congress or Parliament as a whole survives not merely as a 'dignified' charade (like Royal Assent in the United Kingdom), but as something regarded as a matter of right by the representatives themselves and as crucial to the standing and authority of legislation in the community.[76]

I agree that the internal structure of the legislature does not entail that deliberation and passage by the assembly in plenary session is a charade. There is good reason to have a large assembly even when a subset of legislators is disproportionately involved in drafting and debating legislation. However, Waldron is wrong to take the importance of general deliberation and approval to mean that the inegalitarian internal structure of the legislature is irrelevant to how the legislature acts. He does say that 'these practices are important', but his discussion in *Law and Disagreement* suggests otherwise. There is a hint of disapproval in the reference to 'committees, cabals, and corridors', and apart from this extract and its earlier counterpart,[77] he does not mention political parties or the executive at all, and mentions committees only in passing.[78] The internal hierarchy of the legislature is not squarely in view in Waldron's account of legislative action.

Waldron's conception of the legislative process does not address the internal hierarchies that almost all legislatures employ. He may share the widespread suspicion of political parties and the Westminster fusion of legislature and executive. In any event, his model of the legislative process is light on procedural detail and seems very close to Gary Cox's legislative state of nature. Cox imagines an early legislature 'in which all business is conducted in the plenary session (no committees) and members' ability to talk and make motions is largely unrestricted and unregulated'.[79] In this state of nature, it is, he says, much easier to delay than to act. Each legislator has equal, unregulated access to plenary time and any legislator may filibuster (keep debate going endlessly) or introduce continual amendments.[80] If each bill has to be considered and adopted by majority vote in plenary session to be enacted, Cox

---

[76] LD, 50. [77] LD, 29.
[78] Referring to *Law and Disagreement*, Rosenblum notes that 'a recent philosophical defense of legislatures does not mention parties': Rosenblum (n 49) 147.
[79] G Cox, 'The Organization of Democratic Legislatures', chapter 8 in B Weingast and D Wittman (eds), *The Oxford Handbook of Political Economy* (Oxford University Press, Oxford, 2006), 141, 141.
[80] Cox (n 79) 143.

says, there will very quickly be a shortage of plenary time.[81] The de facto decision rule then is closer to unanimity than majority rule, because any legislator may delay enactment.[82] The legislative state of nature, he argues, makes it difficult for legislators to work together, because there is no guarantee when or if any particular bill will make it to the floor.[83] The problem is coordination not cycling, because the effective decision rule is unanimity.

The 'universal features of modern democratic assemblies—agenda-setting offices and parties—arise as a response to the scarcity of plenary time in the legislative state of nature'.[84] Active legislatures are inegalitarian, which is to say that they feature rules that authorize unequal access to plenary time and curb ordinary members' power to delay.[85] That is, the legislature creates offices with special agenda-setting power and resources and procedures for voting on offices and motions.[86] The reason for this structure is that:

At some point, the plenary time constraint binds when important and controversial issues are at stake. Motivated by the desire to enact legislation on these pressing issues, a majority of members are willing to reduce ordinary members' powers of delay and enhance officer-holders' special powers to expedite business. Eventually, the equilibrium reached is distinctly inegalitarian: there are office-holders with privileged access to the plenary agenda, who drive the important legislation; and there are non-office-holders with default access to the plenary agenda, who seek legislative accomplishment chiefly through alliance with office-holders (or by becoming office-holders themselves) and who exercise some residual but reduced power of delay.[87]

Cox refers to three examples that substantiate this account: the nineteenth century House of Commons, the late nineteenth century House of Representatives in the United States, and the transition from the Fourth to Fifth French Republics.[88]

If the assembly may change its own rules, it may seem unclear how any internal structure could be stable, and why the majority do not

---

[81] Cox (n 79) 142. [82] Cox (n 79) 143.
[83] Cox (n 79) 144. [84] Cox (n 79) 141. [85] Cox (n 79) 144.
[86] Cox (n 79) 145. [87] Cox (n 79) 146.
[88] Cox (n 79) 146; see also M McCubbins, 'Legislative Process and the Mirroring Principle', chapter 6 in C Ménard and M Shirley (eds), *Handbook of New Institutional Economics* (Springer, Amsterdam, 2005), 123, 126.

change the rules to marginalize the minority. This is possible, but there are reasons why it may not occur. Cox argues that the rules may sometimes be legally entrenched, the majority benefits from having a stable framework, and legislators are often too busy to change the rules.[89] I add that fairness requires a stable set of rules that does not oust the minority altogether, the legislative process is a repeat game, in which any member of the majority may later find himself in the minority, and finally, legislators have good reason to retain a process that permits them to defend policy and air differences in public.

The legislature may recognize various offices: some are also executive offices, such as ministers, but others are exclusively legislative, such as the presiding officer (Speaker), directing boards (which decide on the legislative agenda), committee chairs and members.[90] I refer to both kinds just as offices. The offices enable the exercise of agenda power, which is the '*special* ability to determine which bills are considered on the floor and under what procedures'.[91] The office in question may confer authority to fashion special rules to frame how a bill is considered or to delay bills by not scheduling them.

The literature distinguishes positive and negative agenda power. Positive agenda power is power to make it more likely, or to guarantee, that a bill will make it onto the legislative agenda.[92] Negative agenda power is power to keep a bill off the agenda: that is, to veto a proposal.[93] The wider the distribution of veto powers, the smaller the set of bills the assembly considers in plenary time. This risks gridlock. The wider the distribution of proposal powers, the more bills must be decided on in plenary time. This increases the risk of cycling. Political scientists outline different models of the legislatures by reference to which persons have proposal rights or veto rights and how they may be exercised.[94] Some offices may be vested with general agenda-control, whereas others are specific to jurisdiction.[95] Different agenda powers may be exercised earlier or later in the process.[96] If

---

[89] G Cox, 'On the Effects of Legislative Rules' (2000) 25 Legislative Studies Quarterly 169, 170–3.
[90] Cox (n 79) 145.
[91] Cox (n 79) 145.
[92] Cox (n 79) 149; McCubbins (n 88) 131–2.
[93] Cox (n 79) 149; McCubbins (n 88) 132–3.
[94] Cox (n 79) 149–50.
[95] Cox (n 79) 150.
[96] Cox (n 79) 150.

many early veto-players exist, then together they filter bills; an office with late positive agenda power has control over the later form of the bill.[97] Agenda power may also be more or less centralized.

The political party is a response to strategic voting and democratic elections. It is also a response to the introduction of legislative offices.[98] Parties are the only way into office in almost all democratic legislatures and are often recognized explicitly in rules of procedure.[99] Certain offices, such as committee places, are allocated directly to the party, and assigned to particular members by the party leadership. Others are distributed by election within the legislature, such as the Speaker or perhaps committee chairs.[100] Independents have almost no chance to attain office in this political framework; party affinity is crucial. A centralized agenda-setter has a great deal of power depending on the reversionary policy, which is to say what obtains in the absence of legislation.[101]

The two features that define modern legislative organization are thus offices and parties. Parties alone are insufficient: no legislature relies exclusively on party voting discipline to control the agenda.[102] The unequal impact of legislative office is significant everywhere.[103] Legislative offices and political parties enable decisive legislative action, avoiding the frustration of the state of nature. They also ground stable decision-making that is not nearly as vulnerable to cycling as one might otherwise expect for a large group voting on a very wide range of issues.[104] Carey argues that 'parties... both limit the policy alternatives among which legislatures formally choose, preventing cycling, and ensure that some alternatives enjoy procedural advantages that prevent bottlenecks'.[105] Empirical study confirms that legislatures without parties are vulnerable to cycling.[106]

---

[97] Cox (n 79) 151.
[98] Cox (n 79) 147; M Laver, 'Legislatures and Parliaments in Comparative Context', chapter 7 in B Weingast and D Wittman (eds), *The Oxford Handbook of Political Economy* (Oxford University Press, Oxford, 2006), 121, 131–3.
[99] Cox (n 79) 147.
[100] Cox (n 79) 148.
[101] Cox (n 79) 155–6.
[102] Cox (n 79) 158.
[103] 'The order of business, both in committee or cabinet and on the floor, is tightly controlled in almost all legislatures—and is usually controlled on a *partisan* basis': McCubbins (n 88) 127.
[104] Laver (n 98) 135; J Carey, 'Legislative Organization', chapter 22 in R Rhodes, S Binder, and B Rockman (eds), *Oxford Handbook of Political Institutions* (Oxford University Press, Oxford, 2006), 431, 444–6.
[105] Carey (n 104) 445.
[106] Carey (n 104) 446.

Agenda-setting is not unfair. Legislators should form alliances in order to act to change the law in ways that they think reasonable. The legislature cannot act by aggregating the preferences of each legislator and so legislators participate in the process in part by authorizing officers (the Speaker, committee members) and party leaders to frame particular proposals, in light of committee deliberation, and consistent with the party's defining ideals and ongoing internal reflection about policy. Those who control the agenda, whether party leaders or independent officers, have a responsibility to put before the assembly well-formed proposals that in their judgment are fit to be considered for enactment. The officers and leaders do have an unequal impact on the legislative process, which impact is authorized by the other legislators and necessary for the legislature to make reasonable, stable decisions, which is the point of the legislature. Agenda-control may be abused, as it is when officers and leaders extract unreasonable concessions, or suppress debate on significant issues, or prevent the assembly hearing well-formed proposals that oppose their private interests. Legislators delegate authority to their officers and leaders and delegation carries risks. The balance between decisive action and loss of independence is difficult to strike and it is a central factor in explaining differences in legislative organization.[107]

No well-formed assembly delegates plenary legislative authority to any subset of its members. The internal hierarchy is not an alternative to the assembly making decisions, with officers and leaders authorized to legislate because the assembly is incapable.[108] Instead, the hierarchy is a means to enable the assembly to act, putting before it proposals that are fit to be considered as legislative choices. Thus, deliberation and voting in open plenary session remain fundamental to legislative action: this is the central moment of the legislative process. The officers of the legislature enjoy a special place in that deliberation, retaining privileged

---

[107] McCubbins (n 88) 128; R Hardin, 'Democratic Aggregation' in H Yung-Ming and C Huang (eds), *Level-of-Analysis Effects on Political Research* (Weber Publication, Taipei, 2001), 7, 28.

[108] The legislature may delegate lawmaking authority to particular persons or bodies—ministers, local government, regulators—for particular purposes, but this is an exercise of its legislative authority not an alienation of it. The legislature does not authorize any one or more legislators to legislate on its behalf. One might argue that the Parliament Acts 1911 and 1949 authorize a subset of the United Kingdom Parliament (the Queen and Commons) to legislate. However, those Acts are better understood to be procedures that settle how the entire legislature acts: see R Ekins, 'Acts of Parliament and the Parliament Acts' (2007) 123 *Law Quarterly Review* 91, 94–108.

control over the development and form of the proposal even in plenary session—they may restrict the extent to which the bill may be amended or they may be decisive in settling the content of amendments, and 'the government or majority party almost always reserves to itself the final motion on a bill'.[109] However, this is all to the end of putting before the assembly as a whole a bill for its consideration, to be adopted only if a majority of members, whose votes count equally, choose it. The bill is an alternative to the status quo and 'in virtually every legislature the final vote taken on a proposal is that for final passage, which forces members to directly compare the proposed change in policy with the status quo'.[110] Thus, the officers frame the issues and set the agenda, especially if agenda-setting power is centralized, but they do not make the final decision.

The legislature effectively authorizes a subset of its members to be a Commission of Legislation or a Lawgiver, placing coherent, reasoned proposals before all. However, the assembly retains authority to amend the proposal in open session, usually at the direction of those legislators who enjoy majority confidence. This unequal structure is not unfair—the assembly adopts it as a reasonable response to the circumstances of legislating and the assembly monitors and may discipline those who exercise agenda-setting power. The legislators who constitute the internal Commission of Legislation or Lawgiver are likely to be more competent than other legislators, having been chosen as leaders by their peers and having developed lawmaking expertise in committee, and perhaps in government. In this way, the legislature makes use of its internal resources to legislate well.

V. Washington and Westminster

Legislatures are structured differently in parliamentary and presidential systems. The key difference is that in the former the executive is drawn from the assembly and requires continued parliamentary support to remain in office: it is an agent of the assembly. In the latter, the executive is directly elected and the president does not require continued congressional support to remain in office: it is an independent

---

[109] McCubbins (n 88) 133.
[110] McCubbins (n 88) 133.

institution, checking and checked by, the assembly.[111] The members of the majority party in a parliamentary system have good reason to unify, because if they divide, at least on questions of confidence, the government falls. Legislative coalitions in presidential systems have less reason to unite, because the legislators are not solely responsible for legislative outcomes or for good government, and the interests of the executive and the party leadership in the legislature may often come apart or be directly opposing.

Polsby distinguishes transformational legislatures from arenas. The former are:

... legislatures that possess the independent capacity, frequently exercised, to mould and transform proposals from whatever source into laws. The act of transformation is crucial because it postulates a significance to the internal structure of legislatures, to the internal division of labour, and to the policy preferences of various legislators.[112]

Arenas 'serve as formalized settings for interplay of significant political forces in the life of a political system'.[113] That is, arenas are talking shops, where politicians continue electoral politics; they are not primarily concerned with legislating and, Polsby asserts, the real legislative power resides elsewhere.[114] The classic example of an arena is the United Kingdom Parliament and the classic example of a transformational legislature is the United States Congress.[115] Polsby argues that Parliament is an arena by noting that it arose not to forge details of legislation, but to assert rights against the sovereign.[116] Further, there is no real internal structure to Parliament, he asserts, save that which is for the convenience of the government.[117] Polsby argues that the

---

[111] M Shugart, 'Comparative Executive-Legislative Relations', chapter 18 in R Rhodes, S Binder, and B Rockman (eds), *Oxford Handbook of Political Institutions* (Oxford University Press, Oxford, 2006), 344, 346; J Carey, 'Presidential versus Parliamentary Government', chapter 5 in C Ménard and M Shirley (eds), *Handbook of New Institutional Economics* (Springer, Amsterdam, 2005), 91, 91–2.
[112] N Polsby 'Legislatures', chapter 7 in P Norton (ed), Legislatures (Oxford University Press, Oxford, 1990), 129.
[113] Polsby (n 112) 129–30.
[114] Polsby (n 112) 130.
[115] Polsby (n 112) 130.
[116] Polsby (n 112) 131.
[117] Polsby (n 112) 132.

legislature will be more transformational if the majority coalition is fractured, unstable, and less subject to party leadership.[118]

Mezey adopts a similar distinction to Polsby, arguing that one should classify legislatures by reference to their capacity to constrain the executive, with active legislatures being able to veto proposals altogether or perhaps extract concessions.[119] Norton finesses Mezey's distinction, distinguishing policy-making capacity, in which the legislature may modify or reject government policy and substitute an alternate policy, and policy-influencing capacity, in which the legislature may modify or reject but cannot substitute its own policy.[120] He argues that the advantage of this finer distinction is that it better explains the divide between Congress and Parliament, because even if Parliament is active, it still lacks the independent policy-making capacity of Congress.[121]

The problem with each of these distinctions is that they take the executive in parliamentary systems to be a body apart from the legislature, whereas of course the defining feature of such systems is that the leading legislators hold executive office.[122] It is no good to consider the legislature's capacity to make decisions and to ignore the subset of the legislature, the majority party leadership, best placed to decide. In a parliamentary system, the government's proposals are those formed and advanced by the majority party leadership. The government is a subset of the legislature, not a separate body, and one should not conclude that parliament only decides when it acts in defiance of that subset.

The legislature's capacity to decide does not reduce to the likelihood that majority party unity will fracture. Leading legislators hold executive office, form the cabinet, and control the legislative agenda. Most parliamentary time is devoted to government business, and 'to a large extent, parliament is a place for debating, amending, and passing government legislation'.[123] This unequal focus is not objectionable. The majority party has the responsibility to govern and it is therefore

---

[118] Polsby (n 112) 142.

[119] M Mezey, 'Classifying Legislatures', chapter 8 in P Norton (ed), *Legislatures* (Oxford University Press, Oxford, 1990), 149, 153–4.

[120] P Norton, 'Parliament and Policy in Britain: The House of Commons as a Policy Influencer', chapter 9 in P Norton (ed), *Legislatures* (Oxford University Press, Oxford, 1990), 177, 178.

[121] Norton (n 120) 179–80.

[122] A King, 'Modes of Executive-Legislative Relations: Great Britain, France, and West Germany' (1976) 1 Legislative Studies Quarterly 11, 12–14.

[123] Laver (n 98) 121, 125.

important that it has sufficient time to place its legislative proposals before the assembly. The voting unity of the majority further warrants disproportionate plenary time, because proposals that issue from the minority have relatively little, which is not to say no, prospect of success. The minority is, however, constantly active in plenary time, questioning and engaging with the majority's programme.

Parliamentary government is not unitary and cabinet does not draft legislation. Instead, most legislative proposals are first initiated by departments under a particular minister's jurisdiction. Laver argues that this means there is a two-stage agenda-setting process: the minister proposes policy to cabinet and that which emerges from cabinet is government policy that sets legislative agenda.[124] The majority authorizes its leaders, ministers, to set the agenda and to frame particular proposals. Ministers need backbench support—especially votes, but also morale—if their legislative programme is to succeed, while backbenchers need ministers to provide leadership, to share information, and to initiate action.[125] The parliamentary majority is thus two coalitions—the government coalition (ministers) and the parliamentary support coalition (backbenchers)[126]—and 'the most important practical politics between elections in parliamentary government systems takes place *inside the majority legislative party*'.[127] The primary political aim of the opposition is to fracture the parliamentary support coalition, defeating proposals that would otherwise enjoy a majority and, more rarely, building a majority for an alternative proposal.[128]

In presidential systems, the president's legislative role is critical. He may have authority to propose bills to the assembly, to veto legislation, to set the assembly's agenda, and to control the reversionary policy, perhaps through authority to issue decrees.[129] The executive's capacity to act independent of legislative support means that party unity in the legislature is likely to often fracture, because legislators are not directly responsible for stability and good government.[130] While Congress is often taken to be the paradigm assembly in a presidential system, the United States president is relatively weak—he has no power to dismiss Congress, limited capacity to set its agenda, and very limited capacity to legislate by decree. At the same time, there is little Congress can do to

---

[124] Laver (n 98) 125–6.
[125] Laver (n 98) 126–7; King (n 122) 15–17.
[126] Laver (n 98) 128.
[127] Laver (n 98) 129.
[128] Laver (n 98) 130.
[129] Carey (n 19) 106–8.
[130] Laver (n 98) 134–5.

control the President.[131] Other systems feature much greater presidential powers.

McCubbins argues that the internal organization of the legislature mirrors the constitutional structure.[132] Thus, the United States legislature has a proliferation of veto-players, with capacity to block many proposals, while the United Kingdom has unified, decisive majority control. In both cases the internal structure of the legislature was settled by the legislators, who it seems chose procedures consistent with their constitution's separation of powers. Agenda-control in presidential systems is thus likely to be more widely distributed than in parliamentary systems. Congressional committees exercise considerable control over legislative proposals in their jurisdiction, especially early in the process, and are very often able to block bills proceeding. Party leadership has more control at later stages. The allocation of agenda-control to committees and parties means that each may check (or frustrate) the other.[133] The more widely veto power is distributed, the more difficult it is to enact legislation. This has two consequences. First, veto-players are able to demand concessions and this means legislation is more likely to be private regarding. More centralized agenda-control means fewer veto-players and more public-regarding legislation.[134] Second, the proliferation of vetoes raises the political cost of enacting legislation, which means that the legislature is less able to make a decision, but the decisions that it makes are harder to change later. There is a trade-off between a legislature being decisive and resolute.[135]

VI. Prospects for Reasoned Action

Legislatures in both parliamentary and presidential systems are capable of reasoned action. However, parliamentary legislatures are better structured to this end; the reasonable person has good reason to choose to introduce and maintain a parliamentary legislature.[136] (For simplicity, I ignore hybrid forms of regime and the important but very complex question of how different electoral systems bear on legislative

---

[131] Laver (n 98) 131.   [132] McCubbins (n 88) 128.
[133] McCubbins (n 88) 138.   [134] McCubbins (n 88) 129.
[135] McCubbins (n 88) 141; Cox (n 79) 151–2.
[136] Like all questions of separation of powers, the choice between a presidential and parliamentary system is highly contingent.

behaviour.) Carey notes that there is a consensus amongst political scientists against presidentialism.[137] The leading work on point is by Linz, who argues that presidential regimes, especially in new democracies, are prone to collapse into authoritarianism.[138] The problem, as Carey puts it, is that 'presidentialism inflames antagonism between the popular branches while proscribing any constitutional mechanism for resolving the most serious conflicts'.[139] The president's direct election tempts him to claim a popular mandate even when he may have only modest popular support, perhaps less than the separately elected assembly. He need not build a coalition of support to enjoy executive authority, as must a cabinet in parliament, and he may respond to deadlock with the assembly by resorting to unconstitutional action.

The parliamentary alternative is to authorize the subset of leading legislators to be the government and to subject them to an ongoing requirement to maintain the confidence of a majority of legislators. The advantage of this alternative is that it does not set up institutions against one another that both have authority to rule. It integrates the two different dimensions of government—legislation and control of administration—in the assembly. The parliamentary legislature authorizes a salient subset of legislators to set the agenda: those who also direct the government. Those legislators act with the support of a majority and may develop and advance reasoned, coherent proposals. The ministers have the capacity to direct the shape of proposals, although they must move the proposal through the legislative process, at which time they must defend its content in public. Proposals may change quite radically in this process. The minister is the leading agenda-setter with respect to the particular proposal, although cabinet as a group controls the wider legislative agenda.

The minister need not satisfy a series of formal veto-players to move a bill forward. He must, however, defend the bill in committee, in the house, and, perhaps in the second house. Anticipated opposition may be very significant in shaping initial proposals.[140] And bills are often amended significantly across the course of the legislative process. Most amendments are moved by the government and passed by the majority party but it does not follow that the minister acts entirely freely in doing so. He may move an amendment to address an argument raised by his backbenchers, the opposition, or interested third parties. He may also

---

[137] Carey (n 19) 94.
[138] Linz (n 1) 3–90; see further section I of this chapter.
[139] Carey (n 19) 94.   [140] Mezey (n 119) 154–5.

adopt intelligent comments that improve or correct proposals. The minister may not wish to acknowledge the source of the modification to the proposal, but he has good reason to incorporate it in a government amendment.[141] Many legislators work on proposals as they make their way through the legislative process, especially but not exclusively in committee. Input from backbenchers from both parties often has a significant impact on the content of the final proposal.[142] The minister then is critical to shaping the ongoing proposal, but he does not work alone, and he does not present a fait accompli to the legislature.

The legislature is, I maintain, a deliberative body, even in a parliamentary system where legislators have good reason to form somewhat unified voting blocs. Ministers and others form legislative proposals, often in response to detailed policy work by officials and widespread consultation, inside parliament and amongst the public at large. The content of the bill, especially its broad principle and purpose, is debated in the house. The bill is considered at committee, often in extensive detail, before being returned to the house for further debate in light of the changes the committee has made, or proposed, to it. The minister and other key legislators—usually but not exclusively from the majority party—work on the bill between stages, discussing its detailed content and its reasoned scheme with backbenchers, opposition leaders, interested third parties, and executive officials. The final debate in the house concerns a bill that has been closely worked over and is in a form that the minister is prepared to move and which he expects will attract majority support. Legislators debate the bill in this its final form, in direct comparison to the status quo. In a bicameral assembly, the second house then considers the proposal. The point of this extended lawmaking process, which may be expedited on occasion, is to open up the proposal to the assembly, improving and testing it until the moment when, in its final form, the legislators must choose whether the legislature should enact it. That is, the legislature deliberates because the laws that it enacts should be a response to reason.

Legislative deliberation also helps the legislature avoid cycles and make stable decisions. Legislators deliberate in public and so are more likely to make sincere judgments, acting strategically less often than would

---

[141] Mezey (n 119) 171–2; J Blondel et al, 'Legislative Behaviour: Some Steps towards a Cross-National Measurement', chapter 10 in P Norton (ed), *Legislatures* (Oxford University Press, Oxford, 1990), 186, 201.

[142] Mezey (n 119) 171–2.

otherwise be the case.[143] The reason for this is that there are penalties, in terms of reputation and capacity to form stable arrangements in the future, for deception. Further, there is some evidence that deliberation about common problems induces a greater cooperative disposition.[144] As I argued in section III of this chapter, deliberation in public narrows the range of possible argument, screening out arguments that plainly cannot withstand scrutiny, and forcing deliberators to appeal to the general rather than private interest.[145] Deliberation may uncover empirical errors that explain disagreement and prompt cycles. Alternatively, deliberation may disaggregate complex issues, identifying the multiple sub-issues in need of resolution.[146] It may be possible to decide these sub-issues without cycling; that is, once disagreement is sharpened, a stable majority may be found.[147] Finally, legislators who deliberate together may identify a cycle and act to avoid it, crafting a new proposal for action that differs from the initial, cycling alternatives and is thus stable.[148]

The Westminster and Washington legislatures are vulnerable to different pathologies. The Washington legislature has many veto-players, and has difficulty exercising its capacity to legislate in response to reasons. It may enact legislation that is not fit to be chosen by a reasoning person, because it is rendered incoherent by the various riders insisted on by veto-players. The Westminster legislature has a dominant party leadership, which may abuse its majority, forcing through measures without adequate deliberation or scrutiny. In this case, the leading legislators act like a cartel, failing to submit proposals to the assembly but instead forcing the assembly to rubber-stamp their decisions. It might seem then that in either case, but perhaps especially in parliamentary systems, legislative deliberation will not in truth be a serious reflection on the reasons for changing the law.

Hardin argues that an inevitable consequence of popular democracy is that legislative deliberation largely collapses to mere posturing,

---

[143] J Dryzek and C List, 'Social Choice Theory and Deliberative Democracy: A Reconciliation' (2003) 33 British Journal of Political Science 1.
[144] Dryzek and List (n 143) 9–10.
[145] Dryzek and List (n 143) 15; J Dryzek, *Discursive Democracy: Politics, Policy and Political Science* (Cambridge University Press, Cambridge, 1994), 54–5.
[146] Dryzek and List (n 143) 18; D Miller, 'Deliberative Democracy and Social Choice' in J Fishkin and P Laslett (eds), *Debating Deliberative Democracy* (Blackwell, Oxford, 2003), 182, 193.
[147] Dryzek and List (n 143) 19.
[148] Dryzek and List (n 143) 20–1.

because Congress is forced to wage a permanent electoral campaign.[149] He says that:

Deliberation often takes place to the side of the congressional main stage, in staff meetings and in expert panels convened to discover various things and to invent policy options. It is a subordinate activity and an activity that might take place as much in a nondemocratic polity in which the search for good policy is taken seriously.[150]

This conclusion may confound deliberative democrats, as Hardin intends,[151] but I take it to be consistent with the legislative assembly being structured to reason and act well. Not all deliberation has to be democratic to be justified: the detailed work of legislative committees and government departments, in close consultation with experts and interested parties, may not take place in the full glare of public scrutiny, but it remains valuable. It is true that the debates in plenary session, especially on questions of general interest rather than the detail of legislative proposals, may at times amount to straightforward campaigning, rather than active engagement in lawmaking. But there is no reason to think, from Hardin's argument, that this is inescapable, especially when, in parliamentary systems at least, the electoral fortunes of each legislator turn in large part on the coherence and competence of the government's policy programme rather than on his particular debating record.

Two spectacles mark parliamentary debate, argue Brennan and Hamlin: a legislator reading a speech to a deserted chamber or everyone shouting at someone who reads a speech.[152] This is unsurprising, they say, for 'in strong party systems: parliamentary debate is either a ritual or a continuation of campaigning by other means'.[153] The legislators do not listen to one another and no one changes their mind because the votes are already settled.[154] Debate cannot plausibly be thought as an attempt to change minds or votes, they say, because the latter are committed.[155] This analysis is, I suggest, mistaken.

---

[149] R Hardin, 'Deliberation: Method not Theory' in S Macedo (ed), *Deliberative Politics: Essays on Democracy and Disagreement* (Oxford University Press, Oxford, 1999), 103, 115.
[150] Hardin (n 149) 115.   [151] Hardin (n 149) 116.
[152] In fact, the practice of the House of Commons is to prohibit members from reading speeches (they may refer to notes) precisely because this frustrates debate.
[153] Brennan and Hamlin (n 2) 188.
[154] Brennan and Hamlin (n 2) 188.
[155] Brennan and Hamlin (n 2) 195.

Deliberation is not confined to plenary session and it need not be relentlessly partisan. Opposition legislators have good reason to aim to improve legislative proposals that are likely to pass in some form. Also, not all debates in plenary session focus on highly contentious partisan issues. The government often has no position on certain issues and is prepared to develop proposals in response to debate. Or, debate may concern change that most agree is needed in some form, with intelligent, constructive debate concerning precisely what form.

Further, Brennan and Hamlin effectively assume that every vote is a confidence vote. This is not so and the voting unity of the majority is accordingly not guaranteed. Majorities fracture and they fracture, sometimes at least, in response to reasons and arguments. Legislators may view debate in the chamber just as a continuation of the electoral campaign, but they may, and should I argue, often participate in serious argument, attacking or defending the merits of some proposed solution.[156] Legislative debate can and should sometimes have this character. Finally, legislators may direct their argument in the assembly towards the voting public, but it would be unwise to assume this did not have a direct feedback to the actions of legislators. If legislators win the argument outside the assembly, this may, and sometimes should, prompt the unified voting majority to reconsider its position, modifying or changing its proposals. Again, it is overly hasty to take party alignment or unity to entail that legislators do not respond to reasons and that deliberation is necessarily an empty dance.

There are very good reasons to authorize an assembly to legislate, for an assembly is less likely than a sole legislator to misuse its authority, makes it possible for citizens to share in government, and is better placed than the sole legislator to legislate well. These reasons bear on who it is that should legislate, not what it is to legislate. The assembly should, like the prince, choose to change the law for good reasons. It is rightly a representative *and* deliberative body, in which the assembly's standing in relation to the community supports rather than frustrates its capacity

---

[156] I say 'often' rather than 'always' because campaigning is not unreasonable and sometimes an argument in the assembly is reasonably addressed not at one's opponents or even at the particular bill, but at more general political considerations (the government's reputation, for example) and the voting public.

to make reasoned choices. The assembly's size and diversity is a prima facie obstacle to its exercise of this capacity and the members of the assembly for this reason institute an internal hierarchy which supports coherent, reasoned joint action. There are real differences between the structure of Washington and Westminster legislatures, but both are capable of reasoned choice and the structure of the latter is especially suited to this end. The well-formed legislative assembly is thus an institution structured to choose for reasons.

7

Language Use and Intention

Many scholars argue that the legislature may act well, and that interpreters may respond reasonably to its act, without the legislature forming and acting on intentions, or at least intentions other than the minimal intention to enact the statutory text.[1] It is a central premise in these accounts that statutory texts (ordinarily) have a clear meaning that is open to legislators to identify if they want to know what they are enacting and which officials and citizens may identify to determine the meaning and legal effect of the statute. This meaning—Raz and Waldron argue—is a function of the legislature's use of a natural language to legislate. They take the conventions that constitute the relevant language, as well perhaps as interpretive conventions specific to a particular legal system, to settle the meaning of the particular instance of language use that is the statute.

I argue that these scholars here make a fundamental mistake about the nature of language and its implications for the relevance of legislative intent to the act of legislating and its legal meaning and effect. Philosophers of language have refuted the argument that conventions settle meaning and explain communication; instead, communicative action centres on the formation and expression of communicative intentions. The scholars' focus on the conventional meaning of statutory texts would frustrate rational legislating and render statutory

---

[1] In addition to the arguments set out in chapters 2 and 4, see also N Stoljar, 'Survey Article: Interpretation, Indeterminacy and Authority: Some Recent Controversies in the Philosophy of Law' (2003) 11 Journal of Political Philosophy 470, 476–7 and 'Is Positivism Committed to Intentionalism?' in T Campbell and J Goldsworthy (eds), *Judicial Power, Democracy and Legal Positivism* (Ashgate, Aldershot, 2000), 169–83; and H Hurd, 'Sovereignty in Silence' (1991) 99 Yale Law Journal 945.

interpretation arbitrary. The way in which language is used in general, and in legislating in particular, supports my argument in chapters 4 and 5 that the legislature must form and act on intentions if it is to legislate well or even acceptably.

I. The Language Code

Raz and Waldron, in different ways, each take statutory texts to have meanings apart from the intention of the legislature to convey a certain meaning. For Raz, the legislature intends (or rather, all the legislators intend) to enact the statutory text, with its conventional meaning. For Waldron, the assembly has no intention but acts to enact the particular provisions, with their plain or ordinary meaning.

Waldron explores the nature of language and its implications for legislating at two points in *Law and Disagreement*. The first of these is in chapter 4, after his argument that the diverse assembly is capable of deliberation only because its proceedings track a detailed text, which has a clear meaning that is the focus of argument and, in the end, voting.[2] Waldron observes that his line of argument is unlikely to persuade those who are sceptical about the determinacy of language and take words to be capable of bearing any meaning. However, he argues that law, for good reason, 'seeks to connect and associate itself as a social institution with another institution—the institution of natural language. In particular, it seeks to associate itself with *whatever interpersonal determinacy there may be in natural language communication*'.[3] He doubts that law or jurisprudence need adopt any particular account of the nature or grounds of this determinacy, and indeed he suggests that most legal philosophers are not competent to pick out a true or plausible account. What matters, he says, is that language seems to enable shared meanings, which may ground deliberative determinacy. How language enables shared meanings is not centrally important to legal philosophy. He puts the point this way:

We may not be able to say why the specification of a given set of signs, identified as meaningful in a natural language, answers certain purposes that may be associated ideally with the sharing of certain meanings; we may not

[2] *LD*, 77–82.   [3] *LD*, 82.

even be able to say much about what sharing a meaning is. But it is indisputable that law makes an investment of exactly this sort in the determinacy-resources of natural language (such as they are, and however they are explained).[4]

This reluctance to explore in detail how language works, Waldron sets aside in chapter 6 when he explains and defends the voting machine model. He notes that a common but mistaken reason to think that the legislature must form and act on intentions is that legislating is a speech act, which he equates with 'the production of a meaningful utterance or text', and so cannot be unintentional.[5] He says:

What is it after all to say 'No vehicle shall be permitted to enter any state or municipal park' but to utter a string of sounds with the intention to produce a certain effect or response in one's audience by virtue of their recognition of that very intention? Even if one were to eschew the idea of a single utterer for cases like this and concentrate just on the meaning of the sentence, it remains the case that our most plausible accounts of sentence-meaning make that notion a function (albeit a complex one) of individual intention.[6]

The first sentence ends with a footnote to Grice,[7] who argued that one acts to communicate by intending to convey a certain meaning, which is to be achieved by means of the person to whom one is speaking recognizing one's intention. The second sentence is not very clear. The claim seems to be that even apart from what a particular speaker may mean, the meaning of a sentence is constituted, somehow, by an individual's intention. It is mysterious who the individual is—it is not the utterer. It is possible that Waldron means to refer to the individual intentions of the many members of some linguistic community.

In any event, Waldron maintains that:

A legislator who votes for (or against) a provision like 'No vehicle shall be permitted to enter any state or municipal park' does so on the assumption that—to put it crudely—what the words mean to him is identical to what they will mean to those to whom they are addressed (in the event that the provision

---

[4] LD, 83.
[5] He thanks Raz for bringing this point to his attention: LD, 128, n 30.
[6] LD, 128-9.
[7] H P Grice, *Studies in the Way of Words* (Harvard University Press, Cambridge, MA, 1989).

THE LANGUAGE CODE 183

is passed). He can entertain that assumption only on condition that there is a community in which it is well known that members of the community commonly use such words to produce a certain effect or response in their audience by virtue of the audience's recognition of that very intention.[8]

At the end of this sentence, a footnote refers us again to Grice and also back to his own earlier discussion,[9] which I considered above. He continues:

That such assumptions pervade the legislative process shows how much law depends on language, on the shared conventions that constitute a language, and on the reciprocity of intentions that conventions comprise. But though they indicate a place for referring to intentions—the intentions of language-users as such—in any comprehensive account of what is going on, they provide no warrant for the view that, simply because a particular piece of legislation has a linguistic meaning, it must embody a particular intention attributable to a language-user.[10]

The first sentence of this extract ends with a footnote, observing that 'Legislation may also rely on certain quasi-linguistic conventions common to legislative draftsmen and the legal/judicial community'.[11] (In the footnote, Waldron thanks Raz for this point.)

There is a striking shift in emphasis across the extracts reproduced above. From an initial, apparently uncontroversial and approving reference to Grice and the centrality of intention, Waldron introduces the assumption that certain words ('such words' he says) are commonly used to produce a certain response. That response is said to be produced by 'the audience's recognition of that very intention'. It is unclear to what intention Waldron refers, unless it is the intention to use words to produce the response that those words are commonly used to produce. The final extract completes the shift from the intention of a particular speaker to the understanding of the community. For now, the legislator's assumption appears to be simply that linguistic conventions apply, and the only intentions that are now understood to be relevant to meaning are those that constitute the conventions. In other words, Waldron has moved from the speaker's intentions—Grice's focus—to the set of the intentions of language users over

---

[8] *LD*, 129.
[9] *LD*, 129, n 32.   [10] *LD*, 129.   [11] *LD*, 129, n 33.

time, which he asserts constitute convention. He then takes the existence of the latter to mean that one need not find the former for a statute (or, presumably, any text) to have a linguistic meaning.

Later, Waldron explains linguistic meaning. Having argued that the legislature produces statutes, acting formally on certain texts, but not forming intentions that go beyond that formal action, he says that we should 'abandon all talk of legislative intentions apart from the intentionality that is part and parcel of the linguistic meaning (i.e. the conventional or, in Gricean terms, "sentence-meaning") of the legislative text itself'.[12] It is not quite clear what Waldron means when he says that intentionality is part and parcel of linguistic (conventional, sentence) meaning. This may be a reference back to his earlier claim, as well as to aspects of Grice's work, that sentence meaning may somehow be reducible to the intentions of many speakers.[13] He spells out the conclusion when he says that the legislature's only intention is 'that such-and-such words were used with their conventional English meaning'.[14] The availability of conventional meanings, he implies, makes it possible for a text to have a meaning without any need to refer to the intentions of a particular person using that language (the author). Therefore, Waldron concludes, the legislature may act on that conventional meaning without forming any more particular intentions. This argument leaves open, I suggest, the possibility that a particular person using language might form an intention to convey a meaning that goes beyond or departs from the conventional meaning. The implication, however, is that this would be a non-standard, unusual instance of language use. And certainly, no reference to a particular language user's intention is needed to ground meaning or indeed communication.

Waldron's final conclusion is very similar to Raz's minimal intention thesis, which states that the legislature must act on the intention to change the law, if legislating is to be intelligible, but that this intention has no practical relevance.[15] The meaning of the statute that the legislature intends to enact, Raz argued, is settled by how the text is understood in accordance with prevailing interpretive conventions.

The minimal intention of the legislature, Raz says, is that which is shared by each legislator, namely: 'an intention that the text of the Bill on which he is voting will—when understood as such texts, when

---

[12] *LD*, 142.   [13] Grice (n 7) 117–37.   [14] *LD*, 143.
[15] See the discussion in chapter 4, section VI.

promulgated in the circumstances in which this one is promulgated, are understood in the legal culture of this country—be law'.[16] The reference to the circumstances of promulgation, Raz observes in an accompanying footnote, is vital because '[t]he law is—so to speak—the meaning of the utterance in a specific context, rather than of a text devoid of context'.[17]

Raz argues that the legislators (and thus, for him, the legislature) cannot intend anything other than to enact the statutory text as it is understood per prevailing convention. It would be irrational to do otherwise—the legislators know that what they enact will be understood in this way, and so they could not rationally intend the text to be understood in any other way. Raz imagines a legislator who might be tempted to intend that the statutory text for which he votes be understood in accordance with the mystic code for interpreting sacred texts of his religion.[18] The legislator would not be rational in forming that intention because he knows that the text will not be understood in this way and one cannot intend what one knows to be impossible. Raz argues that the legislator could make it the case that the mystic code is used to interpret his lawmaking acts. However, to do so, the legislator would have to express an intention to that effect (to change the content of the conventions that settle how the legislator's lawmaking acts are to be interpreted) and he may only do so by conforming to the conventions that are presently in force.

The structure of this thought-experiment is telling—Raz does not imagine a legislator intending to convey a particular meaning but instead a legislator intending to adopt an alternative set of conventions to settle the meaning that his act shall have. That is, Raz understands the meaning of a text to be settled by the relevant conventions, never by the intention on which the author acts, because the rational author is unable to express an intention except in conformity to prevailing convention. He makes the point explicit:

In the cycle of convention and intention, convention comes first. Not in the sense that we follow convention rather than intention, but in the sense that the content of any intention is that which it has when interpreted by reference to the conventions of interpreting such expressive acts at the

---

[16] Raz, *BAI*, 284. [17] Raz, *BAI*, 284, n 20. [18] Raz, *BAI*, 286.

time. And that is the case even with regard to an intention which, once expressed, changes these conventions.[19]

The priority of convention, Raz takes to be common to language use in general as well as to law. He argues that the relationship 'between what people mean (ie intend to say) and what they say ... is that they mean to say what they said'.[20]

Raz notes various cases (the list is not exhaustive) in which people say what they do not mean and mean to say other than what they say. The cases are all instances of failure on the part of the speaker or author, arising out of linguistic ignorance, physical impairment, or confusion of thought.[21] The possibility of these cases does not entail, he argues:

> ... that when we speak we first intend to say something and then attempt to say it, so that it is always an open question whether one said what one intended. Rather, barring exceptions, like those listed, one means what one says. There is no more to having meant to say *p* than that one said that *p* and none of the exceptions obtain.[22]

It follows, Raz concludes, that 'the normal way of finding out what a person intended to say is to establish what he said. The thought that the process can be reversed mistakes the exceptional case, in which action misfires and one fails to say what one tries to say, for the normal case'.[23] In law, interpreters should 'understand the legislation as meaning what the legislator said. What the legislator said is what his words mean, given the circumstances of the promulgation of the legislation, and the conventions of interpretation prevailing at the time'.[24]

Raz never makes explicit what it is to say anything, but the structure of his argument and his explanation for how the meaning of the statutory text is settled by convention, implies that to say something is to express the meaning that the relevant conventions ascribe to the words that one uses. The mystic code example implies, as does the reference to different conventions prevailing at different times,[25] that the conventions are conventions of interpretation not just of word meaning and may differ between law and ordinary social life, as well as amongst legal systems.

---

[19] Raz, *BAI*, 286.
[20] Raz, *BAI*, 286.   [21] Raz, *BAI*, 286–7.   [22] Raz, *BAI*, 287.
[23] Raz, *BAI*, 288.   [24] Raz, *BAI*, 288.   [25] Raz, *BAI*, 288–9, n 25.

It is not at all implausible to think that conventions are of central importance to language; the seemingly arbitrary differences amongst natural languages suggest that they are, at least in part, sets of conventions. However, Raz's 'conventions-settle-all' account is very thinly made out. He gives no examples of an interpretive convention, in law or ordinary life. The rules that stipulate grammar and word-meaning are conventions in his sense, yet they would not suffice for Raz's purposes: the set of conventions that he needs for his argument to be sound has to be comprehensive, so that nothing apart from conventions settles meaning. At this point, the question of how context relates to convention becomes acute. Presumably, Raz understands some or all conventions to be context-specific, so that their application is contingent on certain features of the circumstances in which the particular instance of language use occurs. Yet, Raz does not explain how context bears on how conventions settle what was said. Raz's recognition of the importance of context, which by definition is particular, seems to undercut his general reliance on conventions, which are universal rules. It is certainly plausible to suggest that context and convention are both relevant to meaning, but it is critical to explain how each relates to the other and how in turn both constitute meaning.

The argument that one cannot intend to mean anything other than what one says, which is what conventions ascribe to one's words (relative to context, somehow), has a suffocating logic. In one sense, Raz has gone well beyond Waldron, who was content to argue that the words one adopts have a conventional meaning apart from one's specific intentions in using them in this instance. Raz's conclusion is that it is irrational, because impossible, to intend to convey a meaning other than what one's words say. The conclusion begs several important questions. First, it asserts that one may not express an intention to convey a meaning other than that which convention attaches to one's words, perhaps by flouting convention in a way that makes clear one's intention. Non-literal meanings (or at least non-conventional meanings) would be unintelligible on this analysis.

Second, Raz's conclusion assumes that the set of conventions is exhaustive and formal—algorithmic almost—so that the application of the many conventions generates an answer.[26] Raz does not ask what

---

[26] See L Alexander and E Sherwin, *Demystifying Legal Reasoning* (Cambridge University Press, Cambridge, 2008), 200–4 on 'The Algorithmic Textualist'.

meanings are open, and thus what speakers may intend to convey, when it is, and is known to be, the case that the conventions leave open multiple possibilities or are otherwise inconsistent. His argument was that the speaker cannot but intend what convention dictates. He seems to assume that the set of conventions does not leave open possibilities, and does not involve interpretive judgment, rather than rule-application—for in either of these cases the speaker may rationally intend to mean something other than what he says. And interpretive judgment would then rightly go to the question of what he intended to convey. Third, Raz assumes that the conventions do not refer to the intention of the language user. That is, he understands the conventions to constitute a comprehensive, self-contained code, when it may be that certain conventions are understood by those who introduce and use them to help identify—to be defeasible by reference to, and certainly not to settle decisively—the intention of the speaker in this or that particular instance.

Schauer has a similar understanding of language, for which he argues in more detail than either Raz or Waldron. Aiming to explain how it is that rules do not collapse to their underlying justifications, he argues that instances of language use, including rule formulations, have acontextual meaning or semantic autonomy. He introduces the latter term in contrast to the idea that the meaning of language reduces to the purpose for which it is used on a particular occasion.[27] Schauer says that semantic autonomy is 'the ability of symbols—words, phrases, sentences, paragraphs—to carry meaning independent of the communicative goals on particular occasions of the users of those symbols'.[28] Different theorists, he argues, might ground semantic autonomy in rules of language, conventions, or socially determined reference.[29] I take these alternatives to be indistinguishable and it is clear that Schauer is not interested in the foundation for he goes on to say that its source is immaterial. What matters, he argues, is that 'there is at least something, call it what you will, shared by all speakers of a language that enables one speaker of that language to be understood by another speaker of that language even in circumstances in which the speaker and the understander share nothing in common but their mutual

---

[27] F Schauer, *Playing by the Rules: A Philosophical Examination of Rule-Based Decision-Making in Law and in Life* (Oxford University Press, Oxford, 1993), 55.
[28] Schauer (n 27).
[29] Schauer (n 27).

language'.[30] (I agree with Endicott that there are no such circumstances because one cannot share a language and nothing else.[31])

The term semantic autonomy entails that meaning is acontextual. Schauer qualifies this conclusion somewhat, arguing that the important point is that the meaning of a text, for example, is not wholly determined by the immediate context of its use.[32] He takes contextual understandings to be relevant to the meaning of what someone else has said but argues that 'some number of these contextual understandings, a number sufficient for communication to take place, are similarly understood by both speaker and listener just because they inhabit the same planet and speak the same language'.[33] He terms this subset of context *'universal context'* or *'baseline context'* and argues that it is invariant amongst members of, and thus partly constitutes a, linguistic community.[34] I take 'universal context' to be an oxymoron. However, the point of the term is clear: it is to insist that shared understandings constitute semantic meanings, which are thus not reducible to particular contexts or to the intentions of particular language users.

Semantic autonomy entails that any use of language has an acontextual meaning, which 'can also be called "literal" or "plain". It is often called "utterance meaning" as distinguished from "speaker's meaning"'.[35] Schauer offers two arguments for acontextual meaning. The first he frames as follows:

...the ability of one English speaker to talk to another about whom she knows nothing is the best proof of the fact that at a particular time *some* meaning exists that can be discerned through access only to those skills and understandings that are definitional of linguistic competence.[36]

Introducing semantic autonomy, Schauer set out two examples.[37] The first is his capacity to 'understand *some* of what is written in an Australian newspaper of 1836 and none of what might be written in Chinese in 1991', which is he says made possible by 'something located in the understandings about the uses of symbols that is not totally reducible to what a speaker might wish to communicate on a particular occasion'.[38]

---

[30] Schauer (n 27) 55–6.
[31] T Endicott, *Vagueness in Law* (Oxford University Press, Oxford, 2000), 19.
[32] Schauer (n 27) 56.
[33] Schauer (n 27) 57.   [34] Schauer (n 27) 57.   [35] Schauer (n 27) 58.
[36] Schauer (n 27) 58.   [37] Schauer (n 27) 56.   [38] Schauer (n 27) 56.

The second is his response to discovering a pattern of shells washed up on the beach in the shape of C-A-T, which is to think of certain small furry animals, despite the absence of any language user. Neither example is convincing. Endicott points out that there is a language user on the beach, namely Schauer himself.[39] As for the newspaper, Schauer begs the question when he says that he understands what is written without reference to what the particular language user meant in the immediate context of use. He may understand something, but precisely what is as yet unclear; it may well not be the meaning of the language use—that is, of the language as used by the writer of the 1836 article—when the nature of meaning is properly explicated.

The second argument is that any account of meaning that privileges immediate context or particular purpose is unstable and unsound because semantic autonomy is a necessary premise in successful communication. Schauer says that particular context enables speakers to communicate much more effectively than they would be able to if limited to acontextual meaning alone. Yet, he continues:

... the phenomenon of literal or plain meaning remains the foundation of linguistic communication, and a totally particularistic theory of meaning, under which the meaning of an utterance is completely a function of what that utterance is designed to accomplish on a particular occasion, cannot explain how it is that communication is possible. If the meaning of an utterance were entirely a function of how it was then used (as opposed to how the word is used within a language), it would be impossible to explain how meaning is conveyed, and why it is that we pick one word rather than another to serve a particular communicative task...[40]

This argument is confused. It is certainly plausible to think that communication involves conventions, and that much is shared by persons who speak the same language and yet are not party to the immediate context of a particular communication. However, that successful communication somehow involves conventions does not entail that literal or plain meaning is the foundation of communication, in the sense that particular communications are literal meanings plus immediate context. Proving that words and sentences have some meaning apart from the intentions with which persons use them on particular occasions

---

[39] Endicott (n 31) 18–19. [40] Schauer (n 27) 58.

does not establish how those meanings feature in acts of communication or that these meanings are sufficiently robust to articulate rules. That is, conventions may be indispensable but also quite incomplete.

Schauer's use of 'utterance' equivocates between 'a set of linguistic symbols arranged in a certain way' and 'some person's intentional communicative act on this occasion'. His argument is that the former does not reduce to the latter and that the latter assumes the former as its premise. The meaning of an utterance may turn in part on the conventional meaning of the words uttered, but this does not prove that the meaning of the utterance either is or even plausibly could be that conventional meaning. In no way does the importance of convention prove that the intentions of particular language users are not central to, or constitutive of, the meaning of any utterance.

I argued in section V of chapter 4 that Waldron's account of legislative action did not explain how reasonable legislators would be likely to understand the imaginary Vehicles in the Park Act. Like Waldron, legislators enacting that Act might reasonably understand s 1 to qualify the scope of s 2 even though neither section says this directly. That conclusion is inconsistent with the conventional meaning of the statutory text but might be justified by inferring why the legislature enacted both sections. I do not think Raz or Schauer fare any better in explaining that example. Waldron, Raz, and Schauer are likewise unable to explain how judges and legislators understand real statutes. Consider:

(1) Taxation of Chargeable Gains Act 1992, s 77(8): 'In this section "derived property" in relation to any property, means *income from that property or any other property* directly or indirectly representing proceeds of, or income from, that property or income therefrom'. (Emphasis added.)

The italicized words mean either: (a) income from that property OR income from any other property representing that property, or (b) income from that property OR any other property directly or indirectly representing proceeds from, or income of, that property, That is, (a) catches the extraction of value in the form of income but not capital, whereas (b) extends to both. The court concluded that (b) was the correct interpretation because to adopt (a) would be to ascribe to Parliament a capricious intention, for which there was no good reason and which would undermine the protection the section was intended to confer on the Revenue.[41] Ambiguity of this simple kind is fatal to the language code conception because the legislature cannot, on this account, intend to enact one of two or more alternative formulations.[42]

The problem is not just ambiguity. Consider the following example.

> (2) The statute of 7 Ed. 6 Cap. 1 provided in relevant part: '... if *any treasurer, receiver, or minister accountant*, or their deputy or deputies, do take or receive of any persons, any sums of money, or other profit of and for the payment of any fees, annuities, pensions, duties or warrants, more or otherwise than he or they may lawfully do by foreign laws and statutes therein then provided, that then the said treasurer, receiver, and minister so offending, shall forfeit or lose for every penny or pennyworth so to be taken or received 6s. 8d. to the party grieved to be recovered in any of the King's Courts of Record...'. (Emphasis added.)

The question is whether the statute makes liable one who is a receiver for certain manors, but who is not a receiver for the King. In *Stradling v Morgan*,[43] the court held that notwithstanding the generality of the italicized words,[44] in uttering this phrase Parliament 'intended the treasurers, receivers, and ministers of the King only, and of no other'.[45] There were very good reasons for this conclusion. The Act was to redress the abuses committed by the King's treasurers, receivers, and ministers in the course of administering pensions and annuities that had arisen out of the dissolution of the monasteries. Indeed, the present statute was the successor to a similar statute of Henry VIII's reign,[46] which had clearly applied only to the King's ministers. The present Act was entitled 'An Act for the true answering of the King's Revenues'. All the other parts of the Act concerned the King and his ministers '[a]nd the clauses before, speaking of the King's ministers, are an inducement to us to take the intent of the Legislature in the said clause above recited, to extend [only] to the King's ministers'.[47] Further, the phrase 'more or otherwise than he or they may lawfully do by foreign laws and statutes therein then

---

[41] Bennion, *BST*, 446, example 152.1; *West (Inspector of Taxes) v Trennery* [2005] UKHL 5, [2005] 1 All ER 827 at [10].

[42] W Eskridge, 'The Circumstances of Politics and the Application of Statutes' (2002) 100 Columbia Law Review 558, 565–7.

[43] (1560) 1 Plowd 199, 75 ER 305; for helpful discussion, see J Evans, *Statutory Interpretation: Problems of Communication* (Oxford University Press, Oxford, 1988), 154–6.

[44] (1560) 1 Plowd 199, 75 ER 305 at 311.

[45] (1560) 1 Plowd 199, 75 ER 305 at 312.

[46] The statute of 33 H. 8.

[47] (1560) 1 Plowd 200, 75 ER 305 at 312.

provided' (the court held 'foreign' here had to be taken in the sense of 'former') was significant for only the King's ministers could by any former law or statute receive any sum for the payment of any fees, annuities, pensions, duties, or warrants. The court held that the meaning of this phrase made clear that in saying 'any treasurer', Parliament intended to mean ministers of the King only.

The arguments for the language code are very weak. Waldron's account is the most plausible, because he does not claim that it would be irrational for speakers to intend anything other than the conventional meaning of the words and sentences they employ. Raz and Schauer do advance this more ambitious claim, yet the most that their arguments make out is that conventions are important in language use. Both scholars reach radical conclusions about the nature of language by means of faulty logic about rational communicative action and without determining whether conventions in fact explain (exhaustively or even sufficiently) how persons use language.

II. Language Use Is Rational Action

Persons use language to communicate with one another, that is, to express their thoughts and to convey and request information. The question for the theorist is how persons are able to achieve so much by uttering sounds and inscribing marks. Part of the answer must be that members of a linguistic community share conventions, specifically rules that ascribe meaning to particular words and that settle how words may be combined to form grammatical sentences. These rules—semantics and syntax—are somewhat arbitrary, varying widely amongst natural languages.[48] Bach argues that '[s]emantics is the part of grammar that pairs forms with meanings' and that 'the meaning of a sentence is determined compositionally by the meaning of its constituents as a function of its syntactic structure'.[49] The literal meaning or meanings of a sentence is or are settled by semantics (in which I include syntax) and is or are thus transparent to any competent language user.

---

[48] It is quite likely that certain aspects of syntax and semantics are common to natural languages by reason of our shared biology. That is, the conventional structure of a natural language is not altogether arbitrary.

[49] K Bach, 'Minding the Gap', chapter 3 in C Bianchi (ed), *The Semantics/Pragmatics Distinction* (CSLI Publications, Stanford, 2004), 27, 28.

A person may convey information to another without language use. For example, one may light a flare to indicate one's presence and need for rescue, or wave a weapon and roar loudly to warn an intruder to depart. Success in these cases turns on making clear to the other person why one is acting. The possibility of this form of interaction is interesting: the way in which it proceeds suggests that one conveys information by making one's intention known. However, this is not language use because the person does not employ or exploit linguistic conventions. A person uses language when he employs sentences, with semantic content, to convey what he means to another.

The complexity, stability, and importance of linguistic conventions may mislead the theorist who aims to explain language use. It is possible to isolate sentences and their semantic properties and to study them in relative abstraction from their use by particular persons. This study may yield insights into semantics or, possibly, formal logic. However, the abstraction is a technical stipulation, adopted to advance certain kinds of scholarly work, and does not entail that the meaning of particular instances of language use is or may be settled by convention. Perhaps Raz and Schauer are right and convention exhausts what a person may rationally mean in uttering a certain sentence. The truth of that conclusion turns on its capacity to explain rational language use. Therefore, a theory of language use and meaning should focus on what it is that a rational speaker (or author) does when he uses language and how his hearer (or reader) understands what it is that he does.

I argue that the use of language is an act, which means that it is undertaken for reasons. What defines the communicative act is a certain type of intention, namely the speaker's intention to convey something—that is, some more or less particular meaning—to his audience by means of the recognition of that very intention with its particular meaning-content. The intention is thus reflexive. For the communication to succeed, the audience must identify and understand the speaker's intention including its highly particular meaning-content, which the speaker intends the audience to identify.

It is quite clear that a speaker may intend to convey something other than what he says. One way in which this might happen, Grice argued, was when a speaker says one thing, but intends thereby to communicate something different or additional. This phenomenon he termed conversational implicature.[50] Imagine that a philosophy professor

---

[50] Grice (n 7) 30–7.

writing a reference for a student applying for an academic position in philosophy utters the following sentence (which is the one evaluative statement in the letter):[51]

(3) John is polite and speaks excellent English.

What he has said is that John is polite and speaks excellent English, but he has implicated that John is not a good philosopher. The semantic content of (3) does not state the latter proposition, which is instead conveyed by the author's act of uttering it. What the professor intends to convey in uttering (3) is that John is not a good philosopher.[52] He acts on an intention to convey this proposition, but does not assert it directly. Instead, the proposition is implicated by what he has done; his intention in uttering (3) is to make it clear without having to state it. The implication succeeds, and the professor conveys what he means, if the reader grasps his intention to this effect. It is not irrational for the professor to form this intention because the reader is likely to think that he must have meant something other than what he said. The professor would not say what is on its face irrelevant, and neglect to address what is relevant, namely John's philosophical acumen, unless he intended to convey something other than what he said, and the proposition in question is, the reader will judge, likely to be what the professor meant.

The observation that a speaker may implicate a meaning that differs from the linguistic meaning of the sentence he utters has significant consequences. It entails that to understand some person's act of language use, that is, to identify what he means, one must attempt to identify the communicative intention on which he acts, which may be an intention to convey something other than the linguistic meaning of the sentence. The meaning of a particular act of language use, on this approach, just is the meaning that the speaker intends to convey. The speaker may intend a non-literal or figurative meaning, rather than the literal sentence meaning. He may also intend indexical terms to have a fixed reference, so that he intends 'he' or 'this' or 'here' to refer to certain objects. Further, when a sentence has more than one linguistic meaning its literal content is ambiguous. In this case, what the speaker

---

[51] Grice (n 7) 33.
[52] He may also mean that John is polite and speaks excellent English, but he need not mean this, despite it being the literal meaning of the sentence.

means may be the particular literal meaning that he intends to convey, unless the ambiguity is intentional.

Grice argued that rational communicative action is framed by 'the Cooperative Principle', which directs the speaker to '[m]ake your conversational contribution such as is required, at the stage at which it occurs, by the accepted purpose or direction of the talk exchange in which you are engaged'.[53] This framing principle is specified by way of four maxims: quantity, quality, relevance, and manner.[54] The maxims, while framed by Grice as directives for speakers, are better understood to inform how hearers judge what it is that the speaker intended to communicate.[55]

III. The Underdetermination Thesis

It may seem that implicature or figurative or non-literal meanings, while possible, are exceptions to the norm, which is that what the speaker means in uttering a sentence is just the literal meaning of that sentence. This is not the case. The semantic content of a sentence underdetermines what a speaker may mean, and indeed what he is likely to mean, in uttering that sentence. There is a very strong line of argument in the philosophy of language in support of this conclusion. Bach's summary is instructive:

> ... the meaning of a typical sentence, at least one we are at all likely to use, is impoverished, at least relative to what we are likely to mean in uttering it. In other words, what a speaker *normally* means in uttering a sentence, even without speaking figuratively or obliquely, is an enriched version of what could be predicted from the meaning of the sentence alone. This can be because the sentence expresses a 'minimal' (or 'skeletal') proposition or even because it fails to express a complete proposition at all.
>
> Indeed, it is now a platitude that linguistic meaning generally underdetermines speaker meaning. That is, generally what a speaker means in

---

[53] Grice (n 7) 26.
[54] Grice (n 7) 26–7.
[55] K Bach, 'Context *ex Machina*', chapter 1 in Z Szabó (ed), *Semantics vs. Pragmatics* (Oxford University Press, Oxford, 2005), 15, 19.

uttering a sentence, even if the sentence is devoid of ambiguity, vagueness, or indexicality, goes beyond what the sentence means.[56]

The same point is made by Neale, who sets out:

The Underdetermination Thesis: What *A says* by uttering an unambiguous, declarative sentence *X* on a given occasion is underdetermined by *X*'s syntax, the meanings [of all] the words (and any other morphemes) in *X* (and the meanings, if any, of prosodic features of *X*), and the assignment of references to any referring expressions in *X*.[57]

This thesis, he argues, is widely held.[58] The point is that the semantic content of a sentence is not capable of settling what a speaker means in uttering that sentence.

If a sentence is ambiguous, what a speaker is likely to mean in uttering the sentence is not settled by its literal meaning. Very many words have multiple meanings—bank (raised portion of ground, bench or platform, counter of money-changer, to border, to act as a banker), pen (hill, enclosure, writing instrument, female swan, prison, to enclose, to develop feathers, to stink), painter (one who paints, nautical rope, cougar), prune (fruit of plum, dark purple colour, preen, cut back).[59] Where a sentence features an ambiguous word (or phrase) the sentence is ambiguous between at least two alternative formulations. A speaker is likely to mean only one of the alternative word or phrase meanings, which hearers aim to identify. That is, the semantic content of the sentence does not settle what it is that the speaker means in using the sentence. The same will be true where the ambiguity is a function of grammar rather than words or phrases. Likewise, while a speaker may intend to be vague and/or ambiguous (riddling), he may also adopt a sentence the literal meaning of which is vague, while intending to convey a more specific meaning.

Speakers may utter sentences that are not grammatical, and so which lack a literal meaning composed from their word-meanings assembled

---

[56] Bach (n 55) 15–16; see also S Soames, *Philosophical Essays, Volume 1: Natural Language: What It Means and How We Use It* (Princeton University Press, Princeton, 2008), 278–83, especially the literature survey at n 1.

[57] S Neale, 'Pragmatism and Binding', chapter 5 in Z Szabó (ed), *Semantics vs. Pragmatics* (Oxford University Press, Oxford, 2005), 165, 193.

[58] Neale (n 57), 193–4, n 40.

[59] This is a short paraphrase of the relevant entries in the OED. For an intriguing study of the ways in which the meanings of words develop, and proliferate, over time, see C S Lewis, *Studies in Words* (Cambridge University Press, Cambridge, 1960).

by syntactical rules, or that are not even sentences at all. These ungrammatical sentences or sentence fragments lack literal meaning, aside from the series of particular word-meanings, and yet may be uttered by a rational speaker seeking to convey what he means.

(4) Family Law Reform Act 1969, Sch 3 para 5(1)(a): 'any interest under an instrument'.

Interpreting this provision, the court noted that the relevant phrase was elliptical because there is no verb connecting 'interest' and 'under an instrument'.[60] The court concluded that the missing verb was 'arising' or 'existing' rather than 'created' or 'constituted'.

Further, not all grammatical, complete sentences express a complete proposition.

(5) Bob has finished.
(6) Police and Criminal Evidence Act 1984, s 10(2): 'Items held with the intention of furthering a criminal purpose are not items subject to legal privilege'.[61]

Sentence (5) is grammatical and yet does not express a complete proposition because it is silent on the object, what it is that Bob has finished. Therefore, the sentence, while grammatical is not what a speaker is likely to mean in uttering the sentence. Sentence (6) is grammatical and yet does not express a complete proposition because the sentence does not specify who holds the items. I return to both (5) and (6) below. It is plain that the semantic content of such sentences does not track or depend on what speakers ordinarily mean in uttering those sentences.

Even when ambiguity, indexicality and the like are set aside, and when one is addressing a complete, grammatical sentence, it is not necessarily the case that the speaker is likely to mean the literal meaning of the sentence he utters. True, he may mean the literal meaning, and true too, whatever meaning he in fact intends to convey could always be restated in literal sentences. However, my claim, following Bach, Neale, and Soames among others,[62] is not that sentence meaning is unintelligible, but that the semantic content of sentences is much thinner than ordinarily assumed. What we are likely to term the

---

[60] Bennion, *BST*, 493, example 173.13; *Begg-MacBrearty (Inspector of Taxes) v Stilwell* [1996] 1 WLR 951 at 958.
[61] Bennion, *BST*, 508, example 179.5.
[62] Soames (n 56) 278–326.

ordinary meaning of many sentences, which is the meaning that speakers are likely to intend to convey by means of that sentence, is not always or even often the literal meaning of those sentences. The semantic content of a sentence underdetermines what a speaker may mean or is likely to mean in uttering that sentence.

The semantic form of the following two sentences is identical:[63]

(7) I have two children.
(8) I have two beers in the fridge.

And yet the speaker is likely to mean by (7) I have exactly two children and by (8) I have at least two beers in the fridge. Yet it is no part of the semantics or syntax that the word 'two' in (7) means exactly two or in (8) means at least two. This is not implicature. The speaker does not say one thing and mean something quite different as in (3). What he is likely to mean, what he intends to assert and convey directly, is that he has exactly two children and at least two beers. This is also not a case of non-literal use. Every word in the sentence is used literally. Two literally means two, not exactly two, or at least two.

(9) Matrimonial Proceedings (Magistrates' Courts) Act 1960, s 2(1): an order may include: 'a provision that the husband shall pay *such* weekly sum as the court considers reasonable'. (Emphasis added.)

The court held that 'the word "such" is not limited to defining the amount of the weekly sum but carries with it an ability to qualify that sum in every relevant respect'.[64] That is, the court could vary the amount of the sum and the duration of payment, and, crucially for this case, could order variable amounts be paid for successive periods. However, it is conceivable that in another statute, 'such' might be used in a more limited sense.

The striking feature of sentences (7–9) is that the speaker uses a sentence literally but states or asserts more than what the sentence says. In one sense, it is true that sentences cannot say anything, because only persons say or imply anything. However, I adopt Bach's helpful terminology and confine 'say' to the literal meaning of a sentence, so that a sentence says its

---

[63] This pair of examples is taken from S Soames, *Philosophical Analysis in the Twentieth Century: The Age of Meaning* (Princeton University Press, Princeton, 2003), 211–12.

[64] F Bennion, *Bennion on Statute Law*, 3rd edn (Longman, Harlow, 1990), 232–3; *Khan v Khan* [1980] 1 WLR 355 at 359.

literal meaning, and to adopt the verbs 'state' or 'assert' for what a speaker conveys directly and the verb 'imply' for what he conveys indirectly.[65]

The gap between what the speaker states and what the sentence literally says is not confined to numbers or quantifiers. Multiple examples abound (the word or phrase in curly brackets is the further content that a speaker is likely to mean in uttering the sentence):[66]

- (10) I haven't had breakfast {today}.
- (11) John and Mary are married {to each other}.
- (12) They had a baby and they got married {in that order}.
- (13) Robin ate the shrimp and {as a result} got food poisoning.
- (14) Everybody {in our pragmatics class} solved the riddle.

The sentences are all used literally, so these are not cases of non-literal use. However, the meaning that a speaker is likely to intend to convey differs notably from the literal meaning of the sentence he utters. A speaker could intend just the literal meaning of what he says, but this is unlikely. In (10) the additional content specifies the temporal scope of the literal meaning. It does not follow that the literal meaning of the sentence is 'I have never had breakfast', which the speaker somehow qualifies to mean 'I haven't had breakfast today'. The literal meaning of the sentence is silent on when the subject has not had breakfast. The added content of (11) determines the relationship between the subjects of the sentence. In (12) it introduces a temporal order between the two events and in (13) what is introduced is a causal relation. Finally in (14), the additional content limits the scope of the assertion, from 'Everybody' to 'Everybody in our pragmatics class'.

There are many similar examples in statutes:[67]

- (15) Witnesses who attest 'any will or codicil {of real estate}' under which they are beneficiaries shall be treated as good witnesses, but the gifts made to them shall be void.
- (16) All drug shops 'shall be closed... at 10 pm on each and every day of the week {and shall stay closed until morning}'.
- (17) It is an offence to 'stab, cut or wound' any person {with a weapon or instrument}.

---

[65] Bach (n 55) 25–6 and Bach (n 49) 31, 33–4.
[66] All five are from L Horn, 'The Border Wars' in K Heusinger and K Turner (eds), *Where Semantics Meets Pragmatics* (Elsevier, Amsterdam, 2005), 21, 24.
[67] All four are from Bennion (n 64) 233–4.

(18) Every person who fraudulently harbours uncustomed goods shall forfeit a specified sum, 'and the offender {or apparent offender} may either be detained or proceeded against by summons'.

In (15), the words 'of real estate' were taken to be implied since, under the state of the law at the time of enactment, wills of personalty did not require attestation.[68] The sentence in (16) does not literally say that the shops must remain closed until morning, but this more detailed temporal condition is what the court takes the legislature to have used the sentence to state.[69] The added content in (17) limits the scope of the literal meaning, so that one does not commit the offence by biting off a person's nose.[70] Finally, in (18) the added content widens the scope of the section, for otherwise guilt would have to be conclusively determined before action could be taken.[71]

The meanings that speakers are likely to intend to convey are very often expansions and completions of the semantic content of the sentences they utter.

(19) I will be home later {tonight}.
(20) Bob has finished {the job}.

The speaker who utters (19) is likely to mean more than the proposition that the literal meaning of the sentence sets out. That is, what he intends is an expansion of that minimal proposition. The speaker who utters (20) completes what is otherwise an incomplete proposition, because it lacks an object. I pick out what it is likely that the speaker means but note that the speaker need not intend to convey the particular proposition that I have set out. A rational speaker may intend to convey a range of alternative possibilities, although the meaning he intends to convey has to be one that he thinks his audience will be able to identify. For example, a speaker might utter (19) intending to mean, and if successful being understood to mean, 'I will be home later this week' or 'I will be home at some indeterminate time' or 'I will certainly return'.

---

[68] *Brett v Brett* (1826) 3 Add 210.
[69] *R v Liggetts-Findlay Drug Stores Ltd* [1919] 2 WLR 1025.
[70] *R v Harris* (1836) 7 C & P 416.
[71] *Barnard v Gorman* [1941] AC 378; *Wiltshire v Barrett* [1966] 1 QB 312.

(21) Criminal Law Act 1967, s 3(1): 'A person may use such force {or threat of force} as is reasonable in the circumstances in the prevention of crime...'.[72]

(22) Police and Criminal Evidence Act 1984, s 10(2): 'Items held with the intention {of either the holder or any other person} of furthering a criminal purpose are not items subject to legal privilege'.[73]

The legislature that enacts (21) is likely to mean more than the proposition that the literal meaning sets out. The legislature that enacts (22) is likely to intend to convey a completion of the incomplete proposition that the literal meaning otherwise sets out. As with (19), the legislature might intend various completions. The court infers which completed proposition the legislature intended to convey.

The literal meaning of the sentence is sometimes a candidate for what the speaker may intend to mean, although often it will be too sparse and uninformative to be a proposition the speaker has good reason to convey. I have said that the words in (most of) the sentences above are used literally. The speaker could, of course, use one or more words non-literally, metaphorically, or figuratively, as well as expanding or completing the semantic content of the sentence.

(23) Offences against the Person Act 1861, s 57: 'whosoever, being married, shall marry any other person during the life of the former husband or wife...is guilty of a felony'.

A person who is already married cannot, in English law, marry. The section focuses exclusively on the case where a married person does 'marry'; therefore, the legislature is likely to intend 'marry' in (23) to mean 'go through the form and ceremony of marriage'.[74]

Neale terms all such cases compressions, because the speaker uses some word or phrase as if it were a compression of some larger formulation.[75] His term refers to the semantic content, which is a compression of what the speaker means, whereas I said above that what the speaker means may be an expansion or completion of that

---

[72] Bennion, *BST*, 555–6, example 197.10; *R v Cousins* [1982] QB 526 at 530.
[73] Bennion, *BST*, 508, example 179.5; *R v Central Criminal Court, ex p Francis & Francis* [1989] AC 346 at 381, 387, 397.
[74] Bennion (n 64) 232; *R v Allen* (1872) 1 CCR 367.
[75] S Neale, 'Textualism with Intent' (UCL-Oxford Colloquia, 18 November 2008) <http://www.ucl.ac.uk/laws/jurisprudence/docs/2008/08_coll_neale.pdf>, 30–1, 58–9.

semantic content. Thus the terms are consistent. He distinguishes two types of compression.

(24) I am a citizen {of New Zealand}.
(25) I assume everybody {in the auditorium} can hear me.

The compression in (24) is a semantic compression. That is, the literal meaning of citizen is incomplete. One cannot just be a citizen; one must be a citizen of some polity. And this is part of the meaning of the word. Therefore, the use of the word signals that it is a compression for what the speaker intends. The compression in (25) is not semantic but pragmatic. That is, no part of the literal meaning of (25) is incomplete. However, it would be odd indeed to ask if 'everybody' can hear. Instead, a speaker who utters that sentence is likely to mean 'everybody in the room' or some such. The word in question is a compression, just as citizen was, but the meaning of the word does not itself point to or require this conclusion. Expanding a compression is always a pragmatic task, because it is a matter of inference to the intention of the speaker, but semantics may make clear the need for such inference whereas in other cases the need is itself inferred.

(26) United States Code, Title 18, Part I, Chapter 44, s 924(c)(1): the section requires the imposition of specified penalties if the defendant 'during and in relation to any crime of violence or drug trafficking crime, uses {for any purpose} or carries a firearm'.[76]
(27) Malicious Damage Act 1861, s 2: 'Whoever shall unlawfully and maliciously set fire to any dwelling house, any person {other than the offender} being therein, shall be guilty of felony'.[77]

Interpreting (26), the US Supreme Court did not recognize that 'uses' is a semantic compression—one cannot just use something, it must be used to some end. The majority argued that the ordinary meaning of use meant any use whatsoever: in effect, they expanded the compression as indicated above. The minority, including Justice Scalia, argued that the ordinary meaning of use meant 'use as a firearm'. The better view, which the minority tracks, is that the legislature said 'uses' but stated 'uses as a weapon'. The compression in (27) is pragmatic. The

---

[76] Neale (n 75) 69–83; *Smith v United States* 508 US 223 (1993).
[77] See D N MacCormick, *Legal Reasoning and Legal Theory* (Clarendon Press, Oxford, 1978), 180 and Evans (n 43) 158–9; *R v Arthur* [1968] 1 QB 810.

literal meaning of (27) is complete, but there are reasons to infer that the legislature intends a narrower proposition. This example is less stark than (25). It would not be senseless for the legislature to intend 'person' to include the offender, but it would be odd. On this interpretation, the section would draw an arbitrary distinction between cases in which the offender sets fire to the house from within or outside it and the likely reason for a distinct offence—punishing those who maliciously endanger others—is absent when the offender is the only person in the house. Again, in both cases, the interpreter expands the compression by inference to intention.

Bach terms the content that a speaker asserts in uttering a sentence, to the extent that it departs from the literal meaning of the sentence, an impliciture, to be contrasted with Grice's implicature.[78] The latter is to say (or state) one thing and mean another. An impliciture, by contrast, is to state more than one says. The content that one intends to convey is implicit in, rather than read off, the fact that one utters the relevant sentence. Soames introduces the term 'pragmatic enrichment' to refer to impliciture.[79] He uses this term to note that the speaker relies on pragmatic facts to adopt and convey a meaning beyond the limited semantic content of the sentence that he utters.

The upshot is that semantics underdetermines the meanings that speakers are likely to or may intend to convey when they utter a sentence. The literal meaning of most sentences is narrower and thinner than the meaning that speakers typically intend to convey in uttering them. The semantic content of a sentence is a skein of meaning, which speakers complete and expand, or use non-literally or to ground implicature, to convey what they mean. The semantic content is a major part of the information that is open to hearers, which speakers in turn exploit. Thus, 'a semantic theory for a language *L* will provide, for each sentence *X* of *L*, a *blueprint* for (a *template*, a *schematic* or *skeletal* representation of) what someone will be taken to be saying when using *X* to say something'.[80]

It is difficult to see how limited semantic content is in part because we often assume that literal meaning explains typical use, so that semantics must explain our intuitions about what a sentence means. The problem is that we are very good at making ourselves understood

---

[78] K Bach, 'Conversational Impliciture' (1994) 9 Mind & Language 124.
[79] Soames (n 56) 278–9.
[80] Neale (n 57) 189.

and at understanding others and this leads to faulty intuitions about semantic content. Neale argues that in fact we have no intuitions about what sentences mean in context but only about what speakers mean in uttering sentences.[81] Likewise, Bach argues that our intuitions about sentence meaning are misleading for they focus on typical cases and trade on pragmatic regularities.[82] This focus obscures the gap between, and often conflates, the literal content and what speakers mean. Yet when one looks closely at semantic content it turns out to be much thinner than one is inclined to assume.

IV. Pragmatics

A speaker conveys the meaning he intends by uttering a sentence with a certain semantic content. The speaker utters that sentence (or sentence fragment) to make clear his intention to convey a certain meaning to his audience. He intends the audience to identify his intention by inferring it from the fact that he utters this sentence at this time. The meaning he intends to convey could be said explicitly, perhaps in a lengthy, complex sentence. However, it is not the case that the speaker first selects that lengthy sentence and then cuts it down to a shorter form, which he then utters, leaving the rest of the lengthy sentence unsaid.[83] Instead, a speaker intends to mean X and utters a sentence that he thinks will make X clear. Likewise, hearers need not focus on the semantic content of the sentence and then infer that X must have been meant. They may do so, but very often will leap directly to the conclusion that X was meant. The literal meaning does not have to be actively entertained to convey one's meaning by uttering that sentence, or to understand what another intends to convey. It does not follow that semantic content is unimportant. The shared knowledge of linguistic information frames the reasoning that is involved in forming and inferring communicative intentions.

Hearers understand speakers, primarily, not by decoding the linguistic information associated with the sentence they utter but by inference about what was intended. The meaning that was intended includes what if anything the speaker implicates and what he states. Identifying

---

[81] Neale (n 57) 183–4, 201, n 50.
[82] Bach (n 55) 29–32.
[83] Bach (n 55) 27–8; Bach (n 49) 30–1.

what a speaker means in an utterance is always a pragmatic exercise, because, as argued above, even if he means to convey the semantic content of the sentence he utters, this is because that is his intention.[84] The subject of semantics is sentences; the subject of pragmatics is utterances, which is to say what speakers do in uttering sentences. What a speaker means by uttering some sentence is a pragmatic fact, not a semantic fact. It is a fact about his intention, which hearers aim to identify. Pragmatic facts about what a speaker intends do not change the semantic content of that which is uttered.[85] The capacity of hearers to determine the meaning that a speaker intends to convey is a pragmatic capacity, a subset of our general capacity to perceive the reasons for, and thus the intentions on, which other persons act.[86]

The Gricean maxims are relevant to the pragmatic exercise of inferring what a speaker intends to convey, but they do not stipulate the pragmatic fact of what a speaker means. While Grice frames 'his maxims as guidelines for how to communicate successfully... they are better construed as presumptions about speaker's intentions'.[87] That is, one should think of the maxims not as a set of rules for how speakers should choose their words, but rather as some standard dimensions of rational action and thus presumptions about intention. Taken to be rules they are inconsistent. However, as presumptions about what is intended, 'they provide different dimensions of considerations for the hearer to take into account in figuring out the speaker's communicative intention', which in turn means they 'ground strategies for a speaker, on the basis of what he says and the fact that he says it, to make what he means evident to the hearer and for the hearer to figure out what the speaker means in saying what he says'.[88] The presumptions may fail: the speaker may be lying, or joking, or recklessly or daringly opining, and so forth.

It is implicit in what I have said, but it is worth making explicit, as Neale does,[89] that communication is asymmetric. The speaker knows what he means because what he means is what he intends to mean.[90] The hearer aims to identify what he means. Having said this, communicative action is a cooperative exercise, where the speaker aims to be understood and the hearer aims to understand.[91] Therefore, the rational speaker is standardly very concerned to utter sentences that

---

[84] Neale (n 57) 190–2.
[85] Bach (n 49) 34–5.   [86] Bach (n 49) 188–9.   [87] Bach (n 55) 19.
[88] Bach (n 55) 19.   [89] Neale (n 57) 179–80.
[90] Neale (n 57) 181, 183.   [91] Neale (n 57) 178.

will make it clear to the hearer, given what is open to the hearer to infer about the speaker and what he is likely to mean, what he in fact means. That is, while asymmetric, communication is reciprocal and feedback is central. The speaker cannot intend the impossible and therefore his communicative intentions are subject to the very important limit that they must take into account what it would be possible for a reasonable hearer (this hearer, if he acts reasonably) to grasp about what the speaker means.[92] It may be, of course, that speakers sometimes or often make mistakes and form communicative intentions that their hearers cannot grasp. In this case, communication fails. However, the rationality of communication does place important limits on what one may intend and this, in turn, grounds the response by hearers to the speaker's action. We judge what is intended by taking into account all that is relevant to rational, reciprocal exchange. Therefore, any information available from our knowledge of the world, this speaker in particular, persons in general, or prior conversation, informs our judgment of what the speaker intended to convey on this occasion.

The semantic content of a sentence provides the linguistic contribution to the pragmatic exercise of inferring what the speaker meant. If this is right, explaining our capacity to communicate requires work in the philosophy of mind as well as the philosophy of language. I cannot attempt an explanation, but will note the following. Much attention has been paid to how hearers infer what speakers mean, but we have little idea how speakers form intentions.[93] It is striking that people simply utter sentences that they expect to convey what they mean; this is an astonishing capacity. There is plainly a close connection between language use and reason, with the exercise of the latter arising with, or at least being greatly sharpened by, competence in the former.[94] Persons convey and understand meaning by inference to intention, rather than by deciphering codes, and it may be that a similar structure obtains in the mind.[95] That is, reasoning may be largely informal and inferential rather than rule-driven and algorithmic. The collapse of the code theory of language removes what would otherwise be a convenient analogy to a computational model of the mind. While induction in

---

[92] Neale (n 57) 180–3, 185.   [93] Bach (n 55) 20, n 11.
[94] J McDowell, *Mind and World*, rev edn (Harvard University Press, Cambridge, MA, 1996), 124–6, 184–6 and M Dummett, *The Seas of Language* (Oxford University Press, Oxford, 1993), 166–87.
[95] D Hodgson, *The Mind Matters: Consciousness and Choice in a Quantum World* (Clarendon Press, Oxford, 1991), Part II 'Against Mechanism', 97–196.

language may be a precursor to sound reasoning, advances in thought outpace language, and novel reasoning extends the boundaries of the language;[96] Bach's coining of the term 'impliciture' is an example of this.[97] There is frequently no need to make one's thought explicit, but it is important that the semantic content of sentences is capable of being employed to make explicit what one thinks. This capacity to employ semantic content, even if seldom exercised, enables precise formulation and articulation of thought.

I have not said much about context save to note that hearers infer what a speaker intends to convey from the fact that he uttered this sentence in this context. An obvious response to my account is to argue that what a sentence or an utterance means is its semantic content relative to context. That is, the gap between literal meaning and what a sentence is ordinarily taken to mean is filled by context rather than by the pragmatic fact of what speakers are likely to mean. It is important to be clear about what one means by context. The claim that context constitutes meaning becomes apparently more plausible the more detail it is taken to include. The context of any act of communication is the set of features of the situation that are salient to both speaker and hearer. These features have an important place in framing the rationality of language use, but they leave room for the open formation of communicative intentions. The context is relevant to what a speaker is likely to mean, but it does not settle what he or his sentence means. His sentence has a semantic content that does not vary by context. He means what he intends to mean, although the context will inform what it would be reasonable for him to mean.

The examples I have outlined throughout this chapter confirm, I think, that context does not settle meaning. The context grounds inference as to what the speaker intends. Recall examples (1) and (2). In (1), the interpreter took the legislature to intend one alternative when the literal meaning was ambiguous. The interpreter reasoned that this alternative was consistent with what the legislature was likely to have intended in enacting this section, because of the impractical and indeed capricious consequences of the other alternative and the apparent objective the legislature otherwise sought in enacting this section. The interpreter inferred what the legislature meant in context, but context did not stipulate what was meant. In (2), the interpreter concluded that the legislature intended to convey a meaning narrower than the literal

[96] Dummett (n 94) 173.
[97] Bach (n 78).

meaning of the words it uttered: specifically, that only the King's receivers were liable. The court reasoned from the mischief, from the title and other parts of the Act, and from another part of the provision itself, to the conclusion that the Parliament was very likely to have intended to speak only of the King's receivers. The mode of reasoning demonstrated in these cases, and very many others, is pragmatic inference to intention, not 'application' of context to produce or generate some meaning.

It is not at all surprising that context does not complete or modify the limited semantic content of a sentence. The latter is a function of conventions, which are rules of general application, whereas context, however understood, is the detail of the particular situation. Semantics and context are both relevant to meaning, because they inform inferences about what the speaker means. However, semantics and context could not together constitute sentence meaning (or 'utterance meaning' perhaps) unless there was some way to explain how they jointly constitute meaning. For the claim to succeed, the semantic rules would have to specify how context modified the semantic content of the sentence. Yet this would just be to have a much more detailed, highly specific set of conventions. No such conventions exist and thus it is implausible to assert that context settles meaning.

What is called context is often extended further, beyond salient features of the situation, to incorporate the language already used, the information that both parties have about one another, and indeed every other relevant fact that might point to one or other intended meaning. At this point, I suggest, context is being used just to capture the best judgment of what the speaker is likely to have intended. It collapses then into an account of the exercise of the pragmatic capacity to identify what was intended.[98] A real difference would remain if context was invoked not as a proxy for what it is reasonable to infer this particular speaker intended but instead to refer to what a reasonable speaker would have intended to convey in uttering this sentence. The latter account of meaning is inconsistent with the nature of communication, in which one person, the speaker, acts to convey his meaning to another. The speaker means what he intends to mean.

The speaker may fail to make his intended meaning clear. In this situation, the hearer will fail to understand the speaker at all or, more

---

[98] Bach (n 49) 36–7; Bach (n 55) 36–9.

likely, will reasonably understand the speaker to mean something other than what he in fact meant. Goldsworthy argues that the meaning of an utterance is just what the hearer reasonably judges the speaker to have intended, and so utterance meaning may be distinguished from speaker's meaning and sentence meaning.[99] I follow Bach and Neale and argue that no such category exists.[100] Goldsworthy's argument founders, in my view, because it takes the premise that 'our language is a social artifact, constituted by our shared practices' to warrant the conclusion that 'there is nothing beyond [those practices] that can settle disagreement'.[101] However, while shared practices are important, it does not follow that 'our linguistic judgments' stipulate the meaning of any particular instance of language.[102]

The primary reality of language use is the rational act of some person in order to convey his meaning to another. A successful instance of communication occurs when the hearer identifies the intended meaning by recognizing the speaker's intention to this effect. An unsuccessful instance is where the hearer fails to identify the speaker's intention, perhaps because the speaker has acted ineptly. In the latter case, there is no third category of meaning, utterance meaning. There is just what the speaker meant and what the hearer wrongly but reasonably understood him to mean. The hearer can do nothing other than judge as best he can what the speaker meant and there may be good reason to hold the speaker to the hearer's mistaken but reasonable understanding. Holding persons to the meaning the hearer reasonably judged them to have conveyed is central to contract law for example. In other cases, we are interested solely in what the speaker meant, as when we determine whether an utterance was in fact a threat to kill. The speaker's communicative intention is the meaning of an instance of language use. At times, it will be impossible to identify that meaning and the hearer may be wholly reasonable in thinking that another meaning is what was intended. But none of this changes what it is for an instance of language use to have a meaning.

It is instructive to return briefly to Raz and Schauer's accounts of the nature of language. Raz's thesis that rational speakers intend only the conventional meaning of the sentences they utter is plainly false. His claim that context is relevant to conventional meaning is incoherent

---

[99] J Goldsworthy, 'Moderate versus Strong Intentionalism: Knapp and Michaels Revisited' (2005) 42 San Diego Law Review 669, 671–5.
[100] Bach (n 49) 35; Neale (n 57) 181–2.
[101] Goldsworthy (n 99) 677. [102] Goldsworthy (n 99) 677.

(unless he just means word order): he cannot explain how context and convention jointly constitute meaning. The rational speaker intends to convey a meaning that very often is not the literal meaning of the sentence that he utters. Indeed, it would very often be irrational for the speaker to intend the literal meaning of the sentence, because it is an incomplete proposition, is ambiguous, includes indexicals, or is otherwise not fit to be meant.[103] Schauer is right that semantics grounds sentence meanings that are constant apart from the occasion of particular use by particular persons. However, the semantic content of sentences is much thinner than he appreciates. The importance of semantics does not entail that literal meanings exhaust or may suffice for meaningful language use. Instead, speakers employ and exploit the semantic content of the sentences they utter to convey their meaning,[104] which hearers identify by inference.

The underdetermination thesis refutes Raz and Schauer's accounts. What a speaker means in uttering a sentence is what he intends to mean, which is a pragmatic fact identified by the hearer through inference as well as semantic decoding.

V. Legislative Language Use

The well-formed legislature acts for reasons to change the law in certain specific ways. It enacts a particular statutory text to convey to the community—to promulgate—its complex choice of how to change the law. The legal content that the legislature acts to introduce, which is what it intends to introduce, might very often be different to the semantic content of the sentences that it utters. The meaning-content that the legislature intends to convey is the legislature's formulation of the legal propositions that it chooses to introduce. Interpreters understand the meaning of the legislature's lawmaking act, the Act of Parliament or Congress that is this enactment, to be that which the legislature intends to convey. In practice, interpreters understand the meaning of the Act to be what they reasonably judge the legislature to have

---

[103] The literal meaning may be a complete, unambiguous proposition and yet not be a proposition that any rational person would mean, so that the sentence is used to convey some other, reasonable proposition.

[104] J Evans, 'Sketch of a Theory of Statutory Interpretation' [2005] New Zealand Law Review 449, 457–8.

intended to convey.[105] (I refer at times to what the legislator says or means, assuming at such points that this one person is the legislature.)

The legal content that the legislature acts to introduce may sometimes, perhaps often, be identical to the semantic content of the sentences it utters, but when this is the case the reason is that this is what the legislature intended to convey. It is unreasonable for interpreters to stipulate, or even to presume, that the legislature intends to convey only this semantic content. I thus maintain that the act of legislating is some person's rational act of language use, to be understood in the same general way as other rational acts of language use. There are differences between legislative communication and other forms of communication, which I shall consider in this section, but they do not entail that the legislature does not act to convey the meaning-content that it intends to convey or that the legislature may rationally intend only to convey the semantic content of the sentences that it utters. Waldron was right to say 'law makes an investment... in the determinacy-resources of natural language (such as they are, and however they are explained)'.[106] The explanation, however, is that speakers exploit semantics in context to convey intended meanings.

The legislature has good reason to draft statutes carefully and to say directly and precisely what it means: legislation that is misunderstood will fail to change the law in the way that the legislature thinks warranted, clear legislation is a requirement of the rule of law, and doubt over what legislation means will give rise to pointless litigation. Legislation is detailed and precise in a way that many instances of ordinary language use—such as many of the examples set out in section III of this chapter—are not. It may seem that whatever may be the case with ordinary conversation, inference about pragmatic facts is not centrally important in legislative communication. The statutory examples set out above strongly suggest that the contrast between statutes and other forms of speech is overstated. It is true and important that legislators draft statutes with care and that interpreters read statutes very closely. In any particular instance of statutory interpretation, it is not open to interpreters to ask the legislature what it intended to convey or for the legislature to answer by restating its intended meaning. (Over time the legislature may amend statutes to correct misunderstandings.) However,

---

[105] In this I agree with Goldsworthy (n 99) 683; see also J Evans, 'Questioning the Dogmas of Realism' [2001] New Zealand Law Review 145, 161.
[106] *LD*, 83.

in one sense the same is true for any interpretation of any instance of language use, for the interpreter must judge what was meant before deciding whether to ask for clarification. And very many instances of language use are, like statutes, not part of a conversation—a public speech, an advertisement, a book, or even a letter to a friend. Many language users also have good reason to speak precisely, to choose their words with care—an author articulating a complex point, a lawyer arguing a brief, a friend in an otherwise informal conversation delicately raising a sensitive issue. Legislation is thus not quite as unusual as the stark contrast with ordinary conversation at first suggests.

It is logically possible that the legislature might act to convey only the semantic content of the sentences that it utters. Were this the case, interpreters would rightly understand the meaning of the legislative act, the legislature's use of language, to be found in and exhausted by the semantic content of the statutory text. No legislature of which I am aware has ever sought to enact only the semantic content of its texts and there is very good reason for no legislature to act in this way: it would frustrate reasonable legislative action and reasonable interpretation of legislative action.

The proposal to limit the enactment and interpretation of statutes to semantic content effectively counsels using a natural language as if it were a formal language, in which meaning is fully settled by conventional rules. The problem with the proposal is that legislators and interpreters are persons and they understand language as a natural language, in which speakers act to convey their intended meaning to others. It may be that many legislators and interpreters do not self-consciously adopt this understanding, but this is how they themselves use language and respond to uses of language. Most language users are not skilled at distinguishing the semantic content of the sentences they or others utter (semantic facts) from the meaning that they or others intend to convey (pragmatic facts). Therefore, if legislators attempted to legislate literally, adopting only the semantic content of the texts they enact, they would very often say something different to what they intended to say even though, by hypothesis, they intend to convey only what they say. That is, the legislators would often be wrong to think that what they say, the semantic content of the text they enact, is precisely what they meant to say.

Further, interpreters responding to the language the legislators used will very often understand the legislators to have meant other than what they said, either because the interpreters rightly recognize that the legislators were mistaken in thinking they meant what they said or because the interpreters wrongly think that what is likely to be meant is what is said. Legislators write for interpreters, who interpret what they write. Neither set of persons is well placed to stipulate that a natural language is to be treated as a formal language. The very real likelihood that neither legislators nor interpreters will consistently understand statutory language to convey only what is said, in the strict semantic sense, has the consequence that legislators and interpreters should not adopt this approach. It is unstable and unworkable because persons communicate by using and exploiting semantic content to convey pragmatic content.

I do not want to suggest that the semantic content of the statutory text is unimportant. On the contrary, the legislator has good reason to attend very closely to the semantic content of what he utters, because that content is critical if he is to convey his intended meaning and if he is not to misdirect the community. The legislator has to promulgate complex choices in precise form, so must take much greater care in articulating the meaning he intends to convey and in disambiguating the sentences he utters than is the case for most, but not all, other language users. And he will often rightly mean exactly what he says. There are, however, two reasons to expect the legislator to convey a meaning-content that is not identical to what he says. The first is that the legislature may express itself imprecisely, adopting a form of words that is unintentionally ambiguous or confusing.

> (28) Lands Clauses Consolidation Act 1845, s 9: 'The *purchase money or compensation* to be paid for any lands to be purchased or taken from any party under any disability... and the *compensation* to be paid for any permanent damage or injury *to any such lands* [shall be as specified]'. (Emphasis added.)

The section dealt with two kinds of compensation for compulsory acquisition of land payable to persons under a disability, such as insanity: compensation for taking land and compensation for severance and injurious affection for land that is not taken but remains with the landowner. The section is poorly drafted, for the grammatical reference of 'any such lands' is 'any lands to be purchased or taken', yet the section already provides for compensation for seizure of those lands, which because they are seized do not suffer 'any permanent damage or injury' that attracts compensation. Bennion argues compellingly that the legislature intended to use 'any such lands' to refer back to lands retained by any party under any disability, which is thus how the phrase should be understood.[107]

The legislature may also adopt words that are wholly unfit to express directly what it intends to convey—as when it purports to repeal the statutes listed in Sch 4 to the Act, which does not exist, rather than Sch 3, which does exist and is entitled 'Repeals'.[108] Failures in precise, direct expression are likely to occur when legislators form and enact complex statutory texts.[109] What the legislature says is not always what would best serve to convey the meaning that it intends to convey. Interpreters strive to grasp the meaning that the legislature intended to convey because they realize that what the legislature means does not reduce to what it says. The reasonable interpreter aims to identify and give effect to the content of the legislature's lawmaking act, hence his inquiry into what the legislature intended to convey and his constant refusal, evident in countless judicial opinions, to accept that what is said must be what is meant.

The second reason why the legislature may not mean just what it says is that the legislator has good reason to be brief and to rely on interpreters to infer correctly what he means.[110] He should speak as directly and clearly as possible, framing the text that he enacts to be straightforward and accessible to the legally trained reader rather than verbose and exhaustively explicit. The statutory text should be clear and clarity is not in general best achieved by exacting, exhaustive precision.[111] The problem with always stating explicitly what one intends to convey is that one must articulate much that need not be said, which lengthens and may greatly complicate the semantic content of one's utterance. One's audience may fail to decode that semantic content accurately because it is now much longer and more complex than is strictly necessary. Further, in making explicit what may otherwise be conveyed by impliciture or implicature the legislator, like any speaker, risks failing to say part of what he otherwise intends to mean.

---

[107] Bennion, *BST*, 454, example 155.5.
[108] House of Commons Disqualification Act 1975, s 10(2); Bennion, *BST*, 451, example 155.1. The example is apocryphal for the 1975 Act contains neither a s 10(2) nor a Sch 3. Bennion likely had in mind the Northern Ireland Assembly Disqualification Act 1975, s 5 of which repeals the enactments specified in Sch 3.
[109] J Goldsworthy, 'Legislative Intentions, Legislative Supremacy, and Legal Positivism' (2005) 42 San Diego Law Review 493, 499–500.
[110] Goldsworth (n 109) 500–2.
[111] Aquinas, *ST*, I–II, q. 96 a. 6 ad. 3; see further P Yowell, 'Legislation, Common Law, and the Virtue of Clarity', chapter 6 in R Ekins (ed), *Modern Challenges to the Rule of Law* (Wellington, LexisNexis, 2011), 101, 104–8.

For persons to understand the legislature's act, the statutory text should be direct and well structured. That is, it should be clear how and to what extent the sections that constitute the statute form part of a larger scheme and the content of any particular section should be stated as clearly and simply as possible. The importance of clarity in legislation by no means entails that legislation should be written in 'plain English' or that the legislature should enact general principles rather than detailed rules. Legislating requires complex, specific choices—even if there is sometimes good reason to posit vague standards rather than a detailed code—and these choices must be carefully framed and expressed, which means that the ordinary citizen will find it difficult to understand the precise legal meaning and effect of most statutes. The legislator should enact texts that say as much as needs to be said to convey the meaning-content he intends to enact, but no more. The legislator, like other speakers, gauges what needs to be said by asking what it is reasonable for his audience to infer from what he says in the context that he says it. If he doubts that his audience will infer his meaning, he may say explicitly what he means, although he must also take care to defeat the possible inference that he means other than what he says.

The legislator has good reason to adopt terms that convey meanings that he would otherwise have to spell out For example:

(29) Prices and Income Act 1966, s 29(4): introduced a wage-freeze by prohibiting an employer from paying remuneration 'at a rate which exceeds the rate of remuneration {actually} paid {or contracted to be paid, though not actually paid} to him for the same kind of work before 20th July 1966'.[112]

The legislator uses 'paid' to convey more than the literal meaning of the term. The legislature may, and very often does, reasonably leave it to interpreters to infer that it intended to imply part of the legal content of its legislative act, such as the conditions on a statutory office (vacating the office in the event of the incumbent's death or resignation) or the scope of statutory powers (implying ancillary powers when necessary).[113] I conclude that the well-formed legislature often intends to convey meanings that depart from the semantic content of the texts it

---

[112] Bennion (n 64) 232; *Allen v Thorn Electrical Industries Ltd* [1968] 1 QB 487.
[113] Bennion (n 64) 231–2.

utters—in interpreting any statute interpreters should remain open to the possibility that the legislature uses language in this way.

The nature of language use does not provide a secure foundation for theories of legislating which maintain that the legislature is incapable of using language for reasons. On the contrary, the failure of the code theory of language, and the centrality of intention in the use and understanding of language, sharply undermines those theories. The semantic content of any utterance underdetermines what its author intends to mean. One understands language use by inferring what the relevant agent intended to convey. This general truth extends to the use of language to legislate, for it would be unreasonable for the legislature to enact only the semantic content of the texts it promulgates. The well-formed legislature is thus likely to use statutory language to convey its intended meaning to the community.

8

The Nature of Legislative Intent

For the legislature to act well it must respond to good reasons for changing the law by choosing to introduce certain propositions into the law. The legislature promulgates this lawmaking choice by adopting a text, the semantic content of which, in context, frames what interpreters infer the legislature decided and intended to communicate. The legislative assembly is able to form and act on intentions that constitute reasoned plans of action, fit for choice by a reasonable sole legislator, which discharge the legislative function. I argued in chapter 6 that the reasons for authorizing an assembly to legislate change who it is that legislates, but not what it is to legislate, and that the internal hierarchy of the well-formed assembly helps enable reasonable, coherent decision-making. I now explain how the assembly, which is a group of legislators, forms and acts on intentions which arise from, but do not collapse to, the intentions of legislators.

My approach departs from those accounts of legislative intent in which scholars aim to reduce the legislature's intention, somehow, to that of some subset of the legislators.[1] The reason for the move is that it seems plausible to these scholars that a group smaller and more cohesive than the entire assembly might form intentions, which might then be attributed to the legislature. Some scholars attribute to the legislature the intention shared by the majority;[2] others, the intention of those

---

[1] MacCallum outlines, without clearly endorsing, several accounts of this kind: see G MacCallum, *Legislative Intent and Other Essays on Law, Politics, and Morality* (University of Wisconsin Press, Madison, 1993), 26–33.

[2] For example, Marmor, *ILT*, 163–5 and L Alexander and E Sherwin, *Demystifying Legal Reasoning* (Cambridge University Press, Cambridge, 2008), 171.

legislators to whom others are said to delegate authority.[3] Both approaches fail because legislating is not an act taken by some subset of legislators that is then somehow attributed to the institution. It is instead the joint act of the whole group, acting on an open proposal. A sound account of legislative intent has to explain how all legislators, including those in the minority, participate in a joint act, which is an action on an intention that does not reduce to the lowest common denominator.

I. The Standing Intention of the Legislature

The legislature is a complex group that uses a set of procedures to structure its coordinated action to the end that defines the group, the end for which the group acts. Therefore, to understand how the assembly forms the intentions on which it acts one needs to differentiate the group's standing intention from its particular intentions. The group's standing intention is to adopt the procedures that characterize the legislative process as the means by which it will act towards its defining purpose. It is important to state carefully this defining purpose. I have argued already that the group exists to exercise legislative capacity for the common good. By this I mean not that the group's purpose is to legislate, such that a failure to legislate (or to legislate often) is a failure to attain its purpose. Instead, the group stands ready to legislate as and when required: its purpose is to exercise voluntary control over the law and thus to legislate to change the existing set of legal propositions when there is good reason to do so. It may be that a legislature attains its purpose by legislating rarely. The group is structured to legislate when appropriate.

The defining end of the assembly is the exercise of legislative capacity, which is to be in a fit state to legislate on particular occasions for the common good. The standing intention of the group is to seek this end by means of a set of procedures that frame the group's deliberation and decision-making and settle how or if the group is to legislate in particular cases. The procedures include most notably the use of a majority voting rule to decide whether to adopt some proposal for

---

[3] For example, L Solan, 'Private Language, Public Laws: The Central Role of Legislative Intent in Statutory Interpretation' (2005) 93 Georgetown Law Journal 427, 439–48.

legislative action. The standing intention of the central case of a legislative assembly is to legislate by acting on proposals for action that are fit to be chosen by a reasonable sole legislator—coherent, reasoned plans to change the law. The assembly has good reason to form a standing intention to act on proposals of this kind because the exercise of legislative capacity calls for complex choice in response to reasons. The legislature cannot legislate well by aggregating a series of majority votes on the issues that call for decision or by intending only to change the law or to enact only the semantic content of the statutory text. The legislators should thus adopt a structure that enables them to make joint decisions that are reasonable legislative acts.

The particular intention of the group is the intention on which it acts in any particular legislative act, which is both that for which it acts—changes in the law that are means to valuable ends—and the plan it adopts to introduce those changes—a complex set of meanings that expresses a complex set of propositions. This particular intention arises from within the standing intention, in that it is formed by following the structure the group has adopted as its means to the end of being ready and able to legislate. Each particular legislative act may be said to be a more specific means to that same end. However, this depiction is somewhat misleading. A particular legislative act is best seen not to be a means to the end of reasonably exercising legislative capacity, but to be an instantiation of that end.[4] Thus, the group intends to exercise legislative capacity by means of this set of procedures and its legislative action in any particular case is an instantiation of the legislature acting, as it should, in fulfilment of its reason to be.

The standing intention of the assembly arises out of the interlocking intentions of the individual legislators. The legislators form a purposive group. The legislators all understand themselves to make up the group that exists to legislate when need be. They will also be identified as members of the legislature by law and custom, but this is of secondary interest. The individual legislators each assert that they are members of the legislature—they are sworn into office, they participate in the legislative process, and they adopt the title of legislator (or local equivalent). Thus, the legislators are not just deemed to be members of the legislature, rather they understand themselves, acting jointly, to be the legislature. The law formalizes entry requirements and

---

[4] D Wiggins, 'Deliberation and Practical Reason' in J Raz (ed), *Practical Reasoning* (Oxford University Press, Oxford, 1978), 144, 148.

authorizes the group to legislate, according to a rule of legislative competence, but it does not create the acting group.

All the members of the group share the defining end of the group. The legislators' joint acceptance of the need to exercise legislative capacity is the common end, the shared purpose, of their joint action, which directs and coordinates the group action. In the central case of legislative action, each legislator takes the fulfilment of the legislature's purpose to be an end that he seeks, so that all the legislators have reason to participate in, and thereby to create or maintain, a group that acts to realize that common purpose. The legislative process is the means to that shared end and the group's standing intention is, as I have said, to take particular legislative acts in accordance with that procedural framework.

Each legislator forms the intention 'I intend that we legislate by means of the relevant set of procedures, in which majority vote for a complete statutory proposal on the third reading counts as the legislature enacting the proposal'. The intention interlocks with the intentions of other legislators to similar effect, so that 'I intend that we legislate ... because of and in accordance with your intention that we legislate'. The legislators have good reason to form and maintain procedures to structure their joint action because they share a common purpose, which is to stand ready to legislate for the common good.

The well-formed legislative assembly is a special kind of purposive group, an institution, which has a stable nature that extends beyond its particular membership. New members join a group that has a defining purpose and a set of complex procedures that it employs for that purpose. The institution is formed to maintain a purposive group over time and when it works well all members of the institution act jointly as a group. For the legislators to act jointly, their intentions to legislate together by means of certain procedures must be unanimous. If a legislator asserted that he did not belong to the group (or that the legislature did not exist) then, even though identified as a member by law or convention, he would not belong to the acting group. Thus, if the legislature were to include persons who publicly rejected the legislative purpose, say anarchists or Sinn Fein members, then the set of those identified by law as members of the institution (those certified to have been duly elected, for example) would not be a purposive group capable of joint action. The remaining legislators who had not rejected the legislative purpose could continue to legislate, acting as the institution. However, the legislative action would be non-central in that it would not be a joint act of the purposive group that the institution should be.

The group could still act jointly despite a lack of unanimity if the disaffected or alienated legislators did not make known that they did not hold the relevant interlocking intentions. Their continued participation in the legislative process would be parasitic, but, as I argued in chapter 3, section III, secret defection need not frustrate joint action. The point of establishing the legislature as an institution is to ground its purpose and procedures with a stability that endures beyond the vagaries of particular members. My interest is in the central case and I assume that all members of the legislature hold interlocking intentions to legislate together.

The unanimity of the interlocking intentions of all legislators, from which arise the group's standing intention, is consistent with majority voting and disagreement over particular actions. The interlocking intentions of the legislators create majority voting procedure. Thus, part of the intention of each legislator is: 'I intend that a majority vote to enact a proposal shall count as the act of the group'. Majority voting is central to the structure of the assembly because it enables action in spite of disunity while also respecting the formal equality of each legislator.[5] The majority vote only settles how the group acts because all the legislators intend that 'we' the group shall legislate by means of majority vote. I say more below about the relationship between the intentions of members of the minority, members of the majority, and the group.

Legislators consider and respond to legislative proposals intending the legislature to exercise rational agency, like a reasonable sole legislator. I do not suggest that each legislator consciously forms the intention 'I intend that we legislate like a sole legislator'. Instead, I argue that all reasonable legislators share an understanding of what it is to legislate— of what legislative authority is for—central to which is a conception of a coherent, reasoning authority choosing what shall be done. The rational legislator, reflecting on the nature of the institution he joins, will grasp that this is the purpose that explains and justifies the legislature. I agree with MacCormick that the idea that 'Parliament itself is contemplated as an intelligently purposive actor' is 'implicit in the

---

[5] A rule that required a qualified majority vote (say 75 per cent) would be equally consistent with formal equality although it might be undesirable for other reasons (bias to status quo, frustrating good government).

ongoing discourse of the legislature'.[6] Legislators intend that they shall legislate, jointly not individually, and that is to aim to be an authority that responds to reasons by choosing complex schemes that are means to valuable ends: in short, a rational sole legislator.

It follows that the standing intention of the legislature is to form an agent capable of reasoned choice, to change the law for reasons. The legislators intend each lawmaking act of the legislature to be reasoned and coherent. I consider in section IV of this chapter the extent to which the acts of the legislature are likely to be consistent over time. My point now is that the legislators intend to act coherently and for reasons and they make provision to act jointly in this way: that is, they adopt means to this end, which is itself a means to the further end of standing ready to change the law when need be. The internal hierarchy of the legislature, discussed in chapter 6, section IV, is a central part of this means, for the disproportionate control that some legislators enjoy relaxes anonymity, in List and Pettit's terminology, which limits the prospect of incoherence. Likewise, the careful, staged way in which proposals for legislative action are introduced, considered, amended and then adopted makes it possible for legislators to attend to the reasoned plan that each proposal, as developed over time, makes out. Specifically, the way in which deliberation is structured invites legislators to consider proposals as reasoned plans for legislating and to act to ensure that the plan in question is coherent and consistent. The legislative process relaxes systematicity, for legislators are willing and able to attend to the relations amongst various parts of the complex proposal that is the bill, with an eye to forming and later adopting workable, reasoned plans to change the law. The legislature's standing intention is thus to form and consider proposals in this way, such that its acts are reasoned choices.

The assembly's standing intention is its plan to adopt particular plans, which is to say its plan for how to legislate on particular occasions. The group exercises legislative authority by choosing plans of action for the community that are put to the assembly and which, after due deliberation, including the opportunity to change their content, a majority votes to adopt. This standing intention is not what is ordinarily meant

---

[6] D N MacCormick, 'Legislative Deliberation: Notes from the European Parliament', chapter 13 in L Wintgens (ed), *The Theory and Practice of Legislation: Essays in Legisprudence* (Ashgate, Aldershot, 2005), 285, 295.

by the term legislative intent. Instead, legislative intent is taken to refer to the group's intention in a particular legislative act, that is, the ends for which the legislature acts and the means it adopts to them. I shall use the term in this way. The structure of group action is such that the legislature's particular intentions, like those of any other group, may only be understood by reference to the standing intention within which they are framed and formed. The standing intention of the assembly entails that the legislature's particular intention in any legislative act is the plan that the bill set out for the community, which there is good reason to expect to be coherent and reasoned, as if chosen by a sole legislator. It is this plan on which the legislators act in legislating. This is the proposal held in common, which explains their legislative act; this is how they propose, and decide, to act together. The legislature is structured to act by choosing such plans of action. Its intention in the particular legislative act is the reasoned choice that it was proposed that the assembly make.

II. Parliamentary Procedure

The custom and practice of the legislature, including standing orders and decisions of the legislature's officials that frame subsequent practice, largely constitute the detail of its standing intention. However, the standing intention is more than the custom and practice alone, because one must grasp the reason for these procedures, the end to which they are ordered. The procedures that structure the well-formed assembly frame the formation and adoption of proposals for action that are complex, reasoned, and coherent.

Consider the procedures of the House of Commons. The House is but part of the legislative assembly and it may be that Parliament is not truly a well-formed legislature. However, many legislatures have adopted the structure and procedures of the Commons and Parliament often succeeds in legislating well. Reflection on the standing orders that structure the House's deliberation and decision confirms, I suggest, that its standing intention is to form and enact complex, reasoned, coherent proposals, which set out and constitute its particular intention in any legislative act. I rely extensively on *Erskine May*, the magisterial treatise on parliamentary procedure that is updated by successive Clerks of the House of Commons.[7]

Not all legislators may initiate legislative proposals. Ministers direct parliamentary counsel to draft complex, detailed bills after extensive discussion with departmental officials and, often, consultation with cabinet colleagues, other legislators, and interested parties. The minister, or private member in rare cases, tables the bill in the House at its first reading. The first reading introduces the proposal to the assembly's proceedings, arranging for the publication and distribution of the draft text to all legislators and the timetabling of the next stage of its consideration, the second reading.[8] The bill is framed as a draft statute, with a short title, stating its object, and a long title, which 'sets out in general terms the purposes of the bill, and should cover everything in the bill'.[9] The bill may also include a preamble, '[t]he purpose of [which] is to state the reasons for and the intended effects of the proposed legislation'.[10] Few modern statutes now include preambles. However, constitutionally significant statutes may still include a preamble and purpose clauses have a similar function. The bill is divided into numbered clauses, which will be sections if enacted, and a table showing the structure of clauses, and any internal divisions into parts, is prefixed to the bill.[11] Government bills may also include explanatory notes that aim to explain briefly and non-technically the content of the clauses.[12] The formality and detail of introduction, publication, and timetabling notifies legislators of the content of a proposal, giving them time to study it, consult relevant persons, and prepare their response. The bill is drafted to help legislators perceive the nature of the proposed act. Legislators may quickly grasp the overall shape of the scheme from the long title, the preamble or purpose clause, the table outlining the structure of the bill, and the explanatory notes.

The second reading stage is the principal opportunity for legislators to debate the reasons for the proposal. The minister or private member is likely to outline the key provisions of the bill but debate is not focused on the detail of the bill, clause by clause, but on the purpose or policy that animates the scheme.[13] That is, the argument amongst legislators concerns whether the proposal is well conceived in general, whether it

---

[7] Sir W McKay (ed), *Erskine May's Treatise on The Law, Privileges, Proceedings and Usage of Parliament*, 23rd edn (LexisNexis, London, 2004).
[8] McKay, *Erskine May*, 575–6.   [9] McKay, *Erskine May*, 535.
[10] McKay, *Erskine May*, 536.   [11] McKay, *Erskine May*, 537.
[12] McKay, *Erskine May*, 538–9.   [13] McKay, *Erskine May*, 582–3.

outlines a reasonable scheme to address a real problem or whether alternative methods would better attain this object. The bill may be opposed at this second reading and if defeated it lapses altogether. There is no opportunity to amend the bill at this stage. However, after the second reading all bills are sent to committee.[14] Most bills are allocated to standing committees, in which sixteen to fifty legislators consider the detail of the bill and proceed by debate and decision.[15] Alternatives are possible. The Committee of the whole House is used for bills that are either constitutionally very important, when all legislators should constitute the committee, or uncontroversial or urgent, so that their consideration in committee is cursory. Select committees also consider some bills; they proceed by hearing evidence, deliberating and issuing reports.

The committee considers the detail of the bill clause by clause and debates and decides on proposed amendments or new clauses, both of which should be notified in advance. The chairman, usually from the majority party, structures the committee's agenda. He may permit debate on several related amendments at once, to avoid repetition, but will also structure decision 'to encourage consistency (and to avoid inconsistency) in the committee's subsequent decisions'.[16] This approach is consistent with the rules that limit the changes that committees may make to bills. The committee is bound by decisions of the House at the second reading and must not make amendments that fall outside the principle of the bill or the scope of its subject matter.[17] Further, the committee may not adopt amendments that are irrelevant or outside the scope of the clause in question,[18] that are inconsistent with decisions the committee has already made,[19] which would make a clause unintelligible or 'incoherent and inconsistent with the context of the bill',[20] or which are proposed at the wrong place in the bill.[21] The committee may not remove subclauses that undermine a clause.[22] The committee decides on new clauses after debate and decision on amendments to the bill.[23] After deciding on new clauses, the committee may consider the preamble or title, which may be amended only to the extent necessary to reflect amendments properly made.[24]

---

[14] McKay, *Erskine May*, 589.
[15] McKay, *Erskine May*, 799.
[16] McKay, *Erskine May*, 606.
[17] McKay, *Erskine May*, 600–1, 607–8.
[18] McKay, *Erskine May*, 607.
[19] McKay, *Erskine May*, 607–8.
[20] McKay, *Erskine May*, 609.
[21] McKay, *Erskine May*, 609.
[22] McKay, *Erskine May*, 611.
[23] McKay, *Erskine May*, 613–14.
[24] McKay, *Erskine May*, 615–16.

The House may issue instructions to the committee, authorizing it to introduce amendments that go beyond the objects of the bill as disclosed at the second reading, but 'the objects must be cognate to the general purposes of the bill'.[25] The House may also instruct the committee to consider whether to divide the bill, if its internal structure lends itself to division into parts, or to consolidate two bills.[26] The Speaker will rule proposed instructions impermissible 'if they attempt to embody in a bill principles that are foreign or not cognate to it', or if their objects are inconsistent with the House's decision at second reading, or if they 'seek to replace that decision by means of an alternative scheme' or if they attempt to introduce 'a subject which should properly constitute a distinct measure'.[27] Deliberation and decision at committee stage is thus structured and limited by reference to the general scheme and principles accepted at the second reading and the importance of advancing a coherent, workable scheme.

The committee returns the amended bill to the House, which considers it at the report stage. The bill is nearly always reprinted before this stage. Sometimes, it is printed to show the effects of amendments yet to be proposed by the government.[28] The bill is fully open to review, but the House decides on proposed new clauses first and then amendments to clauses.[29] New clauses proposed by the member in charge of the bill have priority for consideration.[30] Thus, that member retains an important agenda-setting advantage, for he may frame the initial consideration of a change to the bill. Again, members should give notice of proposed amendments and the Speaker is unlikely to call on latecomers.[31] When all amendments are disposed of, the member in charge names a day for a third reading. After the report stage, the bill or part of the bill may still be recommitted to committee (of any kind). Again, the member in charge of the bill has priority in framing the motion for recommittal. It is rare to recommit a bill, but it may be thought advisable if a new clause is needed after the House has passed that point in the report stage, or to reconsider amendments earlier made, or to make amendments, on the instruction of the House, which would otherwise be outside the scope of the bill.[32] Thus, opportunities remain for the proposal to be revised and improved prior to the third reading.

---

[25] McKay, Erskine May, 595.
[26] McKay, Erskine May, 597.
[27] McKay, Erskine May, 597–8.
[28] McKay, Erskine May, 620.
[29] McKay, Erskine May, 621.
[30] McKay, Erskine May, 622.
[31] McKay, Erskine May, 623.
[32] McKay, Erskine May, 625–6.

The debate on the third reading is more limited than that at second reading, for it is limited to the contents of the bill. Only verbal amendments may be made on a third reading; for material amendments, the proper procedure is to discharge the third reading and recommit the bill to allow a committee to introduce amendments.[33] If the bill in its final, complete form is passed on third reading, it proceeds to the House of Lords.

I take the procedures of the House of Commons, which legislators created and maintain, to be grounded on the premise that legislators should consider and respond to proposals as reasoned schemes. The standing orders recognize bills to be distinct measures that address certain objects for specific reasons. Proposed amendments, like contributions to debate, are only permitted if they are relevant to the subject matter of the bill.[34] The House does not form bills in plenary session. It debates the general shape and purpose of an already well-advanced proposal, which is put before it by a single member, usually a minister, and then authorizes a committee to consider the proposal in detail, perhaps acting on specific instructions that may widen or narrow, but cannot fundamentally change, the scope of the bill.

Parliamentary procedure is framed to advance bills slowly.[35] The content of the bill changes as it advances but the changes are made carefully. Each stage is structured to permit changes that are consistent with the developing scheme of the bill, rather than to transform or undercut that scheme. The rules that structure how bills may be amended focus on the relevance of the proposed amendment to the scheme before the assembly, as well as on the likely coherence and intelligibility of the resulting scheme. Legislators consider and address the effect of changes on the overall scheme, as the amendment of the long title and preamble confirms.

The rules that frame the committee stage take the bill to be a complex means to some end, the general purpose and outline of which the House has already approved. The committee stage and report stage, as well the possibility for recommittal, mean that there are multiple opportunities for legislators to consider the developing scheme and to propose its amendment, to improve but not to undercut

---

[33] McKay, *Erskine May*, 628.
[34] McKay, *Erskine May*, 400–1, 433–4.
[35] Rules permitting bills to proceed under urgency, while by no means always unreasonable, do threaten rational legislative deliberation and action.

or replace it, before it is put to the assembly for final decision. The way to replace an unreasonable scheme is not to amend it wholesale, but to reject it and propose an alternative measure, which then falls to be carefully considered and amended in its own right. When the bill is finally voted on at third reading, its content has been settled, and debate and decision focus on the bill as a complete proposal.

The minister who proposes the bill has disproportionate control over how it is changed. He enjoys this control because he moves the bill, and has an agenda-setting advantage, but also because the majority party shares with him a common agenda and is disposed to support his choice of how to frame any particular changes that there is good reason to make to the bill as it proceeds. In turn, he directs parliamentary counsel and departmental officials, who study the developing scheme and alert him to the possibility of incoherence. The significance of the minister's central role is that he has the capacity to coordinate legislative deliberation and decision around a scheme that is coherent and complete, which is workable and reasoned, even if, as is very often likely, it is not the scheme that he would choose were he the only legislator. The minister does not legislate alone, but his central role in the process helps the assembly form proposals that are fit to be chosen by a reasonable sole legislator.

The House's final decision is on a proposal that has a stable content, the purpose and detail of which has been carefully scrutinized, with the decision at third reading comparing the complete proposal to the status quo. This contrast between a complete proposal and the status quo is fundamental to reasoned legislative action because it means that the way in which the legislature will act to change the law, if a majority votes in favour, is open to legislators at the time of vote;[36] they need not wait until after the vote to identify the content of their joint lawmaking act.[37] The question for the legislator then is whether to help make it the case that the legislature acts in the way that it is proposed it acts. Parliamentary practice, I conclude, is structured to enable legislators to advance and to consider detailed, coherent, reasoned proposals.

This conclusion about parliamentary practice is not undercut by the fact that the Commons is but one chamber in a bicameral legislature. The reasoned scheme for lawmaking change worked up in the

---

[36] M McCubbins, 'Legislative Process and the Mirroring Principle', chapter 6 in C Ménard and M Shirley (eds), *Handbook of New Institutional Economics* (Springer, Amsterdam, 2005), 123, 133.
[37] Cf. Waldron, *LD*, 128.

Commons, which is intended on enactment to be made known to members of the community, is put to the Lords, which considers, perhaps amends, and then adopts the (amended) proposal, always with a view to how the proposed legislative act will reasonably be understood by the community. If amended, the proposal is returned to the Commons for further consideration—the proposal is enacted only if both Commons and Lords adopt it. The second chamber, whether Lords or Commons, works over a proposal that originates in the other, but to which the second chamber may and often does make an important contribution. Legislators from each chamber very often cooperate and confer,[38] which further helps the whole assembly deliberate about and choose a proposal open to all. In other bicameral legislatures, the two chambers may develop related proposals independently of each other, which are then integrated in a joint committee and put again to each chamber for deliberation and adoption. In such cases, there are at first two legislative proposals, which in due course are reduced to one, the origin of which is in two chains of reasoning, but which is intended to be itself a complete, consistent proposal, sourced in the deliberation of the whole assembly and open to all.

III. Legislative Intent in Particular Acts

Legislative intent is the legislature's intention in a particular legislative act, which is the proposal for legislative action that it adopts. The proposal for legislative action is the plan that the statute as enacted is to set out for the community, being a set of propositions adopted for reasons as a coherent means to the end of certain valuable states of affairs. The legislature intends (its standing intention is) to choose to adopt proposals that are put before it and for which a majority of its members vote. It thus intends to act like a sole legislator and on a majority vote the legislature truly chooses the proposal. The legislature's choice then is to change the law in the specific ways and for the specific reasons that the bill proposes.

---

[38] S Kalitowski, 'Rubber Stamp or Cockpit? The Impact of Parliament on Government Legislation' (2008) 61 Parliamentary Affairs 694, 705–6.

My argument is that legislative intent is what is proposed for legislative action. I conclude that this intention coordinates how the group acts and is what the legislators jointly intend in acting to legislate. I do not accept the sharp distinction that Manning makes between objectified intent, which is what a reasonable reader concludes was intended, and actual or subjective intent, which is what a majority of legislators wanted.[39] He has no good reason to assume that actual, subjective legislative intent must be the shared preference of the majority. I have argued that what is held in common amongst legislators and what structures how they act together is not the sum of the intentions held by each member of the majority, but an open proposal. The legislators truly intend to act jointly on this proposal. What is open to them may, at the risk of confusion, be said to be objective, because the content of the proposal turns on how it is reasonably to be understood. Yet the joint intention to act on that proposal is an intention that truly arises out of the interlocking intentions of all legislators and, to that extent, is fully actual and subjective. The distinction purports to open up a gap between what the legislators jointly do and what interpreters say that they intended to do. However, the object of legislative deliberation is a proposal that is transparent to legislators and the community, so that what interpreters infer the legislature intended to do should be what was open to and thus chosen by the legislators.

I have said little thus far about the intentions of individual legislators in respect of particular legislative acts. The reason for this is that I take those intentions to be irrelevant to the content of the joint act. The legislative intent in any particular act is the plan on which the legislature acts, not some summation of each legislator's reasoning in voting for or against the particular statutory proposal, none of which is open to other legislators or understood by any of them to be the object of joint action. It is the plan or proposal that is held in common by all legislators and which explains the joint action. However, a sound account of legislative intent must situate and explain the irrelevance of the intentions of individual legislators, not least to beat back the recurring misconception that the intention of the legislature can only be the intention of the majority.[40] This I now attempt.

---

[39] J Manning, 'What Divides Textualists from Purposivists' (2006) 106 Columbia Law Review 70, 83, 90, 97, 100, 102–3, and 'Textualism and Legislative Intent' (2005) 91 Virginia Law Review 419, 421, 423–4, 430, 432–4, 436, 438, 448–50.

[40] See nn 1–2 above and my discussion in chapter 3, section I.

The legislator who votes in the majority to enact a statutory proposal is likely to act on the particular intention 'I intend that we enact this proposal'. His intention cannot be 'I intend to enact this proposal' because he alone may not legislate and hence an intention to that effect would be futile. A full analysis of his reasoning may reveal that he takes the ends that define the statutory proposal to be his ends. That is, he votes for the proposal intending that the group enact the proposal and intending thereby to realize the valuable ends to which the proposal purports to be a means. This legislator, who I will call an enthusiastic legislator, adopts as his own the chain of reasoning that defines the group's action. His is the simplest case of participation in the legislative act because he votes intending the group to enact the proposal so that the ends that the statute aims for may be realized.

Not all those who vote for an enactment will reason in quite this way, and of course the minority, who vote against enactment, will not do so. The minority legislator plainly does not act on 'I intend that we enact this proposal'. Instead, he votes 'no' intending to defeat the proposal and thus intending the group not enact the proposal. Perhaps surprisingly, a legislator in the majority may also vote intending to defeat the proposal. This is possible if he reasons that his support for the bill may lead others to vote against it. His reasoning is parasitic on the usually sound assumption that legislators vote for a proposal intending the group to enact it;[41] however, it is certainly possible. A legislator may also vote to adopt a proposal intending thereby to achieve some tangential aim (to avoid party discipline; to earn his bribe). More interesting, however, is the position of the reluctant member of the majority who may vote for the proposal intending to realize only some of the ends that define the proposal. That is, he does not adopt as his own the chain of reasoning on which the legislature acts but is instead prepared to vote to enact the whole proposal in order to introduce the particular provision or provisions he values.[42]

Two common scenarios in legislative practice confirm that legislators often vote for a proposal intending to realize only part of it. The first is the enactment of a proposal that includes a so-called poison pill, or wrecking amendment, which is a provision attached to the proposal by its opponents, who hoped that this would ensure the entire proposal

---

[41] Raz, *BAI*, 282, n 16.
[42] J Finnis, 'Helping Enact Unjust Laws Without Complicity in Injustice' (2004) 49 American Journal of Jurisprudence 11, 31–3.

would be rendered unattractive and therefore be rejected. The second is legislative compromise, where legislators put forward proposals that may partly but not fully satisfy the factions that form a majority in support of the entire proposal. Where the legislature acts on a proposal that includes a poison pill or that is a compromise, then the voting majority is likely to be made up of reluctant legislators.

These scenarios are still consistent with most or all of the legislators in the majority voting on the intention 'I intend that we enact this proposal to be law'. The reluctant legislator votes to enact the statutory proposal to attain only certain of the ends that the proposal sets out. However, the necessary means to the ends he seeks is the enactment by the group of the proposal. Therefore, he intends that the group enact the proposal, but he does not intend, for his part, the full set of ends for which the group act aims. Thus, while the full statement of his reasoning differs from the intention on which the assembly itself acts, which intention will be shared by the enthusiastic legislator (if he is not ignorant of the detail of the proposal), he nevertheless acts intending the group enact the proposal.

In a well-formed legislature, one would expect legislators to take seriously their duty to cooperate to exercise legislative authority and only to vote for a proposal when they intend the legislature to enact it. In a corrupt or dysfunctional legislature, the legislators might vote for a statutory proposal without intending it be enacted, instead intending only to earn a bribe, to impress the electors with a show of resolve, or to frustrate the minority. This is possible even if it is not the central case. However, in neither case would the legislature's particular intention arise from the interlocking intentions of the majority. The legislature's particular intention instead follows from the fact of the majority vote understood by reference to the group's standing intention that the vote shall count as the act of the group. The assembly intends the majority vote to count as enactment. The legislators' reasons for voting 'aye' or 'no'—the ends they each seek for their part in the particular act of voting—are irrelevant to the group action.

The majority is not a purposive or an acting subgroup at all. Certainly an intention may be common to all members of the majority, such as 'I intend that we enact this proposal' or 'I intend that we enact this proposal to be a means to the ends that define the proposal'. However, each individual legislator holds this intention for his part only. There is no coordination amongst the legislators who happen to be in the majority to some shared end. Of course, very often legislators in the majority do cooperate to adopt a plan to advance a proposal, to defeat the minority, and convince the public. My point is that the standing intention of the assembly has no place for the action of a purposive subgroup known as the majority. And indeed the intentions on which legislators act confirm that the majority is not conceived to be a purposive group. The rational legislator intends that 'we' act, where the pronoun refers to the assembly not the majority.

The legislative minority does not trouble my account. The legislator in the minority shares the unanimous interlocking intention to legislate in accordance with procedures that include majority voting, from which arises the group's standing intention to that effect. He votes against the particular proposal intending to defeat that proposal, but intending also that the outcome of the vote, whether for or against, shall count as the act of the entire group. Therefore, he will not understand the resulting legislative act to be the act of the majority, but will instead understand it to be the act of the legislature to which he belongs. He may object to the legislative act and campaign for its repeal, but he will not deny that the legislature has chosen the proposal that he voted against.

The open proposal that legislators vote to adopt defines the legislative act. The content of that proposal must be capable of being known, but need not in fact be known by all legislators.[43] The legislators act on a plan to choose plans for others. The former plan must be common knowledge because the legislators must coordinate to play their part in it. The latter plan need not be common knowledge because the act of the legislature is to make the choice that the plan sets out. For the choice to be rational what is chosen must be open to all members, but the (common) failure of many to grasp the point or detail of the plan does not preclude the group from acting, on a majority vote to act on the plan. Legislators coordinate by reference to the open plan. Some legislators will be more or less aware of the content and detail of the proposal. Legislative action is possible because the plan is open to all legislators, for them to vote to adopt or not.

An individual legislator, usually a minister, introduces any particular proposal. Like all texts the bill is understood by reference to the intentions of its author. The initial meaning of the proposal is the meaning its proposer intended to convey, first to other legislators and

---

[43] Raz, *BAI*, 283–4.

then to the community if it is enacted. I say the initial meaning because the group's further consideration of a proposal may change its content. The legislator who advances the proposal determines its content in the same way that a draftsman prepares a text for another person to consider and perhaps adopt as his own. That is, the legislator's intentions are important but not decisive. Whoever reads the text will understand its meaning by reference to the proposer's intentions. But the proposer must write a text that is fit for adoption by the person to whom it is submitted, and thus the text is written on behalf of that person, with the author attempting to capture the meaning that the text will have if that person utters it.[44] The need to write on behalf arises because any action on the proposal will be that of the group (the legislature that aspires to act like a sole legislator) rather than the author. The legislator who advances a proposal is in the same position as a speechwriter who selects phrases for his principal knowing that the phrases will have a different meaning by virtue of their adoption by the principal than would be the case were the speechwriter to deliver his own lines. This analysis is consistent with the proposer remaining free to determine the content of the proposal, for the author may propose anything so long as he is very careful in his explication. However, the proposal that is open to the legislators is not necessarily identical to the proposal the particular legislator put forward. The other legislators may know full well that the proposer intended a different meaning, or they may simply assume that the text has the meaning it appears to them to have, even though that meaning in fact differs from that which the author intended to convey. Either way, the group may act on a proposal that is sourced in, but is not determined by, the intentions of the particular legislator.

Most legislation is drafted by one or more parliamentary counsel, working under the direction of the minister and in close consultation with departmental officials. The minister proposes the bill that his officials, under his direction, draft. They write on behalf of the minister who writes on behalf of the legislature. Rational drafters, whether legislators or officials working for legislators, select the semantic content that they judge will, if uttered by the legislature, convey the meaning that they intend the legislature to convey. It is possible for drafters to convey more than the semantic content of the bill alone because

---

[44] See also the very interesting discussion in Bennion, *BST*, 474–9, ss 165–6.

legislators have good reason to understand proposals for action to be the choice that a rational legislator would be likely to make in enacting this text. I have said that the bill moves slowly through the legislative process, its general outline being approved at second reading, before detailed committee work and then subsequent consideration in plenary time. The importance of this lengthy, careful process is that the complex choice that the text discloses is put before the legislators and is open to them. It is this reasoned scheme that is the object of debate and decision.

The intentions of the bill's sponsor, the way in which debate proceeds, and the assumptions that legislators at committee stage and in plenary session fairly make about the content of the scheme before them, all inform what is open to legislators. Equally, judgments about what a reasonable sole legislator should intend in uttering this text inform how the bill's sponsor forms his intentions, how debate is framed, and what is fair for legislators to assume. Reasonable legislators intend the choice that they jointly make to be transparent to the community. The standing intention to legislate like a reasonable sole legislator frames how legislators reasonably understand the content of the proposal at each stage in the process.

The examples set out in chapter 7 (and that follow in chapter 9) support my argument. It is likely that what was open to the legislators in each of the statutory examples was not just the semantic content of the relevant section. What was open was the meaning that a reasonable sole legislator who attends to the context—including the overall statutory scheme, the rest of the law, especially that which he aims to change, and the nature of the mischief he addresses—would be likely to intend to convey in uttering the semantic content of the section. The particular legislator who aims to understand how the bill proposes the legislature act reads the bill in this way; he then decides whether this is what the legislature should choose and votes accordingly.

IV. Agency and Compromise

The legislative process is structured to develop coherent, reasoned plans of action, such that there is reason to presume that each clause in the bill forms part of a complex scheme fit to be chosen by a rational sole legislator. Legislators jointly act to make the reasoned choice that the proposal seems to make out, when read as a whole, and in this way the legislature forms a group agent. The exercise of legislative agency is, I maintain, consistent with the importance of legislative compromise. Many scholars argue otherwise; the live question, I say, is how legislators should compromise, which informs what (in a well-formed legislature) is open to them at third reading.

I argued in chapter 5, section IV that a sole legislator might well have good reason to compromise and that interpreters should not rule out the possibility that the prince's choice, in any particular section or statute, does not fully cohere with (which is not to say it contradicts) the choices that he or his predecessors had made in other sections or statutes. That is, while it is sound to presume coherence, interpreters should sometimes infer that the prince chose to compromise. Further, the legislature very often acts on a complex set of intentions, involving several sets of means-ends chains, such that one intention limits what would otherwise have been the expected means to some end, in the interest of another end. It is quite possible then that what is open to legislators at the time of enactment, and what interpreters reasonably infer was intended, is a (partial) compromise.

The argument from compromise takes many forms. Marmor argues that because 'legislation is typically a form of strategic behavior... it would seem rather unlikely that the prescribed content of an act of legislation is obviously and transparently different from what it says'.[45] The conversation between legislators is strategic and 'legislation ... is almost always a result of a *compromise* [which] often consists in ... *tacitly acknowledged incomplete decisions*—that is, decisions that deliberately leave certain issues undecided'.[46] The different factions, he then says, 'deliberately leave some formulations of the bill open to conflicting interpretations, hoping that the interpretation they favor will eventually prevail'.[47] Jorgensen and Shepsle argue to similar effect that legislators often choose to enact contradictory propositions, rather than a compromise proposition. This choice, they say, is 'precisely parallel to choosing a lottery [for] the members of the enacting coalition are effectively choosing to "take their interpretive chances" in subsequent litigation lotteries'.[48] They argue further that factions may fail to agree

---

[45] A Marmor, 'The Pragmatics of Legal Language' (2008) 21 Ratio Juris 423, 429.
[46] Marmor (n 45) 436.
[47] Marmor (n 45) 437.
[48] M Jorgensen and K Shepsle, 'A Comment on the Positive Canons Project' (1994) 57 Law and Contemporary Problems 43, 45.

how to settle some issue, so that a statute's apparent silence on point should not be assumed to be capable of clarification by inference to a compromise the legislators must have intended to enact.[49]

The legislature may act well, I argue, in enacting a compromise, but it should not choose an interpretive lottery. The legislature may be unable to decide precisely what should be done, either because its members disagree or because of the nature of the issue and the paucity of information. In either case, it may be reasonable for the legislature to authorize another person or body to decide, either by creating a statutory power, or by enacting a vague standard which calls for specification at a later stage. If this is what should be done, this is what the legislature should decide; the legislature should not simply fail to make a decision, or worse, purport to make a contradictory decision. Reasonable legislators form and consider proposals to be capable of unified choice, which means they act on a disposition to read proposals in a way that avoids internal contradiction or failure to decide. Interpreters rightly seek to infer what was open to legislators and transparent to the community, which is the proposal read in this same way.

The conversation between legislature and community is also strategic, Marmor argues, which undermines the possibility of reliable pragmatic inference. He points to 'those cases... in which the legislature deliberately speaks with several voices, so to speak'.[50] Marmor says this is an example of the strategic nature of the 'conversation' between the legislature and the community, but it is his only example and it is not clear what more general class the example may represent. He has in mind legislation where 'the legislature intends to convey one message to the public at large, and a different one to agencies, or the courts'.[51] Like Hurd,[52] he cites Dan-Cohen's distinction between conduct and decision rules,[53] which Dan-Cohen argues explains duress in the criminal law. Marmor puts the argument this way: the law may 'give the impression that it does not recognize duress as a defense' but also

---

[49] Jorgensen and Shepsle (n 48) 46–7.
[50] Marmor (n 45) 437.
[51] Marmor (n 45) 437.
[52] H Hurd, 'Sovereignty in Silence' (1991) 99 Yale Law Journal 945, 979–80.
[53] M Dan-Cohen, 'Decision Rules and Conduct Rules: On Acoustic Separation in Criminal Law' in M Dan-Cohen, *Harmful Thoughts: Essays on Law, Self, and Morality* (Princeton University Press, Princeton, 2002), 37–93.

'instruct the courts to grant the defense' in certain circumstances.[54] This device may be frequently used, he says, for '[l]egislators may wish to create the impression that they are doing one thing—e.g. seriously restricting campaign finance contributions—while actually trying to do the opposite—allowing such contributions to flow freely but less transparently'.[55]

This legislative double-talk argument fails adequately to distinguish the legislature from the legislators. Marmor talks loosely about both the legislators and the legislature creating impressions and saying one thing but doing another. However, the legislature does not give impressions—it acts to change the law. Legislators may mislead the community about the legislature's act, but the premise of Marmor's analysis is that the joint act of the legislators, which is the legislative act, is to change the law in a particular way. The wider community may be deceived, but for the legislators to achieve their ends they must also, acting jointly as the legislature, communicate to interpreters the legislature's choice of how to change the law. The legislative process is in a bad state if legislators routinely lie about their legislative acts or if they frame legislation to mislead, perhaps, for example, inserting purpose provisions into statutes that are then wholly undercut by more detailed provisions. However, the temptation that legislators may have to mislead the community about the nature of their law-changing act does not refute (but rather presupposes) the truth that the legislature acts as a rational agent, using language for reasons.

More challenging than the interpretive lottery or double-talk arguments is Manning's claim that legislators cannot compromise unless the statutory text is read strictly, aiming to capture what a reasonable speaker would be likely to mean in saying these words, but not what a reasonable legislator would be likely to mean in enacting this statute.[56] Manning conceives of the legislature as an institution that enables many individual legislators to insist on concessions before bills are enacted. This conception has more traction in explaining presidential than parliamentary legislatures and indeed Manning's focus is solely on Congress. I argued in chapter 6, section VI that the presidential legislature has difficulty legislating well because veto-players may frustrate the coherence of the legislative act, making it less likely that proposals will be reasoned and workable. The practice of parliamentary

---

[54] Marmor (n 45) 447.   [55] Marmor (n 45) 448.
[56] Manning (2006) (n 39) 99–109.

legislatures is quite different. However, even in the presidential legislature, the wide distribution of veto powers, while it does inhibit coherence, does not entail that what is open to legislators at the third reading is a proposal that they should assume not to be a complex, reasoned, coherent scheme. Legislators have good reason, I argue, to insist that compromises should be clearly articulated in the final proposal rather than assumed to explain the semantic content (in Manning's broad sense) of the statutory text. That is, one enacts a compromise not just by framing the semantic content of the provision (say to satisfy a committee chairman early in the process), but by making it clear that the legislature's choice, to be inferred from the semantic content in the rich legislative context of the final complex proposal, is to enact this compromise proposition.

The upshot is that legislators should compromise not by drafting provisions in isolation, and then expecting other legislators to refrain from understanding them to form part of a complex reasoned scheme. Instead, legislators agree to form proposals that capture what they think is a compromise worth choosing, with the legislature acting for reasons that support this compromise.[57] The stability of legislative office and party affiliation, as well as the fact that legislating is a repeat game, means that legislators may make support early in the process contingent on the likely content of the final proposal. It follows then, that even in presidential systems legislators may rationally conceive of the open proposal in the way I outline and yet also continue to compromise about what should be done.

Legislators *agree* to change the law in certain ways. McNollgast reasons that 'the "original intent" of legislation ... [is] the actual agreement about policy among those enacting a statute'[58] and accordingly that to discover the legislative intent one must first 'identify the members of an enacting coalition and, in particular, the political actors who were pivotal in that their preferences had to be taken into account in order for a legislative agreement to be made'.[59] In a striking phrase, McNollgast says '[t]he language of a statute can be regarded as a

---

[57] See further H Richardson, *Democratic Autonomy: Public Reasoning About the Ends of Policy* (Oxford University Press, Oxford, 2002), 143–61 and R Bellamy, *Political Constitutionalism* (Cambridge University Press, Cambridge, 2007), 192–4 and 241–2.

[58] McNollgast 'Legislative Intent: The Use of Positive Political Theory in Statutory Interpretation' (1994) 57 Law and Contemporary Problems 3, 5; McNollgast is M McCubbins, R Noll, and B Weingast—three distinguished political scientists—writing jointly as a single author.

[59] McNollgast (n 58) 7.

statement of the preferences of a fictitious decisionmaker who embodies the compromises that solved the collective action problem'.[60] This line of thought partly perceives the reality of legislative agency, but wrongly reduces the intentions of the legislature to the deal struck amongst a subset of legislators. I say legislators cannot legislate by making private deals apart from the legislative process. An agreement amongst a subset of important legislators, or even amongst a majority, does not settle what *the legislature* enacts unless what is agreed is proposed to all legislators—articulated in a proposal for legislative action—and adopted by them on majority vote. That is, for a bargain amongst legislators to be enacted, the legislators have to persuade the legislature to act on a proposal with that content. McNollgast implies that the coalition legislates by drafting a text and then framing the legislative history to imply that this text means what they agreed it should mean.[61] Yet without some reason for other legislators to accept that the text means what the pivotal legislators say it means, the public statements of those legislators cannot settle what the assembly enacts.

It is true that a bill cannot be enacted without the support of pivotal legislators and this means that those legislators have capacity to frame the content of the bill. It does not follow that the bill means what those legislators agree it shall mean, for they must put the bill that they frame before the other legislators as a proposal for their joint action. The minority's reasonable understanding of the act that it is invited to support, but chooses not to support, cannot be set aside merely by noting the importance of majority voting or pivotal legislators. What the legislators do jointly in their lawmaking act turns on what is open to all legislators. This conclusion follows from the rational structure—the standing intention—that alone makes possible joint legislative action. Legislative compromise thus takes its place within a larger theory of how and why legislators jointly act.

The legislature forms an agent, such that the proposals for action it develops and enacts are likely to be reasoned, coherent plans of action. This rational agency is consistent with the truth that the lawmaking acts of the legislature over time, even within the same legislative session, may

---

[60] McNollgast (n 58) 12.
[61] McNollgast runs together an account of the nature of legislative intent—the enacting coalition's implied agreement—and a prescription for how one identifies it—studying the statements of pivotal members of that coalition: McNollgast (n 58) 24–6. It is helpful to separate the two, not least because not all systems permit interpreters to refer to legislative history. See further chapter 9, section V.

manifest quite different responses to reason and fail jointly to cohere. I argued in chapter 5, section IV that the legislature should not strive for integrity in any strong sense, but should rather change the law in the ways there now seems good reason to choose. The assembly exercises its authority by considering to what extent the law serves the common good. The legislature therefore has good reason to consider closely past legislative acts, as well as relevant case law and custom, and to examine how social life has changed because of those acts. Legal stability is important, but this goes to the reasons the legislature has for acting; it is no part of the legislature's standing intention to act consistently with past legislative acts, for this does not help it exercise legislative capacity. The assembly over time is like a succession of princes, each of whom should act to change the law as he thinks warranted, having considered the existing law and the importance of legal stability. The legislature should form and enact workable plans of action, which requires at the very least avoiding contradiction. This requirement of rational legislative agency supports the practical conclusion that the legislature repeals by implication (earlier) existing legal propositions inconsistent with its present (latest) choice.

While different legislatures make different reasoned choices, such that the set of statutes over time is unlikely fully to cohere, each enacting legislature is structured to exercise rational agency in changing the law, which means that there is good reason to expect each of the legislature's particular acts to make out a complex reasoned choice. The deliberation and choice of the assembly, like the succession of princes, is likely to be framed and closely informed by common principles that persist over time and by the set of legal propositions existing at the time of enactment, which while changing with successive lawmaking acts is in many ways continuous. Therefore, while each legislature acts for reasons its members judge sound, there is likely to be some unity across time in the character of the agents that are successive legislatures.

Legislative intent is the intention of the one who legislates, which is neither the majority nor leading legislators, but the assembly. The assembly forms and acts on intentions because its members jointly intend to (stand ready to) legislate together. More precisely, the standing intention of the legislature is to form, consider, and adopt lawmaking proposals, such that on majority vote the legislature acts on the relevant proposal. All legislators, whether in majority or minority, participate in this act. The standing intention of the legislature is to form and choose proposals for action that are coherent and reasoned, which is to say the legislature aims to exercise rational agency. The detail of parliamentary procedure illustrates how the well-formed assembly may conceive of and deliberate about proposals for lawmaking choice in this way. The legislature's intention in any particular lawmaking act—*the legislative intent*—is to change the law in the complex, reasoned way set out in the open proposal for legislative action. It is this plan of action that is the object of legislative deliberation and which the assembly chooses. This account of legislative intent, as the exercise of the legislature's rational agency, does not rule out, and is not frustrated by, legislative compromise. The well-formed legislature over time is a succession of agents, each of whom reasons and chooses, acting on complex intentions to change the law.

9

Intentions in Interpretation

This chapter outlines further how legislative intent changes the law. I explain how citizens and officials, including authoritative adjudicative institutions, ought to understand the legislative act to change the law. My aim is to explore the significance for statutory interpretation of the truth that the well-formed legislature is a rational agent, which acts publicly to choose complex, reasoned schemes. The nature of legislative action entails that interpreters should infer the legislature's intended meaning in uttering the relevant statutory text. This process of inference is informed by, and in turn informs, reflection on the reasoned choice the legislature likely acted to make and is grounded in the rich context of enactment. Legislative history—*travaux préparatoires*—does not form a main part of this context and indeed reference to this history is not entailed by the centrality of legislative intent in statutory interpretation. In exceptional cases, interpreters have good reason to recognize that the legislature's intended meaning is qualified or extended by its reasoned lawmaking choice.

I. The Object of Interpretation

There are good reasons, I have argued, for the legislature to have authority to change the law by making known its intention to this effect: the constitution of any well-formed legal system makes provision for the legislature to act in this way and to this end. It follows that in the central case of interpreting a statute interpreters will aim to infer and understand the legislature's lawmaking intention, which intention (as expressed in the enactment) changes the existing law in some way, a change which persists until it expires on its own terms or is amended or repealed by a subsequent legislature.

The central axiom of well-formed interpretive practice is that the legislature is an institution that aims to act responsibly for the common good. This axiom is no fiction for it responds to the rationale for legislative authority, giving subjects of the law reason to understand the legislature's act to change what they should do *and* also animating and explaining the structure and operation of the legislature. The legislature is a type of institution that is capable of acting responsibly for the common good and in understanding particular exercises of legislative authority interpreters should presume that the legislature was what it should be and is capable of being: a rational, reasonable lawmaker. It follows that there is an important difference between how a court (or citizen) interprets an authoritative legislative act and how a historian or political scientist explains legislators and their acts and intentions.[1] The subject of the law should be slow to hypothesize, and even slower to conclude, that the legislative act is vicious, arbitrary or irrational.[2] For, while possible, any such hypothesis or conclusion is a postulation or judgment that the legislature has failed to do its duty. A mistaken or unjust exercise of legislative authority has intra-systemic validity, yet fails to be a central case of authoritative lawmaking. The relevant lawmaking choice changes the law in the way made clear, but fails fully to bind in conscience.

'Interpretation', Timothy Endicott argues, 'is a creative reasoning process of finding grounds for answering a question as to the meaning of some object'.[3] This definition is, I suggest, less than helpful, at least as it pertains to language use in general and legislating in particular (it may be entirely fitting for dreams or sculpture). The problem is that it obscures the central point of interpreting some person's use of language or some legislature's lawmaking act: to understand what they have said and done, which means to identify the intentions on which they acted and which they aimed—meant—to make recognizable. Endicott argues that interpretation is to be distinguished from understanding,

---

[1] J Finnis, 'Priority of Persons', chapter 1 in J Horder (ed), *Oxford Essays in Jurisprudence* (Oxford University Press, Oxford, 2000), 1, 13.

[2] T Hobbes, *Leviathan*, ed A Martinich (Broadview Press, Peterborough, 2005), chapter XXVI.

[3] T Endicott, 'Legal Interpretation', chapter 8 in A Marmor (ed), *The Routledge Companion to Philosophy of Law* (Routledge, London, 2012), 109.

but in elaborating the point he makes clear that this is a stipulation.[4] Likewise, while his term 'creative' may suggest that the interpreter in some way constructs the meaning of the object in question, Endicott uses it to mean that the relevant interpretation involves stating not just that which is obvious to everyone who is 'familiar with the object', but rather a meaning that might be in dispute.[5] The very expression 'the meaning of some object' obscures the fact that in interpreting (understanding) some instance of language use one interprets (understands) a rational act (of using language with intent to convey some meaning). Endicott at times suggests that what falls to be interpreted (understood) is something distinct from an agent or its action—say an order or a bylaw—yet in the end, he rightly says that the interpreter's task is to elucidate some speech-act, which is to understand the speaker.[6]

I speak interchangeably of interpreting a statute and understanding the legislative act. The statute is, as the terms 'Act of Parliament' or 'Act of Congress' make clear, the legislature's lawmaking act—or at least it is that act considered in its communicative and communicated content. When the legislature enacts a statute it chooses to change the law in specific ways for specific reasons. The legislature acts on a lawmaking proposal that sets out a plan for the community, a plan that consists in a set of propositions to be adopted by citizens and officials. The legislature promulgates its lawmaking intention—its choice that this set of propositions is to form part of the law—by uttering the statutory text in the relevant context and making clear its intention to convey this or that propositional meaning-content in uttering—the legislative act qua activity—the sentences (statements) that form the statutory text—the legislative act qua content and communicative product. The legislature's intended meaning expresses the propositions it has chosen, which is of central importance precisely because it articulates the object of the legislature's choice. The subjects of the law should respond to the legislature's exercise of lawmaking authority by inferring the propositions it chose, which it acted to introduce into the law. Hence, interpreters should aim to infer the legislature's intended meaning, which is how it formulates the set of propositions it intends to introduce into the law. This intended meaning is the central object of statutory interpretation.[7]

---

[4] Endicott (n 3) 121.   [5] Endicott (n 3) 110.   [6] Endicott (n 3) 120.
[7] Contrast J Goldsworthy, *Parliamentary Sovereignty: Contemporary Debates* (Cambridge University Press, Cambridge, 2010), 247: 'The object of interpretation is the statute actually

The exercise of legislative authority is the making and promulgation of a choice. This truth frames how the legislature's act changes the law. The legislature forms and acts on intentions, which it acts to make and make publicly known, and what the legislature adopts and promulgates is thereby transformed from a proposal to law. The significance of the public act of lawmaking, of promulgating one's authoritative intention, is that a well-formed legal system has good reason—consistent with full recognition of legislative authority—to provide that the meaning of the statute turns on what one *reasonably* infers the enacting legislature intended. I do not mean at all that interpreters may substitute their judgment of what the legislature in fact intended for what they think it would have been better for the legislature to have intended. Rather, the interpreter's best inference about what was in fact intended is decisive— he or she can do no other—even if this departs from what is in fact the legislative intent. The legislature changes the law by promulgating its intention to this effect. My discussion in chapter 7 and in this chapter makes very clear, I trust, that this does *not* mean that the semantic content of the text must explicitly assert as much, for the legislature's intended meaning is readily open to be inferred from the utterance of the text in context. The importance of promulgation is that the legislature's intended meaning falls to be inferred from publicly available evidence, which is to say evidence that is open to the community.

Interpreters should aim to understand the legislature's intended meaning. They should also aim to understand the reasoned choice that finds expression in this intended meaning. This may seem surprising. It is true that the legislature aims to make clear the practical conclusions of its deliberations—the set of propositions that confer (or remove) powers and impose (or cancel) duties—and does not aim to promulgate the chain of reasoning that supports those conclusions. However, the legislature's lawmaking act is a reasoned choice of some scheme or plan for the common good. The reasons that the legislature had for acting in some or other way—for choosing some or other set of propositions—are highly relevant to the meaning it was likely to intend to convey in uttering the statutory text and hence to the inferences about intended meaning that it is plausible to make from what the legislature says in context. Further, there is good reason to think each provision, and each particular set of propositions it introduces, forms part of a larger reasoned

enacted, not some other statute that members of Parliament may have mistakenly believed they were enacting'.

scheme, inference about which scheme thus informs inference about the likely intended meaning of each particular part.

The importance of inference about the reasoned scheme that the legislature chooses, in order to understand the propositions it acted to introduce into the law, is made clear in cases where the legislature adopts an especially poor formulation of the propositions it acts to choose. Consider *Inco Europe Ltd v First Choice Distribution*,[8] in which the House of Lords had to determine whether the Court of Appeal had jurisdiction to hear an appeal from a decision of the High Court to stay legal proceedings in relation to an arbitration. The High Court's jurisdiction was conferred by s 9 of the Arbitration Act 1996, which was silent on the question of whether an appeal lay to the Court of Appeal. However, s 18(1) of the Supreme Court Act 1981, as amended by s 107 and Sch 3, para 37 of the 1996 Act, provided:

No appeal shall lie to the Court of Appeal—... (g) except as provided by Part I of the Arbitration Act 1996, from any decision of the High Court under that Part.

The prima facie meaning of this provision is that the Court of Appeal has no jurisdiction to hear appeals save where Part I of the 1996 Act expressly confers a right of appeal. Nowhere in Part I does this occur. Various provisions, such as ss 12(6) and 32(6) for example, specify restrictions on a right of appeal, but they take for granted that the right already exists. The prima facie meaning thus rules out *any* appeal from a decision under Part I, making pointless the phrase 'except as provided by Part I' and the various restrictions on appeal specified in Part I. However, the words 'provided by' might be used to convey either 'authorized (and controlled) by' or 'controlled (but not authorized) by'. The latter avoids the absurdity of the former and is consistent with the reasoned scheme of the 1996 Act, in which Part I takes for granted that there is, and does not aim to limit save as expressly specified, a right of appeal apart from the 1996 Act: that is, the Act itself did not create such a right, which instead arose from the grant of general appellate jurisdiction in ss 15 and 16 of the 1981 Act.

Section 107 made a series of amendments to other statutes consequential on the main provisions of the 1996 Act. The relevant part of s

---

[8] [2000] 1 WLR 586.

107, reflecting the changes made by the rest of the Act, was intended to bring the 1981 Act *expressly* into line with the 1996 Act, subjecting the jurisdiction of the Court of Appeal, which the 1981 Act establishes, to the limitations set out in the 1996 Act. (I say 'expressly' because the terms of the 1996 Act would in any case have limited the general grant of appellate jurisdiction in the 1981 Act by necessary implication; ironically, Parliament presumably chose to make this express to avoid the possibility of doubt.) The draftsman failed to express this lawmaking intention as clearly as he should have in the text of the amended s 18(1)(g), yet it was still open to inference. The point of s 107 was to make such changes to other statutes as would bring them into line with the main terms of the 1996 Act, which means that the changes that section introduced are to be understood by reference to those main terms. Hence, the structure of the reasoned scheme that is the 1996 Act, in which general appellate jurisdiction is subject only to such limits as are specified, makes clear Parliament's choice in s 107. Notwithstanding the awkwardness of its semantic content, the intended meaning of s 18(1)(g), which one infers by reasoning about the likely lawmaking choice, was that the Court of Appeal's otherwise general jurisdiction was limited by the restrictions on appeal expressly set out in Part I of the 1996 Act.

The significance of the example, and of many similar cases, is that the focus of the interpretive inquiry is rightly on what it is plausible to infer Parliament intended in enacting the relevant statutory text—that is, what meaning-content it intended to convey, which is the primary and direct source, and prima facie the content, of the set of propositions the legislature acts to make law. Particular provisions fall to be understood as part of the reasoned scheme that the legislature acts to introduce. The legislature acts for reasons and uses language rationally, which means that interpreters have good reason to reflect on the legislature's likely chain of reasoning in order to determine the meaning that the legislature likely acted to convey, which sets out authoritatively some changes to the law—to the set of duties and powers otherwise in force.

II. Intentions, Purposes, and Applications

I argue in section VI of this chapter that there is good reason in exceptional cases to qualify and to extend the propositions chosen by the legislature, which the legislature's formulations, understood in their intended meaning, articulate, by reference to the reasons for which the legislature acted. Apart from such exceptional, equitable interpretation, which itself responds to lawmaking choice, interpreters should focus on the legislature's intended meaning. Importantly, it is unsound to abandon the legislature's intended meaning (and hence its lawmaking act) in preference for either the further end or ends for which the legislature acts, commonly termed the statutory purpose, or for the beliefs of some legislators about the likely particular applications of the propositions the legislature chooses to enact.

The lawmaking choice, which the legislature aims to articulate and promulgate by way of the statutory statements (text) taken in their intended meaning, does not collapse to the legislature's reasons for action. The legislature does not aim to make fully known—to promulgate—to the community the reasons for each particular choice, instead intending to articulate the proposition it has chosen, the conclusion of its reasoning. The point is not that the legislature intends to obscure the reason for its choice or that inferring those reasons is irrelevant to inferring its choice. Rather, the point is that the legislature acts to make clear what it has chosen shall be done, the plan of action for the community that each is to adopt as if it were his own.

The reason to create and maintain a legislature is so that some agent shall have the capacity to choose how to change the law. The legislature acts to choose some plan of action, which it is unsound for interpreters to set aside by reference to some aspect of the legislature's further reasoning. Yet some of what is termed purposive interpretation has this character, with the court taking one end for which the legislature acts, referring to it as the statutory purpose, and concluding that the statute creates the propositions the court thinks best attains that end. This mode of reasoning fails to respect the structure of legislative action, in which the legislature selects a complex means—this set of propositions—to some complex ends. (Indeed, this unmoored 'purposive' interpretation often trades on scepticism about legislative intent, such that the interpreter is indifferent to the legislature's reasoning, being content instead just to adopt some purpose that the interpreter thinks sound.)

Raz and Marmor argue that interpreters have good reason to set aside the legislature's intended meaning when they judge this to be an unfit means to the legislature's intended end, for the alternative would seem to be an irrational preference of means to end.[9] However, that some choice is not in fact supported by the reasons on which the legislature acts does not warrant the interpreter substituting some alternative plan of action in its place (on reflection, the mismatch between ends and means might warrant adopting the same means but intending different ends; the means may also constitute a valuable intermediary end in their own right). Any such interpretation would fail to grant the legislature's authority to choose, by a choice which may be mistaken or unsound and yet be authoritative. This is not to rule out the possibility that in exceptional cases respect for the substance and grounds of the legislature's choice may call for qualification of its precise terms (see section VI). But this is quite different to taking the ends for which the legislature acts to license the substitution of alternative means. The legislature does not just choose purposes, which interpreters are then free to choose the means to attain. Instead, the legislature chooses a complex plan and while reflection on the end or ends may be highly relevant to determining the legislative choice and working out its consequences, it is the chosen plan that is authoritative.

The legislature may and usually does have a quite complex set of intentions, involving several sets of means-ends chains, such that one intention limits what would otherwise have been the expected means to some end, in the interests of some quite different end. It is unsound for interpreters to take 'the statutory purpose', detached from the full chain of reasoning on which the legislature acted, to settle the content of the law.[10] The better approach is to reflect on the further ends for (which are also often means by) which the legislature is likely to have acted in order to support inferences about the more particular ends and means for which it acted and hence the meaning it likely acted intending to convey. The following two examples help make clear the standing risk of unsound reference to statutory purpose.

The Fair Employment (Northern Ireland) Act 1976 made it unlawful for an employer to discriminate and s 16(1) provided:

---

[9] Raz, *BAI*, 291–4 and Marmor, *ILT*, 171–2. Raz refers with approval to Marmor's argument on point in n 27, 291.

[10] *Rodriguez v United States* 480 US 522, 525–6 (1987): 'no legislation pursues its purposes at all costs. Deciding what competing values will or will not be sacrificed to the achievement of a particular objective is the very essence of legislative choice—and it frustrates rather than effectuates legislative intent simplistically to assume that whatever furthers the statute's primary objective must be the law'.

In this Act discrimination means—
(a) discrimination on the ground of religious belief or political opinion; ...
and 'discriminate' shall be construed accordingly.

The Act did not define 'political opinion'. In *McKay v Northern Ireland Public Service Alliance*,[11] the applicant sought review of a decision of the Fair Employment Tribunal declining jurisdiction to hear his claim of discrimination on the grounds that 'political opinion' meant only political opinions having some connection to religion. The Tribunal held that the statutory purpose was to deal with problems of religious discrimination and that Parliament, recognizing the close connection between religion and politics in Northern Ireland, was acting to make sure that any measures for dealing with religious discrimination did not leave loopholes for its practice in another guise.[12] The Tribunal thus took 'political opinion' in this subsection to refer only to political opinion pertaining to religion. This reading is an implausible inference about the intended meaning of 'political opinion', when used in contradistinction to 'religious belief', and ignores the structure of the legislative choice, which seems to have been an intention to capture both religious belief *and* political opinion, with the proscription of discrimination on non-religious political grounds either a necessary means to the end of proscribing religious discrimination or an intermediary end in its own right. Either way (for either reason supports the lawmaking choice so intended and made), the intended meaning of political opinion here is an opinion about questions of politics, whether or not they are opinions that shade into or involve questions of religion. The interpreter's duty, which a focus on purpose at large may obscure, is to give effect to the chosen means, conveyed by way of the intended meaning of the statutory text.

A second example. Section 34(1) of the Evidence Amendment Act (No 2) 1980 (NZ) provided:

A registered patent attorney shall not disclose in any proceeding any communication between himself and a client or any other person acting on the client's behalf made for the purpose of obtaining or giving any protected information or advice, except with the consent of the client or, if he is dead, the consent of his personal representative.

---

[11] [1995] IRLR 146.
[12] The Tribunal referred to *Hansard* to make this inference, but I set this aside for present purposes.

In *Frucor Beverages Ltd v Rio Beverages Ltd*,[13] the court had to determine whether s 34 extended the two limbs of solicitor–client privilege to patent attorneys and their clients. Those two limbs are: a duty on the solicitor not to disclose communications, subject to the client's power to lift that duty, and an immunity on the part of the client, in respect of certain communications with the solicitor, from the ordinary rules of evidence. The subsection seems to extend only the first limb and says nothing about the client enjoying an immunity in respect of communications with the attorney.

The majority in *Frucor* opined that the purpose of enacting s 34 was to extend solicitor–client privilege to patent attorneys and their clients, that extending only the first limb of the privilege was absurd, and that one could take the second limb of the privilege to be implied. What is freely asserted is freely denied. No rational language user would utter the text of s 34 intending to imply, or taking for granted that interpreters would infer, that the second limb of the privilege extends to the clients of patent attorneys. And extending only the first limb is patently *not* absurd, as ss 31–33 show in forbidding clergy, doctors, and psychologists from disclosing information and yet in not conferring any immunity on the penitent or patient.

Imagine the majority is right about the legislative purpose, the legislature's further end. Still, the legislature seems not to have chosen the means to this end, and therefore has not changed the law to this effect, for in uttering this text in this context, the means it has (by hypothesis) chosen is to refer only to one of the two limbs. If this apparent choice were truly senseless that would provide some support for the argued implication, for one would then have to strive to determine what it was that the legislature did intend to convey. But the choice is not at all senseless, even if it may be unwise. Further, the intelligibility of the legislature introducing only one limb, which is wholly consistent with what one would otherwise infer was the intended meaning of the subsection, supports the inference that in truth the legislature acted to introduce part but not all of solicitor–client privilege or (implausibly) that it acted on poor advice about (or was simply overlooking) what that privilege involved. Either way, inference about the legislature's ends should only inform, not displace,

---

[13] [2001] 2 NZLR 604.

inference about the chosen means. The majority here invokes purpose to license departing from the legislature's limited choice.

The imprecision of 'purposive interpretation' makes it likely that courts will often focus on one or more (abstract) legislative ends, without attending to or identifying the more specific means the legislature has chosen to that end. Yet it is this chosen means, which inference about the end or ends may illuminate or clarify, that is authoritative.

It is thus wrong to conflate purpose and meaning. It is also wrong to conflate meaning and application. The legislature does not specify the particular instances to which the general rules it chooses apply. The claim that legislative intent is no more than the series of particular applications that the legislators have in mind is a recurring argument in the sceptical literature. Max Radin argued that legislative intent, if it existed, would be the pictures in the mind of the legislator, which determined whether any particular case (instance) was a determination of the determinable that was the legislative rule.[14] William Eskridge and others have likewise assumed that legislative intent, if it exists at all, quickly ceases to be relevant, because the terms the legislature chooses quickly outpace the specific applications the legislators foresaw and intended.[15] This is a misconceived explanation of language use, thought, and legislating. What the legislature chooses are general rules or propositions that employ open types and classes, that is, universals. The legislature does not choose the set of particular instances that fall within the general rules that it chooses, such that this set exhausts the scope of the general rule or such that when one applies the general rule to a particular (or specific class of particulars) not foreseen by the legislature one is no longer following and giving effect to the legislature's choice. An example of Lon Fuller's makes the point clear: a statutory rule proscribing possession of dangerous weapons applies to weapons (firearms, death ray projectors, lasers, light sabres...) yet to be invented at the time of enactment.[16] The reason for this is that the legislature refers to a class, a universal.

---

[14] M Radin, 'Statutory Interpretation' 43 Harvard Law Review (1930) 863, 871–2.
[15] W Eskridge, *Dynamic Interpretation* (Harvard University Press, Cambridge, MA, 1994), chapters 1–2.
[16] L Fuller, 'American Legal Realism' (1934) 82 University of Pennsylvania Law Review 429, 445–7.

The scope of the legislative choice does not collapse to the assumptions or expectations any particular legislator or legislators may have about the application of the chosen term or class. Those expectations do not form part of the proposal open to all legislators, which defines the legislative intent. This is not to say that the legislature is unable to act to make clear that a general class or type includes some sub-type or other. Imagine a section reproducing the jurisprudentially ubiquitous 'no vehicles' rule and consisting of four subsections:

(1) It shall be an offence to take a vehicle into a public park.
(2) The park warden has authority to seize a vehicle taken into a public park.
(3) Notwithstanding subsections (1) and (2), a licensed bus may be driven into the park between 10am and 3pm.
(4) Any bicycle seized under subsection (2) shall be released on payment of $50.

Subsections (3) and (4) imply that the legislature uses 'vehicle' to include the sub-types (which are also universals) 'bicycle' and 'bus': the legislative plan is to extend the proscription in (1) and the power in (2) to buses and to bicycles, as well as to other, unspecified vehicles. The legislature's lawmaking act makes it the case that citizens have a legal duty not to take vehicles (licensed buses aside) into the park. The legislative act does not exhaustively specify the set of particular devices that count as vehicles. This is entirely unsurprising, for the act refers to a type—vehicles—the scope and reach of which is open.

Further, and for the same reasons, the intention of the legislature plainly does not settle all questions about the application of the set of legal propositions the legislature acts to introduce. The interpreter's duty is to find and give effect to the chosen plan of action, but this plan may, often for very good reason, be incomplete or vague in some respects. Here the legislative intent frames subsequent action, including perhaps by affirming ends and a structure of means that the interpreter must adopt or respect in precising the vague standard or in elaborating that which is incomplete.[17]

---

[17] S Soames 'What Vagueness and Inconsistency Tell Us about Interpretation' in A Marmor and S Soames, *Philosophical Foundations of Language in the Law* (Oxford University Press, Oxford, 2011), 31, 55.

III. Legislative Context

The legislature makes known its intended meaning by uttering sentences that in context give interpreters good reason to infer that meaning (which may be the literal meaning). The nature of the context in which the legislature acts is thus central to understanding how the legislature conveys its lawmaking decisions and how interpreters should infer them. Marmor argues that the 'the context is not rich enough to make it obvious and transparent that the legislature could not have meant/asserted what it said'.[18] Manning argues to similar effect that 'semantic context' has priority over 'policy context',[19] such that the 'metric' for sound interpretation is 'the understanding of a hypothetical reasonable person conversant with applicable social and linguistic conventions', rather than a 'hypothetical reasonable policymaker'.[20] Each argument turns on an unsound account of the legislature qua agent, accounts that I criticized in chapter 8, section IV in the course of outlining my own theory of legislative action. The well-formed legislature is a single, rational agent, which there is good reason to presume acts for good reasons rather than for any reason or no reason (as Manning's account entails). I now argue that the context in which this agent acts is not thin or opaque, but rich and complex. Like other language users, the legislature exploits the context to frame how interpreters infer what it means.

Viscount Simmonds says that the context of a statute includes 'its preamble, the existing state of the law, other statutes *in pari materia*, and the mischief which I can, by those and other legitimate means, discern the statute was intended to remedy'.[21] Likewise, Bennion says that 'the context of an enactment comprises, in addition to the other provisions of the Act containing it, the legislative history of that Act, the provisions of other Acts *in pari materia*, and all facts constituting or concerning the subject-matter of the Act'.[22] The final phrase is an overstatement: the relevant facts must at least have been known to the legislature. Indeed, the context of legislation consists in what is known and of concern to legislature and community, for it is this that

---

[18] A Marmor, 'The Pragmatics of Legal Language' (2008) 21 Ratio Juris 423, 429.
[19] J Manning, 'What Divides Textualists from Purposivists' (2006) 106 Columbia Law Review 70, 92.
[20] Manning (n 19) 96.
[21] *Attorney-General v Prince Ernest Augustus of Hanover* [1957] AC 436 at 461.
[22] *BST*, 588, s 202. For Bennion, 'an enactment' is a particular proposition: *BST*, 394–401, ss 137–138.

bears on what the legislature is likely to intend to convey in uttering the text. The legislature partly responds to context when selecting the semantic content it is to utter, intending thereby to make plain to citizens and officials some meaning-content, and hence its choice about how the law is to change. However, the legislature also frames the context, because it adopts a complex scheme, which it intends to be read as a whole. The various parts of the statute inform and constrain how each is to be read.

Legislators craft the statutory text intending it to be interpreted as a presumptively coherent whole.[23] Interpreters will infer what the legislature intends to mean in this particular provision by reference to what they infer the legislature intended to convey in the other provisions of the statute. One reads the set of provisions to avoid surplusage, to make sense of the legislature's decision to use the same or some different word or phrase, and to resolve apparent repugnance, inferring the legislature's intended meaning in light of its decision to adopt this set of provisions as part of one scheme. Interpreters also rightly take it for granted that the legislature does not intend to impose contradictory duties or otherwise to introduce incoherence into the body of law. This holds too in relation to (apparent) conflicts between statutes enacted at different times, where interpreters resolve inconsistency between earlier and later statutes by inferring that the legislature has repealed (in a specialized sense of that term) the earlier statute by implication, but also presume that an earlier, relatively narrow proposition is intended to be preserved when or if inconsistent with a later, general proposition. Likewise, the legislature's decision to enable some mode of action may by implication proscribe alternative modes.[24] For example, in making statutory provision for some action, the legislature is taken to imply that the prerogative power to carry out that action and to make provisions relating to its subject matter is abridged.[25]

The legislature acts for reasons and the facts pertaining to the subject matter of the Act are relevant to what the legislature is likely to intend to mean because the legislature acts to convey its decision in this field. Therefore, what the legislature is likely to intend to mean is heavily informed by the nature of the mischief that it acts to address and the facts about this mischief which are known at the time of enactment.

---

[23] *BST*, 1155–67, s 355.
[24] *Blackburn v Flavelle* (1881) 6 App Cas 628.
[25] *R v Home Secretary, ex p Fire Brigades Union* [1995] 2 AC 513.

The interpreters infer what the legislature was likely to have meant by reference to what it would have been rational for it to decide, especially given the general scheme that its other choices disclose. That is, the interpreter reflects on the relevant problem, aiming to understand the legislative response to it, which means inferring the complex means-end packages on which the legislature acts.

For similar reasons, the interpreter 'seeks to avoid a construction that produces an absurd result, since this is unlikely to have been intended by Parliament'.[26] The presumption that the legislature does not intend absurd or anomalous consequences, while sound, is of course consistent with the legislature making mistakes or acting on reasons that interpreters find unpersuasive. Hence, the presumption informs inference about the legislature's reasoning and likely intended meaning, but does not warrant departing from settled judgment about what it is plausible to think the legislature chose. Importantly, as with language use in general, the context of legislation does not produce the meaning of the statutory text. Rather, the context in which the legislature acts is highly relevant to inferring the meaning the legislature acted to convey. It follows that the context of legislation is what is known and salient at the time of enactment, for it is this which is relevant to inferring what the legislature was likely to intend. Foreseeable consequences are relevant (and wholly unforeseen, exceptional consequences may be relevant in any event on the grounds of equity: see section VI below), but only because they inform inference about likely intention.

The context, Bennion says, includes the legislative history of the Act, by which he means the record of the proceedings within the legislature as well as the pre-enactment history of the relevant field of law. The use of *Hansard* (or equivalent) is a recent development in the common law world (outside the United States) and I consider it further in section V of this chapter. However, whatever the relevance of *Hansard*, the state of the law prior to the legislature's act has always been of central importance in understanding how the legislature has acted now to change the law. The interpreter cannot soundly infer what the legislature intended to convey 'unless he or she knows the previous state of the law, the defects found to exist in that law, and the facts that caused the legislator to pass the Act in question'.[27] The legislature often uses words that have particular meanings under

---

[26] *BST*, 969, s 312.
[27] *BST*, 599, s 209; *Heydon's Case* (1584) 3 Co Rep 7a.

the pre-enactment law and interpreters ask whether the legislature intended to use the relevant word to convey that meaning.[28]

Acts *in pari materia* constitute a common scheme: addressing a particular subject matter along the same lines, having identical titles or a collective title, or being deemed by the legislature to be construed as one.[29] The provisions of such Acts constitute part of the context because they are salient to legislature and interpreter, and are relevant to what a rational legislator would intend to convey. It is true also that the law in general forms the context—the legislature acts in response to and takes advantage of the complex set of legal propositions and principles that forms the law. The point of the legislative act is to change this complex set of propositions: to infer which changes the legislature intends one has to think carefully, as the legislature is likely to have, about the detail of the existing law. This argument holds for all propositions relevant to the subject matter of the legislative act, for it is this set that the legislature intends to modify, to some extent and for some reasons. The argument also holds in relation to legal principles that form part of the constitutional order, for such principles may loom large in deliberation or their continued force may be taken for granted. Hence, in England one presumes that statutes do not bind the Crown, that clear and explicit authorization is required before the Crown is permitted to levy charges for services, that there is exclusive parliamentary control over the supply of funds to the Crown, that (per the *Carltona* doctrine[30]) statutory authorization of a minister or Secretary of State extends to his officials, that commencement of primary legislation is to be achieved by statutory instrument rather than mere administrative action, and that individuals have a right to know of a decision adverse to their interests before it takes effect against them.[31]

The presumptions of statutory interpretation are important. However, contra Waldron and Raz among others, the 'canons of construction' are not rules that stipulate how a statute is to be interpreted; they do not stand to legal meaning and effect as semantic rules stand to semantic content. Llewellyn famously argued that the canons were contradictory rules and that they could rationalize but never justify

---

[28] *BST*, 601–3, s 210.
[29] *BST*, 603–4, s 210.
[30] *Carltona Ltd v Commissioners of Works* [1943] 2 All ER 560, CA.
[31] These six examples are drawn from P Sales, 'A Comparison of the Principle of Legality and Section 3 of the Human Rights Act 1998' (2009) 125 Law Quarterly Review 598, 601–2.

how a court interprets a statute.[32] The better view is that the canons are presumptions about what the legislature is likely to intend.[33] The presumptions are defeasible, but they helpfully formalize part of what the interpreter takes into account in inferring what the legislature means. This formalization is valuable because it is salient and helps frame how the legislature forms and conveys its intention.

The legislature may safely leave various points unsaid, say that the offence its enactment creates or regulates is limited to acts within the jurisdiction, does not apply retrospectively and does not oust the standard criminal law defences.[34] These points, which bear on the scope and content of the propositions the legislature introduces, will be taken for granted such that the legislature's act will not disturb them unless it is possible to infer that it intends as much or that this is a necessary implication of the meaning it intends to convey. Other presumptions point to some value or interest that it is likely the legislature took into account, such as the presumptions that the legislature intends to act consistently with international law and intends not to interfere with common law rights. The canons are pointers towards legislative intent. They jointly constitute an interpretive regime, which varies by jurisdiction, but none purports to or is capable of replacing inference about what the legislature intends in this particular legislative act. No legal system adopts a set of rules that settles what any legislative act means, for no set could respond to the range and complexity of legislative acts. The legislature may exploit the canons, like Grice's maxims, or make clear its departure from one by manifesting (more *or less* explicitly) its intention to that effect.

The legislature may explicitly cancel implications to which its choice of language in context may otherwise seem to give rise.[35] The craft of legislating is to formulate a statutory text that makes clear—in light of the previous state of the law, relevant general principles, the content of the rest of the statutory scheme and the law at large, and the ends that the statute seeks to realize—what the legislature intends to convey.

---

[32] K Llewellyn, 'Remarks on the Theory of Appellate Decision and the Rules or Canons about How Statutes Are to Be Construed' (1950) 3 Vanderbilt Law Review 395.

[33] J Evans, 'Questioning the Dogmas of Realism' [2001] New Zealand Law Review 145, 165–6.

[34] F Bennion, *Bennion on Statute Law*, 3rd edn (Longman, Harlow 1990), 230–1.

[35] For example, the Administration of Justice Act 1960, s 12(4) provides: 'Nothing in this section shall be construed as *implying* that any publication is punishable as contempt of court which would not be so punishable apart from this section'. (Emphasis added.)

The overwhelming importance of statutory context, as well as the capacity of legislators to frame part of that context, confirms that one does not legislate just by stating explicitly what the content of the law shall be. Rather one makes clear how precisely one intends to change the law.

IV. The Use and Misuse of Context: Some Examples

In understanding and interpreting legislative action, one goes wrong if one fails to see the depth of the context in which the legislature acts, which makes it possible for the legislature to promulgate its intention to make some particular change or changes to the law. This way of going wrong is made clear, I suggest, in a recent analysis of an example of Lon Fuller's, outlined in his famous reply to Hart, who imagined a statute saying:

It shall be a misdemeanour, punishable by a fine of five dollars, to sleep in any railway station.[36]

How does this provision bear on (1) the tired traveller waiting for a delayed train who nods off in his seat and falls asleep, and (2) the man who is stopped with pillow and blanket bedding down for the night, but not yet asleep? Scott Soames argues that what the legislature says in this statute seems to apply to (1) and not to (2) and yet these outcomes seem wrong.[37] He says one can imagine pragmatic enrichment of the sentence (that is, an intended meaning) which provides linguistic content to this effect, yet such enrichment may well be fanciful if in truth the legislature simply did not consider such cases (which, he says, is difficult to determine).[38] In such cases, Soames argues,[39] as do

---

[36] L Fuller, 'Positivism and Fidelity to Law: A Reply to Professor Hart' (1957) 71 Harvard Law Review 630, 664.
[37] S Soames, *Philosophical Essays, Volume 1: Natural Language: What It Means and How We Use It* (Princeton University Press, Princeton, 2008), 415–16.
[38] Soames (n 37) 416; Marmor (n 18) 428–9 endorses Soames analysis.
[39] Soames (n 37) 417.

Marmor and Schauer,[40] there is a judicial power to fix minor infelicities or oversights in legislative language use.

This conclusion is overly hasty. The intended meaning of 'to sleep' is very likely 'to sleep intentionally', which entails a voluntary act (actus reus) and a guilty mind (mens rea), rather than the mere state of falling or remaining asleep even without fault (if drugged or knocked unconscious). The legislature reasonably takes for granted, and thus intends, that all offences entail mens rea and voluntary action. This presumption is beaten back when one infers that the legislature intended the relevant offence to impose strict or absolute liability. One draws this inference in part from the semantic content of the statutory text but also from the nature and relative seriousness of the wrong and the prescribed sanction. It is likely then that (1) does not fall afoul the intended meaning. For (2), there are good reasons not to convict for he does not sleep in the station but rather takes acts preparatory to sleeping in the station, and one presumes that in specifying the criminal law the legislature speaks precisely, such that preparing to sleep is not a culpable act of sleeping. However, the legislature's enactment of this principal offence may entail that any such acts, if sufficiently close to the act of sleeping, are culpable attempts, by virtue of the standing proposition, which the legislature takes advantage of and does not intend to modify or set aside, that attempts are offences. Soames wrongly overlooks the richness of the context, in which the central distinctions about the structure of criminal law, and the operation of ancillary rules (here, about attempts) that turn on one's lawmaking act, shape the intentions on which the legislature likely acts and make it possible for the legislature to speak with relative precision and concision.

For an analysis fully attentive to legal context, consider this statutory provision:

Criminal Evidence Act 1898, s 4(1): 'The wife or husband of a person charged with an offence under any enactment mentioned in the schedule to this Act *may be called as a witness* either for the prosecution or defence and without the consent of the person charged'.

---

[40] Marmor, *ILT*, 179–80 and F Schauer, *Playing by the Rules: A Philosophical Examination of Rule-Based Decision-Making in Law and in Life* (Oxford University Press, USA, 1991), 209–10; for critical discussion see J Goldsworthy, 'Legislative Intentions, Legislative Supremacy, and Legal Positivism' (2005) 42 San Diego Law Review 493, 504–6.

One might utter the italicized words intending to mean that the defendant's wife or husband is a competent and compellable witness like any other. However, in *Leach v R*,[41] the appellate court held that the defendant's wife was competent but not compellable. The judges reasoned that a fundamental change in the common law should not be taken to have been made in the absence of express language. Hence the case is sometimes taken to stand for the presumption that Parliament does not intend to change the common law.

More interesting is the detail of the argument by counsel for the appellant, who carefully outlined the legal context in which Parliament acted, which informed what it is plausible to think the provision meant. At common law the husband and wife were in law one person, which entailed that neither was competent to testify in any proceedings against the other, subject to three recognized common law exceptions: high treason, personal injuries inflicted by one on the other, and forcible abduction followed by marriage. That unity could be broken by statute but otherwise the wife was not competent to testify against her husband (or vice versa). Various statutes before the 1898 Act had made provision for further exceptions, that is for further kinds of case in which the husband or wife was competent but not compellable, including some of the enactments included in the Act's Schedule.

Section 1 made the wife a competent witness for the defence but recognized the continued unity of husband and wife by way of para (b), which provided that the prosecution can no more comment on her absence than on the defendant's absence, and para (c), which provided that she cannot be called save upon the defendant's application. Section 4(1) provided that in relation to certain offences the wife may be a witness for prosecution or defence even without the consent of the husband. The offences concerned neglect, matrimonial property, cruelty to children, rape, and abduction. Subsection (2) provided that the Act did not change the existing common law exceptions, under which the wife was competent but not compellable even without the consent of the accused. It followed that there is good reason to infer Parliament used the phrase 'may be called as a witness' to convey just that the wife was a competent witness. The law prior to the 1898 Act was that the wife was not in general a competent witness. Sections 1 and 4 of the Act partly changed that legal position, making the wife

---

[41] [1912] AC 305.

competent for the defence in all cases (but in a way consistent with respect for marital unity) and competent for prosecution and defence, even without the consent of the accused, in relation to some offences, specifically those in which the wife (or husband) was likely to be the victim. The latter change in effect widened the scope of the common law exceptions, extending them to analogous offences, and doing so in terms that maintained the continuity with the common law, by providing that the wife was in such cases a competent—but not an ordinary, compellable—witness.

This line of argument is, I suggest, closely attentive to the full context of s 4, identifying with care the set of legal propositions, and justifying legal principle, which the legislature acted to change, which closely inform what the legislature was likely to have intended to mean in uttering s 4, which meaning it is reasonable for interpreters to infer.

Nothing in this discussion is intended to suggest that one may infer the legislative intent without very careful attention to the semantic content of the statutory text, for it is this that the legislature utters in the relevant context to make its intended meaning clear. Interpreters fail to infer legislative intent when they are insufficiently attentive to the rationality of uttering the semantic content in question. For example, consider *Yemshaw v London Borough of Hounslow*,[42] which concerned s 177 of the Housing Act 1996:

(1) It is not reasonable for a person to continue to occupy accommodation if it is probable that this will lead to domestic violence or other violence against him, or against—(a) a person who normally resides with him as a member of his family, or (b) any other person who might reasonably be expected to reside with him.
(1A) For this purpose 'violence' means—(a) violence from another person; or (b) threats of violence from another person which are likely to be carried out; and violence is 'domestic violence' if it is from a person who is associated with the victim.

Lady Hale concluded:

The purpose of the legislation would be achieved if the term 'domestic violence' were interpreted [to include] 'physical violence, *threatening or*

[42] [2011] UKSC 3, [2011] 1 WLR 433.

intimidating behaviour and any other form of abuse which, directly or indirectly, may give rise to the risk of harm.[43]

The italicized words convey an unsound conclusion about the intended meaning of s 177 (in fact it is no such conclusion at all, because Lady Hale purports to 'update' the statute, which is in truth to amend it by judicial fiat). The interpretation makes no sense of the legislature's definition of violence as either 'violence' or 'threats of violence... likely to be carried out'. Lady Hale's interpretation makes the second redundant for any threat of violence would already constitute violence. The reference to threats likely to be carried out plainly limits the class of threats capable of constituting violence for the purposes of s 177—threats not likely to be carried out, however abusive or injurious they may otherwise be, do not constitute violence. The semantic content the legislature utters limits sharply what it is plausible to infer it intended.

A more complex example is *Sellers v Maritime Safety Inspector*,[44] in which the court had to consider s 21(1) of the Maritime Transport Act 1994 (NZ):

No master of a pleasure craft shall permit that pleasure craft to depart from any port in New Zealand for any place outside New Zealand unless—

(a) the Director [of Maritime Safety] has been notified in writing of the proposed voyage... and

(b) the Director is satisfied that the pleasure craft and its safety equipment are adequate for the voyage...

The Director had ruled that pleasure craft must have a radio and an emergency location beacon before he would grant consent to depart from New Zealand. The court held that it was contrary to the 1982 UN Convention on the Law of the Sea for a port state (as opposed to the flag state) to regulate safety equipment carried by a ship on the high sea. The court rejected the argument that the provision (on its obvious reading) only created an offence in respect of action within New Zealand internal waters and so did not interfere with the freedom of the high seas. For, '[t]he effect, if not the purpose, of the provision is to place requirements on the exercise of the freedom to navigate on the

---

[43] [2011] UKSC 3, [2011] 1 WLR 433 at [28]. Emphasis added.
[44] [1999] 2 NZLR 44.

high seas by reference to the adequacy of the ship, her crew and her equipment for the voyage'.[45] The Director conceded that the point of the requirements was to facilitate New Zealand's responsibility for search and rescue in some six million square miles of ocean. The court concluded that the position at international law is 'that a port state has no general power to unilaterally impose its own requirements on foreign ships relating to their construction, their safety and other equipment and their crewing if the requirements are to have effect on the high seas'.[46]

The court then sought to read the provision to avoid any breach of international law. It considered taking 'a pleasure craft' in s 21(1) to mean only New Zealand registered ships. However, the court concluded that the context of the Act as a whole made this reading untenable. The Act distinguishes for different purposes between a ship, a New Zealand ship, a foreign ship, and a foreign ship in New Zealand waters. In using 'pleasure craft' in s 21 it is clear that Parliament did not intend to refer only to New Zealand ships.

Instead, the court took the powers of the Director to be limited by reference to the relevant rules of international law, such that 'adequate for the voyage' is read to mean 'adequate for the voyage so far as at international law it lies in the power of a port state to regulate this'. The court concedes that the conclusion that the Director's power differs in respect of foreign and local craft seems difficult to square with the general words of s 21 (and indeed its own argument that pleasure craft cannot mean only New Zealand ships).[47] The court relies on the presumption that Parliament legislates consistent with international law. This is unsound. True, there is (defeasible) reason to think it unlikely that Parliament would intend to place New Zealand in breach of international law (at the time of enactment). And true, part of the point of the Maritime Transport Act is to give effect to New Zealand's international obligations on point. However, the Act gives effect to those obligations, to the extent that it does (the presumption is defeasible!), by setting out a complex scheme, not by affirming in law the relevant conventions, such that the propositions otherwise chosen in the Act are subject to them. Indeed, at various points the Act does refer to the conventions, directing that rule-making power is to be subject to, or exercised by reference to, such. For example, s 47(2) provides

---

[45] [1999] 2 NZLR 44 at 48. [46] [1999] 2 NZLR 44 at 57.
[47] [1999] 2 NZLR 44 at 61.

that 'The Director shall not grant an exemption... unless he or she is satisfied... that—(a) the granting of the exemption will not breach New Zealand's obligations under any convention'. Nothing of the kind is to be found in s 21.

It is implausible to infer that the legislature uttered 'adequate for the voyage' intending to convey 'adequate for the voyage so far as at international law it lies in the power of a port state to regulate this'. No reader familiar with the context would infer this was intended. The court refers to cases in which general rules are taken to apply only within jurisdiction (or if outside jurisdiction only to acts of citizens)[48] and in which diplomatic immunity is held to preclude civil or criminal prosecution.[49] However, cases of this kind are not evidence of a general qualifying rule that domestic law is subject to international law. Rather, that statutes apply within jurisdiction is a proposition taken for granted because the legislature is responsible for *this* community; that diplomatic personnel enjoy immunity to prosecution for breach of some legal duty is a particular proposition of law which the legislative act does not change unless, by necessary implication, it ousts its continued application.[50]

It might be unwise for the legislature to authorize action that risks placing New Zealand in breach of its international obligations and it might repent of the legislative choice were that to come to pass. However, the court's task is to infer, from what was said in context, the choice that was made. The court's interpretation is unsound because it wrongly fixes on (and distorts) one element of the context and so adopts a highly implausible inference about what Parliament intended in uttering this semantic content. Also, the court's conclusion that the obvious meaning of s 21 is inconsistent with international law is dubious, for it only imposes a duty within New Zealand internal waters not to depart port without the consent of the Director. At best, the point is a subtle one. This is significant for the legislature very likely reasoned that the offence pertained only to what took place in New Zealand and hence that enacting the offence helped the authorities exercise their responsibility for search and protection consistent with the freedom of the high seas. The context of enactment leads me to

---

[48] *R v Keyn* (1876) 2 Ex D 63.
[49] *Governor of Pitcairn and Associated Islands v Sutton* [1995] 1 NZLR 426.
[50] Compare Evans (n 33) 156–7 who argues that diplomatic immunity is a qualifying doctrine that carves out an exception to the statutory rule.

infer that Parliament chose to authorize the Director to require *adequate* safety equipment, not adequate in so far as consistent with international law.

V. The Relevance of Legislative History

The main implication of a sound understanding of the nature of legislative intent for the practice of statutory interpretation is that there is good reason to read statutes with a view to inferring—at least as one's primary task—the meaning the legislature acted intending to convey, which meaning was chosen for reasons. This implication says nothing about the use to which legislative history—by which I mean the proceedings of the legislature recorded in *Hansard* or equivalent—is put. This is unsurprising for legislative history is at best partial evidence of legislative intent, an intent which the interpreter should strive to infer from the legislature's utterance of this text in this context. The legislative history may form *part* of the context in which the legislature acts. Alternatively, it may not be part of what is relevantly of concern to legislature and community, but may be further, private evidence of the legislature's intentions—just as the discovery of an author's personal correspondence may cast light on what he likely intended to mean in publishing some manifesto. In either case, the legislative history records some of the deliberation that culminates in the legislative choice, which is in principle relevant to understanding that choice.

Legislative intent may remain of central importance in statutory interpretation even if interpreters observe a rule excluding reference to legislative history, for the legal meaning and effect of the statute continues to be settled by inference about intended meaning.[51] Such inference is made from the text in its context, apart from the legislative history itself. Legislative intent is not discerned only or even primarily (if at all) from some distinct body of evidence, gleaned from the legislative history, which falls to be weighed *alongside* the text, the context, and the statutory purpose. Rather, it is that to which the semantic content and the context are relevant and of which the statutory purpose at best forms part, viz. the proposal for legal change on which the legislature acts. The interpreter strives to infer the

---

[51] See also Goldsworthy (n 7) 249–50.

legislature's choice, of the content of which the text and context are relevant evidence. The interpreter infers this choice from what is salient at the time of enactment, which includes public reports, official advice, and decisions of the superior courts, to which the legislature may have responded in some way. Hence, it is never safe to read a statute in isolation from the time of enactment,[52] for the exercise of the legislature's authority is to be understood in its relationship to that context, even if the application of its chosen propositions is not exhausted by what is foreseen at enactment.

The distinction between legislative intent and legislative history is made stark by considering two possibilities. Imagine first a prince who promulgates statutes but says nothing (outside the preamble, if any) about his prior deliberation. Imagine second a legislative assembly that does not retain a formal record of its proceedings, or which record is only made public years after enactment. In either case, interpreters aim to infer the legislature's intended meaning. The unavailability of the legislative history does not at all frustrate this. Indeed, it would be quite rational for the prince to decline to release a record of his deliberation (his notebook or diary or private correspondence), reasoning that the changes to the law that his act makes should turn on what is reasonably inferred from what he has made public. And the point of publishing the assembly's proceedings is centrally to make provision for public scrutiny and criticism of legislators, not to supplement or elaborate the intended meaning otherwise inferred apart from reference to such material. Likewise, it may be feasible to promulgate copies of statutes, but not to make readily available copies of the full legislative record, in which case it is sound to posit a rule that in inferring the legislature's intent in enacting this or that statute no reference is to be made to that record.

That the legislature's intended meaning falls to be inferred only from publicly available evidence entails that the secret diary or private correspondence of the prince is irrelevant (even if discovered and published) to the legal meaning and effect of his enactments. The same holds for the legislative assembly. However, one must add that the intention of the assembly is constituted by the proposal for action

---

[52] Contrast J Bell and G Engle (eds), *Cross on Statutory Interpretation*, 3rd edn (Butterworths, London, 1995), 52: 'the ordinary legal interpreter of today...expects to apply ordinary current meanings to legal texts, rather than to embark on research into linguistic, cultural and political history, unless he is specifically put on notice that the latter approach is required'.

that is open to the legislators and on which they jointly act. While it is logically possible for the legislators to all agree to a course of action that is defined by a secret proposal, known only to them, which is not intended to be transparent to the community, this is practically impossible not to mention self-defeating, for the proposal (by hypothesis, to change the law in some way) could not succeed unless it is capable of recognition. Hence, the secret diary or private correspondence of any particular legislator is not evidence of legislative intent, for it does not illuminate what was open to legislators at large.

Unlike the prince, the legislative assembly standardly deliberates in public and the record of its proceedings captures part (plainly not all) of this deliberation. Where the record of proceedings is readily available (at or about the time of enactment), legislative history is in principle relevant to interpretation. For the record may ground inferences about the proposal that was open to the legislature and on which it acted and this information is publicly available and so distinguishable from private knowledge. However, this proposition requires significant qualification. In the central case of legislative action, one need not refer to the record, because the proposal on which the legislature acts is transparent to the community, which is to say open to be inferred from the utterance of this text in this context, apart from the (partial) record of deliberation that culminated in this enactment. The reason for this is that deliberation and action centre on that which is open to legislators at third reading (or equivalent), which is in turn transparent to the community, members of which may infer the intended meaning without reverting to the record of the legislative deliberation, in which the focus was on that transparent meaning. Further, it is reasonable to presume that enactments are drafted (and considered, adopted) with the specific intention that the legislature's intent in enacting them be sufficiently intelligible to any competent lawyer who reads them, without reference to the deliberative record. That is, if the legislature acts well there is no need to refer to the record and the legislative intent will be what it is reasonable to infer it is—the reasoned choice of the scheme the text in context appears to make out.

It is unsound to assume that what the legislature *truly* intends is best gleaned from the legislative history rather than from the text uttered in context. The legislature is structured, for good reason, to make clear its intended meaning, such that its choice is very likely to be what it is reasonable for interpreters to infer. The legislature may act on a proposal that differs somewhat from that which interpreters reasonably infer it acted on, but this is a non-central instance, where the legislative deliberation has gone astray such that what is open to legislators differs from what is transparent to the community. It follows that legislative history is capable of making a difference only when what is intended is not otherwise clearly promulgated, which is a failure of legislative action. Further, the legislative history is a record of only part of legislative deliberation and does not exhaust the reasoning of the legislators, who reasonably understand their joint action to centre on the open proposal. It is entirely possible then that attending to what is said by particular legislators at various points in the process may distract one from the object of joint legislative action.

The standing risk of using legislative history to understand the legislative act is that the interpreter will fail to reflect carefully on what proposal was open to all legislators, and hence on which they jointly acted, and will instead take what some particular legislator or legislators say, at some point in the process, to constitute the legislative intent. A related risk is that what some legislator or legislators say about the purpose of some enactment or about its likely application will be taken to constitute the legislative intent, despite the truth that what the legislature does in exercising its authority is to choose means to ends, consisting in universal propositions rather than a series of particular applications.

The risks are made clear in *Frucor*, where the majority traced the origin of s 34 to a report recommending extension of solicitor–client privilege to patent attorneys and their clients (and drafting a provision to that end), a recommendation that the explanatory note to the bill purported to adopt, while saying that the bill attempted to prescribe the privilege in its own terms. This was at best equivocal, as the minority noted, and it certainly does not stipulate how legislators understood their joint action in enacting the bill. Indeed, the flat inconsistency between the report's recommendation and the text of the bill would have made very clear to the careful legislator that, notwithstanding the explanatory note, the open proposal was to extend only the first limb of solicitor–client privilege.

For legislative history to be used to help infer what the legislature intended, one must see clearly the structure of legislative action, in which the focus is on the proposal that is open at third reading and in which no particular legislator has authority to stipulate what the legislature is doing. The discussion amongst legislators, and the history of amendments moved and adopted or rejected, may help one infer the shape of the proposal as it develops throughout the process. But what is open to be understood at third reading, which should be transparent to the community at large, is decisive. Hence, one should not refer to the history in search of a statement by some legislator that stipulates what the bill means.

The focus of legislative deliberation and action is on the proposal for lawmaking that is open to legislators and which on third reading they jointly adopt. In the central case of legislative action, the open proposal is transparent to members of the community, which is to say it may be inferred from the statutory text uttered in the context of enactment. There are good reasons for legislators to understand their joint action to be defined in this way. There are also good reasons for the community, including its authoritative adjudicative institutions, to take what the legislature seems to have done to change the law. Hence, there is a standing problem in permitting reference to legislative history, in that it threatens to unsettle what is transparent to the community (for now, citizens and their advisers must refer to the record before concluding how the statute changes the law), which also displaces, or at least changes and complicates, the focus of legislative deliberation (for now, legislators must reflect on how the record of their deliberation is likely to inform inference about what they have done). The problem would be avoided if legislative history were only used when there was no other way to infer what the legislature has decided. It is uncertain whether it is possible to limit the use of legislative history in this way, for after all one may always attempt to infer what was intended. The landmark case of *Pepper v Hart* attempts such a limitation, providing that *Hansard* may only be considered when the legislation is ambiguous, obscure, or leads to an absurdity;[53] however I doubt this is effective.[54]

The problem is made clear in *Chief Adjudication Officer v Foster*,[55] a case decided immediately after *Pepper*. The case concerned a challenge to the vires of a regulation made under s 22(4) of the Social Security Act 1986:

---

[53] [1993] AC 593 at 640, per Lord Browne-Wilkinson.
[54] Bennion, *BST*, 623–7, s 217, concluding (at 626) that '[i]n every case involving the construction of an enactment, there must be a search in Hansard. This is because it is rarely if ever possible to be sure, without full knowledge of the background, that the *Pepper v Hart* conditions are not satisfied'.
[55] [1993] AC 754.

Regulations may specify circumstances in which persons are to be treated as being or not being severely disabled.

The relevant regulation set out circumstances not relating to the extent of disablement, but rather to the independence of the claimant. Taken in isolation, the subsection seems ambiguous for it could confer a deeming power to stipulate that some person is or is not 'severely disabled' or a defining power to make more precise the conditions under which a disabled person counts as a 'severely disabled' person. The court referred to *Hansard* and found that the origin of this subsection (and subs (3), on which more below) was in an amendment passed in the Lords making provision for further income support for severely disabled persons living independently. The government moved an amendment, which formed subss (3) and (4), which the minister said was intended to provide a premium for severely disabled persons living independently, that is, with no one else providing support or care for them. The court concluded therefore that s 22(4) was a power to deem persons to be or not be severely disabled (whether in fact severely disabled or not) rather than a power to define more precisely which persons are or are not severely disabled. The problem is that this conclusion is inconsistent with s 22(3):

In relation to income support...the applicable amount for a severely disabled person shall include an amount in respect of his being a severely disabled person.

What does 'severely disabled' mean in this subsection? If it means a person deemed to be such by s 22(4), then the provision is redundant or obscure. Further, if the effect of s 22(3) is contingent on the exercise of s 22(4) then a failure to make regulations means the subsection (and the duty to pay the amount in respect of severe disability) is defunct. Read jointly, one has very good reason to infer that s 22(4) is a defining power only. This intended meaning is what it is plausible to infer from the text and context. The court departs from this meaning on the grounds that s 22(4) is ambiguous, which it is not if read in context (this confirms the obscurity of the condition in *Pepper*, as well as the judicial difficulty in applying it).

It is arguable that what was open to legislators was a proposal to make provision for payment of a premium to severely disabled persons living independently, for this is how the discussion about the series of amendments proceeded. However, the careful legislator reading the amended text would be likely to see that the joint effect of the two subsections, understood to form part of a coherent, rational whole, was that all severely disabled persons were entitled to an additional payment, with s 22(4) serving to permit further definition. Perhaps the legislators who spoke in the relevant debate took 'severely disabled' to be elliptical for those living independently or perhaps they just assumed that there was power to deem only such to be entitled to the premium.[56] Either way, this understanding was not transparent to the community, for it did not follow from the joint adoption of the two subsections, and it is arguable that for this reason it was not open to legislators at third reading. In relying on *Hansard* to infer that the legislature acted on this proposal, which was not grounded in the statutory text or the context, the interpreters unravelled what citizens and officials had good reason to think was promulgated and what legislators other than those who spoke in the relevant exchange had good reason to understand themselves to be doing.[57]

I conclude then that there is a principled argument for the old exclusionary rule. While the use of the record of legislative deliberation is in principle relevant to understanding what legislators intended, the structure of legislative action, with its central focus on what is transparent to the community, militates against such use. Instead, interpreters should infer what the legislature intends from the text uttered in context, apart from the record of deliberation itself, and legislators should accordingly reflect all the more carefully on how they are likely to be understood and should choose their words carefully to that end. The integrity of legislative deliberation and action, in which legislators reflect and act on what is open to all, warrants excluding subsequent reference to that deliberation, for this unsettles what is open. It is sound then to protect reasonable inferences about what, legislative history aside, the legislature seems to intend, for such inferences are valuable not only to citizens and officials but also to legislators acting jointly in the exercise of their lawmaking authority.

---

[56] J Evans, 'Controlling the Use of Parliamentary History' (1998) 18 New Zealand Universities Law Review 1, 40–1.

[57] See also J Baker, 'Statutory Interpretation and Parliamentary Intention' (1993) 52 Cambridge Law Journal 353, 356–7.

VI. Equitable Interpretation

I argued in section I of this chapter that the central object of statutory interpretation is the legislature's intended meaning. I argue now that in some exceptional, *unforeseen* cases the reasoned choice on which the legislature acts comes apart from the legislature's intended meaning and that the reasoned choice is authoritative and should be taken to qualify or extend the law otherwise made out by the intended meaning. Interpreters should *recognize* exceptions or extensions to the statute's intended meaning in such cases. This recognition is a response to the legislative intent in enacting the relevant statute; it is not the exercise of a power on the part of interpreters to change the law that the legislature enacted. That is, what the legislature acts to make law is the set of propositions articulated in its intended meaning, taking that meaning as qualified by reference to its reasoned choice, a qualification which is apparent in exceptional cases. This way of understanding and giving effect to statutes is equitable interpretation, or at least one important kind of equitable interpretation.

The legislature acts to introduce into law a set of propositions that it judges there is good reason to introduce. The legislature chooses the propositions it articulates by way of the intended meaning of the statutory text for these reasons. However, the intended meaning may capture (or fail to capture) *types* of case that are unforeseen, in which the reasons that explain the choice of this intended meaning are absent (or are present). In such cases, the application of the rule made out in the intended meaning—the letter of the rule—may cause injustice, not because the rule is generally unsound, nor for some adventitious facts or circumstances apart from the legislative plan, but rather because the rule extends to cases that fall outside, or fails to extend to cases that fall within, the legislature's reasoned choice—a choice that could be called the spirit of the rule. The injustice of the rule's application to such unforeseen cases is in a sense an unintended side-effect of the legislative choice. The injustice is avoided, and the justice Aristotle termed *equity* is done,[58] if one understands the exercise of legislative authority as introducing such propositions as are articulated in the intended

---

[58] Aristotle, *Nicomachean Ethics*, V.10; see also Aquinas, *ST*, II–II q. 120 aa. 1 and 2, of which Finnis' paraphrase is illuminating: 'the radical justice of equity...departs from the common rule in its common (usual) meaning in order to uphold the rule in its true sense all things considered': Finnis, *Aquinas*, 216.

meaning subject to qualification (exception or extension) by reference to the reasoned choice. That is, the spirit of the rule qualifies the letter.

The legislative predicament is how to make law despite limited foresight.[59] This predicament entails that in relation to some cases, the legislature's intended (and expressed) meaning may come apart from its reasoned choice. The point of exercising legislative authority is to change the law for good reasons, which in turn entails that when intended meaning comes apart from reasoned choice the latter should take priority, for the point of the intended meaning is to articulate this reasoned choice. It would be unreasonable to exercise legislative authority with a view to making one's intended meaning law 'come what may'.[60] Instead, one should act to introduce the propositions made out in the intended meaning subject to an unarticulated proviso that the set of propositions is to be taken to be qualified by reference to the reasoned choice that explains the act, which is to say that the legislature should take for granted that its intended meaning will be qualified in exceptional, unforeseen cases. And interpreters should understand the legislature's exercise of authority accordingly.

The proviso 'in exceptional, unforeseen cases' is important because my argument is that only in such cases is it possible for intended meaning and reasoned choice to diverge. Equitable interpretation is not rule scepticism. It does not involve the collapse of every rule to its reasons, such that, per Raz and Marmor,[61] one is free to change or jettison a rule whenever one concludes it is an inept means to the rule maker's ends. Rather, it involves determining the rule that the legislature enacted while being alert to the possibility that the rule otherwise made out by the intended meaning may not reflect the choice that the legislature made, a choice which there is good reason to prefer to the intended meaning.

Endicott argues that '[e]quitable interference with legal duties or powers or rights' is not interpretation.[62] He works with the example of a bylaw that prohibits vehicles in the park and in which an ambulance enters the park to save an injured person. The driver of the ambulance is exempt from the bylaw, Endicott maintains, not because the bylaw is

---

[59] H L A Hart, *The Concept of Law*, 2nd edn (Oxford University Press, Oxford, 1994), 128.
[60] J Evans 'Sketch of a Theory of Statutory Interpretation' [2005] New Zealand Law Review 449, 450.
[61] Raz, *BAI*, 291–4 and Marmor, *ILT*, 271–2.
[62] Endicott (n 3) 120.

best interpreted as subject to an implicit exception, but rather because it would be unconscionable for the driver's action to be proscribed and because his action was 'compatible with respect for the role of the local authority in regulating the use of the park'.[63] I agree that there is no implicit exception, for there are no grounds to infer any such implication; the problem is rather that this type of case, in which there is a pressing reason to enter the park, was not foreseen by the legislature (whether or not some individual members of the legislature did foresee it). However, the absence of any such implication does not prove that equitable *interpretation* is a misnomer. Endicott wrongly assumes that interpretation concerns only the linguistic meaning of the bylaw. The interpreter should aim, I say, to understand the reasons on which the local authority acted, for this is highly relevant to whether an exception is compatible with the rule maker's authority. Apart from such reflection, the interpreter is left simply to assert that an exception is warranted, which fails entirely to address, face up to, and acknowledge the authority of the lawmaker to choose what is to be done. Endicott's is not an uncommon position.[64] It is nonetheless unsound for when one sees that the legislative act is a reasoned choice, reflection on the legislature's reasons helps one determine whether an exception is consistent with what the legislature chose.

It is telling, I think, that Endicott deals only with the one example,[65] thus collapsing the variety of equitable interpretations into one type, lending support to the claim that interpreters make exceptions to rules whenever this is morally justified. In truth, there are three types of equitable interpretation (a fourth is only a distorted instance), the variety of which helps make clear the importance of reasoning about the legislature's reasoned choice.

The legislature's intended meaning picks out various general classes by way of a set of propositions, which regulate or provide for some types of case to be regulated in a certain way. The reasons for this choice are that the members of the relevant class are taken to have certain features, to form a certain type or types, which warrant the regulation. Some exceptional, unforeseen cases may fall within the intended meaning, which picks out the relevant class, and yet lack

---

[63] Endicott (n 3) 119.
[64] See n 40 of this chapter.
[65] His treatment of administrative law is a tangent, interesting and important though it is in its own right.

the relevant features. Alternatively, some cases may fall within the relevant class and, while they possess the relevant feature, there is also present an unexpected feature which provides a powerful reason to act otherwise. There are also cases in which the intended meaning is thought to capture all cases of a certain type, yet where an exceptional, unforeseen case is of this type (within the legislative choice) and yet falls outside the scope of the intended meaning.

Cases of the first of these types call, I shall say, for corrective exceptions, the second for outweighing exceptions, and the third for corrective extensions.[66] The first and third are more obviously cases where the legislature's reasoned choice comes apart from its intended meaning. This is less obvious for outweighing exceptions, because the reasons for the choice do obtain. However, the analysis holds because the legislature chose the relevant course of action after considering reasons apart from the very pressing reason that arises in this exceptional case. For example, in making it an offence for persons to take vehicles into the park the lawmaker did not take into account the importance of emergency vehicle access. If it had, it would have made an exception to this effect. Hence, the legislature's reasoned choice does not support the application of its intended meaning to this case. It follows that in considering outweighing exceptions, unlike corrective exceptions or extensions, one is reflecting in part on what the legislature would have intended had this new reason been before it.[67] Still, equity centres on what the legislature chose, for an outweighing exception is only warranted if it is likely that the legislature that enacted the rule would qualify it in this new case, which requires one first to infer the reasons for which it acted.

Quite different is extension by analogy, or what was once termed interpretation 'on the equity of the statute',[68] in which the statute is taken to extend to all cases to which the reasons for this statute are also relevant. This is not equitable interpretation as I have outlined it for it does not aim to capture and give effect to the reasoned choice on which the legislature acted, which is to introduce some particular set of propositions for some reasons, not to stipulate ends for action which may then be extended to any relevant case. Evans rejects extension by

---

[66] J Evans, 'A Brief History of Equitable Interpretation in the Common Law System' in T Campbell and J Goldsworthy, *Legal Interpretation in Democratic States* (Ashgate, Aldershot, 2002), 67, 68.
[67] Finnis, *Aquinas*, 257–8, n 19.   [68] Evans (n 66) 68, 74–5.

analogy, in part because it is difficult to subject to principled limits and because extension of different statutes would create frequent contradiction.[69] This is true, but more important is its detachment from what the legislature has chosen. Extension by analogy does not respond to the exercise of the legislature's authority, in which what is chosen (which may be a compromise and/or a set of complex, limited means-ends chains) settles what is to be done. Hence, it is not a licit mode of interpreting legislative acts.

I will not trace the history of equitable interpretation in judicial practice.[70] I will, however, consider some examples to elaborate how equitable interpretation should proceed. I begin with corrective exceptions. An example of Blackstone's, which he attributes to Cicero, is instructive:

There was a law, that those who in a storm forsook the ship should forfeit all property therein; and the ship and lading should belong entirely to those who staid in it. In a dangerous tempest all the mariners forsook the ship, except only one sick passenger, who by reason of his disease was unable to get out and escape. By chance the ship came safe to port. Now here all the learned agree, that the sick man is not within the reason of the law; for the reason of making it was, to give encouragement to such as should venture their lives to save the vessel: but this is a merit, which he could never pretend to, who neither staid in the ship upon that account, nor contributed anything to its preservation.[71]

The lawmaker acted to reward those who risk their lives to save their ship and by means of that end (which is valued in its own right) to encourage others not to forsake the ship (which is in turn a means to the end of avoiding loss of life and property by shipwreck). The happy accident of the sick passenger's survival was an exceptional, unforeseen case that fell within the letter (the intended meaning) of the rule but not within its spirit (the reasoned choice, the means-ends chain that explains the rule), which warrants recognizing an exception to the rule.

---

[69] Evans (n 66) 70–1.
[70] For an illuminating survey of that history, to which I am much indebted, see Evans (n 66); see also S E Thorne, 'The Equity of a Statute and *Heydon*'s Case' (1936) 31 Illinois Law Review 202.
[71] W Blackstone, *Commentaries on the Laws of England* (Oxford, 1765–9) cited to 9th edn (1783), the last revised by Blackstone, Book I, 61.

Consider also the case of *Re Bidie (Deceased)*.[72] The Inheritance (Family Provision) Act 1938 allowed a widow to apply to court to set aside the provisions of her husband's will. Section 2(1) provided that '... an order under this Act shall not be made save within six months from the date on which representation in regard to the testator's estate for general purposes is first taken out'. In this case, letters of administration were taken out on the assumption the deceased died intestate. Fifteen months later, but before distribution, a lost will was discovered disinheriting the widow. The widow immediately applied under the Act. The court at first instance ruled the application out of time. The appellate court reversed, holding that in this context 'representation' meant 'representation in relation to a will', that is probate. This reading avoided the present (unintended!) injustice but would not suffice if a second will were discovered, for the time limit would run from the date of probate for the first will. The court suggested that one might read 'representation' to mean 'representation in relation to the will that is the subject of an application under the Act'. However, this is a tenuous inference about the intended meaning of 'representation'.

The case warranted a corrective exception. The point of the 1938 Act was to qualify testamentary freedom where testators had made insufficient provision for their dependants. The point of s 2(1) was to provide sufficient time for the widow to call testamentary provision into question, to encourage prompt applications, and to enable certain distribution of the estate. The means to this set of ends was a six-month time limit to run from the date of representation. The legislature failed to foresee the prospect of a will (or a second will) being discovered after representation had been taken out. This subsequent will might fail to provide adequately for the widow and should, on the legislature's reasoning, be open to challenge. However, the intended meaning of s 2(1), which the legislature took to express its reasoned choice, entails that no application is possible because the time limit runs from the initial representation. In this way, the intended meaning applies, and the time limit bites, while the reasoned choice that explains the time limit (that it makes possible a fair, certain period of time in which one may contest an unfair will) does not. It is sound to make an exception to the intended meaning of the rule on the grounds that the reasoned choice does not apply. (This is in fact a mixed case, calling also for a

---

[72] [1949] Ch 121; see Evans (n 66) 82–3.

corrective extension to make the time limit run from the date of representation in relation to the later will.)

Consider now corrective extensions. The statute 9 G. 4, c. 40, s 38(a) authorized justices to order lunatic paupers to be removed to the county lunatic asylum 'and if no such county lunatic asylum shall have been established, then to some public hospital or some house duly licensed for the reception of insane persons'. In *R v Ellis*,[73] there was a county asylum, but it was full and by law could not take additional persons. The court held there was no jurisdiction to order removal to a duly licensed house. I say the case called for a corrective extension. The point of the statute was to provide for the care of lunatic paupers. The means to this end was to authorize their removal to an appropriate institution—in the first instance an asylum, but if no asylum had been established then a hospital or licensed house. The legislature took for granted that if an asylum had been established it would be capable of receiving lunatic paupers, who should therefore be sent to the asylum rather than elsewhere. What the legislature did not foresee was that an asylum might not be able to receive someone, because full, or damaged by fire, etc.

The intended meaning of the statutory provision is narrower than the legislature's reasoned choice, for the meaning of the rule ousts the relevant jurisdiction whenever there is an asylum, even if it is incapable of receiving persons. And this entails that in such cases the justices are unable to send the lunatic pauper *either* to an asylum *or* to an alternative institution. This conclusion defeats the object of the Act and more importantly departs from the chosen means. The reasoned choice that animates and goes beyond the intended meaning is that justices should have authority to remove lunatic paupers to an appropriate institution, in the first instance to an asylum, but failing this to a hospital or licensed house. There is good reason to extend the proposition made out in the intended meaning to better capture what the legislature thought there was reason to do and indeed thought it was doing, viz. making provision for removal either to an asylum or, if impossible, to an alternative.

In *Lloyd v Saddler*,[74] two women held a joint tenancy together. One left to be married and the other remained in possession. The landlord applied for possession and the remaining tenant relied on the statutory protection open to 'the tenant'. However, the landlord argued,

---

[73] (1844) 6 QB 501, 115 ER 187; see Evans (n 66) 68–9.
[74] [1978] 2 WLR 721.

logically enough, that 'the tenant' had been the joint tenants and that the remaining woman had never been the tenant. The court refused his application, noting that in conferring protection on 'the tenant' Parliament had overlooked the problem that joint tenants may not remain together over time: one may die, for example. The court held that it should understand 'the tenant' to include each joint tenant considered alone. In effect, this was to extend the intended meaning of 'the tenant' to better capture Parliament's reasoned choice, which was that all persons in a tenancy should be entitled to the relevant protection. Thus, the court rightly recognized, without full explanation, a corrective extension.

Outweighing exceptions are more difficult. In *R v Registrar General, ex p Smith*,[75] the court had to consider s 51(1) of the Adoption Act 1976, under which the Registrar General had a duty to disclose to the applicant his birth certificate. The Registrar refused to provide the certificate on the grounds that the applicant was detained in a mental hospital after having killed two persons, one of whom he had thought was his foster mother, and was very likely to use the information provided in the certificate to attempt to kill his birth mother. The court upheld his refusal, reasoning that the statute was subject to an implied exception based on public policy, i.e. that statutory rights do not hold when their use may facilitate the commission of serious crimes. Sir Stephen Brown said, 'It is clear that the facts giving rise to this application and to this appeal are wholly exceptional. I do not believe that Parliament intended to provide an absolute right to the relevant information "come what may"'.[76] Staughton LJ reasoned that otherwise absolute duties may be subject to implied limitations; hence he thought this was an interpretation of the meaning intended by Parliament.[77]

It is true the facts were exceptional. But it is not plausible to infer that the intended meaning of s 51(1) was that the Registrar's duty was subject to public policy in this way. Rather, the legislature enacted a general duty to disclose (subject to specified exceptions, which were not relevant in this case), reasoning that persons were entitled to the information made out in their birth certificate. However, the legislature (understandably) had not foreseen that an applicant might be a murderous madman intent on killing his mother. It is true in a sense

---

[75] [1991] 2 QB 393; see Evans (n 66) 83.   [76] [1991] 2 QB 393 at 401.
[77] [1991] 2 QB 393 at 402.

that Parliament did not intend the right to be absolute, but only in that its choice to confer a general right to one's birth certificate was not informed by a consideration and setting aside of the reason not to disclose that is apparent in this case. That is, it had not intended the right to be absolute in the sense that it had considered such cases and chosen an absolute right anyway. This exceptional case falls within the scope of the intended meaning of the rule, but not within the scope of the legislature's reasoned choice in the special sense that the unforeseen feature changes, and would be accepted by the legislature to change, what should be done, such that the initial lawmaking choice does not extend to this (type of) case. In this way, the legislature's choice warrants recognition of an exception to the rule.[78]

Allusions to public policy all too often license unprincipled exceptions. For an example, consider *R v Secretary of State, ex p Puttick*,[79] on which the court in *Smith* relied. The case concerned s 6(2) of the British Nationality Act 1948, which provided that: 'a woman who has been married to a citizen of the United Kingdom... shall be entitled... to be registered as a citizen of the United Kingdom'. The court held this did not entitle a woman to be registered as a citizen who had been married in the United Kingdom under a false name, using forged documents to support her false identity. However, the forgery was not to secure that her husband married her or to secure entitlement to marry—she could have married under her own name—and importantly the marriage under a false name was valid. The court made an exception to the statutory right to citizenship. Parliament's choice seems to have been that all women married to citizens shall be entitled to be citizens. That the woman in question committed an offence in the course of marrying—an offence that did not concern her entitlement to marry or the validity of the marriage—is not a reason that obviously outweighs the reasons for the statutory rule (contrast the force of the reason in *Smith*) and warrants inferring that Parliament too would have made an exception.

Equitable interpretation is important and difficult. However, it remains an interpretation of the legislative act, for it centres on

---

[78] The case is strikingly similar to an example Aquinas uses in explaining the virtue of equity: '... the law requires deposits to be restored, because in the majority of cases this is just. Yet it happens sometimes to be injurious—for instance, if a madman were to put his sword in deposit, and demand its delivery while in a state of madness'. Aquinas, *ST*, II–II q. 120 a. 1.

[79] [1981] QB 767; see Evans (n 66) 85.

understanding what the legislature chose. It follows that to legislate is not to make one's intended meaning law, but rather to make a reasoned choice, one which is articulated in one's intended meaning but which may depart from that meaning, and hence may in exceptional cases warrant qualification of that meaning. Thus, I conclude that to interpret a statute is to understand the legislative intent, which means to infer the intended meaning the legislature acts to convey and the reasoned choice it makes.

Bibliography

Alexander, L and Sherwin, E, *Demystifying Legal Reasoning* (Cambridge University Press, Cambridge, 2008)

Anscombe, E, 'On Frustration of the Majority by Fulfillment of the Majority's Will' (1976) 36 Analysis 161

Aquinas, St, *Summa Theologica of St Thomas Aquinas* [A Summary of Theology]

Aristotle, *Nicomachean Ethics*

Arrow, K, *Social Choice and Individual Values* (Wiley, New York 1963)

Atienza, M, 'Practical Reason and Legislation' (1992) 5 Ratio Juris 269

—— 'Reasoning and Legislation', chapter 14 in L Wintgens (ed), *The Theory and Practice of Legislation: Essays in Legisprudence* (Ashgate, Aldershot, 2005), 297

Bach, K, 'Conversational Impliciture' (1994) 9 Mind & Language 124

—— 'Minding the Gap', chapter 3 in C Bianchi (ed), *The Semantics/Pragmatics Distinction* (CSLI Publications, Stanford, 2004), 27

—— 'Context *ex Machina*', chapter 1 in Z Szabó (ed), *Semantics vs. Pragmatics* (Oxford University Press, Oxford, 2005), 15

Baker, J, 'Statutory Interpretation and Parliamentary Intention' (1993) 52 Cambridge Law Journal 353

Beer, S, 'The British Legislature and the Problem of Mobilizing Consent', chapter 4 in P Norton (ed), *Legislatures* (Oxford University Press, Oxford, 1990), 62

Bell, J and Engle, G (eds), *Cross on Statutory Interpretation*, 3rd edn (Butterworths, London, 1995)

Bellamy, R, *Political Constitutionalism* (Cambridge University Press, Cambridge, 2007)

Bennion, F A R, *Bennion on Statute Law*, 3rd edn (Longman, Harlow, 1990)

—— *Bennion on Statutory Interpretation*, 5th edn (LexisNexis, London, 2008)

Blackstone, W, *Commentaries on the Laws of England* (Oxford, 1765–9) cited to 9th edn (1783), the last revised by Blackstone

Blondel, J, et al, 'Legislative Behaviour: Some Steps Towards a Cross-National Measurement', chapter 10 in P Norton (ed), *Legislatures* (Oxford University Press, Oxford, 1990), 186

Bratman, M, *Faces of Intention* (Cambridge University Press, Cambridge, 1999)

Brennan, G and Hamlin, A, *Democratic Devices and Desires* (Cambridge University Press, Cambridge, 2000)

Brennan, G and Pettit, P, 'Unveiling the Vote' (1990) 20 British Journal of Political Science 311

Brest, P, 'The Misconceived Quest for the Original Understanding' (1980) 60 Boston University Law Review 204

Burke, E, 'Speech to the Electors of Bristol' [1774] in R Hoffmann and P Levack (eds), *Burke's Politics, Selected Writings and Speeches* (AA Knopf, New York, 1949), 115

Carey, J, 'Presidential versus Parliamentary Government', chapter 5 in C Ménard and M Shirley (eds), *Handbook of New Institutional Economics* (Springer, Amsterdam, 2005), 91

—— 'Legislative Organization', chapter 22 in R Rhodes, S Binder and B Rockman (eds), *Oxford Handbook of Political Institutions* (Oxford University Press, Oxford, 2006), 431

Christiano, T, *The Rule of the Many: Fundamental Issues in Democratic Theory* (Westview Press, Boulder, 1996)

Coleman, J and Ferejohn, J, 'Democracy and Social Choice' (1986) 97 Ethics 6

Condorcet, M, *Selected Writings*, ed K Baker (Bobbs Merrill, Indianapolis, 1976)

Cox, G, 'On the Effects of Legislative Rules' (2000) 25 Legislative Studies Quarterly 169

—— 'The Organization of Democratic Legislatures', chapter 8 in B Weingast and D Wittman (eds), *The Oxford Handbook of Political Economy* (Oxford University Press, Oxford, 2006), 141

Cyrul, W, 'How Rational is Rational Lawmaking?', chapter 5 in L Wintgens (ed), *The Theory and Practice of Legislation: Essays in Legisprudence* (Ashgate, Aldershot, 2005), 93

Dan-Cohen, M, 'Decision Rules and Conduct Rules: On Acoustic Separation in Criminal Law' in M Dan-Cohen, *Harmful Thoughts: Essays on Law, Self, and Morality* (Princeton University Press, Princeton, 2002), 37

Dryzek, J, *Discursive Democracy: Politics, Policy and Political Science* (Cambridge University Press, Cambridge, 1994)

—— and List, C, 'Social Choice Theory and Deliberative Democracy: A Reconciliation' (2003) 33 British Journal of Political Science 1

Dummett, M, *Voting Procedures* (Oxford University Press, Oxford, 1984)

—— *The Seas of Language* (Oxford University Press, Oxford, 1993)

Dworkin, R, 'Social Sciences and Constitutional Rights – the Consequences of Uncertainty' (1977) 6 Journal of Law and Education 3

—— *Taking Rights Seriously* (Duckworth, London, 1977)

—— *A Matter of Principle* (Harvard University Press, Cambridge, MA, 1985)

—— *Law's Empire* (Fontana, London, 1986)

—— *Freedom's Law: the Moral Reading of the American Constitution* (Harvard University Press, Cambridge, MA, 1996)

—— 'The Arduous Virtue of Fidelity: Originalism, Scalia, Tribe and Nerve' (1997) 65 Fordham Law Review 1249

—— 'Reflections on Fidelity' (1997) 65 Fordham Law Review 1799

—— 'Comment' in A Scalia, *A Matter of Interpretation: Federal Courts and the Law*, A Gutmann (ed) (Princeton University Press, Princeton 1998) 115

——*Sovereign Virtue: The Theory and Practice of Equality* (Harvard University Press, Cambridge, MA, 2000)
Easterbrook, F, 'Statutes' Domains' (1983) 50 University of Chicago Law Review 533
——'Method, Result, and Authority: A Reply' (1985) 98 Harvard Law Review 622
——'The Role of Original Intent in Statutory Construction' (1988) 11 Harvard Journal of Law & Public Policy 59
Ekins, R, 'Acts of Parliament and the Parliament Acts' (2007) 123 Law Quarterly Review 91
——'Legislative Intent in *Law's Empire*' (2011) 24 Ratio Juris 435
Elster, J, *Explaining Social Behavior* (Cambridge University Press, Cambridge, 2007)
Endicott, T, *Vagueness in Law* (Oxford University Press, Oxford, 2000)
——'Legal Interpretation', chapter 8 in A Marmor (ed), *The Routledge Companion to Philosophy of Law* (Routledge, London, 2012), 109
Eskridge, W, 'The Circumstances of Politics and the Application of Statutes' (2000) 100 Columbia Law Review 558
——*Dynamic Interpretation* (Harvard University Press, Cambridge, MA, 1994)
Estlund, D, *Democratic Authority: A Philosophical Framework* (Princeton University Press, Princeton, 2008)
Evans, J, *Statutory Interpretation: Problems of Communication* (Oxford University Press, Oxford, 1988)
——'Controlling the Use of Parliamentary History' (1998) 18 New Zealand Universities Law Review 1, 4
——'Questioning the Dogmas of Realism' [2001] New Zealand Law Review 145
——'A Brief History of Equitable Interpretation' in T Campbell and J Goldsworthy (eds), *Legal Interpretation in Democratic States* (Ashgate, Aldershot, 2002), 67
——'Sketch of a Theory of Statutory Interpretation' [2005] New Zealand Law Review 449
Farber, D and Frickey, P, 'The Jurisprudence of Public Choice' (1987) 65 Texas Law Review 873
——*Law and Public Choice: A Critical Introduction* (University of Chicago Press, Chicago, 1991)
Ferejohn, J, 'Law, Legislation, and Positive Political Theory', chapter 7 in J Banks and E Hanushek (eds), *Modern Political Economy: Old Topics, New Directions* (Cambridge University Press, Cambridge, 1995), 191
Finnis, J, *Natural Law and Natural Rights* (Oxford University Press, Oxford, 1980)
——'The Authority of Law in the Predicament of Contemporary Social Theory' (1985) 1 Notre Dame Journal of Law, Ethics & Public Policy 115
——J Boyle and G Grisez, *Nuclear Deterrence, Morality and Realism* (Oxford University Press, Oxford, 1987)

—— 'Persons and their Associations' (1989) 63 Aristotelian Society Supplementary Volumes 267

—— 'On Conditional Intentions and Preparatory Intentions' in L Gormally (ed), *Moral Truth and Moral Tradition* (Four Courts Press, Dublin, 1994), 163

—— *Aquinas: Moral, Political, and Legal Theory* (Oxford University Press, Oxford, 1998)

—— 'Priority of Persons', chapter 1 in J Horder (ed), *Oxford Essays in Jurisprudence* (Oxford University Press, Oxford, 2000), 1

—— 'Helping Enact Unjust Laws Without Complicity in Injustice' (2004) 49 American Journal of Jurisprudence 11

Fuller, L, 'American Legal Realism' (1934) 82 University of Pennsylvania Law Review 429

—— 'Positivism and Fidelity to Law: A Reply to Professor Hart' (1957) 71 Harvard Law Review 630

Gardner, J, 'Rationality and the Rule of Law in Offences Against the Person' (1994) 53 Cambridge Law Journal 502

—— 'Some Types of Law', in D Edlin (ed), *Common Law Theory* (Cambridge University Press, Cambridge, 2007), 51

Gilbert, M, *On Social Facts* (Routledge, London, 1989)

Goldsworthy, J, 'Dworkin as an Originalist' (2000) 17 Constitutional Commentary 49

—— 'Legislative Intentions, Legislative Supremacy, and Legal Positivism' (2005) 42 San Diego Law Review 493

—— 'Moderate versus Strong Intentionalism: Knapp and Michaels Revisited' (2005) 42 San Diego Law Review 669

—— *Parliamentary Sovereignty: Contemporary Debates* (Cambridge University Press, Cambridge, 2010)

Goodin, R, *Motivating Political Morality* (Blackwell, Oxford, 1992)

Grice, H P, *Studies in the Way of Words* (Harvard University Press, Cambridge, MA, 1989)

Guest, S, 'Interpretation and Commitment in Legal Reasoning' in M Freeman (ed), *Legislation and the Courts* (Ashgate, Dartmouth, 1997), 133

Hardin, R, 'Deliberation: Method not Theory' in S Macedo (ed), *Deliberative Politics: Essays on Democracy and Disagreement* (Oxford University Press, Oxford, 1999), 103

—— 'Democratic Epistemology and Accountability' (2000) 17 Social Philosophy and Policy 110

—— 'Democratic Aggregation' in H Yung-Ming and C Huang (eds), *Level-of-Analysis Effects on Political Research* (Weber Publication, Taipei, 2001), 7

Hart, H L A, *The Concept of Law*, 2nd edn (Oxford University Press, Oxford, 1994)

Hobbes, T, *Leviathan*, ed A Martinich (Broadview Press, Peterborough, 2005)

Hodgson, D, *The Mind Matters: Consciousness and Choice in a Quantum World* (Clarendon Press, Oxford, 1991)

Horn, L, 'The Border Wars' in K Heusinger and K Turner (eds), *Where Semantics Meets Pragmatics* (Elsevier, Amsterdam, 2005), 21

Hurd, H, 'Sovereignty in Silence' (1991) 99 Yale Law Journal 945

Jorgensen, M and Shepsle, K, 'A Comment on the Positive Canons Project' (1994) 57 Law and Contemporary Problems 43

Kalitowski, S, 'Rubber Stamp or Cockpit? The Impact of Parliament on Government Legislation' (2008) 61 Parliamentary Affairs 694

Kavanagh, A, 'The Role of Parliamentary Intention in Adjudication under the Human Rights Act 1998' (2006) 26 Oxford Journal of Legal Studies 179

Keith, K J, *Interpreting Treaties, Statutes and Contracts* (Occasional Paper No 19, New Zealand Centre for Public Law, Wellington, 2009)

King, A, 'Modes of Executive-Legislative Relations: Great Britain, France, and West Germany' (1976) 1 Legislative Studies Quarterly 11

Kirby, M, 'Towards a Grand Theory of Interpretation: The Case of Statutes and Contracts' (2003) 24 Statute Law Review 95

Kousser, T and McCubbins, M, 'Social Choice, Crypto-Initiatives, and Policy-making by Direct Democracy' (2005) 78 Southern California Law Review 949

Kutz, C, *Complicity: Ethics and Law for a Collective Age* (Cambridge University Press, Cambridge, 2000)

——'Parliamentary Self-Government: Comment on Waldron' in E Villanueva (ed), *Legal and Political Philosophy* (Rodopi, New York, 2002), 39

Kyritsis, D, 'Representation and Waldron's Objection to Judicial Review' (2006) 26 Oxford Journal of Legal Studies 733

——'Principles, Policies and the Powers of Courts' (2007) 20 Canadian Journal of Law and Jurisprudence 379

Laver, M, 'Legislatures and Parliaments in Comparative Context' chapter 7 in B Weingast and D Wittman (eds), *The Oxford Handbook of Political Economy* (Oxford University Press, Oxford, 2006), 121

Lewis, C S, *Studies in Words* (Cambridge University Press, Cambridge, 1960)

Linz, J, 'Presidential or Parliamentary Democracy: Does it Make a Difference?' in J Linz and A Valenzuela (eds), *The Failure of Presidential Democracy* (Johns Hopkins University Press, Baltimore, 1994), 3

List, C and Pettit, P, *Group Agency* (Oxford University Press, Oxford, 2011)

Llewellyn, K, 'Remarks on the Theory of Appellate Decision and the Rules or Cannons about How Statutes Are to Be Construed' (1950) 3 Vanderbilt Law Review 395

Locke, J, *Two Treatises on Government*, ed P Laslett (Cambridge University Press, Cambridge, 1988)

MacCallum, G, *Legislative Intent and Other Essays on Law, Politics, and Morality* (University of Wisconsin Press, Madison, 1993)

MacCormick, D N, *Legal Reasoning and Legal Theory* (Clarendon Press, Oxford, 1978)

——'Coherence in Legal Justification' in A Peczenik, L Lindhal, and G van Roermund (eds), *Theory of Legal Science* (Reidel Publishing Co, Boston, Dordrecht, 1984), 235

——and Summers, R S, 'Interpretation and Justification', chapter 13 in D N MacCormick and R S Summers (eds), *Interpreting Statutes: A Comparative Study* (Dartmouth Press, Aldershot, 1991), 511

——'Legislative Deliberation: Notes from the European Parliament' in L Wintgens (ed), *The Theory and Practice of Legislation: Essays in Legisprudence* (Ashgate, Aldershot, 2005), 285

Maitland, F W, *Constitutional History of England* (University Press, Cambridge, 1908)

Madison, J, Hamilton, A and Jay, J, *Federalist Papers*, ed I Kramnick (Penguin, Harmondsworth, 1987)

Manin, B, *The Principles of Representative Government* (Cambridge University Press, Cambridge, 1997)

Marmor, A, *Interpretation and Legal Theory* (Oxford University Press, Oxford, 1992)— *Positive Law and Objective Values* (Oxford University Press, Oxford, 2001)— *Law In the Age of Pluralism* (Oxford University Press, Oxford, 2007)

——'The Pragmatics of Legal Language' (2008) 21 Ratio Juris 423

Manning, J, 'Textualism and Legislative Intent' (2005) 91 Virginia Law Review 419

——'What Divides Textualists From Purposivists' (2006) 106 Columbia Law Review 70

Mashaw, J, 'The Economics of Politics and the Understanding of Public Law' (1989) 65 Chicago-Kent Law Review 123

McCubbins, M, 'Legislative Process and the Mirroring Principle', chapter 6 in C Ménard and M Shirley (eds), *Handbook of New Institutional Economics* (Springer, Amsterdam, 2005), 123

McDowell, J, *Mind and World*, rev edn (Harvard University Press, Cambridge, MA, 1996)

McKay, Sir W, (ed), *Erskine May's Treatise on The Law, Privileges, Proceedings and Usage of Parliament*, 23rd edn (LexisNexis, London, 2004)

McNollgast, 'Legislative Intent: The Use of Positive Political Theory in Statutory Interpretation' (1994) 57 Law and Contemporary Problems 3

Mezey, M, 'Classifying Legislatures', chapter 8 in P Norton (ed), *Legislatures* (Oxford University Press, Oxford, 1990), 149

Mill, J, *Considerations on Representative Government* (Longman, London, 1865)

Miller, B, 'Justification and Rights Limitation' in G Huscroft (ed), *Interpreting the Constitution* (Cambridge University Press, Cambridge, 2008), 93

Miller, D, 'Deliberative Democracy and Social Choice', chapter 9 in J Fishkin and P Laslett (eds), *Debating Deliberative Democracy* (Blackwell, Oxford, 2003), 182

Mueller, D, *Public Choice II* (Cambridge University Press, Cambridge, 1989)

Neale, S, 'Pragmatism and Binding', chapter 5 in Z Szabó (ed), *Semantics vs. Pragmatics* (Oxford University Press, Oxford, 2005), 165

——'Textualism with Intent' (UCL–Oxford Colloquia, 18 November 2008) <http://www.ucl.ac.uk/laws/jurisprudence/docs/2008/08_coll_neale.pdf>

New Zealand Law Commission, *A New Interpretation Act to Avoid "Prolixity and Tautology"* (NZLC R17, 1990)

Norton, P, 'Parliament and Policy in Britain: The House of Commons as a Policy Influencer', chapter 9 in P Norton (ed), *Legislatures* (Oxford University Press, Oxford, 1990), 177

Oliver-Lalana, A, 'Legitimacy through Rationality: Parliamentary Argumentation as Rational Justification of Laws', chapter 11 in L Wintgens (ed), *The Theory and Practice of Legislation: Essays in Legisprudence* (Ashgate, Aldershot, 2005), 239

Panning, W, 'Formal Models of Legislative Processes' (1983) 8 Legislative Studies Quarterly 427

Paulson, S, 'Statutory Positivism' (2007) 1 Legisprudence 1

Pettit, P, 'Collective Persons and Powers' (2002) 8 Legal Theory 443

——'Deliberative Democracy, the Discursive Dilemma, and Republican Theory', chapter 7 in J Fishkin and P Laslett (eds), *Debating Deliberative Democracy* (Blackwell, Oxford, 2003), 138

Pitkin, H, *The Concept of Representation* (University of California Press, Berkeley, 1967)

Polsby, N, 'Legislatures', chapter 7 in P Norton (ed), *Legislatures* (Oxford University Press, Oxford, 1990), 129

Quinton, A, 'Social Objects' (1975) 75 Proceedings of the Aristotelian Society 67

Radbruch, G, *Einführung in die Rechtswissenschaft* (Quelle & Meyer, Leipzig, 1910)

Radin, M, 'Statutory Interpretation' (1930) 43 Harvard Law Review 863

——'A Short Way with Statutes' (1942) 56 Harvard Law Review 388

Raz, J, *Practical Reason and Norms*, 2nd edn (Princeton University Press, Princeton, 1990)

——*Ethics in the Public Domain: Essays in the Morality of Law and Politics*, revd paperback edn (Oxford University Press, Oxford, 1995)

——*Between Authority and Interpretation: On the Theory of Law and Practical Reason* (Oxford University Press, Oxford, 2009)

Rhodes, R, Binder, S and Rockman, B (eds), *Oxford Handbook of Political Institutions* (Oxford University Press, Oxford, 2006)

Richardson, H, *Democratic Autonomy: Public Reasoning about the Ends of Policy* (Oxford University Press, Oxford, 2002)

Riker, W, *Liberalism Against Populism* (W H Freeman, San Francisco, 1982)

——*The Art of Political Manipulation* (Yale University Press, New Haven, 1986)

Rock, E B, 'The Corporate Form as a Solution to a Discursive Dilemma' (2006) 162 Journal of Institutional and Theoretical Economics 57

Rodriguez, D, 'Legislative Intent' in P Newman (ed), *The New Palgrave Dictionary of Economics and the Law* (Macmillan, London, 1998), Vol 2, 563

Rosenblum, N, *On the Side of the Angels: An Appreciation of Parties and Partisanship* (Princeton University Press, Princeton, 2008)

Rousseau, J, *The Social Contract*, ed G Cole (Everyman, London, 1973)
Ruben, D, *The Metaphysics of the Social World* (Routledge, London, 1985)
Sales, P, 'A Comparison of the Principle of Legality and Section 3 of the Human Rights Act 1998' (2009) 125 Law Quarterly Review 598
Scalia, A, *A Matter of Interpretation: Federal Courts and the Law*, A Gutmann (ed) (Princeton University Press, Princeton, 1998)
Schauer, F, *Playing by the Rules: A Philosophical Examination of Rule-Based Decision-Making in Law and in Life* (Oxford University Press, Oxford, 1993)
Searle, J, 'Collective Intentions and Actions' in P Cohen, J Morgan and M Pollack (eds), *Intentions in Communication* (MIT Press, Cambridge, MA, 1990), 401
—— *The Construction of Social Reality* (Penguin Press, London, 1995)
Shapiro, S, 'Law, Plans, and Practical Reason' (2002) 8 Legal Theory 387
Shepsle, K, 'Institutional Arrangements and Equilibrium in Multi-dimensional Voting Models' (1979) 23 American Journal of Political Science 27
—— 'Congress is a "They," Not an "It": Legislative Intent as Oxymoron' (1992) 12 International Review of Law and Economics 239
Soames, S, *Philosophical Analysis in the Twentieth Century: The Age of Meaning* (Princeton University Press, Princeton, 2003)
—— *Philosophical Essays, Volume 1: Natural Language: What It Means and How We Use It* (Princeton University Press, Princeton, 2008)
—— 'What Vagueness and Inconsistency Tell Us about Interpretation' in A Marmor and S Soames, *Philosophical Foundations of Language in the Law* (Oxford University Press, Oxford, 2011), 31
Solan, L, 'Private Language, Public Laws: The Central Role of Legislative Intent in Statutory Interpretation' (2005) 93 Georgetown Law Journal 427
Shugart, M, 'Comparative Executive-Legislative Relations', chapter 18 in R Rhodes, S Binder and B Rockman (eds), *Oxford Handbook of Political Institutions* (Oxford University Press, Oxford, 2006), 344
Steyn, J, '*Pepper v Hart*; A Re-examination' (2001) 21 Oxford Journal of Legal Studies 59
Stoljar, N, 'Is Positivism Committed to Intentionalism?' in T Campbell and J Goldsworthy (eds), *Judicial Power, Democracy and Legal Positivism* (Ashgate, Aldershot, 2000), 169
—— 'Survey Article: Interpretation, Indeterminacy and Authority: Some Recent Controversies in the Philosophy of Law' (2003) 11 Journal of Political Philosophy 470
Thorne, S E, 'The Equity of a Statute and *Heydon*'s Case' (1936) 31 Illinois Law Review 202
Tollinson, R, 'Public Choice and Legislation' (1988) 74 Virginia Law Review 339
Uslaner, E and Zittel, T, 'Comparative Legislative Behavior', chapter 23 in R Rhodes, S Binder and B Rockman (eds), *Oxford Handbook of Political Institutions* (Oxford University Press, Oxford, 2006), 455
Vermeule, A, *Law and the Limits of Reason* (Oxford University Press, Oxford, 2008)

Waldron, J, 'Legislators' Intentions and Unintentional Legislation', chapter 9 in A Marmor (ed), *Law and Interpretation* (Clarendon Press, Oxford 1997), 327
—— *The Dignity of Legislation* (Cambridge University Press, Cambridge, 1999)
—— *Law and Disagreement* (Oxford University Press, Oxford, 1999)
—— 'Legislation by Assembly' (2000) 46 Loyola Law Review 507
—— 'Legislating with Integrity' (2003) 72 Fordham Law Review 373
—— 'Judges as Moral Reasoners' (2009) 7 International Journal of Constitutional Law 2
Wiggins, D, 'Deliberation and Practical Reason' in J Raz (ed), *Practical Reasoning* (Oxford University Press, Oxford, 1978), 144
Wintgens, L, (ed), *The Theory and Practice of Legislation: Essays in Legisprudence* (Ashgate, Aldershot, 2005)
Wollheim, R, 'A Paradox in the Theory of Democracy' in P Laslett and W Runciman (eds), *Philosophy, Politics and Society* (2nd series Blackwell, Oxford, 1962), 71
Yowell, P, 'A Critical Examination of Dworkin's Theory of Rights' (2007) 52 American Journal of Jurisprudence 93
—— 'Legislation, Common Law, and the Virtue of Clarity', chapter 6 in R Ekins (ed), *Modern Challenges to the Rule of Law* (Wellington, LexisNexis, 2011), 101

Index

Act of Congress 126, 223, 246
Act of Parliament 38, 126, 223, 246
Acts *in pari materia* 256, 259; *see also* context
adjudication 16, 69, 78, 119, 121, 132
agency, *see* group agency, legislative agency
agency model of legislative intent 6n
agenda-setting 13, 36, 41–2, 44–6, 89, 162, 165, 167–9, 172, 174, 227, 229
aggregation
   intention of the group as 75
   legislative intent as 9–10, 15–16, 20, 23–6, 29–30, 46, 47
   of preferences 77, 79, 81–90, 92–4, 97, 105n, 116, 168
   of votes 24, 67, 147, 220
   voting machine and 35, 39, 97, 100, 105n, 106
Alexander, L and Sherwin, E 50n, 187nn 218n
ambiguity 32, 192, 195, 196–8, 211, 214, 272, 273
amendment 27–8, 34, 36 8, 44, 120, 164, 169, 174–5, 226–8, 248, 271, 273
anonymity condition 71, 223
Anscombe, E 86
Aquinas 1, 52n, 64, 125n, 130, 148, 215n, 275n, 283n
arena, legislature as 170
Aristotelian synthesis 98–9, 106
Aristotle 162, 275
Arrow, K 41–2, 46, 85, 89
assembly; *see also* legislature
   agency over time 241–2
   Athenian 124
   bicameral 143–4, 146n, 149–50, 175
   community personified in 161
   compared to sole legislator 94, 121n, 144, 148, 151, 155–8, 178
   definition of 30, 146
   distinct from majority 51–2, 233–4

   doubts about capacity to legislate well 117, 161–3
   membership 31, 39, 149–50, 159, 221
   modern legislature as 3, 7, 12, 15, 33, 156
   of all citizens 146, 148
   open voting and 147n
   reason(s) to authorize an 12, 127, 143–4, 146, 155–62, 178
   record of proceedings 269–70
   representative and deliberative 148–154, 158; *see also* representation
   size of 12, 30, 97–8, 149, 157, 160–3, 179
   structure of 30–32, 39, 118, 156, 228–30
   well-formed 117, 143, 179, 243
association 10, 50, 52–3, 64, 75
Atienza, M 123n, 133
attributing intentions
   to a group 47–8, 50
   to the legislature 3, 12, 39, 45–6, 110–1, 114, 218–9
authority; *see also* legislative authority
   delegation of 168
   indirect, arguments for 102, 105, 115; *see also* voting machine
   nature of 94–6, 112–16, 124
   of sole legislator 136–7, 139
   procedures 52, 57–62; *see also* complex group action
   Razian 33, 94

Bach, K 193, 196–200, 204–10
backbenchers 26, 172, 174–5
Bellamy, R 141n, 240n
Bennion, F A R 2, 32n, 192n, 198–200nn, 202n, 214–5, 216n, 235n, 256, 258, 260n, 272n
bicameral(ism) 124, 144, 175, 229–30; *see also* second chamber

bill(s) 13, 21, 26, 28, 34, 36, 43–5, 51–2, 108, 110–1, 113–4, 116, 158n, 163–7, 169, 172–5, 178n, 184, 223–30, 232, 234–7, 239, 241, 271–2
Blackstone, W 2, 279
Bratman, M 49, 53–7, 59, 63
Brennan, G and Hamlin, A 145, 147–8nn, 150, 156–7nn, 177–8
Brennan, G and Pettit, P 24n, 147n
Burke, E 152
Burkean 155

cabinet 167n, 171–2, 174, 225; *see also* executive, government, minister(s)
canons of construction 111, 259–60; *see also* presumptions
Carey, J 149n, 160n, 167, 170n, 172n, 174
case law 121–2, 125, 242
cases
   A-G for Canada v Hallett & Carey Ltd 2n
   A-G v Prince Ernest Augustus of Hanover 256n
   Carltona Ltd v Commissioners of Works 259
   Chief Adjudication Officer v Foster 272–4
   Corocraft v Pan-Am 2n
   Frucor Beverages Ltd v Rio Beverages Ltd 253–4, 271
   Inco Europe Ltd v First Choice Distribution 248–9
   Leach v R 263–4
   Lloyd v Saddler 281–2
   McKay v Northern Ireland Public Service Alliance 252
   Momcilovic v The Queen 4n
   Pepper v Hart 18n, 32, 110, 272
   R v Ellis 281
   R v Registrar General, ex parte Smith 282–3
   R v Secretary of State, ex parte Puttick 283
   Re Bidie 280
   Rodriguez v United States 251n
   Sellers v Maritime Safety Inspector 265–8
   Stradling v Morgan 192–3
   Yemshaw v London Borough of Hounslow 264–5
central case of
   interpreting a statute 244–5
   joint action 47, 65–6
   law 121
   legislative action 127, 138–9, 221, 245, 270, 272
   the legislature 118, 121, 127, 161, 220, 222, 233
chain novel 17
choice-sensitive and -insensitive issues 80–1, 90, 92
Christiano, T 153–4
clarity in legislation 215–6
classical method of social theory 118
classical understanding of social action 64
coalition(s) 44, 170–2, 174, 237, 240–1
code theory of language 207, 217; *see also* language code
coherence 10, 40–2, 71, 175, 100–2, 139–41, 228–9, 237, 239–40, 242, 257
collective (ir)rationality 11, 66–8, 70–2, 75, 99–100, 106, 116, 148
coincident intention 49, 51, 53, 55, 86, 114; *see also* shared intention, summative accounts
Commission of Legislation 163, 169
Committee of the whole House 226
committee stage 227–8, 236
committee(s) 6, 26, 44–5, 114, 160, 163–4, 166–9, 173–5, 177, 226–8, 230, 236, 240
common good 14, 84, 90, 97, 99, 102, 105, 119–28, 130, 135, 142–6, 148–52, 154–6, 159, 219, 221, 242, 245, 247
common knowledge 48–50, 53–4, 63, 234; *see also* joint action
common law 16–17, 69, 260, 263–4
communication 17, 24, 52, 180–1, 184, 189–91, 194, 206–7, 209–10, 212

296 INDEX

communicative intentions 25, 180, 195, 205–8, 210
community personified 19–20, 161
company, acts and intentions of 58, 60, 74–5
compromise 13, 34, 37–8, 44, 81, 83, 87, 93, 102, 141, 153–4, 161, 233, 237–41, 243, 279
conditional intentions 26, 56
Condorcet, M 162
Condorcet's Jury Theorem 97–9, 105, 155
Condorcet's voting paradox 41
Congress 16, 21, 43–5, 120, 144, 164, 169–73, 177, 239; *see also* presidential system(s), Washington
consent 148–9, 159
constituency 88, 90, 150, 154, 156
constitutional limits 120
constructive interpretation 16–18, 29
context 2, 12–13, 185, 187, 189–90, 205, 208–12, 216, 218, 236, 240, 244, 246–7, 253, 256–64, 266–70, 272–4
conventions 111, 180, 183–8, 190–1, 193–4, 209, 256; *see also* language code, meaning, interpretive conventions
conversational implicature, *see* implicature
conversational intentions 19, 29
coordination
    in joint action 49, 52n, 65
    in legislative action 162, 165, 233
    social 126, 129, 136, 141–2; *see also* common good
corrective exceptions, *see* equitable interpretation
corrupt(ion) 84, 101, 127, 134, 144, 156, 159, 233
Cox, G 37 164–7, 173
craft of legislating, the 132–3, 260
criminal law 135, 238, 260, 262; *see also* offence(s)
Cross, R 4, 16n, 269n
customary legal change 121–2, 125
cycling 41–3, 86, 88–9, 101, 165, 166–7, 176

Dan-Cohen, M 238
deadlock 174
debtor's prison 133–5
defeasibility of presumptions 188, 260, 266
defection from group action 65–6, 222
delegate, legislator as 92, 152–4; *see also* representation, representative(s)
delegation theories of legislative intent 219
deliberate lawmaking 9, 122
deliberate legal change 120, 127
deliberation; *see also* legislative reason(ing)
    abstract moral reasoning and 130, 135
    at committee stage 227
    continuity over time 242
    and cycling 89, 101, 175–6
    and democracy 9, 94, 176–8
    feedback and 127, 132
    in plenary session 168, 178
    inadequate 176–8, 228n, 270–1
    integrity of 274
    and legislative procedure/structure 44, 164, 219, 223–4, 229–30
    and number of legislators 33, 149n, 157–8
    object of 128, 231, 243, 270, 272
    of assembly, representing the community 152–4, 160–1
    openness of 125, 152
    principle in 259
    public nature of 89, 175–6, 270
    and reasoning of the prince 127–8, 268–9
    record of 268–72, 274
    and voting machine 36, 99, 101
democracy 79–81, 84, 93–4, 148–50, 155, 158, 162, 174, 176–7; *see also* election, parties
determinatio 130–1
disagreement 30–1, 89, 94, 98, 151, 176, 222
discursive dilemma 69–70, 72; *see also* doctrinal paradox, collective (ir)rationality, group agency

dispositions 11, 72, 75, 131, 238
doctrinal paradox 67–9; *see also* discursive dilemma, collective (ir)rationality, group agency
document as author 25–6
double-talk, legislative 239
drafter 25–6, 235; *see also* draftsman, parliamentary counsel
draftsman 6, 249; *see also* drafter, parliamentary counsel
Dummett, M 86–7
Dworkin, R 9–10, 15–32, 33n, 40, 48n, 77–85, 90–3, 101–2, 140n

Easterbrook, F 22n, 41n, 81
economic analysis of the legislative process 83–4
Ekins, R 8n, 15n, 29n, 168n
election(s) 44, 70, 74, 83–4, 144–7, 149–52, 156–9, 167, 172, 174; *see also* democracy, electoral constraint, electoral system, electorate, voters
electoral constraint 144–5, 157
electoral system 150, 156, 173–4
electorate 88, 94, 145, 147–8
Elster, J 155
empirical reasoning 125, 130–1, 134
Endicott, T 189–90, 245–6, 276–7
equality, *see* legislators, formal equality of; political equality
equitable interpretation 14, 116, 137, 250, 275–283
equity 258, 275–6, 278
Erskine May 224–8
Eskridge, W 192n, 254
Estlund, D 94
Evans, J 116n, 192n, 203n, 211n, 212n, 260n, 267n, 274n, 276n, 278–9, 281n
exclusionary rule 274; *see also* legislative history
executive 143, 146n, 163–4, 166, 169–72, 174–5; *see also* cabinet, government, minister(s)
extension by analogy, *see* equitable interpretation

factions 34, 87–8, 114, 162, 233, 237; *see also* coalition(s), party, political parties
false personification 45
Farber, D and Frickey, P 42
feedback 72, 132, 178, 207
fiction, legislative intent as 3, 5, 19–20, 29
final reading 35, 158n; *see also* third reading
final vote 12, 106–7, 169, 229; *see also* third reading
Finnis, J 1n, 38n, 50n, 52n, 56n, 58n, 61–2, 64, 65n, 88–9nn, 118n, 125–66nn, 130n, 140n, 146n, 148n, 159n, 232n, 245n, 275n, 278n
first reading 225
formal language 213–4
formulation and proposition 126
forum of policy 78–9
four orders of knowledge 130
freedom to change the law 11, 120, 123, 141; *see also* voluntary control
Fuller, L 6n, 254, 261

Gardner, J 15n, 107–11, 113–4, 123, 126n, 132n
general welfare 78–9, 81, 90; *see also* preferences, utilitarianism
Gilbert, M 48–9, 53, 56
Goldsworthy, J 16n, 210, 212n, 215n, 246n, 262n, 268n
goods 124–5, 130; *see also* practical reasoning
government 144, 152, 155, 160, 169–72, 174–5, 177–8, 225, 227, 273; *see also* cabinet, executive, minister(s)
Grice, H P 182–4, 194, 195n, 196, 204, 206, 260
gridlock 166
group, two types of 50; *see also* purposive group
group action 13, 47–50, 52–67, 69, 71–3, 75, 98, 100, 117, 127, 158, 219, 221–2, 224, 231, 233

INDEX

group agency 11–12, 67, 72–4, 237;
see also collective (ir)rationality
group intention 10, 47–50, 52–8, 61–3,
75, 97; *see also* joint intention
group letter example 25–6
group(s), complex 10, 47, 57–8, 60–1,
63, 76
  legislature as 219

Hansard 252, 258, 268, 272–4; *see also*
legislative history
Hardin, R 92, 147, 155, 176–7
Hart, H L A 22n, 31, 119–20, 123n
hearer(s) 25–6, 194, 196–7, 204–11
Hermes 19–24, 26–9
Hercules 16–7, 20–1, 28–9
Hobbes, T 1–2, 33, 162, 245n
House of Commons 143–4, 165, 168n,
177n, 224–5, 228–30
House of Lords 143, 228, 230, 273
House of Representatives 144, 165
Hurd, H 136n, 180n, 238

implicature 194, 196, 199, 204, 215
impliciture 204, 208, 215
incoherence, *see* coherence
indexicality 197–8
indexical(s) 195, 211
individual acts and group action 53,
60, 64
institution, as special kind of purposive
group 221
institutional matrix 10, 43
integrity 16–17, 19, 20, 28, 78, 101–2,
140, 242, 274
intended meaning 12, 137, 209–10,
212; *see also* speaker's intention
  legislature's 12–14, 116, 212–4, 217,
244, 246–8, 250, 252, 256–8,
268–70, 274–8, 284
  statutory examples 192, 249, 252–3,
261–2, 264–5, 273, 279–83
intention of the group, *see* group
intention
intention(s) and hopes/
expectations 26–7, 139; *see also*
means-end(s)
interlocking intention(s)

and joint action 10, 54–6, 58–60,
62–3, 65
of all legislators 13, 220, 222,
231, 234
of the majority 233
internal hierarchy of the legislature 12,
89, 143, 164, 168, 179, 218, 223
internal point of view 84
interpretation
  nature of 245–6
  statutory 1–2, 4, 13–14, 16, 30,
137, 212, 244, 246, 259,
268, 275
interpretive conventions 181, 184, 187
invisible hand argument 98, 108

joint action 10, 47, 52, 54–7, 61–2,
65–6, 71–2, 74–6; *see also* group
action
  of legislators 161, 179, 221–2, 231,
241, 271–2
joint intention 10, 12, 46–7, 49, 52,
54n, 55, 57–8, 66, 73–4, 114, 231;
see also group intention, group
agency, shared intention
Jorgensen, M and Shepsle, K 237–8

king 149, 192–3, 209
Kirby, M 3
Kutz, C 65–6, 158, 159n
Kyritsis, D 78–9, 152n

language code 192–3; *see also* code
theory of language
language use 9, 12, 40, 111, 180, 184,
186–8, 190, 193–5, 207–8, 210–3,
217, 245–6, 254, 258, 262
language user(s) 12, 35–6, 183–4,
188–91, 193, 213–4, 253, 256
law, nature of 125
Lawgiver 162–3, 169
legal change, need for 119–22,
124–5, 127
legal content 211–2, 216
legal system(s) 3, 31, 112, 119–21, 126,
180, 186, 244, 247, 260
legislation, nature of 83–4, 123, 125–6,
212–3

legislative act as reasoned choice 13, 117, 128, 131, 142, 224, 236, 242, 247, 270
legislative agency 10–11, 14, 223, 236–7, 239, 241–3, 244, 250, 256
  denial of 35, 37, 40, 97
legislative agenda 12, 114, 166, 171–2, 174
legislative assembly, *see* assembly
legislative authority, exercise of 14, 77, 101, 108, 123–4, 245, 247, 275–6; *see also* authority
  by group 223, 233
  by one person 114–5, 144–5
legislative capacity 123, 127, 143, 147, 162, 172, 176 219–21, 242; *see also* legislative function
legislative deliberation, *see* deliberation
legislative function 7–8, 90, 98, 122, 124, 126, 138–9, 141, 218; *see also* legislative capacity
legislative history 13–14, 17–18, 32, 45, 241, 244, 256, 258, 268–72, 274; *see also* Hansard, *travaux préparatoires*
legislative integrity 78, 140, 242
legislative intent, defined 230–1, 242–3; *see also* particular intention(s), standing intention(s)
legislative offices 4, 12, 147, 158, 160, 165–7
legislative proposal(s) 36, 78, 124, 151, 162, 172–3, 175, 177–8, 222, 225, 230
legislative reason(ing) 93, 98, 125, 130, 132–4, 143, 152–3; *see also* deliberation
legislative state of nature 164–5, 167
legislative structure 11, 82; *see also* internal hierarchy, legislative offices, standing intention(s)
legislators
  enthusiastic and reluctant 232–3
  formal equality of 23, 163, 222
  ignorant 13, 114, 233
  large number of 156–8, 160, 162–3
  leading 12, 89, 171, 174, 176, 242
  minority 13, 21, 23, 51–2, 110–11, 114, 219, 232, 241–2

  and ordinary speakers 24–5, 27–8, 30
  reasonable 13, 77, 102, 107, 154, 191, 222, 236, 238
legislature; *see also* assembly, sole legislator
  agent 4, 10, 13, 14, 113, 140, 161; *see also* legislative agency
  arena vs. transformational 170–1
  capable of reasoned choice 117, 179, 223
  central case 118, 121, 127, 161, 220, 222, 233
  deliberative 4, 12, 93, 151–2, 155, 175, 178
  focus of democratic political life 9
  machine 4, 83–5, 88; *see also* voting machine
  representative 4, 12, 93, 121, 148, 149, 155, 158, 178
  responsive to numbers 79, 82–3, 93
  self-starting, self-directing 123; *see also* voluntary control
  well-formed 9, 14, 40, 77, 107, 127, 211, 216–17, 224, 233, 237, 243–4, 256
linguistic community 182, 189, 193
linguistic conventions 183, 194, 256
Linz, J 144–5nn, 174
List, C and Pettit, P 67–9, 71–3, 223
Llewellyn, K 259–60
lobbyists 21, 27, 81–3
Locke, J 156n, 157, 159n, 162–3
logrolling 37–8, 46

MacCallum, G 6n, 23n, 51, 218n
MacCormick, D N 153, 203n, 222–3
MacCormick, D N and Summers, R S 3
McCubbins, M 148n, 165–9nn, 173, 229n, 240n,
McKay, W, *see* Erskine May
McNollgast 240–1
Madison, J 162–3
majority intention model of legislative intent 6n, 52, 218; *see also* summative accounts
majority party 169–71, 174–5, 226, 229

majority voting procedures 31, 41, 52, 58, 67, 219–20, 222, 234
Manin, B 150n, 155n
Manning, J 2n, 41n, 231, 239–40, 256
Marmor, A 32n, 47–8, 50–2, 98n, 139–40, 218n, 237–9, 250, 251n, 256, 261n, 262, 276
Mashaw, J 41n, 43
meaning; *see also* meaning-content, intended meaning, semantics, pragmatics, code theory
  acontextual 188–90
  conventional 12, 32, 38–40, 104, 107, 113–4, 180–1, 184, 187, 191, 193, 210
  figurative 195–6
  intuitions about 204–5
  literal 12–13, 190, 193, 195n, 196–205, 208, 211, 216, 256
  non-conventional 187
  non-literal 187, 195–6
  sentence 102, 182, 184, 195, 198, 205, 209–11
  shared 181
  speaker's 189, 210; *see also* speaker's intention
  utterance 189, 190–1, 209–10
meaning-content 194, 211–2, 214, 216, 246, 249, 257; *see also* intended meaning
means-end(s) 58, 62, 136–8, 142, 154, 237, 251, 279
membership of assembly 31, 39, 149–50, 159, 221
membership of legislature 22
Mezey, M 171, 174n, 175n
military, acts and intentions of 61–4
Mill, J 98, 162–3
Miller, B 78n
Miller, D 81, 156n, 176n
minimal intention 77, 107, 109–15, 180, 184
minister(s) 26, 166, 168n, 172, 174–5, 225, 228–9, 234–5, 259, 273
minority party 156–7, 165–6, 172
mischief 32, 209, 236, 256–7; *see also* purpose, statutory

monarch 155, 162; *see also* king, prince, queen
motives and intentions 38
mystic code 185–6

natural language 180–2, 187, 193, 212–4
Neale, S 197–8, 202–7, 210
non-literal use 199–200, 202, 204
Norton, P 171

objectified vs. subjective intent 231
offence(s) 200–2, 204, 255, 262–4, 265, 267, 278, 283
open proposal 13, 219, 231, 234, 240, 243, 271–2
outweighing exceptions, *see* equitable interpretation

Parliament 109–11, 120, 124, 143–4, 147, 149, 152, 154n, 157, 164, 168n, 170–1, 174, 191–3, 209, 223–4, 247n, 249, 252, 258, 263, 266–8, 282–3
parliamentary counsel 225, 229, 235; *see also* drafter, draftsman
parliamentary procedure(s) 35, 107, 177, 224–5, 228–9, 243
parliamentary sovereignty 120
parliamentary system(s) 169–77, 239–40
particular intention(s) 58, 60, 76, 183–4; *see also* means-end(s)
  of the legislature 110, 219–20, 224, 232–3
party 3, 69–70, 74, 145, 150–2, 154, 156–7, 163, 167–78, 226, 229, 232, 240; *see also* majority party, minority party, political parties
party unity 171–2
personification of groups, in *Law's Empire* 19–20
Pettit, P 63n, 69–70, 100, 148; *see also* List, C and Pettit, P
pivotal legislators 241
plan of action 10, 47, 52–3, 55, 57–8, 61–3, 65, 102; *see also* open proposal

and legislating 11, 102, 136–8, 140, 243, 250–1, 255; *see also* legislative proposal(s)
plenary
  legislative authority 168
  session 164, 168–9, 177–8, 228, 236
  time 162, 164–5, 172, 236
poison pill 232–3; *see also* wrecking amendment
policy, distinction between principle and 78, 81, 91
political equality 94, 158–9
political parties 48, 50, 164, 167
political party, *see* party
political scientist(s) 40–1, 163, 166, 174, 240n, 245
Polsby, N 170–1
popular participation 94, 143, 158
practical reason(ing) 62, 102, 125–6, 128–31, 136–7
pragmatic enrichment 204, 261
pragmatics 203–9, 211–4, 238, 261
preamble 225–6, 228, 256, 269
preferences 41–2, 44–6, 77, 79–94, 97, 105n, 116, 150, 168, 170, 240–1
premise-based procedure 67, 69, 72; *see also* sequential priority procedure
president 21, 145, 149, 155–60, 169, 172–4
presidential system(s) 145n, 169, 170, 172–4, 239–40; *see also* Washington, Westminster
presidential veto 44, 144
presumptions 258–60, 262–3, 266; *see also* canons of construction
primary intention, *see* particular intention(s)
prince 11–12, 127–8, 130–5, 137, 139–45, 148, 151, 155–9, 160–1, 178, 237, 242, 269–70; *see also* king, monarch, sole legislator
promulgation 125, 185–6, 247
propositions, interlinked 11, 75, 133
public act, legislating as 138, 247; *see also* promulgation
public choice theory 83–4, 92, 100
purpose, statutory 250–2, 268

purposive groups 50, 107
  assembly as 146
  legislative assembly as 221–2; *see also* institution
  legislators forming 220
  majority is not 234
  party as 156
purposive interpretation 137, 250, 254; *see also* purpose, statutory

Queen 21, 144, 168n
Queen-in-Parliament 31, 144

Radbruch, G 4–5, 7–9
Radin, M 5–10, 38, 254
Raz, J 31, 33, 94, 107–15, 121, 124n, 140n, 141, 180–1, 182n, 183–8, 191, 193–4, 210–11, 220n, 232n, 234n, 250–1, 259, 276
Razian authority, *see* authority
reader(s) 194–5, 215, 231, 267
reasonable sole legislator 115, 127, 139, 218, 220, 222, 229, 236; *see also* prince, sole legislator
reasoned scheme 13, 175, 228–9, 236, 240, 244, 248–9
reasoning in public 155
referenda 91–2, 124, 147–8
repeal 22, 119, 123, 128, 135, 215, 234, 245
  by implication 137, 242, 257
representation 92, 149n, 152, 155; *see also* delegate, deliberation, trustee
representative(s) 92, 149–50, 152–4, 157–8, 162–4
representative democracy 80–1, 155
reversionary policy 167, 172
Richardson, H 94, 141n, 240n
Riker, W 85, 88n
Rock, E 74n
Rousseau, J 162–3
rule of adjudication 119
rule of change 120–1
rule of law 125, 132, 138, 140, 144, 212
rule of legislative competence 22, 120, 221
rule of recognition 31, 120

302 INDEX

sanction(s) 89, 129, 133, 262
Sales, P 259n
Scalia, A 3, 203
Schauer, F 188–91, 193
Searle, J 48n, 50n, 53, 56–8, 59n, 61
second reading 225–8, 236
Shapiro, S 65–6
standing intention(s) 58, 60–1, 63, 76
　of the legislature 219–24, 230, 233–4, 236, 241–3
second chamber 143, 150, 230; *see also* bicameral(ism)
secondary intention, *see* standing intention(s)
semantic autonomy 188–90; *see also* meaning, acontextual; code theory
semantic content 12, 194–9, 201–9, 211–7, 218
　of the statutory text 220, 235–6
semantic context vs. policy context 256
semantics 193–4, 199, 203–4, 206, 209, 211–2
Senate 45, 144, 157
Senator Smith 24, 27
sequential priority procedure 72
shared intention 12, 24, 47–8, 50–2, 54, 110, 184, 218
Shepsle, K 41–6, 83, 84n, 89n, 237, 238n
slavery 154
sleeping in railway hypothetical 261
Soames, S 197n, 198, 199n, 204, 255n, 261–2
social action, classical understanding of 64
social choice theory 9, 40–1, 46, 85
sole legislator 33, 115, 127–9, 137, 139, 142, 144–5, 157n, 158, 160, 178, 218, 220, 222–4, 229–30, 235–7
sovereign 7, 141, 162, 170
Speaker, the 166–8, 227
speaker, rational 194, 198, 201, 206, 210–11
speaker's intention 183, 188, 194, 203, 206, 210; *see also* intended meaning
speaker's meaning theory of legislative intent 17–20, 21n, 24, 26, 29, 30

specification 130, 132, 152, 154, 238; *see also* determinatio
standing orders 224, 228
statute, checkerboard 101–2
statutes
　7 Ed. 6 Cap. 1 192–3
　9 G. 4, c. 40 281
　Adoption Act 1976 282–3
　Arbitration Act 1996 248–9
　British Nationality Act 1948 283
　Criminal Evidence Act 1898 262–4
　Criminal Law Act 1967 202
　Endangered Species Act 18
　Evidence Amendment Act (No 2) 1980 (NZ) 252–3
　Fair Employment (Northern Ireland) Act 1976 251–2
　Family Law Reform Act 1969 198
　Finance Act 2008 37
　House of Commons Disqualification Act 1975 215
　Housing Act 1996 264–5
　Inheritance (Family Provision) Act 1938 280
　Lands Clauses Consolidation Act 1845 214
　Malicious Damage Act 1861 203–4
　Maritime Transport Act 1994 (NZ) 265–6
　Matrimonial Proceedings (Magistrates' Courts) Act 1960, 199
　Northern Ireland Assembly Disqualification Act 1975 215
　Offences against the Person Act 1861 202
　Parliament Acts 1911 and 1949 168n
　Police and Criminal Evidence Act 1984 198, 202
　Prices and Income Act 1966 216
　Slave Trade Act 1807 154n
　Slavery Abolition Act 1833 154n
　Social Security Act 1986 272–3
　Supreme Court Act 1981 248–9
　Taxation of Chargeable Gains Act 1992 191–2
　United States Code, Title 18, Part I, Chapter 44 203–4

INDEX 303

strategic action 43–4, 46, 84, 86–8, 156, 175, 237–8
summative accounts 48–50, 53, 55; *see also* coincident intention
syntax 193, 197–199
systematicity condition 71–2, 223

third reading 12, 221, 227–9, 237, 240, 270, 271–2, 274; *see also* final reading, final vote
time of enactment 20–1nn, 111, 201, 237, 242, 254, 257–8, 266, 269–70; *see also* legislative context
transformational legislatures 170–1
travaux préparatoires 13, 244; *see also* deliberation, record of; *Hansard*; legislative history
trustee, legislator as 152–3; *see also* representation, representative(s)
tyrant/tyranny 127, 143–5, 155–7

unanimity and joint action 55, 57–60, 62–4, 71
unanimity of legislators 165, 221, 234
underdetermination thesis 197, 211
unintentional legislation 30, 34, 40, 97, 102, 105, 108–9; *see also* voting machine
unitary model of legislature 9–10, 31–2, 40
universal domain condition 71–2
universals 254–5
utilitarianism 79–81, 97, 105n

vagueness 32, 125, 132, 197, 216, 238, 255
Vehicles in the Park Act 1993 34, 36–7, 103–5, 191
(no) vehicles in the park rule 255, 276–7
veto power 44, 166, 173, 240
veto-players 167, 173, 174, 176, 239
voluntary control over the law 109, 112, 124, 127, 132, 141, 219
voters 85–6, 94, 147, 149–50; *see also* elections, electorate
voting 24, 29, 37, 43, 85–8, 100, 105–6, 147n, 167
voting machine 10, 34–8, 40, 77, 94–5, 97–107, 148, 182

Waldron, J 9–10, 15, 30–40, 42, 52n, 93–8, 100–08, 121–3nn, 148, 149n, 151n, 158, 159n, 161–4, 180–4, 187–8, 191, 193, 212, 229n, 259
Washington 12, 176, 179; *see also* Congress, presidential system(s)
we-intentions 53–4, 56–7
Westminster 8, 12, 120, 143, 164, 176, 179; *see also* Parliament, parliamentary system(s)
will of the prince 143
Wollheim, R 35, 100–1
wrecking amendment 232; *see also* poison pill

Yowell, P 78n, 215n

Printed in Great Britain
by Amazon